Reading Strategies and Practices
A Compendium
Second Edition

Robert J. Tierney
University of Illinois

John E. Readence
Louisiana State University

Ernest K. Dishner
Southwest Texas State University

ALLYN AND BACON, INC.
Boston   London   Sydney   Toronto

Credits:

Series Editor: Susanne F. Canavan
Production Administrator: Jane Shulman
Editorial Coordinator: Lauren Whittaker
Text Designer: Cynthia Andrews
Cover Coordinator: Christy Rosso
Cover Designer: Lynne Abell

Library of Congress Cataloging in Publication Data

Tierney, Robert J.
    Reading strategies and practices.

    Bibliography: p.
    Includes index.
    1. Reading. I. Readence, John E., 1947-
II. Dishner, Ernest K., 1943-   . III. Title.
LB1050.T57 1985   428.4   85-7439
ISBN 0-205-08485-0

Printed in the United States of America

10 9 8 7 6 5 4 3   90 89 88 87 86

About the Authors

Robert J. Tierney is currently a senior scientist at the Center for the Study of Reading at the University of Illinois, where he is conducting research on reading-writing relationships and reading comprehension, as well as teaching graduate and undergraduate courses in language arts and reading. He received his Ph.D. from the University of Georgia and has been a member of the faculty at Harvard University and the University of Arizona. A teacher, consultant, and researcher in both the United States and Australia, Dr. Tierney has written books and numerous articles dealing with theory, research, and practice. He has been a major coauthor of three reading series published by Scott, Foresman and Company.

John E. Readence received his M.A. at Ohio State University and his Ph.D. in reading education from Arizona State University. A teacher at both the public school and college levels, and a consultant for numerous school districts, Dr. Readence has published many articles in the education field. He has held positions at Ohio University, Kansas State University, the University of Georgia, and currently serves as Associate Professor of Education at Louisiana State University. His current instructional/research interests focus on reading comprehension and metaphorical interpretation.

Ernest K. Dishner received B.S. and M.A. degrees from East Tennessee State University and a doctorate in reading education from the University of Georgia. Since 1973 Dr. Dishner has held teaching and administrative positions at Arizona State University, Delta State University, and the University of Northern Iowa. Currently, Dr. Dishner serves as Professor and Dean of the School of Education at Southwest Texas State University. A former elementary and secondary reading teacher, Dr. Dishner is coeditor of Reading in the Content Areas, published by Kendall/Hunt Publishing Company and has written articles in a variety of professional journals. His primary professional interests are in the areas of preservice and inservice teacher education and in content reading.

Contents

Unit 10 Word Identification Strategies   313

Unit 11 Multisensory Strategies for Teaching Reading 339

Preface

Reading Strategies and Practices: A Compendium represents a revision of the 1980 edition, *Reading Strategies and Practices: A Guide for Improving Instruction*. The revision represents a significant improvement over the earlier edition. Some of the changes that were made include:

- the addition of over 20 new strategies.
- the addition of several new units, including a Meaning Vocabulary Unit, a Responding to Reading as Writers Unit, a Study Skills Unit, and a Text-Based Comprehension Unit.
- the revision of existing descriptions of strategies, especially the cautions and comments for each strategy.
- The incorporation into the body of the text of suggestions for the diagnostic use of strategies.
- a discussion of each strategy in terms of current research findings, which addresses their utility.

It should be noted that the book is a compendium of strategies; the book is not a description of a single approach, nor is it intended to be eclectic. The inclusion of a strategy in this book should not be perceived as an endorsement of that strategy by the authors. There are some strategies that all of the authors view as problematic; there are others on which we disagree.

We appreciate those of you who have used the book, and especially those colleagues who gave us feedback for this revision. We hope you will find this new edition even more useful than its predecessor. Ideally, we hope the book stimulates reflection, discussion, evaluation, and intelligent use of instructional procedures. We especially want the book to fill a void by being a ready reference for teachers and prospective teachers who want a clear overall perspective of instructional procedure. The first edition was used in numerous courses at the undergraduate and graduate level for such purposes; we think the new edition will have even greater utility. We also recommend the book to administrators and others concerned with reading improvement—including parents.

How to Use This Book

INTENDED PURPOSES

There are certain purposes that the authors do not intend in this volume, namely, to suggest that users of this text change strategies or practices as they might change clothes. Likewise, the authors do not expect our readers to become familiar with all of the strategies or practices presented in the text, nor do the authors even advocate reading the text from cover to cover.

Rather, the purpose of this volume is to afford the reader an active role in examining and evaluating instructional techniques. To this end, the text should be read selectively and reflectively. Readers should select from the units and strategies those they wish to review and to critically evaluate.

HOW IS THIS BOOK ORGANIZED?

For organizational purposes the text is divided into an Introduction and eleven Units. The Introduction is designed to aid the reader in using the textbook. The authors delineate their intent, and provide recommendations for using various strategies and practices. The eleven units under which the strategies and practices have been classified are:

Unit One: Lesson Frameworks
Unit Two: Comprehension and Content Area Reading Strategies
Unit Three: Strategies for Responding to Reading as Writers
Unit Four: Text-Based Comprehension Strategies
Unit Five: Meaning Vocabulary Strategies
Unit Six: Study Skills Strategies
Unit Seven: Strategies and Practices for Teaching Reading as a Language Experience and with Shared Books
Unit Eight: Practices for Individualization and Recreational Reading
Unit Nine: Oral Reading Strategies and Practices

Unit Ten: Word Identification Strategies
Unit Eleven: Multisensory Strategies for Teaching Reading

Some readers may disagree with the separation of teaching strategies and practices into these particular strands. This breakdown is intended as one viable method of organization; it is not suggested as a "divinely inspired" division of reading or curriculum.

The eleven units of this text describe over fifty strategies and practices. As an aid to examining and evaluating these techniques, each unit provides the reader with an overview and a consistent organizational pattern. The following describes how these aids might be used.

Unit Overview

At the beginning of each unit, an overview provides an introduction to the various strategies and practices presented in that section. This overview serves three essential purposes:

1. since only selected strategies have been included within the various units, the overview provides information on the basis for selecting strategies;
2. since several strategies could be classified in more than one unit, the overview provides information on the basis for the present classification; and
3. the overview provides the reader with a brief orientation, which enables purposeful reading of each section and thus facilitates the evaluation, comparison, and intelligent selection of strategies and practices or their adaptations.

Strategies and Practices

In detailing the major features of the various strategies and practices, the discussion of each adopts the following framework:

Purpose,
Rationale,
Intended Audience,
Description of the Procedure, and
Cautions and Comments.

Where further information is desired, each unit provides an annotated list of references to guide readers in their research. Additionally, a unit appendix, which gives information concerning the diagnostic use of selected teaching strategies, is provided for some units.

Strategies and Practices

1

Lesson Frameworks

The Unit and Its Theme

In most classrooms, teachers approach reading instruction and content area learning (e.g., social studies and science) with a general framework within which the teachers do a variety of activities. The focus of these activities may be either a text that students are given to read or skills instruction that usually is related or applied to a selection. If a text is the focus of the lesson, then the framework may involve preparing students to read a text, or guiding their reading of a selection, or extending their skills and understandings following the selections. If skill activities are the focus, then there will usually be an attempt to relate the skills to the text by using the text as a source of examples or a basis for application.

The Strategies

The present unit describes three strategies that we have labeled lesson frameworks. Two of the three strategies, the Directed Reading Activity and the Directed Reading–Thinking Activity, are used primarily with basal reading material. The third strategy, the Instructional Framework, is used with content area material.

Directed Reading Activity (DRA)

Over the years, the Directed Reading Activity has been probably the most widely used framework for a "total" reading lesson. There are five basic steps that constitute a DRA. These steps provide the structure for the improvement

3

of a wide spectrum of reading skills—the most important of which is comprehension. This strategy may be applied to reading selections that vary in both length and readability and is suggested for use with students at all grade levels.

Directed Reading–Thinking Activity (DR–TA)

Assuming that critical reading performance requires the reader to become skilled at determining purposes for reading, the Directed Reading–Thinking Activity emphasizes that the reader declares his or her own purposes for reading. As with the DRA, the Directed Reading–Thinking Activity may be applied to reading selections that vary in both length and readability and is suggested for use with students at all grade levels.

Instructional Framework

The three major phases of the instructional framework—preparation, guidance, and independence—provide the content teacher with a viable design for presenting a unit of study. The framework provides a means for teaching both the important reading skills (process) the students need and the important concepts (product) of the unit. Thus, process and product merge in the development of independent learners. The strategy is appropriate for both fictional and expository materials and would appear most suitable for students in grades four and above.

DIRECTED READING ACTIVITY

Purpose

The purpose of the Directed Reading Activity (DRA) (Betts 1946) is to:

1. Give teachers a basic format from which to provide systematic instruction on a group basis;
2. Improve students' word recognition and comprehension skills; and
3. Successfully guide students through a reading selection.

Rationale

The DRA is synonymous with the basal reader lesson. Betts (1946) compiled the guidelines that various authors of basal readers generally recommended for teaching their reading selections. Betts described a plan to follow when there was general agreement among the authors:

> First, the group should be prepared, oriented, or made ready, for the reading of a story or selection. Second, the first reading should be guided silent reading. Third, word-recognition skills and comprehension should be developed during the silent reading. Fourth, the reading—silent or oral, depending upon the needs of the pupil—should be done for purposes different from those served by the first, or silent, reading. Fifth, the follow-up on the "reading lesson" should be differentiated in terms of pupil needs. (P. 492)

Thus, the general plan of instruction in basal readers, what became known as the Directed Reading Activity,* originated as a comprehensive means to provide reading instruction to children through a reading selection.

Intended Audience

The DRA is normally associated with basal reader instruction in the elementary grades, but the teacher may adapt it for any reading selection. For example, Shepherd (1978) has illustrated the use of DRA with content area textbooks from the middle school level through high school.

Description of the Procedure

Although there may be minor differences as to what constitutes the DRA, it usually contains the following components, all of which the teacher may modify to fit a student's needs:

1. Readiness;
2. Directed silent reading;
3. Comprehension check and discussion;
4. Oral rereading; and
5. Follow up activities.

Stage 1: Readiness

The readiness, or preparation, stage of the DRA involves getting students ready to enter the story by relating the story selection to their past experiences, developing their interest in reading it, and setting their purposes for reading. Four components comprise the readiness stage of the DRA.

   a. *Develop concept background.* Here it is suggested that the teacher connect the new concepts that the students will be exposed to in the reading selection with their previous experiences or readings. Any misconceptions or

---

*An example of the DRA applied to a story is given on page 10–14.

hazy understandings by the students are expected to be clarified before they read the story.

The teacher may build background through various means, including discussions centering around the story title and illustrations in the selection, personal experiences of the students related to the story content, films, pictures, maps, or other audiovisual displays.

b. *Create interest.* Starting with the notion that children must be interested, or motivated, to read a selection in order to maximize their comprehension and enjoyment of its contents, the teacher attempts also to create interest in the early stages. The mechanical side of the selection alone, its title and the various illustrations, many times may serve to arouse students' interest; however, the teacher may also have to keep creating enthusiasm for students to read the story effectively. In this case, a thorough job by teachers in developing conceptual background (the previously discussed section) may suffice. If not, the teacher may choose to read a short, introductory portion of the selection and thus inspire the students to want to read the rest. At other times, the teacher may wish to use multimedia material and/or experiences to stimulate interest.

c. *Introduce new vocabulary.* Here the teacher's task is to prepare students for any words they will encounter that are outside the students' reading vocabularies and word recognition abilities. To emphasize word meanings and not just word pronunciations, the teacher may introduce new vocabulary in context, both orally and visually. For example, the teacher might first use the word *orally* in a sentence, followed by a visual presentation on the chalkboard using meaningful phrases or sentences. The introduction of new vocabulary is not a time for drill or for emphasizing word attack skills. Instead, it is the time to give students oral familiarity with selected words. Typically, a teacher introduces no more than five words at once.

d. *Establish purpose.* Based upon the notion that the establishment of clear, concise purpose for reading a selection determines the quality of the readers' comprehension, at this point the teacher should pose questions for the students to answer in their silent reading. The overall question the teacher should consider is, "What are the students reading for?" For example, the teacher must decide whether to set a general purpose for the entire selection, such as "Read to find out the series of events that led to the downfall of the dictator," *or*, if the teacher decides to set more specific purposes for each part of a selection, another example is "Read to find out how the dictator came to power before you go on to other parts of the selection."

The presentation of the readiness stage of the DRA should take approximately five to fifteen minutes but will vary in length and emphasis according to the ability of the students and to the complexity of the selections. For less advanced students, it may be necessary to spend a longer time preparing them to read the selection than when preparing more advanced students. Depending upon how the teacher approaches the readiness stage, one component may encompass other aspects of this step. For instance, introducing new vocabulary may create interest and develop concept background simultaneously. With the exception of establishing purpose, which should conclude the readiness stage, the teacher need not present the other components in any established order.

Stage 2: Directed Silent Reading

Following the readiness stage of the DRA, the students should read the selection silently to seek answers to the purpose-questions that the teacher has set. It is emphasized that the teacher have students read the selection silently, and not orally. This way is more rapid, it is more characteristic of everyday reading needs, and it gives the students an opportunity to use their work attack skills without expressed effort.

If readiness activities have been thorough, many students will work efficiently with very little, if any, teacher help. The teacher should encourage students to work out word recognition problems independently; however, he or she might also be available in the event a student requests help with confirmation or analysis. Since silent reading is not a time for word attack drills, it is suggested that teachers guide students who require help to clues that will aid them in unlocking the meaning of unknown words. If students seem unable to decode certain words, the teacher usually will provide these words so that reading may proceed. The teacher can make note of those words that give students particular difficulty and/or those specific skill needs of students as they attempt to decode words. Later, teachers can plan appropriate individual and/or group activities to counteract those difficulties.

Stage 3: Comprehension Check and Discussion

Discussion activities follow each silent reading segment that is assigned. An obvious start of the discussion can be answering the purpose-questions set during the readiness stage, although discussion may begin naturally on the other aspects of the selection.

During the discussion it is appropriate to stress and develop comprehension abilities. For example, teachers might formulate discussion questions on the interpretive or critical levels (thinking questions) to extend the ideas students glean from their reading to set purposes.

Stage 4: Oral Rereading

This stage of the DRA may occur in conjunction with the previous stage (comprehension check and discussion) or the teacher may use it to set new purposes for reading. The teacher may set these purposes independently, or new purposes may develop out of the discussion, or they may serve as a preparation for a follow-up activity. Rereading may also occur if students are confused about one of the discussion questions. If such is the case, the new purpose is for students to read to solve problems that have resulted from the discussion. Students reread rapidly to locate information under question and then orally reread to the group to alleviate the confusion or to verify a point.

Stage 5: Follow-up Activities

Follow-up activities include those experiences that build and extend skill development and those activities that add to, or enrich, students' understanding of the concepts in the story. Activities that extend skill development include introducing new word attack skills, establishing the new terms of the story firmly in students' vocabulary, and further developing the students' comprehension abilities. This is also an appropriate time for the teacher to review any skills that were noted to have produced difficulties during the silent reading. Such activities are suitable on an individual basis, in a small group, or in a whole class situation.

The rationale behind this type of follow-up activity is that practice with, and opportunities to use, those skills that present difficulty to students will provide them the reinforcement necessary to master those skills. As such, the use of basal reader workbooks, teacher-made worksheets, or commercially available material is often suggested to strengthen those specific skills that the DRA showed to be of concern.

Activities that can enrich or extend students' understanding of the story's concepts start with the premise that the application of newly learned concepts to other types of activities will further enhance and broaden new learning. Such extension activities may involve creative work, study activities, or extended reading. Creative work may include writing about personal experiences related to the story, dramatization, and making illustrations for the story. Study activities may include workbook exercises and teacher-made practice material. Students may also do research into the information they gain from the selection in order to organize it into a chart or table format. Examples of extended reading might include selected readings in other texts or library books on related topics, or reading to find answers to questions that arise in the discussion of the story.

Cautions and Comments

The effective use of the DRA requires the teacher to be sensitive to the students' needs, to the differential demands of text, and to the adequacy of the DRA as a lesson framework. In this respect, the DRA seems to have one shortcoming; namely, it seems to be too teacher-dominated. Teacher–pupil interactions flow mainly from the questions and activities that the teacher prescribes. As a result, the DRA could develop students who are overly dependent on teacher direction rather than on their own self-initiated reading–thinking processes. Indeed, studies by Davidson (1970) and Petre (1970) compared the DRA with the Directed Reading–Thinking Activity (DR–TA) found results favoring the DR–TA.

Another concern about the use of the DRA involves skill development, including oral reading, word recognition, comprehension, and study skills. If implemented properly, and related to the actual reading assignment, skill instruction can be purposeful and relevant. However, if skills instruction is rote or isolated from a selection, as worksheet exercises often are, then it is often meaningless. Indeed, Sachs (1981) and Osborn (1984) put forward arguments about the worthlessness of many such activities.

Despite these limitations, the DRA has adaptive potential to teach almost any reading selection. Aspects of other strategies described in this book may serve as supplements to the DRA. For example, teachers can effectively utilize ReQuest (see Unit 2) as a replacement for the readiness stage of the DRA.

Part of the DRA's adaptive potential has to do with classroom management and ability grouping. For example, when basal reading programs are used, teachers can use the DRA for a week with various ability groups. An example of such a schedule follows.

A WEEK-LONG SCHEDULE FOR A DIRECTED
READING ACTIVITY

Day One

Minutes	Group I	Group II	Group III
3–5	Teacher briefs students he or she does not work with directly. Students working directly with teacher organize themselves.		
25–30	*Stage I—Introducing the Selection* (Teacher present) Teacher introduces new story. *Stage II—Directed Silent Reading* (Teacher present) Students read story silently. *Stages III & IV— Comprehension Check and Oral Rereading* (Teacher present) *Stage V—Follow-up* Students reread and write an alternative ending.	*Independent Reading* (Students independently) or *Bookmaking*	*Stage V—Follow-up* (Students independently) Students work through activities reviewing outline. Students check own work. *Independent Work* (Students independently) Students begin work on a research problem.
5–10	Teacher checks those students working independently, giving individuals help if needed.		
20–25	*Stage V—Follow up* (Students independently) Workbook activities. *Independent Reading* (Students independently)	*Stage I—Introducing the Selection* (Teacher present) *Stage II—Directed Silent Reading* (Teacher present) *Stage III—Comprehension Check* (Teacher present) *Stage IV—Oral Rereading* (Teacher present)	*Stage V—Follow-up* Students skim story to locate answers to questions. They create questions and ask them of each other. *Independent Reading*

Day Two

Minutes	Group I	Group II	Group III
3–5	Teacher organizes for instruction and briefs students.		
	Stage V—Follow-up (Teacher present) Teacher goes over work exercises. *Stage IV—Oral Rereading* (Teacher present) Oral rereading of selected conversations in story. *Stage V—Follow-up* (Teacher present) Word identification instruction.	*Independent Reading* (Students independently)	*Independent Reading* (Students independently)
3–5	Teacher organizes for instruction and briefing.		
15–20	*Stage V—Follow-up* (Students independently) Workbook activities. *Independent Reading* (Students independently)	*Stage V—Follow-up* (Students independently) Students complete dealing with context clues. *Independent Work* Research project.	*Stage V—Follow-up* (Teacher present) Review work from previous day. Students classify information from story and summarize.
5–10	Teacher checks work of groups, organizes for instruction, and briefs students.		
15–20	*Independent Reading* (Students independently)	*Stage V—Follow-up* (Teacher present) Teacher reviews use of context and other word identification skills.	*Stage V—Follow-up* (Students independently) Students continue work. *Independent Reading of Work*

Day Three

Minutes	Group I	Group II	Group III
3–5	Teacher organizes for instruction and briefs students.		
15–20	*Independent Reading* or *Independent Work* (Students independently) Dictated story; Bookmaking.	*Stage V—Follow-up* (Students independently) Students reread story silently to answer thought questions. Students prepare dramatization.	*Stage V—Follow-up* (Teacher present) Review classifying and summarizing. Reread parts of story for a radio show.
5–10	Group III shares reading experiences with Groups I and II (radio play).		
20–25	*Stage V—Follow-up* (Teacher present) Teacher checks workbook exercises. *Stage I—Introduces the Story* (Teacher present) *Stage II—Directed Silent Reading* *Stages III & IV* (Teacher present) Stage III & Stage IV *Comprehension Check & Oral Rereading* (Teacher present)	*Stage V—Follow-up* (Students independently) Continue on previous activities. *Independent Reading* *or* *Independent Work* (Students independently) Research project.	*Stage V—Follow-up* (Students independently) Read related stories. Students use reference books to look for answers to questions related to stories.
3–5	Teacher checks with other two groups and organizes class.		
10–15	Group II presents dramatization of story.		

Day Four

Minutes	Group I	Group II	Group III
3–5	Teacher organizes for instruction and briefs students.		
20–25	*Stage V—Follow-up* (Students independently) Students skim story to locate answers to specific questions. Students organize events from story into the correct sequence. *Independent Reading* (Students independently)	*Independent Reading* (Students independently) *Independent Work* (Students independently) Research project.	*Stage V—Follow-up* (Teacher present) Discussion of previous work. *Stage I—Introduces the Selection* (Teacher present) *Stage II—Directed Silent Reading* (Teacher present) *Stage III—Comprehension Check &* *Stage IV—Oral Rereading* (Teacher present)
3–5	Teacher checks work of groups, organizes for instruction, and briefs groups.		
20–25	*Independent Reading* (Students independently) *Independent Work* Students move to learning center for research work.	*Stage V—Follow-up* (Teacher present) Teacher discusses students' answers to thought questions from previous day. *Stage I—Introduces Selection* (Teacher present) *Stage II—Directed Silent Reading* (Teacher present) *Stage III—Comprehension Check* *Stage IV—Oral Rereading* (Teacher present)	*Stage V—Follow-up* (Students independently) Students organize information they recall from story into an outline. *Independent Reading* (Students independently)
3–5	Teacher introduces several new books for independent reading. Children share books they have read and enjoyed.		

Day Five

Minutes	Group I	Group II	Group III
3–5	Teacher briefs class and organizes for instruction.		
15–20	All three groups participate in independent reading. This may be through the use of U.S.S.R. (see Unit 8)		
3–5	Children terminate reading. Organize for class activity.		
15–20	Selected students may elect to continue reading for a few minutes. Remainder of class shares personal reading through book reports, posters, dramatizations, or displays. Teacher and children list five favorite magazine or newspaper articles.		
15–20	*Stage V—Follow-up Activities* (Teacher present) Students discuss and develop a mural based upon story.	*Independent Reading or Work* (Students independently)	*Independent Reading or Work* (Students independently)
Note:	The above pattern is suggestive rather than prescriptive. For each group the sequence would vary from week to week. Depending upon the nature of activities and the students' needs, the teacher might alter group structure in terms of size, membership, and number.		

REFERENCES

Betts, E. A. 1946. *Foundations of reading instruction.* New York: American Book. Presents one of the original descriptions of the general principles and assumptions behind the DRA.

Davidson, J. L. 1970. The relationship between teachers' questions and pupils' responses during a directed reading activity and a directed reading-thinking activity. Unpublished doctoral diss. University of Michigan. Presents a research study in which the efficacy of DRA is questioned.

Karlin, R. 1975. *Teaching elementary reading: Principles and strategies.* 2d ed. New York: Harcourt, Brace, Jovanovich, 146–51. Describes the steps involved in the DRA when used with a basal reader.

Miller, W. H. 1977. *The first R: Elementary reading today.* 2d ed. New York: Holt, Rinehart & Winston, 59–78. Provides general guidelines for using the DRA in the guise of a basal reader lesson.

Osborn, J. 1984. The purposes, uses, and contents of workbooks and some guidelines for publishers. In *Learning to read in American schools: Basal readers and content texts*, edited by R. C. Anderson, J. Osborn, and R. J.

Tierney. Hillsdale, N.J.: Erlbaum. Discusses the strengths, weaknesses and use of workbooks accompanying basal reading lessons.

Petre, R. M. 1970. Quantity, quality and variety of pupil responses during an open-communication group directed reading–thinking activity and a closed-communication structured group directed reading activity. Unpublished doctoral diss. University of Delaware. Presents a research study in which the efficacy of DRA is questioned.

Sachs, A. W. 1981. The effects of three prereading activities on learning disabled children's short-term reading comprehension. Unpublished doctoral diss., George Peabody University. Presents a research study in which the effectiveness of the DRA was examined.

Shepherd, D. L. 1973. *Comprehensive high school reading methods.* Columbus, Ohio: Charles E. Merrill, 132–38. Outlines steps to adapt the DRA for use in the content fields.

Spache, G. D., and E. B. Spache. 1977. *Reading in the elementary school.* 4th ed. Boston: Allyn and Bacon, 46–53. Provides an outlined procedure for teaching a typical basal reader lesson.

Stauffer, R. G. 1969. *Directing reading maturity as a cognitive process.* New York: Harper & Row, 35–86. Describes an alternative procedure to the DRA–The Directed Reading–Thinking Activity. Using the same fundamental steps as the DRA, this strategy promotes more student involvement.

DIRECTED READING–THINKING ACTIVITY

Purpose

The Directed Reading–Thinking Activity (DR–TA) is intended to develop students' ability to read critically and reflectively. Broadly speaking, it attempts to equip readers with:

1. The ability to determine purposes for reading;
2. The ability to extract, comprehend, and assimilate information;
3. The ability to examine reading material based upon purposes for reading;
4. The ability to suspend judgments, and
5. The ability to make decisions based upon information gleaned from reading.

Rationale

Russell Stauffer (1969) developed the DR–TA to provide conditions that would produce readers who could think, learn, and test. Stauffer suggests these readers

> . . . will learn to have the strength of their convictions and the
> courage to deal with ideas. They will not be fearful but courageous;
> not blind, but discerning; not hasty, but deliberate; not deceitful,
> but honest; not muddled, but articulate; not acquiescent, but mili-
> tant; not conceited, but modest; not imitative, but original. (P. 84)

Stauffer based his notions upon the belief that reading is a thinking
process that involves the reader in using his or her own experiences to recon-
struct the author's ideas. The reconstruction begins with the generation of
hypotheses based upon the reader's doubts and desires. It continues with the
reader's acquisition of information and the generation of further hypotheses
during reading. The reconstruction terminates with the resolution of the
reader's doubts and desires. Stauffer puts this into practice with the DR–TA as
follows:

> . . . either the reader declares his own purposes or if he adopts the
> purposes of others, he makes certain how and why he is doing so.
> He also speculates about the nature and complexity of the answers
> he is seeking by using to the fullest his experience and knowledge
> relevant to the circumstances. Then he reads to test his purposes
> and his assumptions. As a result, he may: one, find the answer he is
> seeking literally and completely stated; two, find only partial an-
> swers or implied answers and face the need to either restate his
> purposes in light of the new information gained or to suspend
> judgment until more reading has been done; three, need to declare
> completely new purposes. (P. 40)

Intended Audience

As with the Directed Reading Activity, the teacher can easily adapt the
DR–TA for any selection at any level of difficulty. Toward a balanced reading
program, Stauffer suggests the extension and differentiation of the DR–TA
for both group and individual use. With groups, he suggests using it with from
eight to twelve students. Shepherd (1978) has also suggested using the DR–TA
with content fields.

Description of the Procedure

The DR–TA has two parts—a process cycle and a product. The process cycle
involves the reader in the following: setting purposes for reading, adjusting the
rate and the material for these purposes, reading to verify purposes, pausing to
evaluate understanding, then proceeding to read with the same or with different purposes. The product of the DR–TA is the extension and refinement of
students' ideas and thinking.

In describing the DR–TA, Stauffer suggests procedures for a group
DR–TA, which the teacher can extend and adapt into an individualized
version.

1. Group DR–TA

There are certain essential phases in the implementation of a group DR–TA. The first phase involves directing reading-thinking processes. The second phase involves fundamental skill training.

a. *Phase One: Directing the reading-thinking process.* Directing the reading-thinking process involves the reader in three steps: predicting, reading, and proving. As students proceed through a selection, they predict or define purposes for reading; they read and select relevant data; and they evaluate and revise predictions, using the information they acquire.

The teacher, the material, and the group are all essential to the success of this activity. The teacher has to create an environment that will arouse students' curiosities and meet their reading needs. The group serves to audit and extend the thinking of its members. The material provides, Stauffer states, "the substance for cognition" (1969, 46). To this end, he suggests the material should be well-written, appealing in content, and of an appropriate difficulty level. For the purpose of directing the reading-thinking processes, the teacher may treat the selection in segments. Here is an example of how teachers might implement this phase with a selection divided into segments.

1. Each student either receives or locates a copy of the selection; the teacher directs the student to study either the title or the pictures on the first page.

   a. What do you think a story with this title might be about?
   b. What do you think might happen in this story?
   c. Which of these predictions do you agree with?

   The teacher encourages students to make several different suggestions and to discuss agreement or disagreement with one another's suggestions. The teacher promotes this interaction.

2. When the teacher introduces the DR–TA, he or she first familiarizes students with the strategy for dealing with unknown words. That is, if students encounter unknown words, the teacher would expect the students to implement the following steps in the specified order:

   a. Read to the end of the sentence;
   b. Use picture clues, if available;
   c. Sound out the word; and
   d. Ask the teacher for help.

   Before asking for teacher assistance, the student should try to figure out the word and, according to Stauffer, the teacher should give the student the opportunity to do so.

3. The teacher directs the students to read a segment of the story silently to check their predictions. The teacher is responsible for ensuring students read for meaning, observing reading performance, and helping students who request help with words. When the latter occurs, the teacher might have the student

suggest a word it might be, explain what the student did to figure out the word, and, if the word is still unknown, the teacher provides the word. Note that the teacher introduced no vocabulary prior to reading the story. Stauffer suggests this is unnecessary, given the vocabulary controls and systematic word identification programs found in basal readers.

4. After students have read the first segment, the teacher asks them to close their books and the comprehension check begins.

   Questions serve to guide the students' examination of the evidence, their evaluation of their previous predictions, and their generation of new predictions.

   "Were you correct?" or *"What do you think now?"* force students to examine the proof of their predictions. Oral reading of a particular sentence directs students to share their evidence with other group members.

   "What do you think now?" or *"What do you think will happen?"* encourage students to screen their ideas and to make predictions about events to come.

5. The students read the next segment of text and with each new segment of reading material, continue the predicting-reading-proving cycle. As students proceed, they come upon more and more information; divergent conjectures begin to converge. At the beginning of the selection, predictions usually tend to be divergent. Toward the end of the reading, predictions should tend to converge.

   b. *Phase Two: Fundamental Skill Training.* After the students have read the selection, the teacher has completed first phase of the DR–TA—directing the reading-thinking of the selection. Now the second phase begins. Stauffer refers to this phase as the phase when "skill training of a different kind is accomplished" (1969, 64). The second phase entails reexamining the story, reexamining selected words or phrases, and pictures or diagrams, for the purpose of developing systematically and concurrently the students' reading-thinking abilities and other reading-related skills. These might include word attack, the use of semantic analysis, concept clarification and development, power of observation, and reflective abilities. The format of these activities varies, but, in many cases, is also similar to the suggested exercises in the teacher's edition, the workbooks, or the skillbooks that accompany most basal reading systems.

2. Individualized DR–TA

Individualized DR–TAs apply, extend, and refine the skills and abilities that students acquire in group DR–TAs. Stauffer claims that individualized DR–TAs afford a systematic method by which students can learn about themselves in terms of their own interests, tasks, judgments, and thinking abilities.

Teachers can introduce individualized DR−TAs after group DR−TAs or in conjunction with them. Familiarity with group DR−TA procedures is a prerequisite for introducing an individualized DR−TA.

There are several features that distinguish an individualized DR−TA:

1. It does not use traditional grouping; instead, each student is free to work with a minimum of interruption, in pursuit of his or her interests. If interests coincide, students may occasionally work together.
2. The teacher expects students to know why they are to select materials, what materials they might select, and how they should select them. To this end, the teacher schedules time for selection of material and for discussion of selection techniques. The teacher may help students either individually or in groups to formulate interests, needs, and methods for selection.
3. Students should generate their own reading purposes and be familiar with the predicting, reading, proving cycle of the DR−TA. Either worksheet or student record cards might direct these processes.
4. At scheduled times, students should share their work or what they have read with others. This process might involve the use of posters, bulletin boards, dramatizations, reports, and the like.
5. As the need arises, students receive incidental or systematic skills instruction, individually or in groups.
6. Students should abide by class rules that are established to ensure individual rights and efficient learning.
7. Students should keep meaningful records on a daily or weekly basis. These records might track students' activities, the stories they read, or their skill needs.
8. Students can develop other language-related skills (oral expression, written expression, listening) through presentations, reports, verbal sharing, and other activities.
9. Throughout the individualized DR−TAs, the teacher should serve various functions, including the following:

   a. Organizing groups for projects and skill training;
   b. Organizing the schedule to ensure flexibility and efficiency;
   c. Pacing the various activities to afford maximum success and a minimum of frustration;
   d. Establishing operating rules to facilitate learning and thinking;
   e. Maintaining meaningful records to map individual progress and planning future activities; and
   f. Guiding, directing, and assisting students.

Cautions and Comments

As lesson frameworks, the Directed Reading Activity and the DR−TA are suitable for use with almost any reading selection. But the DR−TA has certain features that distinguish it from the Directed Reading Activity. First, the

DR–TA places a heavy emphasis upon the relationship between reading and thinking. It encourages students to be aware of and to develop their own reading-thinking processes through initiating their own purposes for reading and making predictions. Second, the role of the teacher is different. Unlike the DRA, the DR–TA materials govern teacher-pupil interactions and students' purposes for reading; the teacher's questioning does not prescribe this interaction. The teacher does not assume the role of either questioner or judge. Instead, the teacher becomes a moderator and a facilitator. Third, vocabulary is treated differently; the student does not meet words prior to reading but as they occur in context. In those studies in which comparisons have been made of the two procedures, the DR–TA has fared better (Davidson 1970; Petre 1970). To see some of these differences more clearly, consider the use of both the DRA and DR–TA with a single selection (see the sample lesson plan in this section).

For teachers familiar with traditional reading materials, the DR–TA affords a useful alternative, but one that they should not use repeatedly. For example, teachers might wish to vary both the treatment of the reading-thinking phase and the format of activities within the fundamental skill phase, since with repeated use, children become "programmed" to the strategy rather than become involved in reading-thinking interactions. If teachers find their students unable or unwilling to make predictions, they may supplement the approach with games and activities that encourage predictive behaviors. Teachers may find the presentation of either incomplete pictures, jigsaw pieces, or cartoons useful devices for generating predictions. And teachers may sometimes read a story to students for the purpose of either introducing or supplementing the predicting-reading-proving cycle.

SAMPLE LESSON PLAN FOR A DIRECTED READING ACTIVITY AND A DIRECTED READING–THINKING ACTIVITY

To compare the use of a Directed Reading Activity and a Directed Reading–Thinking Activity, here are two lesson plans for the same selection. One lesson plan represents what a teacher might typically do using a Directed Reading Activity Approach. The other lesson plan represents what a user might typically do with a Directed Reading–Thinking Activity.

The Selection

The selection we chose for this purpose is a story entitled "The Surprise," suitable for use in a second grade classroom. "The Surprise" tells what happened to a child's box of cookies. The child had made the cookies for his or her teacher. The teacher inadvertently sits on the box, crumbling the child's cookies. The story ends happily, with the children and the teacher having a party.

Directed Reading Activity

I. *Introducing the Selection*
In the Directed Reading Activity, the teacher introduces the selection by attempting to do four things: build an interest in the story, build concept background, introduce new vocabulary, set purposes.
Show children a white box. Ask them what they think the box is (create interest). Explain to students that what you have is a surprise. Have them tell about surprises they have received (concept background). Write the words *surprise* and *children* on the chalkboard. Have the students say the words and use them in a sentence (introduce vocabulary). Direct children to the story entitled "The Surprise" and have them read the first page to learn who is getting the surprise (setting purpose).

II. *Directed Silent Reading*
As the students silently read the designated section, the teacher stands by to help. If the student has difficulty with a word, the authors suggest the teacher provide it immediately. Once the students have located the answer to the question, the teacher directs them either to mark with their finger, or to remember the word, sentence, or section that told them the answer

Directed Reading-Thinking Activity

I. *Introducing the Selection*
In the Directed Reading–Thinking Activity, the teacher encourages the students to make their own predictions concerning what they are about to read. The teacher neither introduces vocabulary nor sets purpose.
Show children a white box. Ask them what they think the box is. Explain to students that what you have is a surprise. Have them turn to the story entitled "The Surprise" and have them make predictions about the surprise. Ask questions like: *What do you think a story like this is about? What do you think will happen in this story?* (The teacher might refer them to the picture clues.) Direct students to read the first page to learn about their predictions.

II. *Directed Silent Reading*
As the students silently read the designated section, the teacher stands by to help. If the student has difficulty with a word, there is a set procedure to follow. This procedure involves:

1. Reading to the end of the sentence;
2. Using picture clues, if available;
3. Sounding out the word; and
4. (If the students still do not recognize the word) asking the teacher.

Once the students have finished the designated page, they turn over their books and await the teacher.

III. *Comprehension Check and Skill Building*

IV. *Oral Rereading*

The teacher asks the students to answer this previous question: *Who was the surprise for?* The students share their answers and verify them by orally rereading the sentences or sentence that yielded the answer. The teacher asks other related questions: *Who is Miss Day? Who is Jay?*

Repetition of Phases I, II, III & IV

As the students progress through the rest of the selection in segments, the teacher sets further purposes for their reading, the teacher checks their comprehension, and the students orally reread to verify answers.

III. *Comprehension Check and Skill Building*

IV. *Oral Rereading*

The teacher asks the students how accurate their predictions were. The students produce the proof they used to verify their predictions by orally rereading the sentences or sentence that yielded the answer. The teacher asks students to share what else they now know.

Repetition of Phases I, II, III & IV

As the students progress through the rest of the selection in segments, the teacher asks them to make further predictions, to silently read to verify them, to revise, and to evaluate these predictions. The students refine the predictions with more information, as in the phases described under *Introducing the Selection*. Students repeat Directed Silent Reading, Comprehension Check, Skill Building, and Oral Rereading.

A teacher may use the patterns exemplified here for teaching a story or article at any level; however, there may be some differences. The teacher may or may not break the selection into segments. What the teacher actually does within each phase will vary. These variations depend upon the selection, the students themselves, and their purposes for reading.

Follow-up Activities

In the Directed Reading Activity, various and sundry follow-up activities usually occur. In the main, they center upon developing the following skills:

1. Comprehension;
2. Word identification;
3. Study skills;
4. Literary appreciation and understanding;

Follow-up Activities

In the Directed Reading–Thinking Activities, the follow-up activities are virtually the same as those we propose for a Directed Reading Activity. Indeed, a teacher might use the examples here across both strategies. To follow-up the Directed Reading–Thinking Activity, Stauffer suggests Fundamental Skill Activities that would be

Follow-up Activities (con't.)

5. Vocabulary; and
6. Oral reading.

In addition, typical follow-up activities afford opportunities for enrichment.

Follow-up Activities (con't.)

similar to the follow-up activities suggested in most basal programs.

Here are some examples:

1. *Oral rereading.* Explain to students that the story they have read has plenty of conversation; have them take parts and reread the story.
2. *Comprehension.* Write several sentences that describe events that either did or did not happen in the story. Have the students decide which events did happen and then arrange the order.

   The children did not like the cookies.
   The children had a party.
   Jay made little cookies.
   Jay dropped the box.
   They went to the zoo.

3. *Word identification.* Have students locate the following words in the story: looked, carried, hurried, parties. Have students locate the endings and root words.
4. *Enrichment*

   a. Present the students with a recipe they might follow to make cookies. Make some as a group project.
   b. Have students make a surprise for a friend.
   c. Dramatize the story.

REFERENCES

Davidson, J. L. 1970. The relationship between teachers' questions and pupils' responses during a directed reading activity and a directed reading–thinking activity. Unpublished doctoral diss., University of Michigan. Presents a research study in which the efficacy of DRA is questioned.

Petre, R. M. 1970. Quantity, quality and variety of pupil responses during an open-communication group directed reading–thinking activity and a closed-communication structured group directed reading activity. Unpublished doctoral diss., University of Delaware. Presents a research study in which the efficacy of DRA is questioned.

Shepherd, D. L. 1978. *Comprehensive high school reading methods.* 2d ed. Columbus, Ohio: Charles Merrill. Presents a discussion of how the

Directed Reading–Thinking Activities might be used in the content areas.

Stauffer, R. G. 1969. *Directing reading maturity as a cognitive process*. New York: Harper & Row. Intended for the graduate or advanced student, this text presents a detailed description of the procedure and its rationale.

———. 1970. *The language-experience approach to the teaching of reading*. New York: Harper & Row, 132–76. Presents a readable description of the strategy and its use.

———. 1960. Productive reading-thinking at the first grade level. *Reading Teacher* 13:183–87. Presents a brief description of the use of reading-thinking strategies with first graders.

———. 1976. *Teaching Reading as a thinking process*. New York: Harper & Row. Intended for the less advanced student, this text presents the procedure in detail, but with less theory.

Stauffer, R. G., and M. M. Harrel. 1975. Individualized reading-thinking activities. *The Reading Teacher* 28:765–69. Describes a program for individualizing Directed Reading–Thinking Activities.

INSTRUCTIONAL FRAMEWORK

Purpose

The purpose of the instructional framework (Herber 1970, 1978) is to:

1. Provide content area teachers with a structure for presenting a content lesson; and
2. Teach not only the content (product) of the unit, but also the skills (process) necessary to understand the content.

Rationale

Most content reading materials are written at a relatively high level of sophistication. The introduction of new concepts can be confounded by technicaι vocabulary and complex explanations.

It would seem students need a structure that helps them cope with the process of learning so they can meet the product expectancies of learning. Herber's instructional framework is designed to provide just that structure. Specifically, the instructional framework provides a structure for lesson⌐ that is intended to guide students' reading processes and products. The eventual aim is to enable students to apply these structures independently in their own reading.

Intended Audience

The technique may be used at all levels with students whose learning requires them to understand content reading material. The study guide component allows for individual instruction or for instruction with the entire class.

Description of the Procedure

Before the classroom teacher can implement the instructional framework, decisions are necessary regarding: (1) the major concepts to be emphasized within a given selection; (2) each concept's relative importance to the unit and to the subject as a whole; (3) the major technical vocabulary terms that appear to be important in understanding and communicating the major concepts; and (4) the specific skills the students need in order to learn the concepts. After the teacher has made these decisions (Herber 1970, 1978), the content instructor is ready to prepare the content lesson.

The basic structure of the instructional framework has three major components: (1) preparation, (2) guidance, and (3) independence.

A sample lesson plan for an instructional framework follows the description of these three components.

1. Preparation

Before students are assigned to read the new chapter, the teacher should "prepare" them for the assignment. The amount of time spent on the preparation stage of the lesson depends upon the students' reading and study skills and their background experiences with the topic. The order may vary from one unit to the next, but the specific stages of the preparation phase are:

   a. *Motivation.* Although sometimes difficult to attain, the goal should be to complete the preparation stage of the lesson with each student *wanting* to learn more about the topic. This can be accomplished by involving the students as much as possible in the learning act itself. Field trips, films, filmstrips, records, tapes, study prints, and demonstrations are just a few of the motivational techniques the classroom teacher might use. The remaining steps within the preparation phase of the instructional framework are designed to provide the students with further motivation.

   b. *Background Information and Review.* Authors of content material assume that students have a certain amount of knowledge related to the particular content unit. If this background information is not present, it is the responsibility of the content teacher to "fill the gaps." Otherwise, a review of information already known by the students also is suggested. This segment of the strategy provides the important "mind set" for learning the new information.

c. *Anticipation and Purpose.* At the conclusion of the preparation stage, students should anticipate certain new understandings to be gained. Establishing purposes in two very specific areas—the product (ideas to be discovered) and the process (skills to be applied in order to gain that information)—can heighten students' anticipation.

d. *Direction.* After students understand what skills are necessary to learn the new information, the instructor gives the students specific assistance in ways to use these identified skills. If the students are already accomplished in the specific skill, a brief review may be all that is necessary; however, if the teacher is aware of student skill deficiencies, this would be the time when skills teaching takes place. For example, suppose that the author of the unit under consideration has consistently used the organizational pattern of cause-effect (Niles 1965). An understanding of cause-effect patterns might then be appropriate for students, as it will aid their text understanding.

e. *Vocabulary Development.* A major hurdle for students in content material is the technical language of the particular subject under study. To assist the student in the acquisition of the important concepts, the major vocabulary in any given unit is pretaught. A variety of strategies for preteaching vocabulary can be found in a later unit of this text.

2. Guidance

As a logical follow-up to this purpose setting and direction, the teacher then provides guidance in two important areas—the development of skills (the process), and the development of concepts (the product). This structured form of support is determined by the nature of the material and the abilities of the students. The two components of the guidance phase of the instructional framework are:

a. *Development of Skills.* Here, Herber (1970) suggests the use of reading guides, a special type of study guide "designed to show students how to apply skills as they read" (p. 36). A detailed explanation of the development and use of reading guides, including numerous examples, is available in Herber's *Teaching Reading in Content Areas* (1978).

Using the example from Niles (1965), during the direction portion of the preparation stage, the instructor teaches the students how to recognize and how to glean information from the organizational pattern of cause-effect. A reading guide could then be used to develop that new skill further, while, at the same time, the teacher guides the student to the important information within the unit. For example, the teacher might list in a study guide some possible causes and require the students to supply the effects they gleaned from the selection.

b. *Development of Concepts.* Another type of study guide, designed to improve students' understanding of the major concepts of the unit, is the reasoning guide (Herber, 1970). The reasoning guide involves the development and use of a study guide for postreading extensions. This form of guidance allows the content instructor to lead the student to the major concepts within the selection and to extend the student's understanding both critically and creatively.

3. Independence

Finally, the teacher must provide opportunities for students in the (a) application of skills and (b) application of concepts.

In both instances, it is important that students have occasions to use these newly acquired skills and concepts in other settings. As Herber (1978) suggests, this may entail coaching by the teacher. (For example, indirect questioning by the teacher may implicitly alert the student to the use of the framework in the student's own reading. This may entail recalling prior uses of the framework and a discussion of its possible use with other material.)

Cautions and Comments

The instructional framework provides teachers with a structure for presenting a content lesson; it provides students with a procedure for acquiring understandings from content reading. But the strategy is teacher-dominated rather than student-centered. Indeed, the constant use of the lesson plan format along with study guides and graphic organizers may impose on rather than develop students' own reading-learning abilities and strategies. Toward the goal of increasing student independence, the teacher needs to vary the instructional framework with the differential needs of students across texts.

The constant use of this lesson plan format along with the teacher-developed study guides may result in less-than-exciting lessons. The creative teacher should seek ways to vary the strategy in order to insure total student involvement and eventual student independence.

An individual content teacher may find it extremely difficult and time consuming to develop a program centered around the concept of the instructional framework. For that reason, teacher teams might be formed to develop such a program. Personnel involved in pre- and in-service training sessions could set aside sufficient amounts of time so that teachers could take part in meaningful activities designed to "pay off" in the classroom. Finally, an increasingly large number of school districts are reassigning their more experienced reading teachers to positions as resource teachers. One of the major functions of these individuals could well be to assist the content teachers in the development and use of the instructional framework.

For an extended discussion of this strategy, the reader is directed to the description of study guides found later in this text.

SAMPLE LESSON PLAN FOR AN
INSTRUCTIONAL FRAMEWORK[1]

Example of Instructional Framework

I. PREPARATION

  A. Motivation

    1. Could discuss possible results of "suburban sprawl." What happens each time a new subdivision is built in our community?

    2. Refer to picture on page 232 of a portion of a market-place in Guadalajara, Mexico. "What do you see? What basic need of man could be filled by the items pictured?" (Kimble, Teachers Edition, 233)

  B. Background Information and Review

    1. If available, show film "Foods around the World.' (Coronet Instructional Films, 11 min., color)

    2. Following specific discussion of film, ask, "What is needed in order to use land for growing crops or raising animals?" (Kimble, T. E., 233) List these points on board. List might include: sunlight, soil, water, proper temperature, seed, methods of planting, methods for insuring proper growth, methods for harvesting, food for animals, shelter for animals.

    3. "Can we raise crops or animals in an area that does not have all these things? If so, what is needed to do so?" (Kimble, T. E., 233)

    4. "Can you see how we can relate what we learned in the last chapter on the haves and the have-nots to this chapter on food?"

  C. Anticipation and Purpose

    1. As a result of the above discussion, students should have some notion of the type of information we will be learning in this chapter.

    2. Set purposes in terms of

      a. Content. Example: "In our study of this chapter, we will want to note

        (1) How increased population effects the available land and the actual food supply

        (2) Ways in which dependence on other nations is good and bad

        (3) How improved technology might overcome some of our problems"

1. Developed for "Trailblazers in the Search for Food," in G. H. T. Kimble, *Man and His World*. Morristown, N.J.: Silver Burdett, 1972, Chap. 12, 232–51.

  b. Process. Example: "You will learn much of this
     information if you can
     (1) Accurately interpret the wealth of information
         displayed on the six maps in this short chapter
     (2) Recognize the two writing patterns that the
         author uses throughout this chapter—cause-
         effect and comparison-contrast"
D. Direction
   If students do not possess sufficient map-reading skills or if
   they have not been taught the two organizational patterns
   mentioned above, provide appropriate instruction for one
   or both of these skills. This teaching can be done by using
   the material within this chapter or by using supplemental
   material. If students already possess these skills, such
   instruction will not be necessary.
E. Language Development
   This particular chapter is divided into three segments by
   the text author. The following terms may be pretaught as
   an introduction to each lesson
       Lesson 1.   Arable land, cultivation, tillage, polder
       Lesson 2.   Strains, steppes, plant breeder, animal
                   breeding, mixed farming
       Lesson 3.   Custom, tradition, agricultural specialists

II. GUIDANCE

Guide(s) may be developed to provide students with an opportunity to use the newly acquired skill(s) taught in Direction
phase mentioned above and, at the same time, to learn the
important chapter content.

The following guide could be used with the first portion of this
chapter.

Cause-Effect Relationships

Cause	Effect
1. "In England and Wales, . . . more than 100,000 acres of land are needed yearly for new homes, factories, airfields, highways, parking lots, and playing fields. Nearly all of this land is first-rate farming land." (Kimble, 233)	1.

The following actions resulted in specific changes to land previously thought of as nonproductive (Kimble, 235):

Cause	*Effect*
2. In the Netherlands, they turned the Zuider Zee into land called *polders*.	2.
3. The Egyptians built the High Dam across the Nile at Aswan.	3.
4. The Soviet Union built dams and irrigation canals.	4.

Additional guides may be developed to provide students with the necessary structure for learning both the process of learning the material and the material itself.

Students may use the guides individually, followed by small group discussion, then large group discussion.

III. INDEPENDENCE

The teacher should provide opportunities in which students might use their newly learned skills and concepts in new settings. Here are some of the possibilities with this chapter:

1. Establish research groups to explore more specifically the Netherlands *polder* plan, the Aswan Dam, and other land-reclamation projects.
2. Invite a local agricultural specialist to class ". . . to discuss new strains of plants or animals that are being developed in your own area." (Kimble, T. E. 242)
3. "Divide the class into groups and assign each one a vegetable—rutabaga, broccoli, brussels sprouts, etc. Each group is to plan a campaign that will 'sell' the vegetable to the rest of the class." (Kimble, T. E., 250)

REFERENCES

Herber, H. L. 1970. *Teaching reading in content areas*. Englewood Cliffs, N.J.: Prentice-Hall. The original source of information on the instructional framework.

———. 1978. *Teaching reading in content areas*. 2d ed. Englewood Cliffs, N. J.: Prentice-Hall. The primary and updated source of information on the instructional framework.

Niles, O. S. 1965. Organization perceived. In *Developing study skills in secondary schools*, edited by H. L. Herber. Newark, Del.: International Reading Association. Describes the various organizational patterns in factual writing and provides numerous examples of the four major writing patterns—enumerative order, time order, cause-effect, and comparison-contrast.

APPENDIX

DIAGNOSTIC USE OF
LESSON FRAMEWORKS

Lesson frameworks are presented in Unit One. Diagnostically, they might allow: (1) an analysis of students' reading abilities in the context of these strategies, and (2) a determination of the effectiveness and suitability of the strategies themselves. Specifically, they provide an opportunity to analyze a student's:

1. Reading behavior, including an examination of the student's purposes for reading, ability to read to verify purposes, ability to evaluate and to generate further purposes for reading;
2. Reading products, including the student's recall of details, main ideas, inferences, and organization of information into a meaningful interpretation;
3. Skimming, previewing, scanning, rate-of-reading, and word-recognition skills;
4. Reading-related skills, including vocabulary, oral reading, use of reference skills, and study skills such as outlining, classifying, summarizing, and using reference material;
5. Readiness for a strategy, and the general efficacy of each strategy, by contrasting student responsiveness and abilities across the various frameworks and strategies. (For example, by comparing a student's responsiveness to a Directed Reading Activity and a Directed Reading–Thinking Activity, the student's readiness for and the efficacy of either a teacher-directed approach or a student-centered approach can be determined.);
6. Differential abilities across material varying in difficulty, length, content, and type;
7. Differential abilities across segments of a single selection; and
8. Differential abilities across reading, viewing, and listening modes.

Illustrations

The following examples illustrate the use of selected strategies for these purposes. Illustration One describes the diagnostic use of the Directed Reading–Thinking Activity. Illustration Two describes a comparative analysis of the diagnostic use of the Directed Reading–Thinking Activity across reading, listening, and visual modes.

Illustration One

Using the Directed Reading–Thinking Activity Diagnostically.
Sherry, Michael, and Tony were sixteen-year-old ninth graders who
were having difficulty reading in material intended for their grade
level. Their performances during a Directed Reading–Thinking
Activity were examined with respect to the following reading behaviors: (1) purpose-setting (predictive) capabilities and subsequent modification/confirmation of predictions; (2) motivation to
pursue predictions; (3) use of experiential background; (4) comprehension skills, such as ability to recall details, make inferences, and
derive a main idea; and (5) word identification skills through contextual use.

They were asked to read silently a passage on weather fore-
casting excerpted from a science text. The material was selected
because of the emphasis upon this type of reading in their high
school curriculum. They were directed to stop at various points and
to comment upon their previous predictions and predict forthcoming information. Then they were asked several comprehension
questions and vocabulary questions, and asked to read sections of
the passage orally.

They were fairly successful with the technique. They were
able to make predictions based upon the available information, and
to bring their own experiential base to the process; however, their
subsequent confirmations and modifications of predictions were
made independently of the text, and they had to be redirected to the
material to confirm or refute statements. Questioning at the end of
the passage revealed a good grasp of the main idea, of supporting
details, and of inferences. Sherry's oral rereading, ninety-seven
words in length, contained only one miscue, in which she changed a
verb from active to passive voice. It is interesting to note that
she was able to use context to figure out the meaning of "meteor-
ologist." The other students read equally well.

Conclusions: The students were able to bring their experiential background to the task, process the textual information, and
acquire an understanding from what they had read. Motivation for
continued reading, however, did not appear to be internalized.
Instead, it seemed that the three students needed some encouragement to make predictions through the text. Obviously, if this strategy were to be used successfully with them, adjustments would need
to be made to avoid these lags. Possibly, interactions within a
different group setting or changing the nature of the purpose-setting
activity might prove beneficial.

Illustration Two

*Comparing the use of the Directed Reading–Thinking Activity across
a reading mode, a listening mode, and a visual mode.* Rosa and Peter
were beginning readers in their second semester of the first grade.
To learn more about their reading performance and to assess their

instructional needs, an analysis was made of their responses to the above-mentioned variations of the Directed Reading–Thinking Activity.

Directed Reading–Thinking Activity: Reading Mode. In this activity, Rosa and Peter were directed to read a story and, at appropriate points in the story, make predictions about what was likely to happen on the basis of the events so far. They read two stories selected from their reading series. Their responses throughout this activity were hesitant. They would set purposes and make predictions only after much encouragement, and even then their purposes were specific rather than general. It appeared they were unable to relate personal experiences to those in the stories. Rosa seemed to be afraid to take chances on predicting, for fear her predictions would be incorrect or would not please the examiner. When she ventured a prediction that seemed correct, she was reluctant to try other alternatives. Peter seemed unwilling to suggest even a single prediction.

Directed Reading–Thinking Activity: Listening Mode. Using the procedure in this fashion allows appraisal of purpose-setting behavior and comprehension outside the context of their reading. Using this procedure, the teacher read the title and asked Rosa and Peter to look at the page to determine what the story might be about or what might happen. At first, both Rosa and Peter were very reluctant to raise any kind of questions or to make any predictions. As the story progressed, they were encouraged to raise questions and to check their answers upon hearing the story and viewing the pictures. Rosa made predictions as to who the characters were and what they might be doing. Peter on the one hand, was still quite reticent and only gave one or two predictions. He seemed unable to apply his own experiences and relied entirely upon the pictures to make predictions while using the text to confirm them. For instance, when he viewed a new picture, he would name the people and activity, and would confirm his predictions by listening to the text. At no time did he attempt to read any of the text for himself. Upon hearing the text, he would comment on the validity of his predictions, and he did not wish to guess what would come next until seeing a new picture.

As the activity progressed, Rosa on the other hand, became more interested in the story. She had to be discouraged from turning the page too quickly. As her interest grew, her predictions were more frequent although still specific; that is, within the range of specific events. As Rosa's interest grew, so Peter also became more involved. Many of Rosa's early predictions proved to be inaccurate, although all were reasonable. She did not seem at all discouraged by these errors and freely corrected her predictions. She rather unhesitatingly generated several predictions throughout the selection. Although Peter did not generate as many predictions as Rosa, he generated many more than he had ever done before. They both commented that they had not previously used this activity and usually relied on the teacher to correct their ideas.

Directed Reading–Thinking Activity: Visual Mode. In this activity, Rosa and Peter completed three exercises:

1. Picture jigsaw, in which increasing amounts of a final pattern were displayed; Rosa and Peter were asked to make predictions on final pictures;
2. Cartoon story, in which sequential frames of a pictorial story were shown; they were asked to make predictions as to possible story-endings; and
3. Single picture frame, in which a single picture of an event was shown and the students were asked to conjecture as to what had preceeded the action and what might follow.

On all exercises, Rosa and Peter responded enthusiastically and were able successfully to implement behaviors analogous to those involved in reading: purpose-setting, relating background knowledge, using several comprehension skills, and risk-taking. On the first exercise, both Rosa and Peter were able to make several predictions about potential final pictures, to modify their predictions in the light of further information, and to bring their prior experience and the text to bear upon their predictions. On the second exercise, they were able to make several predictions about a logical story, using similar behaviors to those cited for the first exercise. On the third exercise, both Rosa and Peter used these same skills to offer a number of different, plausible suggestions for events preceding and following the action.

Conclusions: In the reading situation, both Rosa and Peter appear hesitant to participate in activities that require prediction, purpose setting, and involvement. When they make predictions, they tend to hold to them. They seem to lack motivation and are reluctant to trust their own judgment. Outside a reading mode, Rosa's responses are quite different. In a viewing and listening situation, she readily makes predictions and seems highly motivated. Peter's responses are quite different outside either a reading or listening mode. It would appear that Rosa's confidence and reading-thinking abilities would improve if she were given Directed Reading–Thinking Activities using viewing and listening modes. It would seem that Peter could profit from the viewing mode. For purposes of improving their purpose-setting behaviors within these contexts, both Rosa and Peter should be encouraged to make multiple predictions of both a specific and general nature, without being concerned about their correctness. If possible, activities in which there are no correct responses should be used. In general, it would appear that both students need to become involved in reading for meaning. Maybe high-interest material that involves reading and doing (e.g., directions, menus) would prove beneficial.

2

Comprehension and Content Area Reading Strategies

The Unit and Its Theme

The basic goals of reading are to enable children to gain an understanding of the world and of themselves, to develop appreciations and interests, to find solutions to their personal and group problems, and to develop strategies by which they can become independent comprehenders. Logically, comprehension should be considered the heart of reading instruction, and the major goal of that instruction should be the provision of learning activities that will enable students to think about and react to what they read—in short, to read for meaning.

The Strategies

The present unit describes ten strategies for the improvement of reading comprehension. The strategies are designed to help teachers in one or more of the following ways:

1. Activate students' prior knowledge;
2. Guide students' reading of a text;
3. Foster active and engaged reading; and
4. Reinforce concepts gleaned from the text reading.

Many of these strategies may substitute or augment parts of the lesson frameworks described in Unit One. A brief summary of each strategy follows.

PReP Technique

The PReP Technique provides a teacher a means to prepare students to read a text selection and, at the same time, analyze their responses so as to tailor subsequent instruction to student needs.

Anticipation Guide

An Anticipation Guide is designed to activate students' prior knowledge about a topic by having them react to a series of statements related to the major concepts to be encountered in their text reading. Thus, it also provides students a guide for their reading.

Guided Writing Procedure

The Guided Writing Procedure is designed to facilitate the synthesis of text material through the use of free association and writing. Additionally, it is intended to provide teachers a means to improve students' written expression.

Question–Answer Relationships

Question–Answer Relationships are designed to help students answer comprehension questions by providing them a format for analyzing the task demands of questions. This strategy seems to be more appropriate for middle school students.

ReQuest Procedure

The ReQuest Procedure uses a reciprocal questioning technique in an attempt to encourage students to formulate their own questions about material and thereby learn purposeful, thoughtful reading. The ReQuest Procedure can be applied to either a reading passage or a picture, and it is suggested for use with students at all levels.

Study Guides

The backbone of the instructional framework is the study guide, which students use in dealing with the content. Study guides can guide students through their content area textbook reading by focusing their attention on the major ideas presented.

Selective Reading Guide-O-Rama

The Selective Reading Guide-O-Rama provides the content teacher an opportunity to guide the students to the relevant information within the content unit.

This helps the student to see the significant information within the chapter. Suited for students in grades six and above, the technique appears to offer more assistance to those readers who may experience difficulty with the material.

Guided Reading Procedure

Incorporating the techniques of unaided recall of facts, self-correction, recognition of implicit questions, organization of ideas, and brief quizzes, the Guided Reading Procedure attempts to improve attitudinal and skill aspects of reading comprehension. While the Guided Reading Procedure can be used with children at various levels, it seems best suited for grades three and above.

GIST

The GIST procedure provides students a format for generating gist, or summary, statements of paragraphs and short passages. It progresses from a teacher-directed small group strategy to one in which students independently generate their own summary statements.

Explicit Teaching of Comprehension

The Explicit Teaching of reading comprehension is a framework for the direct instruction of reading comprehension. Its intent is to get students to independently apply comprehension skills learned through explicit teaching to other reading situations. The strategy is useful for students at all grade levels.

PReP TECHNIQUE

Purpose

The Pre Reading Plan (PReP) was developed by Judith Langer (1981) with the following goals:

1. To give students an opportunity to generate what they know about a topic and to extend these ideas and evaluate them; and
2. To provide teachers with a procedure for assessing the adequacy of the students' prior knowledge about a specific topic, and for determining the language students use to express their ideas

Rationale

The PReP technique represents an extension of the research of the late 1970s on the relation between prior knowledge and reading comprehension (e.g., Anderson, Pichert, and Shirey 1979; Anderson, Reynolds, Schallert, and Goetz 1977; Anderson, Spiro, and Anderson 1978; Anderson and Freebody 1981). By providing students opportunities for their brainstorming (listing on a chart or the chalkboard the students' ideas), developing associations for, and reflecting and reformulating these ideas, Langer (1980, 1981, 1982) claims that the technique can be used to help students access what they know about a topic prior to reading. For those students who know a lot about a topic, it can be used to help them determine what is relevant and what is irrelevant. For those students who may be unaware that they know something about a topic, the technique helps them access relevant knowledge. For those students who know very little about a topic, the technique helps extend their understandings sufficiently to prepare them for learning from their texts. Alternatively, the technique might be used as a flag for determining the readiness and needs of different students. As Langer (1981) stated:

> When preparing students for a reading activity, we can help them become aware of relevant prior knowledge, while we judge whether or not that knowledge is sufficient for comprehension of the text. And that point we will be able to make knowledgeable decisions about reading assignments and instruction and related concepts. (P. 153)

To guide teachers in their assessment of the response of students, Langer (1982) lists characteristics of the type of associations that students with either a lot or very little prior knowledge will likely generate. Her own research, in collaboration with Nicholich (Langer and Nicholich 1981), suggests that her analyses of prior knowledge are better than IQ or standardized reading test scores in predicting student recall of a specific passage.

Intended Audience

Langer does not specify any particular audience for the technique. It would seem reasonable to use the procedure with groups of students at almost any grade level, either as preparation for reading or in conjunction with other learning experiences such as excursions, films, and the like.

Description of the Procedure

Use of the PReP technique has two facets: (1) engaging students in group discussion around key concepts and (2) analyzing the nature of student responses.

1. Engaging Students in Group Discussion

A group discussion directed at key concepts from a topic that students are to explore represents the heart of the PReP technique. Prior to initiating the discussion, the teacher is expected to determine what are the key concepts that they wish the students to address, and what are ways they might stimulate discussion or associations with those key concepts. For example, a teacher about to embark upon a unit on, or have the students read a text about, underwater exploration might isolate selected key concepts (e.g., geography of the oceans and problems with deep water exploration) and introduce the students to the topic with a photo or an artist's depiction of deep-water sea life. The ensuing discussion involves a three-step process:

Step One: Initial Associations with the Concept (What comes to mind when . . . ?)

Using the picture or some other stimuli the teacher encourages brainstorming (What comes to mind when . . . ? What do you think of . . . ? What might you see, hear, feel . . . ? What might be going on . . . ?). As students generate ideas, the teacher jots them down on the chalkboard.

Step Two: Reflections on Initial Associations (What made you think of . . . ?).

During the second step, students are expected to explain the free associations they generated in Step One. This is intended to encourage students to become aware of the bases of their own individual associations, as well as those generated by their peers. Through this procedure, it is suggested, they are better able to evaluate the usefulness of their ideas during the subsequent reading experience.

Step Three: Reformulation of Knowledge (Have you any new ideas about . . . ?)

In this step the teacher asks the students if they have any new ideas or ideas they wish to change or refine. While Step Two often results in triggering new ideas, Step Three serves to probe if there are any changes, deletions, revisions, or additions. The teacher's role in this and other steps is accepting and inquisitive rather than evaluative and critical.

2. Analyzing Student Responses

To provide teachers with the diagnostic information necessary to determine the instructional needs of students, Langer proposes that teachers pursue an analysis of the free associations generated by the students. She offers guidelines by which they might determine if students have well-formed, partly formed, or ill-formed knowledge structures:

    a. Students with very little knowledge about a concept will generally focus on low-level associations with morphemes (prefixes,

suffixes, or root words; words that sound like the stimulus word, or first but not quite relevant experiences.
   b. Students with some prior information will generally mention examples, attributes, or defining characteristics.
   c. Students with much prior information about a concept will generally offer information that suggests evidence of integration with high-level concepts. Their responses might take the form of analogies, definitions, linkages, and superordinate concepts.

As Langer points out, a reader's responses may vary across the three steps of the technique, so any analysis should not be restricted to one of the steps and not the three. To assist teachers in the use of the technique and in a determination of the level of students' prior knowledge, Langer offers several examples of student responses and discusses how these responses might be analyzed and what they might suggest for teaching. Students with some or much knowledge may need some teacher guidance but are probably quite capable of reading the selection. In contrast, Langer suggests that students with little knowledge will need direct instruction in concepts. An example of such analyses is presented in Figures 2–1 and 2–2.

Cautions and Comments

Langer's PReP technique offers the teacher much that is worthwhile. First, PReP provides teachers with a straightforward framework for preparing students for a selection while, at the same time, it encourages teachers to study the responses of readers and adjust their instruction accordingly. Second, Langer's suggestions are offered as guidelines and include enough exceptions, examples, and interpretations to prompt intelligent use of the technique. Third, Langer's steps go beyond simply allowing students to free associate to having them think about their ideas and revise them. Fourth, Langer provides the teacher with procedures that can be used to apply the strategy to classroom situations, including the suggestions of a grid upon which teachers could map out the responses of a whole class. In addition, the steps involved in the procedure are broad enough to be applied to almost any textbook or instructional activity involving concept development.

Langer's technique has one other feature that distinguishes it. Namely, Langer has subjected to careful study the guidelines for analyzing levels of prior information. In a study with Nicolich (Langer and Nicholich 1981), Langer was able to show that her method for analyzing prior information was a better predictor of reading comprehension of a particular passage than were IQ or a standardized reading achievement measure.

The technique, however, has its limitations. Despite the research data on the procedure, it is questionable whether students' prior knowledge can be so accurately assessed by using the three steps Langer proposes or the guidelines she advocates for analyzing responses. She alludes to exceptions, but we are never sure how many students might be misclassified. Some students may be as

Figure 2–1   Diagnostic Analyses of Student Responses to PReP

General Topic: Underwater Exploration

Key Topic: Geography of the oceans (picture of cross-sectioned ocean topography)

Student	Responses	Level
Robin	1. sandy, dark and cold on bottom.	some—attribute
	2. only a few plants or animals can live there	
	3. not many plants or fish there	
Kim	1. drifting sand and rocks	some—attribute
	2. ocean floor changes	
	3. ocean geography is different from land geography because ocean geography changes more	much—analogies
Terry	1. depth of water varies	some—attribute
	2. plants and fish vary with depth of water	
	3. depth of water must affect the marine life	much—superordinate
Jay	1. plants, fish, and water	little—association
	2. different fish in different places	
	3. fish live where they like, how deep the water is	some—attribute
Casey	1. bacteria, shells, lots of fish and whales	little—association
	2. oceans have lots in them	
	3. oceans have more life in them	much—superordinate

unwilling to free associate as some readers are tentative about inferencing. Possibly the procedure would be better applied after reading a paragraph or two, a synopsis, or a related passage. Ideally, Langer should have determined her classes of response *after* she had determined which students had adequate comprehension and which students had inadequate comprehension. An a priori determination seems less than desirable. Potential users of the technique should realize that, apart from some claims from selected users, the instruc-

Figure 2-2   Diagnostic Analysis of Student Responses to PReP

General Topic: Underwater Exploration

Key Topic: Problems with deep water exploration (picture of deep sea life)

Student	Responses	Level
Robin	1. fish and plants	little—association
	2. some fish aren't friendly	
	3. a diver could be attacked by a mean fish	some—example
Kim	1. lots of things growing and swimming around	some—attribute
	2. fish may not want a diver there	
	3. some animals don't like intruders into their territory	much—superordinate
Terry	1. dark and cold water	some—attribute
	2. ocean isn't an easy place to go	
	3. divers might get cold or lost if a flashlight breaks	some—example
Jay	1. not much air down there	some—attribute
	2. divers have to bring a lot of equipment	
	3. divers are vulnerable because water isn't like land, without air	much—analogy
Casey	1. it's very dark	some—attribute
	2. it's hard to see what is down there	
	3. explorers might not see some things because it's so dark	some—example

tional worth of the procedure has yet to be determined. Whether or not the strategy improves comprehension of a passage, concept development, or greater awareness of what readers know has yet to be determined. Likewise, whether or not the technique improves teacher decision making in this realm is an issue awaiting research validation. In the meanwhile, the technique may serve to point teachers and students in the right direction and the effects of this technique are unlikely to be detrimental.

REFERENCES

Anderson, R. C., and P. Freebody. 1981. Vocabulary knowledge. In *Comprehension and teaching: Research reviews*, edited by J. T. Guthrie. Newark, Del.: International Reading Association. Discusses the role of vocabulary in reading comprehension based upon an extensive review of the literature.

Anderson, R. C., J. W. Pichert, and L. L. Shirey. 1979. Effects of the reader's schemata at different points in time (Tech. Rep. No. 119). Urbana: University of Illinois, Center for the Study of Reading, April. (ED 169 523) Provides research support for the influence of prior knowledge upon reading comprehension.

Anderson, R. C., R. D. Reynolds, D. L. Schallert, and E. T. Goetz. 1977. Framework for comprehending discourse. *American Education Research Journal* 14:367–81. Presents research support for a schema-theoretical point of view of reading comprehension.

Anderson, R. C., R. J. Spiro, and M. C. Anderson. 1978. Schemata as scaffolding for the representation of information in connected discourse. *American Educational Research Journal* 15:433–40.

Langer, J. A. 1980. Relation between levels of prior knowledge and the organization of recall. In *Perspectives in reading research and instruction*, edited by M. L. Kamil and A. J. Moe. Washington, D. C.: National Reading Conference, 23–33. Provides the research bases for using PReP to assess levels of prior knowledge.

———. 1981. From theory to practice: A prereading plan. *Journal of Reading* 25:2. Represents a very practical description of how PReP can be used.

———. 1982. Facilitating text processing: The elaboration of prior knowledge. In *Reader meets author/bridging the gap*, edited by J. Langer and M. Smith-Burke. Newark, Del.: International Reading Association. Discusses the use of PReP including examples of responses by students.

Langer, J. A., and M. Nicolich. 1981. Prior knowledge and its effect on comprehension. *Journal of Reading Behavior* 13:375–78. Represents a research study in which the validity of using PReP as a means of assessing background knowledge was addressed.

Pearson, P. D., and D. Johnson. 1978. *Teaching reading comprehension*. New York: Macmillan. Represents a practical introduction to the theory and practice of teaching reading comprehension.

ANTICIPATION GUIDE

Purpose

The Anticipation Guide (Readence, Bean, and Baldwin 1981) is designed to:

1. Activate students' knowledge about a topic before reading; and
2. Provide purpose by serving as a guide for subsequent reading

Rationale

The Anticipation Guide attempts to enhance students' comprehension by having them react to a series of statements about a topic before they begin to read or to engage in any other form of information acquisition. It utilizes prediction by activating students' prior knowledge, and it capitalizes on controversy as a motivational device to get students involved in the material to be read.

Numerous studies (e.g., Pearson, Hansen, and Gordon 1979) have pointed out the efficacy of activating students' knowledge about a topic before they read in order to enhance comprehension. Other ways to promote better comprehension have also been suggested. Herber (1978) has recommended that statements be used in lieu of questions as an initial means to get students more involved in their learning, because statements require students only to recognize and respond, while questions require students to produce a response. Production of their own questions and statements, which is a more sophisticated learning behavior than recognition alone, becomes the end goal of such instruction. Additionally, Lunstrum (1981) suggested that controversy could be used as a motivational technique for reading by arousing students' curiosity about a topic and getting them to use the text to corroborate their stance on an issue.

The Anticipation Guide incorporates all of these comprehension-enhancing strategies by asking students to react to statements that focus their attention on the topic to be learned. Students' previous thoughts and opinions about that topic are activated by using statements that are carefully worded so as to challenge students' knowledge bases and to arouse their curiosity. Students then become motivated to read to resolve the conceptual conflict. In this way, misconceptions about a topic can be brought out and inaccuracies dealt with. Additionally, the Anticipation Guide can also be used as the basis for postreading discussion wherein students react a second time to the statements, this time dealing with the text information as well.

Intended Audience

The Anticipation Guide can be adapted for use at any grade level and can be used with a variety of print and nonprint media. Statements used in the guide can be modified and read to younger or slower students, who may be unable to read them on their own. Additionally, the Anticipation Guide can be used to introduce a film, filmstrip, lecture, audiotape, or field trip, as well as to introduce a text reading assignment. Thus, the guide can be realistically applied in most learning situations.

Description of the Procedure

Readence, Bean, and Baldwin (1981) recommend the following eight steps to implement an Anticipation Guide:

1. Identify major concepts;
2. Determine students' knowledge of these concepts;
3. Create statements;
4. Decide statement order and presentation mode;
5. Present guide;
6. Discuss each statement briefly;
7. Direct students to read the text; and
8. Conduct follow-up discussion.

1. Identify Major Concepts

The ideas to be learned by reading the text should be determined by a careful perusal of the material and of the teacher's manual, if one is available. This step is analogous to what normally happens in good lesson planning. The following example of constructing and using an Anticipation Guide is adapted from one provided by Head and Readence (1985). Using a text entitled "Food and Health," the following concepts were identified:

    a. Food contains nutrients that your body needs for energy, growth, and repair.
    b. Carbohydrates and fats supply energy.
    c. A balanced diet includes the correct amount of all the nutrients needed by your body.
    d. Every food contains some calories of food energy.

2. Determine Students' Knowledge of These Concepts

In order to determine how the main concepts support or challenge what the students already know, the teacher must consider the students' experiential background. The whole class, as well as individual students, will have to be considered in this step. In our nutrition example, socioeconomic level is one, but only one, factor that may have a bearing on the kinds of statements that eventually result.

3. Create Statements

The number of statements to be created varies with the amount of text to be read and, particularly, the number of concepts that have been identified. Additionally, the ability and maturity levels of the students influence statement making. Three to five statements is usually a good number to aim for. Generally, the most effective statements are those in which the students have sufficient knowledge to understand what the statements say, but not enough to make any of them a totally known entity.

4. Decide Statement Order and Presentation Mode

An appropriate order must be determined to present the guide. Usually, the order follows the sequence in which the concepts are encountered in the text, but that is subject to each teacher's judgment.

The guide may be presented using the chalkboard, an overhead transparency, or a ditto sheet that is handed out individually. A set of directions and blanks for students' responses should be included. The directions must be worded appropriately for the age and maturity levels of the students.

5. Present Guide

Continuing with our Anticipation Guide example on nutrition, the following guide is given the students:

Anticipation Guide: Food and Health

Directions: Below are some statements about food and nutrition. Read each statement carefully and place a checkmark next to each statement with which you agree. Be prepared to defend your thinking as we discuss the statements.

————————— 1. An apple a day keeps the doctor away.
————————— 2. If you wish to live a long life, be a vegetarian.
————————— 3. Three square meals a day will satisfy all your body's nutritional needs.
————————— 4. Calories make you fat.

When presenting the guide to students, it is advisable to read the directions and statements orally. You should emphasize that students will share their thoughts and opinions about each statement, defending their agreement or disagreement with the statement. Students can work individually or in small groups to formulate a response.

6. Discuss Each Statement Briefly

A discussion ensues, with the teacher first asking for a show of hands from students to indicate their agreement or disagreement. The teacher tallies the responses. The discussion should include at least one opinion on each side of the issue per statement. As other students listen to the opinions offered, they can evaluate their own view in terms of the others.

7. Direct Students to Read the Text

Students are now told to read the text assignment with the purpose of deciding what the author would say about each statement. As they read, students should keep two things in mind: their own thoughts and opinions as well as those voiced by others, and how what they are reading relates to what was discussed.

8. Conduct Follow-up Discussion

After reading, the students may respond once again to the statements. This time they should react in the light of the actual text. Thus, the guide now serves as the basis for a postreading discussion in which students can share the new information gained from reading and how their previous thoughts may have been modified by what they understand the reading to say. It should be made clear to the students that agreement with the author is not mandatory, depending on the type of text used. For instance, it may not be necessary to agree with an author's viewpoint expressed in a poem, but it may be so if the text deals with an explanation of a scientific principle.

Cautions and Comments

The Anticipation Guide presents a versatile format for use by teachers to activate students' prior knowledge about a topic to be learned and to motivate them to pursue that information. In essence, the guide provides for the following: (1) active involvement by students in their own learning; (2) the use of prediction as a means to stimulate comprehension; and (3) guidance in the form of purpose-setting behaviors as students interact with the text in their effort to verify their predictions.

In addition, the Anticipation Guide has some diagnostic value for teachers in formulating and executing their instructional plan. As students discuss the statements before reading, teachers can assess the depth and breadth of students' knowledge about a topic. This allows teachers to make tentative instructional decisions about the time required for learning, the kind of materials that may be most appropriate, and what alternative strategies would be beneficial to the students. Lipson (1984) has expressed some concern about the negative effects of inaccurate prior knowledge on learning. Because of this diagnostic character of the Anticipation Guide, teachers can readily take appropriate steps to rectify students' misconceptions when inaccurate or incomplete knowledge is discovered.

Perhaps the most difficult aspect of constructing an Anticipation Guide is selecting appropriate statements to be used. Guide statements must be within students' previous knowledge and, therefore, must be on the experience-based level of comprehension. But the statements must also be on a higher level of generality in order to be an effective teaching and learning strategy. Using statements that are merely fact-based is ineffective. Students should discuss reasons for holding or forming opinions, not simply recite easily found facts.

For instance, if we used a statement in our example guide on nutrition such as "the recommended minimum daily allowance of vitamin A is 1.5 mg," the statement would be virtually useless as a tool to enhance learning. That type of statement is based on fact, not experience. Either students would know it or they wouldn't; in essence, it becomes a true-false statement. If the student does know it, then it has no value as an instructional tool. Conversely, if the student doesn't know it, then it will not serve as a knowledge-activation device. Students must be allowed to use their prior experiences in order to benefit from the use of prereading statements. Teachers are cautioned that, though such statements are more difficult to construct, experience-based statements are crucial to the success of Anticipation Guides or any other guide based on prediction.

REFERENCES

Head, M. H., and J. E. Readence. 1985. Anticipation guides: Enhancing meaning through prediction. In *Reading in the content areas: Improving classroom instruction*, 2d ed., edited by E. K. Dishner, T. W. Bean, J. E. Readence, and D. W. Moore. Dubuque, IA: Kendall/Hunt. Provides a detailed description of the construction and use of Anticipation Guides.

Herber, H. L. 1978. *Teaching reading in content areas.* 2d ed. Englewood Cliffs, NJ: Prentice-Hall. Discusses the use of statements and the role of prediction in learning from text.

Lipson, M. Y. 1984. Some unexpected issues in prior knowledge and comprehension. *The Reading Teacher* 37:760–64. Describes the problem of inaccurate prior knowledge on comprehension.

Lunstrum, J. P. 1981. Building motivation through the use of controversy. *Journal of Reading* 24:687–91. Offers controversy as a means to arouse curiosity and enhance comprehension.

Pearson, P. D., J. Hansen, and C. Gordon. 1979. The effect of background knowledge on young children's comprehension of explicit and implicit information. *Journal of Reading Behavior* 11:201–19. Research study exploring the facilitative effects of prior knowledge on learning from text.

Readence, J. E., T. W. Bean, and R. S. Baldwin. 1981. *Content area reading: An integrated approach.* Dubuque, IA: Kendall/Hunt. Delineates the steps involved in using an Anticipation Guide and provides numerous examples.

GUIDED WRITING PROCEDURE

Purpose

The Guided Writing Procedure (Smith and Bean 1980) is designed to:

1. Activate and assess students' prior knowledge of a text topic before reading occurs;

2. Evaluate students' written expression in a content area;
3. Improve students' written expression through guided instruction; and
4. Facilitate the synthesis and retention of text material.

Rationale

The Guided Writing Procedure (GWP) attempts to use the process of writing as a means to help students learn from text. As a perusal of this volume attests, a number of strategies are offered using the language processes of reading and listening as a means to help students learn from text. Additionally, a number of these strategies advocate the notion that the processes needed to learn content material can be taught concurrently with the content itself. It is precisely this notion that Smith and Bean state also holds true for the development of writing fluency, i.e., the processes of writing can be taught concurrently with the content itself.

Writing takes its own form and style in each content area; it is with this in mind that GWP was developed. Since relatively few specific procedures have been offered by which writing might be integrated with the learning of content, the GWP has been suggested as a means to implement such an approach.

Intended Audience

The GWP was originally intended to be used with students at the middle and secondary levels as an aid to developing writing fluency and enhancing learning from text. Additionally, it can be used with elementary students using basal readers with factual, rather than story-type, content.

Description of the Procedure

Smith and Bean state that using the GWP involves a series of specific procedures spanning several days of content instruction. Two general steps are involved: (1) informal diagnosis of prior content knowledge and written expression, and (2) teaching content and written expression.

1. Informal Diagnosis of Prior Content Knowledge and Written Expression

Begin the GWP by asking students to brainstorm any thoughts they have related to the topic to be learned, for example, "the Solar System." Record everything students say verbatim on the board or overhead projector. The following ideas related to the solar system might be offered by students:

nine planets	Earth
sun is center	revolution around sun
Milky Way	Venus and Mars closest
Jupiter largest	Saturn has rings

Next, have students vote on which ideas seem to be the major ones and which are details. These ideas are organized into an outline or graphic organizer on the board or overhead. The design of the outline is to get students to cluster their ideas. Now, students are ready to write one or two short paragraphs, using the outline or graphic organizer as a guide. Students are told that this will constitute their "first draft." These drafts are collected, and students are assigned to read the text.

At this point, teachers should examine the students' paragraphs rapidly and analyze them for organization of ideas, style, and mechanics. It is suggested that rather than writing any edits on these first drafts, a "Concept and Writing Checklist" be used to record this information for each individual student. Below is an example of a student's paragraph on the solar system and a representative checklist that may be used for recordkeeping purposes.

Fred's Draft

The solar system consists of nine planets and the sun is the center and the earth is one of them. Jupiter is the largest and Saturn has rings while Venus and Mars are the closest.

Concept and Writing Checklist

(=OK; 0=Needs improvement; ?=Can't tell)

Student

Fred

Criteria

Organization of ideas
  Clear topic   ?
  Supporting details/examples   ?
  Logical flow   ?
  Comments: _____ *What do you want the reader to know?* _____

Style
  Shows variety in:
  Word choice   √
  Sentence length   ?
  Comments: _____ *Too many "ads"* _____

Mechanics
  Complete sentences   √
  Capitalization   0
  Punctuation   0
  Spelling   √
  Comments: _____

In this example Fred has shown that he can organize his ideas well. His problems arise in word choice (too many "and's"), sentence length, punctuation (he needs to use commas and periods), and capitalization.

2. Teaching Content and Written Expression

At this point in time, one or more days have lapsed since the initial draft. The teacher now displays an illustrative draft on the board or overhead along with the checklist as a guide. This draft may be an actual student's or a composite of several first drafts. Perhaps the best example to use is one that contains inaccurate text information as well as inappropriate writing criteria. Using the checklist and text information, the class as a whole should contribute ideas to edit the illustrative paragraph.

Students' papers are now returned, and they are asked to use the checklist to help them edit their own drafts. At this point students edit for both content and writing inaccuracies.

This second draft is collected, and a follow-up quiz is given on the material read. As an alternative, a post-reading activity for vocabulary and/or concept reinforcement may be used. As soon as possible, teachers should examine the second drafts and compare them to the initial checklist results. Individual conferences may be used to provide help for students whose writing has not shown growth. Smith and Bean suggest that a positive trend should be noted in students' ability to use ideas and express themselves in writing.

Cautions and Comments

The Guided Writing Procedure presents teachers with a novel way to introduce and teach text material. There is no doubt that writing needs to take its place as a viable means to help students learn from text—the GWP fills a gap in the instructional literature in reading.

At the same time, some concerns about the procedure need to be mentioned. Smith and Bean fail to extend their suggestions to preparing students for writing; for instance, they fail to suggest that students might examine examples of text written by professional authors. Also, they fail to go far enough in how they suggest a teacher might help students deal with their own ideas. Apart from organizing ideas, students should perhaps select those ideas upon which they wish to focus and, prior to writing, they might consider how their ideas could be arranged. In conjunction with helping students develop and refine ideas, Smith and Bean confound revision (i.e., the reexamination and redevelopment of ideas) with editing. Furthermore, their checklists seem more cumbersome than helpful. Nor have the authors discussed the possibility of having students write reports that are more ongoing or that are coauthored.

Another major problem lies with their suggestions for teacher evaluation. In their failure to consider procedures by which peers might offer and obtain feedback, they put the teacher in the unenviable position of being the only source of feedback and of spending a great deal of time grading. Therefore, they leave most teachers with little choice but to use the strategy only occasionally.

Finally, this is not a strategy in which instant results should be expected.

As the authors of this strategy state, fluent writing like fluent reading evolves through constant practice with actual text material.

REFERENCES

Readence, J. E., T. W. Bean, and R. S. Baldwin. 1981. *Content area reading: An integrated approach.* Dubuque, IA: Kendall/Hunt. Describes the GWP and other alternatives.

Searfoss, L. W., C. Smith, and T. W. Bean. 1981. An integrated strategy for second language learners in content area subjects. *TESOL Quarterly* 15:383–89. Research study that shows the efficacy of the GWP with second language learners in content areas.

Smith, C., and T. W. Bean. 1980. The guided writing procedure: Integrating content reading and writing improvement. *Reading World* 19:290–98. The original discussion of the GWP.

QUESTION-ANSWER RELATIONSHIPS

Purpose

Question-answer relationships (QARs) was developed by Raphael (1982b) as a procedure for enhancing students' ability to answer comprehension questions by giving them a systematic means for analyzing task demands of different question probes.

Rationale

Stemming from her concern that students are frequently asked questions in school but receive little or no guidance in knowing how to answer them, Raphael generated a strategy whereby readers are encouraged to analyze the task demands of questions prior to answering them. The system she devised for students to use involves having students identify three types of questions: text explicit or "right there," scriptal or "on my own," and text implicit or "think and search." This system was based upon a taxonomy suggested by Pearson and Johnson (1978) in which comprehension responses were described as follows: text explicit if the information to be used for the most appropriate response is stated explicitly in the text; text implicit if the response information is located in the text but requires the integration of textual material; and script implicit if the response information is located in the reader's knowledge base.

The system itself is presented to teachers and students in a carefully crafted fashion. Using the research on developing independent comprehenders as a basis (see Tierney and Cunningham 1984), Raphael applies four principles of instruction to helping readers analyze the task demands of questions: (1) give immediate feedback; (2) progress from shorter to longer texts; (3) begin with questions for which the task demand is more straightforward to questions that require the use of multiple sources; and (4) develop independence by beginning with group learning experiences and progressing to individual and independent activities.

Raphael's claims about the efficacy of the strategy has been partially substantiated by research. Raphael and Pearson (1982) found that students in the fourth, sixth, and eighth grades who had been taught the strategy by a university researcher were more successful in answering questions than students who had not received the instruction. In a follow-up to this study Raphael, Wonnacott, and Pearson (1983) taught fourth grade teachers how to use the strategy and obtained similar results. They found that the trained teachers were pleased with the strategy and that students outperformed comparable groups of students who received no such directed learning experiences. In a third study Raphael and McKinney (in press) examined developmental differences in children's performance and training requirements. With older students (eighth graders compared with fifth graders), orientation was as effective as training and the performance of students improved by training, but not by simply being reminded to apply QARs at the time of testing.

Intended Audience

Raphael has used the procedure successfully with students of varying ability levels from grades four through eight. With some modification the procedure could be used with students at earlier grade levels. The strategy has worked most effectively with younger students (fifth and fourth graders), especially with those that are less able.

Description of the Procedure

At the heart of QARs is having the student identify the response demands of various questions (either "right there," "think and search," or "on my own"), then using a knowledge of the response demands to generate an answer. For this purpose, Raphael (1982b) offers the following guidelines and student response format as a way of accustoming readers to the strategy. Once the reader has learned the strategy, Raphael suggests that the focus should be on the best possible response to the question.

Initial use of the format entails having students circle the QAR strategy they will use. During this initial period, a student's response to a question is less important than the student's assessment of the task demands. In other words, it would be okay if the reader generated a wrong answer, but correctly identified the task demands. Later, when students move to determining and writing in the answer, the actual answer the reader generates becomes important.

To introduce most students to the strategy, Raphael suggests a week of intensive training followed by maintenance activities. Adaptations are recommended, if a teacher deems necessary. Four lessons make up the first week's intensive training.

Figure 2-3

Three Kinds of Questions
Where is the answer found?

Type 1

RIGHT THERE
The answer is in the story, easy to find. The words used to make the question and the words that make the answer are RIGHT THERE, in the same sentence.

Type 2

THINK AND SEARCH
The answer is in the story, but a little harder to find. You would *never* find the words in the question and words in the answer in the same sentence, but would have to THINK AND SEARCH for the answer.

Type 3

ON MY OWN
The *answer won't be* told by words in the story. You must find the answer in your head. Think: "I have to answer this question ON MY OWN, the story won't be much help."

PASSAGE 1: ALBERT

Albert was afraid that Susan would beat him in the tennis match. The night before the match, Albert broke both of Susan's racquets.

RIGHT THERE

When did Albert break both of Susan's racquets?
(The night before the match.)

THINK AND SEARCH

Why did Albert break both of Susan's racquets?
(He was afraid that Susan would beat him.)

ON MY OWN

Why was Albert afraid that Susan would beat him?
(He knew she had practiced more.)
(The other students might laugh.)

Figure 2-4 Passage—"Lighting a Match"

When lighting a match, it is important to follow these steps carefully. First tear one match out of the matchbook. Second, close the matchbook cover. Third, strike the match against the rough strip on the outside of the matchbook. Finally, after the match has been used, blow it out carefully, and be sure it is cool before you throw it away.

1. What are the first two steps to correctly light and use a match?
   Right There _____
   Think and Search _____
   On My Own _____

2. Why should you be sure the match is cool before you throw it away?
   Right There _____
   Think and Search _____
   On My Own _____

3. What should you do after a match has been used and is still burning?
   Right There _____
   Think and Search _____
   On My Own _____

4. Why should you close the cover before striking the match?
   Right There _____
   Think and Search _____
   On My Own _____

5. What do you strike the match against to light it?
   Right There _____
   Think and Search _____
   On My Own _____

Lesson 1. The first lesson is intended to introduce students to the task demands of different questions and to provide some initial practice at identifying task demands in conjunction with answering questions. For this purpose, Raphael recommends that instruction similar to the following be given in groups.

Using the previously suggested guidelines and response format (see Figures 2-3 and 2-4), the teacher would explain:

We are going to talk about different types of questions and the best way to answer them. Sometimes your workbook or I give questions that ask for information you can find quite easily in the book. Other times you won't find the answer there. I will describe three kinds of questions: "Right There," "Think and Search," and "On My Own." Each type can be figured out by deciding where you get the information for the answer. We call this a Question-Answer Relationship, or QAR for short." (Raphael 1984, 189).

Raphael (1983) recommends that initially the teacher discuss the difference between text-based and knowledge-based responses, prior to discriminating between the two text-based strategies. Following the introduction, she suggests three practice stages can be used with short passages of two or three sentences. In the first stage, she suggests giving students passages to read with questions for which the answer as well as the QARs are identified. During this stage, she suggests discussing the type of QAR each question represents. In the second stage, she suggests giving students passages, questions, and responses to these questions and having students generate as a group the QAR for each. Finally, in the third stage, she suggests having students determine the QARs and respond with answers.

Lesson 2. The purpose of the second lesson is to provide the students with review and further guided practice as they read slightly longer passages (75 to 150 words). Specifically, Raphael recommends that the teacher begin the lesson with a review of each QAR category and then some guided practice with five questions that require different responses with a passage of approximately 75 to 150 words. She suggests the students do the first passage as a group and then, as a group, that they be given feedback after they finish the second passage independently. As the students proceed with subsequent passages, Raphael emphasizes the importance of giving the students feedback, as well as having them justify their answer to the question and their choice of a QAR. Also she suggests that the teacher explain why an answer is acceptable on the grounds of both accuracy and strategy.

Lesson 3. In the third lesson, Raphael suggests extending the QAR task to a passage approximately the length of a basal selection. She suggests dividing the selection into four sections and generating two questions of each of the three types (a total of six questions) for each section. The first section would be completed in conjunction with reviewing the strategy; students would complete the remaining three sections independently, prior to acquiring feedback.

Lesson 4. For the fourth lesson, Raphael suggests using material typically found in the classroom—a basal story or a social studies or science chapter. She suggests giving the students the passage as a single unit with six questions from each QAR category. The student would be expected to read the passage, determine the QAR for each question, and answer them.

Maintaining QARs. To maintain the use of QARs, Raphael recommends a weekly review lesson and suggests some fun activities (e.g., a courtroom game that requires readers to respond to questions from students who role-play lawyers with the source of answers) that might be reinforcing. To supplement the use of QAR, she recommends that the training program might be extended to more systematic use with content material.

Cautions and Comments

The QAR represents one of the more thoroughly researched instructional strategies that has been developed in recent years. Raphael has gone to great lengths to thoroughly explore its utility at different grade levels with students of varying ability. She reports having most success with students of average and below average ability in grades four through eight. She also claims that the strategy can be easily learned by teachers, and she has explored the worth of different in-service training experiences with the technique (see Raphael 1984). What is lacking from her research data are the long-term benefits or detriments that might arise from using the strategy. We do not know whether students who have been trained to do QARs are better at answering questions after some time has elapsed after training. Nor do we know if the students are better monitors of their own ability to read or answer questions. Furthermore, we have no descriptive data of how QARs influence the reasoning processes that readers use to answer questions and continue reading. Raphael (1984) suggests that with older students there may be interference that arises as a result of considering the task demands.

A concern which seems worth mentioning about QAR relates to problems with using the taxonomy in this way. The taxonomy was intended to describe question-answer types rather than to facilitate a determination of correct responses. As readers consider answering a question, they might be better advised to consider the goal of the question and the point of the passage rather than whether or not the answer is forthcoming from such artificial discrete categories as text or reader. It seems possible that QARs miss the mark by not defining the task demands of questions for students in a way that is helpful to readers.

REFERENCES

Pearson, P. D. and D. D. Johnson. 1978. *Teaching reading comprehension.* New York: Holt, Rinehart & Winston. Presents an overview of the nature of reading comprehension and instructional issues. The taxonomy used by Raphael is described in this book.

Raphael, T. E. 1982a. Improving question-answering performance through instruction (Reading Education Report No. 32). Urbana-Champaign, University of Illinois, Center for the Study of Reading, March. Provides an extensive discussion of the procedure, including pages teachers could use as transparencies or duplicating masters.

———. 1982b. Question-answering strategies for children. *The Reading Teacher* 36:186–90. Presents a clear description of how students might be taught to use QARs including lesson plans and guidelines for teachers.

———. 1984. Teaching learners about sources of information for answering comprehension questions. *Journal of Reading* 27:303–11. Presents an overview of the results of several studies that have explored the utility of QAR.

Raphael, T. E., and P. D. Pearson. 1982. *The effect of metacognitive awareness training on children's question-answering behavior* (Tech. Rep. No. 238). Urbana: University of Illinois, Center for the Study of Reading, March. Reports the first of three research studies in which QARs were taught to students in grades four, six, and eight.

Raphael, T. E., C. A. Wonnacut, and P. D. Pearson. 1983. Increasing students' sensitivity to sources of information: An instruction study in question-answer relationships (Tech. Rep. No. 284). Urbana: University of Illinois, Center for the Study of Reading, July. Reports an attempt to have selected fourth grade teachers trained to teach their students to use QARs.

Raphael, T. E., and J. McKinney. In press. An examination of fifth and eighth grade students' question answering behavior: An instructional study in metacognition. *Journal of Reading Behavior*. Reports an exploration of developmental trends in the use of QARs by students.

Tierney, R. J., and J. W. Cunningham. 1984. Research on teaching reading comprehension. In *Handbook of Reading Research*, edited by P. D. Pearson, R. Barr, M. L. Kamie, and P. Mosenthal. New York: Longmans. Reviews the research on teaching reading comprehension, including QAR and related approaches.

REQUEST PROCEDURE

Purpose

The ReQuest procedure (Manzo 1968) is designed to encourage students to:

1. Formulate their own questions about the material they are reading and develop questioning behavior;
2. Adopt an active inquiring attitude to reading;
3. Acquire reasonable purposes for reading; and
4. Improve their independent reading comprehension skills.

Rationale

Manzo, the originator of the ReQuest procedure, suggests that while teacher questioning and purpose setting are important to reading comprehension, of greater importance is the development of the students' abilities to ask their own questions and to set their own purposes for reading. He suggests that these skills facilitate the students' acquisition of an active, inquiring attitude and their ability to examine alternatives and to originate information. These things he considers essential if students are to transfer problem-solving involvement to different contexts.

Intended Audience

ReQuest is suitable for use with students at levels ranging from kindergarten to college. While originally devised for use on a one-to-one basis, it can also work with groups of up to approximately eight persons.

Description of the Procedures

In the ReQuest procedure, an individual student and teacher silently read sections of a selection and then take turns asking and answering each other's questions about that selection. The teacher's function is to model good questioning behavior, to provide feedback to the student about his or her questions, and to assess whether the student has established reasonable purposes for independently completing the passage.

There are six steps teachers should follow in using the ReQuest procedure. These are:

1. Preparation of material;
2. Development of readiness for the strategy;
3. Development of student questioning behaviors;
4. Development of student predictive behaviors;
5. Silent reading activity; and
6. Follow-up activities.

1. Preparation of Material

Preparation of the material entails previewing the selection for the purpose of:

a. Selecting material at an appropriate level for the student;
b. Selecting material appropriate for making predictions; and
c. Identifying appropriate points within the selection where the student could plausibly make predictions.

2. Development of Readiness for the Strategy

Manzo (1969) suggests the following protocol and guidelines as those appropriate for beginning a ReQuest session.

The purpose of this lesson is to improve your understanding of what you read. We will each read silently the first sentence. Then we will take turns asking questions about the sentence and what it means. You will ask questions first, then I will ask questions. Try to ask the kinds of questions a teacher might ask in the way a teacher might ask them.

You may ask me as many questions as you wish. When you are asking me questions, I will close my book (or pass the book to you if there is only one between us). When I ask questions, you close your book. (P. 124)

The teacher might also explain these points during or prior to the session: each question deserves to be answered fully; "I don't know" as an answer is unacceptable; unclear questions are to be rephrased; and uncertain answers should be justified by reference to the text. In addition, it may be necessary at times to introduce some of the vocabulary contained in the selection and/or develop some background for understanding the passage. For example, the teacher may need to give the student oral familiarity with some of the more difficult words in the selection. Also, in order to develop some background for understanding the passage, the teacher might alert the student to the basic concepts involved by a brief and general discussion of the title.

Therefore in introducing the ReQuest procedure, the teacher should be aware of the need to:

a. Build student interest in the procedure;
b. Introduce selected vocabulary;
c. Develop some background for understanding the passage; and
d. Provide the student with an understanding of the rules of ReQuest.

3. Development of Student Questioning Behaviors

At this point, both the teacher and the student participate in the reciprocal questioning procedure. As Manzo's protocol suggests, this procedure entails:

a. *Joint silent reading.* Both the student and teacher read the first sentence of the selection;
b. *Student questioning.* The teacher closes his or her book, and the student questions the teacher. The teacher responds as well as possible, reinforces appropriate questioning behavior and, if necessary, requests rephrasing of unclear questions; and
c. *Exchange of roles.* The student finishes questioning and removes his or her copy of the material. Then the teacher questions the student.

Throughout this phase, the teacher exhibits good questioning behavior and provides feedback to the student about the student's questions. When taking the role of questioner, the teacher should endeavor to extend the student's thinking. To this end, the teacher might use various types of questions, including questions that build upon prior questions and require the student to integrate information. When responding to the student's questions, the teacher could use both verbal and nonverbal reinforcement. For example, a student's question might be reinforced with a statement such as "That's a great question. I really have to . . ." or "I hope I can ask questions that tough that will make you . . ."

4. Development of Student Predictive Behaviors

At an appropriate point in the procedure (i.e., when the student has read enough to make a prediction about the rest of the material), the exchange of questions is terminated. Assuming the role of agitator, the teacher attempts to elicit predictions and validations from the student. At this point, the teacher might ask, "What do you think will happen? . . . Why do you think so? . . . Read the line that proves it." It may prove helpful to develop a list of suggested predictions and a ranking from most likely to least likely.

If the predictions and verifications are reasonable, the teacher and student can move to the next step—silent reading activity. If the predictions are unreasonable, the teacher and student may continue reading and exchanging questions until another opportunity to elicit predictions arises. However, if the student is unable to make a reasonable prediction after having read three paragraphs, the teacher should terminate this activity. As Manzo suggests, "It may be self-defeating to continue beyond this point" (1969, 125).

5. Silent Reading Activity

The teacher now directs the student to read the remainder of the selection. At this point, the teacher might say, "Read to the end of the selection to see what actually did happen." During this period, the teacher can either read along with the student or stand by to assist. It is suggested that an important aspect here is to give aid in a manner that does not disrupt the student's comprehension, that is, do not destroy the student's train of thought.

6. Follow-up Activities

Numerous worthwhile tasks are suitable for follow-up activities. Manzo suggests that readers might engage in activities that verify or apply the information gained from reading. Other useful activities may emanate from a reconsideration and discussion of student predictions. For example, the teacher could encourage the student to consider manipulation of the story.

Cautions and Comments

For those teachers using ReQuest for the first time, Manzo offers a number of suggestions. He advises working with individuals rather than with groups, and for the first encounter, he suggests the use of specific question types: immediate reference, common knowledge, related information, open-ended discussion, personalized discussion, further reference, and translation. Dishner and Searfoss (1974) have also offered an evaluation form that can be used in conjunction with a teacher's use of the procedure. A copy of this form appears at the end of this section.

With children for whom ReQuest is a new experience, a questioning game or activity is often essential for their readiness. Students may wish to underline those ideas about which they want to ask questions; students' confidence in their ability to formulate questions can be vital to their successful involvement in the ReQuest procedure.

At certain times, modifications of the ReQuest procedures may be desirable. For example, in order to provide more varied interactions between questioner and respondent, it may be desirable to alternate the role of questioner after each question. Also, greater flexibility seems desirable in the selection of sections of the passage to be read at one time. Rather than proceed sentence by sentence, one might look for natural breaks within the passage. In a group situation, there are numerous possibilities. One example is where the roles of questioner and respondent either alternate around a circle or proceed at random within the circle. Often a group, as a whole, enjoys challenging the teacher. With kindergarten children, Legenza (1974) has successfully applied a modification of the ReQuest using pictures. The suggested protocol in this situation runs as follows:

> Let's ask each other questions about this picture to see if we can learn all the things we can about it. In order to help us to learn all we can, let's both look at the picture first and ask me any questions you can think of about this picture and I'll see if I can answer them—then I'll ask you some questions and you see if you can answer them. (Manzo and Legenza 1975, 482)

With advanced students, another possible modification is an incomplete questioning technique. This technique requires the student or teacher to initiate an incomplete question, for example, "Why did John . . .?" The other party completes the question and directs it at the initiator.

With or without these modifications, the ReQuest procedure appears to be very effective strategy. The various permutations of the ReQuest procedure provide a viable tool for exploring, extending, and encouraging student hypothesizing. ReQuest facilitates student involvement in problem solving and necessitates teacher awareness of the student's level of involvement.

More recently, Palincsar and Brown (1983) found that reciprocal questioning training, in conjunction with training in summarizing, clarifying, and predicting, proved beneficial in improving students' comprehension. Studies by Manzo, the originator of ReQuest, and Legenza provide empirical support for these claims. In the hands of a sensitive teacher, ReQuest can indeed be an effective means of improving comprehension.

REQUEST EVALUATION FORM

Observer _____
Name _____
Date _____ Grade Level _____

INTERVIEW Before lesson begins: ask these questions; record responses; check the boxes.

Information Accurate

	Yes	No
a) What is the instructional level of students?		
b) What is the reading level of the selected story?		
c) Where will first prediction be elicited?		
d) At what point will eliciting predictions stop?		
e) How long is the story?		
f) Does the story have setting, characters, and an unfamiliar plot?		

	Yes	No
1. Was appropriate material selected?		

OBSERVATION When the lesson begins: answer the questions on the left first.

Record: Time lesson begins

	Yes	No
a. Were the rules accurate?		
b. Were the rules complete?		
c. Were the rules received?		
d. Were the rules understood?		

	Yes	No
2. Were rules given?		

Did teacher

	Yes	No
a. Direct joint silent reading?		
b. Give the correct amount to be read?		
c. Close the book?		
d. Direct students to keep books open?		
e. Direct students to ask questions?		
f. Answer students' questions?		

	Yes	No
3. Was student questioning directed?		

Did teacher

	Yes	No
a. Open books?		
b. Direct students to close books?		
c. Ask students questions?		

	Yes	No
4. Was teacher questioning conducted?		

RECORD During the lesson: record the number of questions from each category.

	Student	Teacher
LITERAL: "What in the story tells . . . ?"		
INTERPRETIVE: "From these clues, why . . . ?"		
APPLIED: "How do you think . . . ?" or "In your opinion, what . . . ?"		

	Yes	No
5. Were all question categories sampled?		

Did teacher

	Yes	No	N/A
a. Ask questions different from students' questions?			
b. Integrate information from previous sentences?			
c. Request rephrasing of unclear questions?			
d. Employ problem-solving strategies when needed?			
e. Select effective strategies?			

	Yes	No
6. Did questions meet specifications?		

Did teacher attempt to

	Yes	No
a. Elicit prediction at earliest point?		
b. Elicit prediction of another story *content*?		
c. Elicit more than one prediction?		

	Yes	No
7. Were predictions elicited?		

Did teacher   Yes   No

a. Ask students to support other
   students' predictions?

b. Request ranking of predictions according
   to likelihood?

c. Refrain from making value judgments
   about students' predictions?

Record: Time-predicting ends

                                               Yes   No

8. Were evaluations of predictions
   elicited?

Did teacher   Yes   No

a. Direct students to read to end of story?

b. Ask students to compare *actual* with
   predicted story *content*?

                                               Yes   No

9. Were predictions compared to
   story content?

Lesson began:	Time	Time Estimate for Grade Level	Well Timed?	
			Yes	No
Predictions ended:				
Lesson ended:				

                                               Yes   No

10. Was lesson well placed?

SUMMARY After lesson ends: Go back and   Was ReQuest
           check 1–10. If all questions   Performed?
           were answered Yes, ReQuest   Yes   No
           was performed.

REFERENCES

Dishner, E. K., and L. W. Searfoss. 1977. Improving comprehension through the ReQuest procedure. *Reading Education: A Journal for Australian Teachers* 2 (Autumn): 22–25. Presents an expanded and more specific set of directions for the ReQuest procedure.

————. 1974. ReQuest evaluation form. Unpublished paper, Arizona State University. Evaluation form that provides step-by step implementation.

Legenza, A. 1974. Questioning behavior of kindergarten children. Paper presented at Nineteenth Annual Convention, International Reading Association. Describes the use and effectiveness of the ReQuest Picture Treatment with kindergarten children.

Manzo, A. V. 1968. Improving reading comprehension through reciprocal Questioning. Unpublished doctoral diss., Syracuse University. Primary reference. Describes the original development of the ReQuest procedure, rationale, piloting, and empirical support of its effectiveness.

————. 1979. The ReQuest procedure. *Journal of Reading* 2:123–26. Manzo's first article based upon the ReQuest Procedure. Describes the rational, procedures, and suggestions for use.

Manzo, A. V., and A. Legenza. 1975. Inquiry training for kindergarten children. *Educational leadership* 32:479–83. Presents the procedures and empirical support for use of the ReQuest procedure with kindergarten children.

Palincsar, A. S., and A. L. Brown. 1983. Reciprocal teaching of comprehension-monitoring activities (Tech. Report No. 269). Urbana: Center for the Study of Reading, University of Illinois, January. Research that found positive results for using reciprocal questioning and other metacognitive strategies for promoting comprehension.

Helfeldt, J. P., and R. Lalik. 1979. Reciprocal student-teacher questioning. In *Reading comprehension at four linguistic levels*, edited by C. Pennock. Newark, Del: International Reading Association, 74–99. Reports a study in which ReQuest was shown to be more effective than teacher questioning.

STUDY GUIDES

Purpose

Study guides (Earle 1969; Herber 1978) are designed to (1) guide a student through reading assignments in content area textbooks, and (2) focus a reader's attention on the major ideas presented in a textbook.

Rationale

Reading in a content area textbook may demand a relatively high level of skill development. As Herber argues, this kind of reading entails the student's acquiring an awareness of levels of comprehension and of how to function at each level. Then, once secure in these levels, the student should acquire the ability to consider and deal with the organizational patterns of the different reading materials. Toward this end, study guides can be useful in developing the ability of students to learn how to read. Specifically, study guides purport to develop the *student's* understanding of, and ability to deal with, levels of comprehension, the organizational patterns of different texts, and the specific skills these might require. Study guides do this by structuring and guiding the reading of textbook material or students' post-reading reasoning.

Intended Audience

Study guides are used mainly in conjunction with content area subjects. They may be used in both individual and group instructional situations and can be adapted to aid students regardless of the students' ability level in reading.

Description of the Procedure

Discussion of study guides as an integral part of a well-planned lesson will include the following three components: (1) development of study guides, (2) construction of study guides, and (3) use of study guides.

1. Development of Study Guides

Before they can construct a study guide for use with their students, teachers must analyze the content material to be read by the students for both content and process (Earle 1969). By analyzing the materials, teachers are assured that the study guide material used by students will be in keeping with the content objectives teachers have in mind.

In analyzing the material for both content and process, teachers themselves should first thoroughly read the material they plan to assign to students. Teachers are then better able to select the content to be emphasized during the lesson. In this way, portions of the assigned material that fit the overall objectives of the subject will be emphasized, and those portions not doing so can be deleted, thus leaving students the opportunity to concentrate on the portions deemed important.

For example, with a reading assignment from a social studies course involving "the Black Revolution," a teacher might decide that the concepts *black, nationalism, nonviolence, black power, separatism*, and the *advocates* of these courses of action, are important for students to master.

Once the content to be emphasized has been decided, teachers then must decide the processes (skills) that students must use in acquiring that content. Earle (1969) and Herber (1978) suggested the decisions made regarding the skills to be used in mastering the material concern an understanding of levels of comprehension and patterns of organization.

Herber (1978) described three levels of comprehension: literal, interpretive, and applied. Literal understanding involves identifying factual material and knowing what the author said. Interpretive understanding involves inferring relationships among the details and knowing what the author meant. Finally, applied understanding involves developing generalizations that extend beyond the assigned material. Herber suggests that it is necessary to master understanding at one level before proceeding to the next. With the content to be emphasized, the teacher must decide what levels of understanding students will need.

Earle (1969) described four patterns of organization in which textual information is frequently found: cause and effect, comparison and contrast, sequence or time order, and simple listing. Dealing with the particular way in which information is organized in a text aids students in mastering the content. Therefore, the teacher must ascertain the pattern of organization for the information in a given text. Together with levels of comprehension, the identification of patterns of organization provides students with the necessary structure to study the assigned material.

Continuing with our example of "the Black Revolution," the teacher might determine that all three levels of understanding are necessary to deal successfully with the portions of the text to be emphasized. In addition, the comparison-and-contrast pattern of organization may be found to be used by the text authors in organizing their information.

One last step must be accomplished before the study guide is constructed. The teacher must consider the students' abilities in relation to the content and processes to be emphasized. By doing this, the teacher can provide differing amounts of assistance to insure that all students complete the assignment successfully.

In this step the teacher must consider two points: the students' competencies and the difficulty of the material itself (Earle 1969). Keeping these two factors in mind, the teacher decides how much structure should be provided each student to address the content. For instance, the teacher can provide aids to locate the desired material in the form of page and/or paragraph numbers. Also, the teacher must decide whether guides should be constructed for only a single level of comprehension or for differential levels, so particular students may be assigned only to deal with those levels commensurate with their abilities. Teachers, knowing the individual needs and abilities of their students, will have to make these kinds of judgments and to vary the structure of study guides to insure the success of their students.

2. Construction of Study Guide

Once decisions have been made regarding the content and process and the types of assistance to be provided, teachers are ready to construct their study guides. Although there is no standard form that a study guide must take, Earle (1969) recommends the following guidelines:

   a. Avoid overcrowding print on the study guide, as overcrowding may overwhelm some students;
   b. Make the guide interesting enough so students will be motivated to deal with the information; and
   c. Be sure the guide reflects the instructional decisions made with regard to content and process.

Continuing with our previous example, study guides can be constructed to aid students in mastering the concepts and in acquiring the skills needed to do so. Here are two examples of study guides, one concerning levels of comprehension and the other involving the comparison-and-contrast pattern of organization.[2]

READING GUIDE #1:
LEVELS OF COMPREHENSION

    *   Literal level
  **   Interpretive level
***   Applied level

    *   1. What are the basic steps of a nonviolent campaign? (p. 634, par. 4)
***   2. Why did the political leaders of Birmingham refuse to engage in good faith?
  **   3. Why does Stokely Carmichael think "integration is a joke"? (p. 636)
***   4. Why do you think the authors say that the SNCC has become more militant since the early 1960s?
  **   5. Why did SNCC choose the black panther as its symbol? (p. 637)
    *   6. What is black nationalism? (p. 639, par. 1)
  **   7. Why did the man in the tavern say the extremists would end up in concentration camps? (p. 640)
***   8. Why do so many people think the racial problem has to be solved in our generation? (p. 640)
    *   9. What does the term "black Jim Crow" mean? (p. 641, par. 4)
    *   10. Who is Thurgood Marshall? (p. 642, par. 3)
  **   11. Why does Thurgood Marshall fear the black militants? (p. 643, par. 2)
***   12. Why do black people think black studies programs are essential?

READING GUIDE #2:
PATTERNS OF ORGANIZATION

Directions: 1. Match the name of a black leader in Column A with his strategy in Column B. Put the number of that name in the blank provided in Column B.

---

2. From J. E. Readence and E. K. Dishner, "Getting Started: Using the Textbook Diagnostically," *Reading World*, vol. 17, October 1977. Copyright © 1977 by the College Reading Association. Reprinted by permission of the College Reading Association, J. E. Readence, and E. K. Dishner. Based on material from M. Sandler, E. Rozwenc, and E. Martin, "Strategies of the 'Black' Revolution," in *The People Make a Nation*. Boston: Allyn and Bacon, 1971, 634–644.

2. Match the name of a black leader in Column A with the ideas in Column C. Put the number in the blank provided in Column C.

A. Names	B. Strategies
1. Martin Luther King	_____ black nationalism
2. Stokely Carmichael	_____ anti-separatism
3. Roy Innis	_____ non-violence
4. Roy Wilkins	_____ leadership through education
5. Thurgood Marshall	_____ black power

C. Ideas

_____ Our philosophy is one of self-determination.

_____ White power has been scaring black people for 400 years.

_____ Direct action is the only way to force the issue. (p. 635)

_____ You can't use color for an excuse for not doing what you should be doing. (p. 643)

_____ Current black studies programs represent another form of segregated education. (p. 641)

_____ Nothing will be settled with guns or rocks.

_____ You must be able to accept blows without retaliation.

_____ We must rehabilitate blacks as people. (p. 639)

_____ Black history is significant only if taught in the context of world history.

_____ Our idea is to put men in office who will work for the people they represent. (p. 638)

It should be noted that these sample guides have been constructed with varying amounts of assistance (page and paragraph numbers) and level of comprehension designated. Teachers may decide to use only one or all of the levels, depending on what decisions have been made with regard to individual students.

3. Use of the Study Guides

Study guides should be used in the context of a well-planned lesson. Students should be prepared for the reading assignment through background development and a purpose-setting discussion. A follow-up discussion also might be provided after the guides have been used. The instructional framework or the Directed Reading Activity (both described in Unit 1) may provide the lesson framework needed to incorporate the study guides as one element in that lesson.

When first using study guides, teachers may need to "walk" students through a portion of a guide so that they will become acquainted with the procedure and will be better able to use the guides. Specifically, this step may aid students in seeing how the relationship between content and process can be fostered.

Groups of students can work on study guides cooperatively in lieu of using them individually. In this way, students can collaboratively arrive at responses to the guide. The activity promotes students' active involvement in the reading/learning process.

Finally, as students develop sensitivity to study guides and begin to transfer their new learning to other situations, the varying structure included in the initial guides may be progressively withdrawn. In this way, students are encouraged toward independence in their reading.

Cautions and Comments

Study guides can provide a means to encourage students to become active participants in the learning process rather than passive observers. Additionally, study guides aid teachers in insuring that the important concepts present in text material are communicated to students. Particularly in group situations, study guides represent a unique opportunity to explore ideas; they do not tie students directly to recall-type learning. Study guides are versatile, and their judicious use may provide the kind of instructional environment necessary to develop students' independence in reading and thinking.

Three cautions should be mentioned with regard to study guides. First, it does take time and effort on the part of the teacher to develop, construct, and use them effectively. This caution, however, should be put into perspective alongside the benefits to students' understanding and the possibility that teachers might work cooperatively on their development.

Second, although study guides are designed to move readers toward eventual independence, they are essentially teacher-directed activities. Teachers, not readers, decide what is important in reading the texts. Decision making, therefore, in this learning situation rests almost entirely with teachers. Those educators concerned with creating a learning environment that involves students as much as possible must bear this factor in mind when using study guides. In partial response to this point, Herber (1970) remarked:

> How much better for students to expend energy using skills to explore content rather that discovering the skills by which the content will eventually be explored. Although we should fear too much structure, we should also fear the lack of it. (P. 131)

Third, various studies have provided substantial support for the efficacy of study guides (see Herber and Barron 1973; Herber and Vacca 1977; Herber and Riley 1979): In comments made by Herber and Nelson (1975), some of the problems with the study guide have been alluded to. For example, the use of questions over statements as prompts has been questioned.

REFERENCES

Dishner, E. K., and J. E. Readence. 1977. Getting started: Using the textbook diagnostically. *Reading World* 17:36−49. Recommends the use of study guides as diagnostic tools for the content area teacher.

Earle, R. A. 1969. Developing and using study guides. In *Research in reading in the content areas: First year report*, edited by H. L. Herber and P. L. Sanders. Syracuse, N.Y.: Reading and Language Arts Center, Syracuse University, 71−92. Provides directions for the content area teacher in how to develop and use study guides as an instructional tool.

Estes, T. H., and J. L. Vaughan. 1978. *Reading and learning in the content classroom*. Boston: Allyn and Bacon, 157−76. Discusses the uses of study guides with examples.

Herber, H. L. 1970. *Teaching reading in the content areas*. Englewood Cliffs, N.J.: Prentice-Hall. Original source for the rationale and use of study guides.

―――. 1978. *Teaching reading in content areas*. 2d ed. Englewood Cliffs, N.J.: Prentice-Hall. Discusses the use of study guides in conjunction with the instructional framework, a teaching strategy for content area teachers.

Herber, H. L., and R. F. Barron. eds. 1973. *Research in reading in the content areas: Second year report*. Syracuse, N.Y.: Syracuse University, Reading and Language Arts Center. Includes studies by Estes and others exploring the effectiveness of study guides.

Herber, H. L., and R. Vacca, eds. 1977. *Research in reading in the content areas: Third year report*. Syracuse, N.Y.: Syracuse University, Reading and Language Arts Center. Includes studies by Berget, Carney, and Vacca that examined the use of study guides.

Herber, H. L., and J. B. Nelson. 1978. Questioning is not the answer. *Journal of Reading* 18:512−17. Discusses the demands that questions place on students and suggests alternatives en route to developing students who question independently.

Herber, H. L., and J. D. Riley, eds. 1979. *Research in reading in the content areas: Fourth year report*. Syracuse, N.Y. Syracuse University, Reading and Language Arts Center. Includes studies by Maxon, Phelphs, and Riley that examined the use of study guides.

SELECTIVE READING GUIDE-O-RAMA

Purpose

The major objectives of the Selective Reading Guide-O-Rama (Cunningham and Shablak 1975) are (1) to lead students to the major ideas and supporting details within a content text chapter, and (2) to teach students flexibility in their reading.

Rationale

The Selective Reading Guide-O-Rama assumes that since most students are not "experts" in the subject, they are not able to select with ease the important textual information. That is, it assumes most students read the material as if everything within the chapter were of equal importance. The subject matter instructor is in a position to guide students through the reading assignment by providing them with clues as to which information is important and which can be skimmed lightly.

Intended Audience

The Selective Reading Guide-O-Rama can be used with students in grades six and above. It would appear to be better suited for use with those students who need additional guidance in their reading.

Description of the Procedure

Before an instructor can design any type of guidance tool for students, several important decisions must be made during the planning stage of the lesson. Of primary importance is the identification of the major concepts and understandings to be derived from the chapter. Subject matter instructors should ask themselves the following questions:

1. What should students know when they finish this chapter?

    a. What are the major concepts that the students should understand?
    b. What supporting information or details should they remember on a long-term basis?

2. What should students be able *to do* when they finish the chapter?

    a. What background information is essential to perform the required tasks?

By making a brief list of the answers to the above questions, content teachers can identify the essential information within the text chapter that they want their students to understand. The next step is to move through the book chapter and identify those portions of the text that provide students with the previously identified important information. After lightly noting the margins of their teacher's edition the letters "M" for main ideas and "D" for important details, content instructors are ready to design the Guide-O-Rama.

Perhaps the easiest way to approach this task is to imagine a group of three or four students. It is assumed that content teachers have already completed the preparation stage of the lesson (see description of the instructional framework in the previous unit). Students will have their texts open to the first page of the chapter to be studied and are now ready to read the chapter. What information should the teacher provide so that the students will key in on the important ideas that have been identified? The response to this question is the type of information that will be written down in guide form.

Several examples might be in order to illustrate the preceding discussion. The teacher might note important information in the following manner:

- p. 93, paragraphs 3–6. Pay special attention to this section. Why do you think Hunter acted in this manner? We will discuss your ideas later in class.
- p. 94, subtopic in boldface print at top of page. See if you can rewrite the topic to form a question. Now read the information under the subtopic just to answer the question. You should pick up the five ideas very quickly. Jot down your answers in the space provided below.
- p. 94, picture. What appears to be the reaction of the crowd? Now read the fifth paragraph on this page to find out why they are reacting as they are.
- p. 95, paragraphs 5–8. Read this section very carefully. The order of the events is very important and you will want to remember this information for our quiz.

The same approach is used when noting information within the chapter that, based upon the content teacher's analysis, is of little or no importance. The following example illustrates this situation:

- p. 179, all of column 1. The author has provided us with some interesting information here, but it is not important for us to remember. You may want just to skim over it and move on to the second column.
- pp. 180 and 181. These pages describe a fictitious family who lived during the Civil War. You may skip this section because we will learn about the lifestyles of the time through films, other readings, and class discussions.
- pp. 221–222. Recent discoveries in science have disproved the information contained on these pages. I will discuss this information with you in class. Now move on to page 223.

By pointing out unimportant information as well as important ideas in the text, content teachers are purported to be effectively communicating to their students that they must be flexible in their reading. Teachers may even wish to communicate literally to their students the notion that all words in print are not necessarily of equal value for the reader who is attempting to ascertain the author's important ideas.

The completed guide should appear in a logical order and should move the student from the beginning of the chapter through the end of the unit. Thus, through the use of the Selective Reading Guide-O-Rama, content teachers are saying to the youngsters (1) pay close attention to this, (2) skim over this material, (3) read this section carefully, and (4) you can read this section rather quickly, but see if you can find out why, and so on.

Cautions and Comments

Like most guidance tools, it should be used sensitively. The Selective Reading Guide-O-Rama might work best with those students who need the assistance and who could profit from structured approaches to developing selected skills. A conscious effort should be made by the teacher to remove this assistance as the students learn the mechanics of reading and studying text material. This weaning process might begin following the use of the Guide-O-Rama for a two- or three-month period. The students should be told when this is taking place and occasionally reminded that, for example, they should continue to pay particular attention to the pictorial information within the unit.

For those students who have difficulty handling the written version of a Guide-O-Rama, the instructor can just as easily design a cassette tape version. Oral direction will now lead the students through the selection. The instructor might advise the student to ". . . turn off the recorder now and read very carefully these first two paragraphs on page 96. When you have finished, turn the recorder on again and I will discuss the material you read." By providing approximately five seconds of dead space on the tape, the student is allowed sufficient time to handle the mechanics of turning off and on a cassette tape recorder. Of course, the student will have all the time necessary to read and study once the recorder is off.

REFERENCES

Cunningham, D., and S. L. Shablak. 1975. Selective reading Guide-O-Rama: The content teacher's best friend. *Journal of Reading* 18:380–82. Introduces the concept of the Guide-O-Rama and provides examples for its construction.

GUIDED READING PROCEDURE

Purpose

As developed by Manzo (1975), the Guided Reading Procedure is designed to:

1. Assist students' unaided recall of specific information read;
2. Improve the students' abilities to generate their own (implicit) questions as they read;
3. Develop the students' understanding of the importance of self-correction; and
4. Improve the students' abilities to organize information.

Rationale

Many teachers expect their students to remember the facts in a story or in a chapter from a content textbook. The Guided Reading Procedure (GRP) is intended to provide the teacher with a logical series of instructional steps that can lead to the majority of the students in a given classroom addressing the content. The group or whole class recalls orally the information they have just read silently. The teacher then asks them to confirm, organize, and note relationships. These, Manzo argues, are essential factors in advancing an attitude of comprehension accuracy and, ultimately, reading comprehension ability. As Manzo (1975) contends:

> . . . the GRP enriches skills by having the teacher allow students to see implicit questions, by strengthening determination to concentrate during reading, and by encouraging self-correction and organization of information with minimal teacher direction. (P. 288)

Intended Audience

Teachers can use the Guided Reading Procedure at the primary level, although it appears most appropriate for students in the middle grades through college level. It also is important to note that GRP is a group activity and may not be effective as a one-on-one strategy.

Description of the Procedure

The Guided Reading Procedure may use narrative selections or informational material. The selection should be short enough so that the majority of the students can complete the reading comfortably in one sitting. Manzo (1975) provides a rule of thumb to use in deciding appropriate length. His suggestions on number of words and amount of reading time for average readers follow. For primary students, allow three minutes or approximately 90 words; for intermediate students, three minutes or approximately 500 words; for junior high students, seven minutes or approximately 900 words; for senior high students, ten minutes or approximately 2,000 words; and for college students, twelve minutes or approximately 2,500 words.

Manzo (1975) outlines six basic steps to be followed for the GRP:

1. Prepare the student for the reading assignment;
2. Students read and recall information;
3. Return to article for additional facts and corrections;
4. Organize the remembered material;
5. Provide students with thought-provoking questions; and
6. Test students on their knowledge of the information.

1. Prepare the Student for the Reading Assignment

As with any good teaching lesson, students should work through some form of readiness task before they plunge into the actual reading assignment. This preparation may take the form described under the Directed Reading Activity (Unit 1), the Instructional Framework (Unit 1), the Survey Technique (Unit 6), or the ReQuest Procedure (Unit 2). Regardless of which strategy the teacher employs, it is vitally important that the students understand why they are reading the printed material before them. The general purpose, at least for this particular lesson, is for them to remember as much of the details as possible. Teacher/student agreement on this purpose is of vital importance to the strategy's success.

2. Students Read and Recall Information

With their purpose clearly in mind, the students read the material silently while the teacher stands by to assist those students who may have difficulty with the reading. Students are advised that, upon completion of their reading, they are to turn the material face down on their desks and wait until their classmates have finished the assignment.

When the large majority of the students have finished the reading, the instructor asks the students to tell what they remember. The emphasis at this point is on unaided recall of the material read. The teacher serves as the recorder and notes on the chalkboard each bit of information suggested by the students. In order to speed the process and avoid extensive writing, an abbreviated form of recording is suggested.

3. Return to Article for Additional Facts and Corrections

When the students are no longer able to recall information from memory, the teacher allows them to return to the selection in order to add additional information and to correct inaccurately recalled details. The teacher adds the new information to the board and corrects inaccuracies noted by the students.

4. Organize the Remembered Material

The teacher now asks the students to organize the material into a modified outline form. Sometimes the instructor may ask questions to lead the students to an outline highlighting the main ideas and supporting details through the locating of more general statements and their supporting details. Sometimes the teacher may have students organize the information and the sequence in which the information was presented. Questions such as the following may be useful: "What happened first in this selection?" "What came next?" "Where does this information appear to fit best?" At other times, the teacher or the student may suggest alternative outline forms.

5. Provide Students with Thought-Provoking Questions

The teacner should direct his or her efforts at this point toward helping the students understand how this new information relates to material they previously learned. Initially, the questions may need to be fairly specific. For example,"How does this new information about Jackson support what we learned about him last week?" As the students become more familiar with this segment of the technique, the teacher may turn to less specific questions that place more responsibility upon the students during this transfer-of-learning stage. Questions of a more general type might include: "Do you see any relation between this information and the material we studied last week?" or "Give me some examples of how this material supports last week's unit." During this step, the teacher serves as a model by asking thoughtful questions that require students to synthesize new information with previously learned information.

6. Test Students on Their Knowledge of the Information

Following this rather intense reading/reacting activity, the teacher should take time to check the students' short-term memory of the ideas they presented. A short quiz will provide the students an opportunity to reveal how much information they have learned as a result of the procedure. Although Manzo suggests no specific test format, the teacher could use either matching, multiple-choice, short answer, essay items, or some appropriate combination of question types.

The teacher may provide students additional opportunities to ". . . manipulate and deliberate" (Manzo 1975, 291) over the material read. The teacher may also wish to check recall over longer periods of time.

Cautions and Comments

The GRP strategy is a rather intense activity, which may prove beneficial when used selectively. For example, with selected "meaty" reading material (i.e., material containing much important information), the GRP affords students an opportunity to read that information, to interact with others' interpretations of the material in the classroom, and to organize the material. The GRP is a teacher-directed but student-dominated activity that can lead to improvements in readers' understandings. Cunningham, Arthur, and Cunningham (1977) describe an interesting variation of the Guided Reading Procedure. They label it simply the Guided Listening Procedure. After sufficiently preparing them for the listening activity, the teacher asks the students to remember as much as they can from the selection. The teacher then reads a short selection orally, taping it at the same time. The remaining steps are similar to those we described earlier, with one obvious exception. Rather than returning to the printed material to confirm student recall, the teacher plays the tape recording and asks the students to raise their hands to stop the tape when they wish to discuss specific pieces of information.

Due to the nature of this particular strategy, Manzo (1975) recommends that the teacher use the Guided Reading Procedure no more than once every two weeks. With appropriate reading selections, a logical variation might be to use the GRP every other week, with the Guided Listening Procedure employed on the off-week (Cunningham, Arthur, and Cunningham 1977).

Finally, the efficacy of the GRP was investigated by Bean and Pardi (1979). They found that the GRP, used in combination with a prereading survey technique, was effective in enhancing the learning from text of poor seventh grade readers.

REFERENCES

Bean, T. W., and R. Pardi. 1979. A field test of a guided reading strategy. *Journal of Reading* 23:144–47. Study that found that the GRP used in combination with a prereading strategy was effective in improving comprehension and retention.

Cunningham, P. M., S. V. Arthur, and J. W. Cunningham. 1977. *Classroom reading instruction K-5: Alternative approaches.* Lexington, Mass.: D. C. Heath, 241. Presents a brief description of a variation of the GRP—the Guided Listening Procedure.

Manzo, A. V. 1975. Guided reading procedure. *Journal of Reading* 18:287–91. Provides the rationale and specific steps that make up the GRP strategy.

GIST

Purpose

The GIST procedure (Generating Interactions between Schemata and Text) was developed by Cunningham to improve students' abilities to comprehend the gist of paragraphs by providing "a prescription for reading from group sentence-by-sentence gist production to individual whole-paragraph gist production" (1982, 42).

Rationale

Cunningham (1982) claims that the GIST procedure is an effective instructional tool for guiding student summary writing, which, in turn, improves their learning from text. The procedure has its roots in three sets of studies. First, based upon the work of Kintsch (1977), Dooling and Christiansen (1977), and Anderson (1978), Cunningham argues for a strategy that engages a reader's background knowledge while using cues from the text in the order in which they were presented. The GIST procedure, Cunningham claims, is such a strategy. Second, justification for the value of summary or gist generation comes from his own research (Cunningham 1982) as well as the research of Doctorow, Marks, and Wittrock (1978) and Taylor and Berkowitz (1980) in which students who wrote summaries following each paragraph increased their learning from text. Third, Cunningham used the work of Day (1980), Brown, Campione, and Day (1981) and, more directly, Doctorow, Marks, and Wittrock (1978) to generate the instructional procedures for guiding students' use of the procedure. The technique represents a teacher-directed small-group strategy that takes students from writing summary statements for sentences to generating gist statements for paragraphs.

Intended Audience

While Cunningham has only investigated the use of the strategy in the fourth grade, the technique might be used with students at higher levels who need guidance in summary writing.

Procedure

There are two versions of the procedure: a paragraph version and short passage version. The steps involved in each version are outlined below.

1. Paragraph Version

In the paragraph version, students are asked to generate summary statements of no longer than fifteen words as they read a paragraph sentence by sentence. After reading the first sentence they are expected to summarize what the text stated. Then as each additional sentence of a paragraph is exposed, students are expected to incorporate the additional information into a new statement of no more than fifteen words. The following illustrates the steps a teacher would follow with a paragraph.

Step One: Selecting appropriate paragraphs. The first step in using the procedure is to select several paragraphs, each with three to five sentences, which have a gist. The following paragraph is representative of the type of text Cunningham has used.

The theory of how planets were formed differs from the one generally accepted a couple of decades ago. At that time, it was thought by most astronomers that the planets formed as the result of a wandering star passing too close to the sun and sucking chunks of matter out of its fiery mass. The decline of this theory occurred on the basis of new evidence and new calculation which suggested that the planets developed from random particles which grew larger as they attracted others by their gravity.

Step Two: Students read the first sentence. Step two involves having students read the first sentence of the paragraph for purposes of retelling it in their own words. Cunningham (1982) recommends that the sentence be displayed on an overhead, chart, or chalkboard with fifteen blanks underneath. The blanks are the spaces in which students are expected to fit their summaries.

Step Three: Students generate summaries. In this step, students are asked to retell in a statement of fifteen or less words what they read in the sentence. Writing one word in every blank, students as a group dictate and revise the statement until they are satisfied with it. The sentence is uncovered if a student wishes to reread the sentence; otherwise, the text is put aside and the students are expected to generate their summary based upon memory. Only after generating their summary are the students encouraged to reread the text. At that time, by comparing their summary statement with the text, students are expected to decide for themselves whether or not they wish to revise their gist further. Once satisfied, the students proceed with step four.

Cunningham (1982) emphasizes that teachers should be careful not to interfere with the students' decision making. He discourages teachers from evaluating the summary or interfering, even if the students' statement represents an exact duplication of the text.

Step Four: Reading the first two sentences. The fourth step involves having students read the first and second sentence and retell them in the same number of words used for the first sentence alone.

Step Five: Generating a summary for sentence one and two. The fifth step involves having students generate a single sentence (no longer than fifteen words) that summarizes both sentence one and two. Again students are encouraged to revise their statement until they are satisfied with it. As a final check on the adequacy of the sentence, students are given an opportunity to compare what they generated with the text prior to proceeding with the next step.

Step Six: Continue with the procedure for the remainder of the paragraph. In step six, the procedure outlined above is continued with the addition of each new sentence until the students have produced a single statement of fifteen words or less that they feel best summarizes the paragraph.

Step Seven: Moving beyond a sentence-by-sentence approach to a paragraphs approach. As students develop in their ability to generate such statements across a variety of different paragraphs, Cunningham suggests moving toward the presentation of paragraphs. In addition, as students develop in their ability to generate summaries, teachers are urged to give students opportunities to produce their own gist statements individually rather than as a group.

2. Short Passage Version

The short passage version parallels the paragraph version.

Step One: Selecting appropriate passages. The teacher selects short passages of an appropriate difficulty level, each with a gist, and three to five paragraphs in length. The passage is placed on an overhead.

Step Two: Reading the paragraph. All the paragraphs are covered over but the first one. Twenty blank spaces are placed on a chalkboard, and the students are directed to read the paragraph so they can retell it in their own words in one statement of twenty or less words.

Step Three: Students generate summaries. When students have finished reading the paragraph, the overhead transparency is removed and students are asked as a group to start writing their summaries. Writing one word per blank, students dictate and edit the statement until it is complete. Students may review the paragraph at any time, but they are expected to dictate and edit from memory. When students feel that their statement is an accurate summary of the paragraph, the step is complete. The teacher is expected to enforce the twenty-word rule; the students are expected to determine how satisfied they are with the final statement.

Step Four: Students read and summarize subsequent paragraphs. The chalkboard is erased and the students proceed to read and summarize the first two paragraphs in no more than twenty words. The same procedures are used for leading them through the entire passage.

Step Five: Generating summaries for whole passages and developing independence. Cunningham recommends using the strategy with as many different short passages as necessary until the students become adept at efficiently producing gist statements. Thereafter, he suggests that the teacher might have the students respond to the whole passage rather than paragraph-by-paragraph. Furthermore, when the students as a group become quite capable of producing gist statements, he suggests that students might be encouraged individually to produce gist statements.

Cautions and Comments

There are positive features and some possible limitations to the procedure. On the positive side, Cunningham has carefully developed a step-by-step procedure for helping students write brief summaries of gists that are accountable to the text. If teachers follow Cunningham's steps, students are expected to move from group summaries to generating their own individual summaries. Furthermore, students are given procedures and encouragement so that they should be able to evaluate for themselves the adequacy of their summaries. In this regard, an important and worthwhile feature of the technique is the discussion and revisions that emerge in conjunction with the group's refinement of their statement. Another positive feature, which should not be overlooked, is Cunningham's (1982) scrutiny of the technique in a research study that involved fourth graders. His findings suggest that, if having students generate summaries is your goal, then the GIST technique is possibly better than nothing or other writing experiences.

In terms of limitations, there are a number of problems that might arise as teachers implement the technique. Can it be assumed that students will be able to readily transfer summarization skills acquired with a sentence to a paragraph to a whole text? Will students be able to judge the adequacy of their summaries without some criteria for so doing? Of overall importance, is summary writing always worthwhile? Even Cunningham alludes to the possibility that some texts do not lend themselves to summarization. Even if it is worthwhile, are there other procedures that expedite the generation of summaries? We tend to think that the procedure is likely to become tedious if used repeatedly. Furthermore, the procedure seems to assume that summaries can be readily developed by reading in a linear, sentence by sentence fashion. This assumption seems questionable.

REFERENCES

Anderson, R. C. 1978. Schema-directed processes in language comprehension. In *Cognitive psychology and instruction*, edited by A. M. Lesgold, J. W. Pellegrino, S. D. Fakkema, and R. Glaser. (Eds.), New York: Plenum Press. Presents a theoretically oriented discussion of the nature of reader-text interactions during reading comprehension. The ideas presented in this paper serve as some of the basis for the GIST technique.

Brown, A. L., J. C. Campione, and J. D. Day. 1981. Learning to learn: On training students to learn from texts. *Educational Researcher* 10: 14–21. Presents a discussion of how past research suggests reading comprehension abilities might be developed.

Cunningham, J. W. 1982. Generating interactions between schemata and text. In *New inquiries in reading research and instruction*, edited by J. A. Niles and L. A. Harris. Thirty-first Yearbook of the National Reading Conference. Washington, D.C.: National Reading Conference, 42–47. Describes a research study and represents the major source for information on the GIST procedures.

Day, J. D. 1980. Teaching summarization skills: A comparison of training methods. Unpublished doctoral diss., University of Illinois. This thesis has proven seminal to other studies of summarization and for purposes of guidelines for teaching reading comprehension.

Dooling, D. J., and R. E. Christiansen. 1977. Levels of encoding and retention of prose. In *The psychology of learning and motivation*, edited by G. H. Bower. New York: Academic Press. Presents a theoretically oriented discussion of reading comprehension. Cited by Cunningham as influential in guiding the basis for developing the GIST technique.

Doctorow, M., C. Marks, and M. Wittrock. 1978. Generative processes in reading comprehension. *Journal of Educational Psychology* 70:109–18. Represents an earlier study of summarization that served partly as justification for the procedure.

Kintsch, W. 1977. On comprehending stories. In *Cognitive processes in comprehension*, edited by M. A. Just and P. A. Carpenter. Hillsdale, NJ: Erlbaum. Provides a discussion of the nature and role of summarization in reading comprehension.

Taylor, B., and S. Berkowitz. 1980. Facilitating children's comprehension of content material. In *Perspectives on reading research and instruction* edited by M. L. Kamil and A. J. Moe. Twenty-ninth Yearbook of the National Reading Conference. Washington, DC: National Reading Conference. Represents an earlier study of summarization that Cunningham (1982) cites as contributing to the justification of his procedure.

EXPLICIT TEACHING OF READING COMPREHENSION

Purpose

The Explicit Teaching of Reading Comprehension is intended as a framework for developing reading comprehension skills and strategies that are capable of applying without teacher support to other reading situations.

Rationale

In the late 1960s and early 1970s, developmental psychologists began to explore the possibility that reading comprehension and other problem-solving abilities were amenable to change with appropriate intervention. Subsequently, throughout the 1970s and early 1980s, several research studies were pursued in which deliberate and carefully planned attempts were made to explore the instructional characteristics of effective reading comprehension instruction. The question governing these pursuits was: Can students be made aware of reading comprehension strategies or be taught skills that will transfer to independent reading situations? What emerged as a response to this question and from these research pursuits was Explicit Teaching of Reading Comprehension. In other words, as researchers explored different procedures for teaching selected reading comprehension strategies and skills (e.g., summarizing, inferencing, self-questioning, relating background knowledge, finding the main idea and relevant details), several recommendations for instructions seemed forthcoming (Brown, Campione, and Day 1981; Day 1980; Gordon and Pearson 1983; Hansen and Pearson 1981; Palincsar and Brown 1983). These have been pulled together and now are labelled by some educators "Explicit Teaching" (Pearson and Leys 1984). The features that constitute Explicit Teaching have been discussed in several papers (Brown, Campione, and Day 1981; Tierney and Cunningham 1984; Pearson and Gallagher 1983; Palincsar and Brown 1983; and Tierney 1982). The features include:

1. *Relevance:* students are made aware of the purpose of the skill or strategy—the why, when, how, when and where about the strategy;
2. *Definition:* students are informed as to how to apply the skills by making public the skill or strategy, modeling its use, discussing its range of utility, and illustrating what it is not;
3. *Guided Practice:* students are given feedback on their own use of the strategy or skill;
4. *Self-regulation:* students are given opportunities to try out the strategy for themselves and develop ways to monitor their own use of the strategy or skill;
5. *Gradual release of responsibility:* the teacher initially models and directs the students' learning; as the lesson progresses, the teacher gradually gives more responsibility to the student; and
6. *Application:* students being given the opportunity to try their skills and strategies in independent learning situations, including nonschool tasks.

Intended Audience

Explicit Teaching is a generic plan for developing a wide range of strategies. It would seem to be an appropriate framework for teaching students at all ages.

Description of the Procedure

During any Explicit Teaching lesson certain key elements will be present; others may be optional. For example, the following is based upon those suggested by Pearson and Leys (1984) as an integral part of explicit teaching:

Step one: Introduction to the skill or strategy through examples and review. Refer or expose the students to examples of the skill in the "real world," including the purpose for using the strategy.

Discuss how, when, where, and why the strategy or skills are used. If possible, contrast them with other skills; for example, contrast main idea with details, fact from opinion, good summaries from poor summaries. If the skill has been treated previously, review what they know about the skill.

Step two (optional): Have the children volunteer additional examples and discuss them.

Step three: Label, define, model, and explain the skill or strategy. In this step, the skill or strategy is given a specific label and its application demonstrated with teacher modeling. As the teacher models, students are given both guidelines by which they might use the skill or strategy and also examples of faulty strategy usage or skill application.

Step four: Guided Practice. In this step, examples are done together in order to prepare the students for independent practice and to determine who is incurring difficulty with the skill or strategy.

Step five: Independent practice. The students work through the same type of exercise, but do so independently.

Step six: Application. Students are given a variety of situations in which they are encouraged to apply the skill and discuss its application. This might entail applying the skill or strategy to other text or to situations outside of school.

What follows are two examples of applying this lesson framework to comprehension skills. The first example illustrates the Explicit Teaching of a main idea; the second is an example taken from a recent research study that looked at the effects of explicit teaching on discerning fact and opinion (Rogers and Leys 1984).

AN EXAMPLE OF EXPLICIT TEACHING APPLIED TO MAIN IDEA

I. Introduction to the Skill or Strategy

In the first part of the lesson, examples are provided and the relevance of the strategy established. This can be done by relating what you are going to do to something with which the child has had experience. At the same time, the purpose for teaching the strategy is established.

Ask: "Have you ever had to give a brief description of something? Have you ever wondered what it would be like to give the news on the radio or television? Imagine it was your turn to give the news. Usually you have a few minutes to present in a nutshell the main idea and a few key facts. Now suppose you have been given lots of stories by your classmates. Your task is to present them, but before you do so, you need to isolate the main idea and most relevant details. What would you do?"

II. Labeling, Modeling, Defining and Explaining

In the next phase the teacher labels, models, defines, and explains the skill. Through teacher modeling and student discussion, the how, when, and where of the strategy is presented. Negative instances (i.e., demonstrations of faulty applications) are given, as well as clear examples of appropriate strategy or skill usage.

The teacher explains that they are going to learn more about how to find the main idea. Students read one of the stories for which the main idea needs to be established.

My name is Sally. I have four gerbils. One is pure white and two have brown spots. The fourth one is all black with a pink nose.

The teacher explains: "The story tells how many different and colorful gerbils Sally has. The reason I know this is the second sentence tells how many gerbils Sally has. The other sentences talk about not the size nor what they eat, but about the color of the gerbils. What is key in finding the main idea is finding out the most important ideas or facts stated about the topic. The main idea is: Sally has four colorful gerbils. Let's look at another story."

III. Guided Practice

In this step the teacher and students walk through an example together.

"Let's do the next story together. This is Juan's story . . ."

IV. Independent Practice

Students should be given the equivalent of a checklist by which they can not only guide their own use of the strategy, but can also check whether they have succeeded.

The teacher directs the children to a third story. The teacher says: "Try one by yourself this time. Remember the main idea is what is important about the topic. Decide whether the main idea of Pam's story is about:

Adela's home run
Adela's best friend
Adela's favorite sport

Before you make a final decision ask yourself:

Did you find the important ideas or facts?
Did you decide what they were all about?
Does your main idea cover all the ideas or facts? If not . . . choose another."

The teacher has children share their choice and explain. Other examples follow.

V. Application

The next essential step is application. Your goal should be

The teacher suggests: "Now try to do some on your own. Re-for the self-initiated and success-ful use of the strategy or skill without the teacher.

member to use the self-help questions."

After checking these exercises, the teacher says: "Today we have learned about main idea. Can anybody think of where else one might use this skill? Let's see if it could help us with our social studies."

Children are encouraged to dis-cuss how it might help in social studies and take out their social studies books to try it out. Other applications are discussed.

AN EXAMPLE OF EXPLICIT TEACHING APPLIED TO FACT AND OPINION

(from Rogers and Leys 1984)

I. Introduction to Skill or Strategy

The teacher discusses with children advertising and newspaper articles that might contain bias writing. The teacher asks students how they judge fact from opinion. For purposes of reviewing previous work, the teacher says:

> Remember when we were here a few weeks ago and you worked on an exercise on statements of opinion and statements of fact. Tell me what you remember about statements of facts.

Possible responses:

> "A fact is a true."
> "A fact is a true thing that someone says."
> "A real thing"
> "What people know"

Write these responses on an overhead (or blackboard). Say:

> Can you remember what you said about statements of opinions?

Possible responses:

> "what somebody thinks"
> "a person's feeling about something"

"something one person thinks and maybe someone else doesn't think that"
"something that's true to one person, but not true to others"
"something that you make up your mind about"
"something that might not be true"
"something that could be true or false"

II. Labeling, modeling, defining, and explaining

Say:

Good, we are going to talk more about opinions in a minute. Now, can you give me some examples of statements of fact?

Write examples on the overhead. Say:

Okay, I am going to add some.
"K-Mart *sells* more pairs of Levis than Jordache jeans"
"It is *faster* to do your math with a calculator than to do it in your head"
"A meter stick is *longer* than a yard stick"
"Tommy's dog *weighs* thirty pounds"

Say:

Let me tell you how I might decide if this is a statement of fact or of opinion. I see the words "sells more" and I know that I could check on this by going to the store and looking at their sales records. Now, how can you tell whether the other statements are statements of fact?

Possible responses (take each sentence at a time):

You can look, count, test, etc.
You can ask, You can read about it, etc.

What are you doing when you look, count, ask, read that something is a fact? (Try to get to idea that you are *proving* that the statement is true, real, etc.)
Say:

Let's look at this next group of sentences and see whether they are statements of fact or opinion.
"Jordache jeans are more "hip" than Levi's"
"It is more fun to do your math with a calculator than in your head"
"A meter stick is better than a yard stick"
"Tommy's dog is meaner than David's"

Say:

> (Model first sentence) Can we check on the rest of these statements like we did with the first ones? We can't test these directly. They are what one person thinks. Therefore they must be opinions.

State rule:

> Statements of fact can be proven to be true. Statements of opinion cannot be proven so easily. For example, Testable: faster, sells more, longer, weight, height, age, temperature, location; less easily tested: beauty, "funness," goodness, niceness, fairness.

III. Guided Practice

Say:

> Now suppose I read "The Metcalf School is in Champaign." Is that a statement of fact, I would ask myself. (What do you think?)

Possible responses:

> It's not a fact because it's not true.

Say:

> How do you know it's wrong or it's not a statement of fact?

Possible responses:

> It's in Normal.

Say:

> How do you know?

Possible responses:

> Town map, Town line, sources.

Say:

> So, you can prove it is wrong. And since we decided before that statements of fact contain things that can be proven, then even if it is proven wrong, it is still a *statement of fact*. (Explain that a statement is not itself a fact but a statement about something that is factual.)

Examples of statements of fact that are false:

> The city of Chicago is in the state of Iowa.
> In Illinois, it snows in the summer.
> The fourth of July is in August.

You need to ask yourself, "Could this be true?" "What do I know about this?"

A statement of fact can be proven true or false.

Review:

> Remember the things we learned about statements of fact and statements of opinion today: (1) Statements of fact can be proven easily (but statements of opinion are difficult or impossible to prove), and (2) Statements of fact can be proven true or false.

IV. Independent Practice

Now you are reading to try some on your own. Read each sentence below. Decide which sentences are statements of true facts, which are statements of false facts, and which are statements of opinion. In the blank before each sentence write the letters *TF* if the sentence is a statement of true fact, write the letters *FF* if the sentence is a statement of false fact, and write the letter *O* if the sentence is a statement of an opinion. For each statement of fact, true or false, give a possible source that you could use to check on this information.

_____ A. The best way to see an ice hockey game is on TV.
Possible Source _____

_____ B. Miss Bradford and Mrs. Behrends are fourth grade teachers at Metcalf School.
Possible Source _____

_____ C. New York City is in the state of California.
Possible Source _____

_____ 1. Columbus discovered China in 1492.
Possible Source _____

_____ 2. Lake Michigan is a large freshwater lake in the United States.
Possible Source _____

_____ 3. The Grand Canyon is one of the wonders of the world.
Possible Source _____

_____ 4. The noise of exploding fireworks on the Fourth of July is frightening.
Possible Source _____

_____ 5. A baseball game usually has 9 innings.
Possible Source _____

_____ 6. Photographs show you the way things and people look.
Possible Source _____

_____ 7. The average male hippopotamus weighs about 5 tons.
Possible Source _____

_____ 8. McDonald's french fries are always better than Burger King's or Wendy's.
Possible Source _____

_____ 9. Any boy between the ages of seven and seventeen can be a Girl Scout.
Possible Source _____

_____10. Football games seem to last forever.
Possible Source _____

V. Application

Remember at the start of the lesson we talked about advertisements. Let's see if we can apply what we just learned to an advertisement. Identify statements of fact that are true, statements of fact that are false, and opinions.

Introducing the Phantom

Our new Phantom is an extraordinary automobile. With one switch is changes from two-wheel to four-wheel drive. You will feel confident in blizzard or sun. And then you get great mileage. It has leather seats, power windows, air conditioning. It is a step beyond past driving machines. Come in. You can't afford not to see it.

Cautions and Comments

As an approach to developing independent reading comprehension abilities, Explicit Teaching has a large number of advocates. In support of this approach are a number of research studies in which considerable success was achieved in teaching students selected skills and strategies. At a time when we are well aware of the shortcomings in our methods of teaching reading comprehension, Explicit Teaching seems a timely solution for upgrading our practices. Furthermore, it is a commonsense approach. It represents a compilation of what many very good teachers have done for some time and what some educators who have looked at effective instruction have specified as key elements (e.g., Rosenshine 1983).

Despite these qualities, Explicit Teaching should not be accepted without question. The results of experiments in which Explicit Teaching was used were not very well sustained beyond the course of the experiment; and evidence of the application of skills or strategies, either spontaneously or planned, was lacking. Unfortunately, there exists no comparisons of Explicit Teaching with learning that is less teacher-centered and more collaborative or discovery-oriented. There exists no data by which a determination can be made as to whether or not an Explicit Teaching procedure might take away from the tendency of some students to self-initiate their own learning strategies. For example, if the approach were more collaborative and less teacher-dependent, perhaps students would be more open to define and use a great many more strategies for themselves at times other than those tied to a teacher's plans.

Apart from these limitations, there are some other issues that stand in the way of the use of the Explicit Teaching model of teaching reading comprehension. Such a model assumes that there are well-defined strategies to teach. Unfortunately, a detailed description of comprehension strategies and skills that are worth teaching—that is, are likely to lead to improvements in comprehension performance—does not exist. The problems facing Explicit Teaching are compounded by problems in describing how readers actually do use some of the skills that might be taught.

REFERENCES

Baumann, J. F. 1983. A generic comprehensive instructional strategy. *Reading World* (May): 284–94. Presents a reading comprehension instruction based on explicit teaching notions.

Brown, A. L., J. D. Campione, and J. D. Day. 1981. Learning to learn: On training students to learn from texts. *Educational Researcher* 10:14–21. Discusses the research related to developing independent comprehension including ramifications for instruction.

Campione, J. 1981. Learning academic achievement and instruction. Paper delivered at the Second Annual Conference on Reading Research and the Study of Reading, New Orleans. Discussed the notion of gradual release of responsibility and other key notions of relevance to Explicit Teaching.

Day, J. D. 1980. Teaching summarization skills: A comparison of training methods. Unpublished doctoral diss., University of Illinois at Urbana-Champaign. Represents a research study in which Explicit Teaching practices were explored.

Durkin, D. 1978–79. What classroom observations reveal about reading comprehension instruction. *Reading Research Quarterly* 14:481–533. Presents a dismal picture of the teaching of reading comprehension in schools.

———. 1984. Do basal manuals teach reading comprehension? In *Learning to read in American schools*, edited by R. C. Anderson, J. Osborn, and R. J. Tierney. Hillsdale, N.J.: Erlbaum. Discusses how basals have approached the teaching of reading comprehension.

Gordon, C., and P. D. Pearson. 1983. The effects of instruction in meta-comprehension and inferencing on children's comprehension abilities (Tech. Rep. No. 277). Urbana: University of Illinois, Center for the Study of Reading. Presents a research study involving Explicit Teaching of reading comprehension.

Hansen, J., and P. D. Pearson. 1981. An instructional study: Improving the inferential comprehension of fourth grade good and poor readers. *Journal of Educational Psychology*. Describes the use of explicit teaching in conjunction with research on the influence of attempting to teach students to develop inferential comprehension strategies.

Palincsar, A., and A. Brown. 1983. Reciprocal teaching of comprehension monitoring activities (Tech. Rep. No. 269). Urbana: University of Illinois, Center for the Study of Reading. Describes the use of Explicit Teaching in conjunction with having students take the teacher's role in their own learning.

Pearson, P. D., and M. C. Gallagher. 1983. The instruction of reading comprehension. *Contemporary Educational psychology* 8:317–44. Reviews the research on reading comprehension instruction and presents a model for teaching based upon the gradual release of responsibility.

Pearson, P. D., and M. Leys. 1984. Teaching comprehension. Unpublished paper, University of Illinois. Describes Explicit Teaching with examples.

Rosenshine, B. 1983. Functions of teaching. *Elementary School Journal* 83:335–51. Presents a framework for teaching based upon the research on effective schools.

Rogers, T., and M. Leys. 1984. Two approaches to teaching a comprehension skill. Unpublished paper, University of Illinois. Presents a research study of different approaches to Explicit Teaching of fact and opinion.

Tierney, R. J. 1982. Learning from text. In *Secondary school reading*, edited by A. Berger and H. Alan Robinson. Newark, Del.: International Reading Association. Presents an extended discussion (both pro and con) of Explicit Teaching.

Tierney, R. J., and J. Cunningham. 1984. Research on teaching reading comprehension. In *Handbook of reading research*, edited by P. D. Pearson. New York: Longman. Presents a comprehensive review of the research on teaching reading comprehension, including studies using Explicit Teaching.

APPENDIX

DIAGNOSTIC USE OF COMPREHENSIVE AND CONTENT AREA READING STRATEGIES

Illustration: Using the Guided Reading Procedure Diagnostically

The Guided Reading Procedure was used with six fifth-graders to evaluate their ability to recall main ideas, details, and sequence through unaided recall and guided rereading. The Guided Reading Procedure was selected as a medium through which the students' capabilities in developing an organizational structure for information might be viewed.

An informational passage, approximately 500 words in length, was selected. It was selected for its historical ordering of information and for its match with the students' reading levels. The material was considered to be reasonably difficult, moderately interesting, and simply organized.

The students were asked to read the story once silently and then to recall verbally everything they possibly could. This was intended to give an indication of the skills used in dealing with a body of information without external direction. Their responses were recorded for them to use for future reference. They then were asked to reread the text and make any additions and/or changes in their recalls. The information was then organized into a simple outline.

The students read the material intently, at an appropriate rate with few hesitations. Their initial recall of the selection was very sketchy and general; each student recalled only isolated pieces of information. Upon rereading the selection, they were able to confirm their choices and add some details to their recall. When asked to organize their material, three students were able to mention outlining as an organizational aid, but none could correctly sequence the information without the addition of irrelevant details. At no point did the students demonstrate a grasp of either the main ideas or the theme of the text. They did seem enthusiastic, however, about the tasks they were asked to perform.

Conclusions: If we can assume that the students' performance on this task was typical, it seems they have difficulty organizing and recalling what they have read. It is possible that classroom activities in which a student is asked to "read this and answer questions at the end" might be inappropriate for them. They may lack the ability to set their own purposes for reading, be motivated to read a passage on their own, and possess the organizational skills to do so. If experiential background is a factor, they may profit from discussions and experiences through which topics can be explored. At present, it would seem that they could all profit from instructional methods and interesting materials that would prompt them to set, focus, and organize their purposes and information-gathering abilities.

Illustration: Study Guide

A study guide was used diagnostically to assess the study skills and content area reading skills of selected high school sophomores, and to determine the suitability of the strategy for use with those students.

A combination of reading-reasoning study guide was given to the students to fill out as they read the passage. The combination of these two types of study guides was used to determine the students' ability to perceive cause-effect patterns in a selection and to classify causes into categories. It also served to assess the suitability of this technique for use with the students as an aid to developing reading and study skills. The reading guide consisted of matching causes with effects. The reasoning portion of the guide consisted of listing causes under various categories. Several of the students were unable to grasp the relationship between cause and effect and had difficulty with the reading guide. These same students were unable to categorize the causes correctly.

Conclusions: Several students seemed to have difficulty with the reading-thinking skills necessary to cope with a reading-reasoning study guide. They were unable to either determine cause-effect relations or to categorize causes. Furthermore, they seemed uninterested in doing so. It is possible that either the guides detracted from reading the text or the students need to explore cause-effect and other relationships through discussion of topics within the realm of their experiences. For example, once an understanding of these relationships is developed with familiar material, the students might be given similar activities through which to apply these understandings to their reading. To this end, they might be encouraged to develop their own study guide for the material being read.

3

Strategies for Responding to Reading as Writers

The Unit and Its Theme

Over the past decade, the results of assessments of reading achievement suggest that students generally do most poorly when they are asked questions that require careful inferential thinking and when they are asked to generate a written summary of a story. These findings are not necessarily surprising. In many classrooms, students receive very little opportunity to write, and if they are asked to write, it is usually done in a writing lesson, not a reading lesson. At the same time, observations of teacher-student interactions have shown consistently that teachers tend not to extend students' responses either by asking them inferential questions or by asking them to substantiate evaluative responses.

The situation, however, is changing. There has been a sudden upsurge of interest in teaching writing, which has included a swing towards providing students with many more opportunities to write, including writing in response to what they read and even interacting with each other about their own writing. As a result of these and other changes in practices, students are not only being encouraged to generate ideas, they are also being given feedback on the quality of their thinking. Furthermore, student responses are being developed and guided using ideas that originate with literary theorists, such as Bleich and Rosenblatt.

The Strategies

The present unit includes five strategies to help students respond to reading as writers. Each of the strategies has emerged in recent years as ways of having students use writing in conjunction with reading and of responding to the writing done by readers.

Author's Chair/Peer Conferencing

The Author's Chair involves having students present to peers their own writing and the writing of other classroom authors or professional authors. In conjunction with peer questioning of what writers did or were trying to do, Author's Chair establishes rich linkages between reading and writing *and* between authors and readers.

Dialogue Journals

Dialogue Journals provide a more private forum for students to write to their teacher about what they are reading and writing and about the problems they are having. It provides the teacher the opportunity to learn not only what students are thinking and doing, but also to share thoughts and suggestions with them.

ECOLA (Extending Concepts through Language Activities)

ECOLA represents an attempt to provide students with careful guidelines for generating a written response to what they read, to use peer input to develop an appreciation of different possible interpretations, and to revise these statements.

Response Heuristic

The Response Heuristic represents a procedure by which students given a structured procedure for responding to text, and then they are given opportunities to interact with their peers, the teacher, and the text as "members of a community of readers and writers."

Readers Theatre

Readers Theatre involves having students develop their own adaptations and interpretation of stories, poems, and other text for presentation to peer groups. The procedure integrates oral reading and interpretation with composition and collaboration. It is suitable for use with students of any age level.

AUTHOR'S CHAIR/PEER CONFERENCING

Purpose

The goal of Author's Chair/Peer Conferencing is to develop readers and writers who have a sense of authorship and readership which helps them in either composing process. This includes developing in students an appreciation of the following: what they read has been written by someone who has certain purposes in mind and control over what they have written; when they write they have a variety of options; and what they write can be interpreted in different ways by different readers.

Rationale

The present description of Author's Chair is taken from the work of several educators (Blackburn 1982; Boutwell 1983; Calkins 1983; Graves 1983; Graves and Hansen 1983) and represents a composite of their ideas. To a large extent, the notion of Author's Chair was shaped in selected classrooms in which teachers had begun exploring the relationships between reading and writing. Most notable among these teachers were Ellen Blackburn and Marilyn Boutwell, whose classrooms are described in several of the articles cited in this section. The term "Author's Chair" was first applied by Graves and Hansen (1983) to activities that took place in these classrooms.

Essentially, the concept of Author's Chair grew from attempts to give writers the opportunity to hear feedback from their peers about their writing. Sometimes this feedback would be used to provide suggestions to a writer who was in the process of writing a story or report and who wanted help; or it would be a sounding board for ideas before proceeding further. Sometimes this feedback would be used to respond to a finished piece of writing or to several works written by a classmate. In time, these peer conferences also were used to enable students to discuss professional authors, ranging from C. S. Lewis to Judy Blume.

Researchers interested in reading-writing relationships support such experiences after examining the outcomes (Graves and Hansen 1983; Tierney, Leys, and Rogers 1984). They note that children who are involved in peer conferences acquire several abilities and sensitivities that seem desirable and are relatively unique. These include (1) an appreciation that reading and writing involve ongoing constructive activities in which both readers and writers have many options, (2) a richer sense of what the relationship between readers and writers might be, (3) an appreciation of peer input and of the extent to which collaborations might contribute to enhancing both reading and writing skills, and (4) a better sense both of the quality of their own interpretations or written selections and of the strategies that can be used when problems are encountered during reading and writing.

Intended Audience

While most of the descriptions of Author's Chair or Peer Conferencing emanate from the elementary school, Author's Chair or Peer Conferencing can be used at any age level and in almost any learning situation—from a second grade reading class to writing an official business memo for a corporation.

Procedures

The use of peer conferences requires a change in the typical approach used by most teachers. In most reading lessons, teachers guide students through a reading selection with a variety of questions to ensure they are engaged and come to understand the selection. Upon completing the selection, the teacher is likely to assign more questions, or some activities, or develop some comprehension, word recognition, or study skill. Likewise in many classrooms, the teacher assigns students to write on a topic, and as the writing progresses, she may help the students. Upon completing the writing assignment, the student submits the assignment to the teacher for evaluation. These scenarios represent an approach to reading and writing that is in sharp contrast to the use of Peer Conferences or Author's Chair.

The major difference is in the role of the teacher. In Peer Conferencing, the students act as advisors and evaluators along with the teacher. The teacher might orchestrate or facilitate Peer Conferences, but students are given control of many of the questions and other ideas that get introduced. At the heart of Author's Chair or Peer Conferencing is collaboration.

As classes begin to use Peer Conferences and collaboration, various permutations can emerge. For example, in a single class the range of possibilities might include coauthoring, coreading, class discussions of a peer's problem or work in progress, and small group or a paired sharing of work, ideas, or interests. To illustrate the use of Author's Chair or Peer Conferences, three variations of the group conference will be described. They include (1) reading and writing in progress conference, (2) end of book conference and (3) peer author conference.

Reading and Writing in Progress Conference

At any stage during the reading or writing of a story or a report, it may be appropriate to conference. For example, as readers and writers begin to read or write a story or report, they may wish to seek some input on what they are about to read or write. A writer might be unsure as to how he might begin a story, so he might meet with peers to acquire their feedback. Another child might be about to begin reading a book and he would like advice from peers who have read this same or similar books. Sometimes if groups of students are to read the same book or write on the same topic, they might share their plans or simply brainstorm together.

As readers and writers progress through a story or report, they may encounter a problem or want to share what they have done so far and what they plan to do next. Again peer conferences might be organized in which students define the help they need (their reason for asking for a conference), present what they have accomplished so far, and explore reasons for being stuck, or consider what they plan to do next. The student who desired the conference is responsible for entertaining the questions and ideas of their peers. This might involve calling for questions from classmates as well as from the teacher. Below is a segment from a conference in which a student is wrestling with a problem in a story he is reading.

> **FRED:** I wanted to conference because I having trouble finding information on robotics for my report. I have all these books and I started reading them. It seems that there is just too much information. I don't know what to do
>
> **HELEN:** Why did you decide upon robotics?
>
> **FRED:** I'm real interested in robots and how people might use them in everyday life. Also I thought it would be interesting.
>
> **SAM:** Maybe you could just do one idea of using robots. Sometimes when I do reports I get too much information, so I try to decide what I really want to say. Then I usually just take part of a big idea and use only a few books.
>
> **HELEN:** You could write about just a few kinds of robots or just a few kinds of things they can do.
>
> **FRED:** Umhmm. Yeah, that would help. Mr. Flores?
>
> **MR. FLORES:** So what do you plan to do?

As you can imagine, similar conferences—with or without the teacher—might be held with a variety of different goals in mind. The key is providing peers an opportunity to get an issue on the floor, acquire input, and then discuss how they might use the advice.

End of Book Conference

These conferences provide students the opportunity to share their reading and writing experiences and products. When students finish the stories they have been reading or the reports they have been writing, they can set up a conference for purposes of sharing their accomplishment with their peers. This might involve providing their peers a synopsis of what they have written or read. It might involve reading the entire story or report or interesting sections of a book aloud. Also, it might include discussing what it was like to read or write this story. After sharing, the writer or reader opens the floor to peer reactions, comments, and questions. As Graves and Hansen (1983) suggest sometimes a reader or writer might need to develop confidence, in which case peers are encouraged to give supportive comments more than interrogative questions. Hansen (1984) has illustrated two such conferences in some examples of writing conferences that took place in Ellen Blackburn's first grade classroom. As Hansen (1983) described them:

> When Scott sits on a little chair . . . and reads his published book to the whole class clustered on the floor in front of him, with their eyes glued upon him, he's scared. Scott is a fragile author. But knows that when he has finished reading, they will clap. Then lots of hands will go up. However, Scott need not fear because no one plans to ask a question. His friends want to make comments. Regardless of whom Scott calls upon, the child will accept his writing. "My favorite part was when you rode in the ambulance." Or, "The part I liked best was when you looked in the doctor's glasses and under your skin it looked liked fish eggs." His friend didn't ask him to read that part again, but it is also Scott's favorite part and he intends to share it again. . . .
>
> When Jamie shared her book about her nana, a classmate asked, "Why does your Nana have a lump on her back?" Some questions are more pointed. Daniel read his book about his babysitter's cat who got stuck in the dryer, and a friend asked, "Why didn't you tell how the cat got in the dryer?" (Pp. 972-73)

Again, such conferences can be used in conjunction with stories and reports that are read by students, as well as written by them. Sometimes such conferences might involve presenting reactions to published authors similar to the following:

> **LISA:** I loved this Judy Blume book. She tells a story about a girl who was overweight. I particularly like the way she let you know the girl's feelings. Let me read you a section. Blume is an excellent author, the only section which I thought she could have improved was her description of the eating by the girl. Also sometimes she left out some important facts. Anyhow I would recommend the book, in fact, I am planning to write a book similar to it.
> **FLOR:** Who do you think would like this book?
> **LISA:** Anybody who enjoys Blume or stories about people who are real and have everyday problems. I think you would like it.
> **PETER:** How come you didn't like so much of the book and still recommend it.
> **LISA:** No book is perfect.
> **ELIZABETH:** In what ways will your book be similar? etc.

In contrast to reporting on professional authors, conferences about peer work might also be conducted. These are described next.

Peer Author Conferences

Unlike the conferences in which students report on professional authors or their own efforts, peer author conferences refer to conferences that are given by classmates on peer writing. In this situation, the author is present and might be questioned occasionally, but somebody else—a peer reader—reports on the book and fields most of the questions and comments. The author has an opportunity to hear somebody else represent the book, including what they enjoyed, found confusing, and might use. In addition, the author along with peers has an opportunity to ask questions of the readers about their recommendations and evaluation of the book. The person who reads the book has a unique opportunity to share a book of an author whom they know and with whom they may have conferenced about the book.

Cautions and Comments

As was mentioned earlier, researchers have suggested that the collaborative experiences afforded by the Author's Chair or Peer Conferencing result in improvements in a student's sense of readership and authorship, as well as an ability to evaluate and problem solve. Apart from these benefits, the opportunity to conference provides students with a rich resource that often goes untapped in classrooms—namely, one's own peers. Furthermore, if conferencing opportunities extend to works in progress, they provide a vehicle by which teachers can move away from just assigning and assessing reading and writing to developing strategies for use as reading and writing actually occurs. By providing a forum for making public any difficulties and strategies, as Graves and Hansen (1983) and Tierney, Leys, and Rogers (1985) have argued, readers and writers are likely to become both better self-monitors and more flexible strategy users.

There appear to be three obstacles likely to stand in the way of successful conferencing in many classrooms. First, most teachers place themselves on center stage; a conferencing approach requires them to establish quite a different social setting for reading and writing. Second, a teacher may find that children do not automatically take to the approach. Their comments may seem off-base, too general or too tentative. Some students need encouragement, support, and repeated opportunities before the conferences seem worthwhile. In a recent study, Hittleman had a great deal of success establishing more effective peer conferences, using a combination of peer and teacher modeling (Hittleman 1983). Third, many of the conferences that were described are based on two tenets: (1) students should have the opportunity to write for longer than 30 minutes twice a week (they should be given enough time to write extended stories and reports of their own choosing); and (2) writing experiences contribute to reading. Unless these two tenets are observed in a classroom, some of the conferences described could not have taken place.

REFERENCES

Blackburn, E. 1982. The rhythm of writing development. In *Understanding writing*, edited by T. Newkirk and N. Atwell. Chelmsford, MA: Northeast Regional Exchange. Describes several of her experiences in the first grade as she observed her students writing and interacted with them.

Boutwell, M. 1983. Reading and writing: A reciprocal agreement. *Language Arts* 60:6. Describes the features of her classroom that supported a reciprocal agreement between reading and writing, including the conferences that were initiated.

Calkins, L. M. 1983. *Lessons from a child*. Exeter, N.H.: Heineman. In this story of one child's growth in writing, Calkins illustrates what influences and classroom procedures are woven into the child's development.

Graves, D. 1983. *Writing: Teachers and children at work*. Exeter, N.H.: Heineman. Provides a full description of how teachers might teach writing in conjunction with the use of a conference approach. Graves provides extensive guidelines for how teachers might conference with students, which can be applied to peer conferencing.

Graves, D. and J. Hansen. 1983. The author's chair. *Language Arts* 60: 176–83. Describes the nature and benefits derived in a first grade classroom that initiated the use of Author's Chair.

Hansen, J. 1983. Authors respond to authors. *Language Arts* 60: 970–76. Describes several different types of conferences with examples from her observations in classrooms.

Hawkins, T. 1977. *Group inquiry techniques for teaching writing*. Urbana, Ill.: ERIC Clearinghouse on Reading and Communication Skills/NCTE. Describes several procedures for organizing and developing discussion of writing by peers.

Healy, M. K. 1980. *Using student writing response groups in the classroom*. Berkeley: University of California, Bay Area Writing Project. Describes the use of peer response groups in classrooms.

Hittleman, C. G. 1983. Peer conference groups and teacher written comments as influences on revisions during the composing processes of fourth grade students. Unpublished doctoral diss., Hofstra University. Presents a thorough study of the use of peer conferencing in the fourth grade.

Tierney, R. J., M. Leys, and T. Rogers. 1985. Composition, comprehension, and collaboration: An analysis of two classrooms. In *Contexts of literacy*, edited by T. Raphael and R. Reynolds. New York: Random House. Describes the classroom parameters for a conferencing approach for both reading and writing, as well as the comments and responses of selected fourth grade students who have been involved in such experiences.

DIALOGUE JOURNALS

Purpose

Dialogue Journals, as described by Staton (1980), are intended to provide students an opportunity to share privately in writing their reactions, questions, and concerns about school experiences (and sometimes personal matters) with the teacher without any threat of reprisal or evaluation. It affords the teacher an opportunity to learn what each individual child is doing and thinking and then to offer counsel.

Rationale

While the term "Dialogue Journal" has a rather recent history, the use of Journals per se has a long history dating back to when individuals began using writing as a means of record keeping and of reflecting upon their lot in life. In school situations, journal writing has often assumed a life of its own as English teachers, and sometimes science teachers, have introduced it into the daily or weekly life of their students. Often journals were used to encourage diarylike entries of what took place in the way of progress on a project; sometimes they were used to give students the opportunity to respond freely to what took place at school or home, or to respond to a book or some other form of literature. The negative side of journals is that they can become tedious or, with some students, never take hold. Some students don't enjoy the experience and find the task boring; some may be very withdrawn or are not sufficiently introspective to talk "to themselves." Also, if journal writing becomes a preoccupation, then both the students and the teacher will likely find the experience a chore. On the positive side, and what accounts for the widespread advocacy of journal writing, are testimonies of the benefits. As Kirby and Liner (1981) suggest:

> Simply stated, the journal is the most consistently effective tool for establishing fluency that I have found. True believers swear that the journal works on some mystical principle because some nonfluent, nontalking, and apparent nonthinking students have blossomed so dramatically through journal writing. (P. 45)

Other testimonies attest to further advantages: (1) the opportunity that journal writing provides for more open responses to classroom assignments; (2) the vehicle that it provides for teacher feedback, counseling and response; and (3) the chance that it gives for dealing with each student individually.

The notion of Dialogue Journals is a partial refinement of Journal writing. The major characteristic that distinguishes Dialogue Journals from other forms is the importance given to communications between the student and the teacher. Dialogue Journals are more like a daily letter or memo to the teacher. While the teacher might not respond to every entry, the intent of Dialogue Journals is to have students write to the teacher and to have the teacher write a genuine response to the student. Often the Dialogue Journal is quite open-ended and the student includes letters on all sorts of matters, from diets to schoolwork to sporting events. Sometimes students have journals that are intended to record reactions and concerns to specific experiences, such as reading and writing. If the latter be the case, the teacher might ask the students to include, either occasionally or on a regular basis, specific types of information in their journals. In all of these situations, the child writes and the teacher responds. The advantage is that the teacher and student can share, on a one-to-one basis, matters that, in the course of the day, most classroom situations do not allow sufficient time for.

Intended Audience

Dialogue Journals can be used with students at any age level.

Procedures

To illustrate the procedures for Dialogue Journals, the following examples are taken from a third grade classroom in which the teacher provided time every day for students to write entries in two journals: a reading journal and writing journal. The original entries have been rewritten and the names of the student and teacher changed to ensure their privacy. Otherwise they are reproduced exactly.

The four journal entries represent some of the different types of comments students might be prompted to make in their journals. They include examples of comments by the students about what they have been reading and writing and their experiences in so doing. They include reflections about peer relationships, and responses to and inquiries directed at the teacher.

The teacher's entry represents a rich assortment of reflections in response to what the student has shared, and an attempt to extend the child's thinking. One of the comments offered by the teacher discusses how the student's experiences were similar to her own (I also picture in my head as I read); at the same time the teacher's comments reflect an attempt to extend these ideas (it is a sign of good writing) and offer some advice (tell the author). It is interesting to note the teacher's written comments following one student's lengthy discussion of a classmate with whom there is some enmity. The teacher does not evaluate the student's comments as either right or wrong. The student's feelings are accepted as legitimate, and the teacher offers a couple of suggestions as to how she might deal with her feelings. What is important to note is the teacher's respect for the privacy of the journal as well as the nonjudgemental and nonprescriptive nature of the teacher's reaction. Decisions to be made are left up to the student.

Getting Started

Nancy Atwell has discussed beginning Dialogue Journals in her eighth grade classroom (Atwell 1984). She described how she initiated the journals:

> This folder is a place for you and me to talk about books, reading, authors, and writing. You're to write letters to me, and I'll write letters back to you.

Figure 3-1   Examples of Dialogue Journal Entries

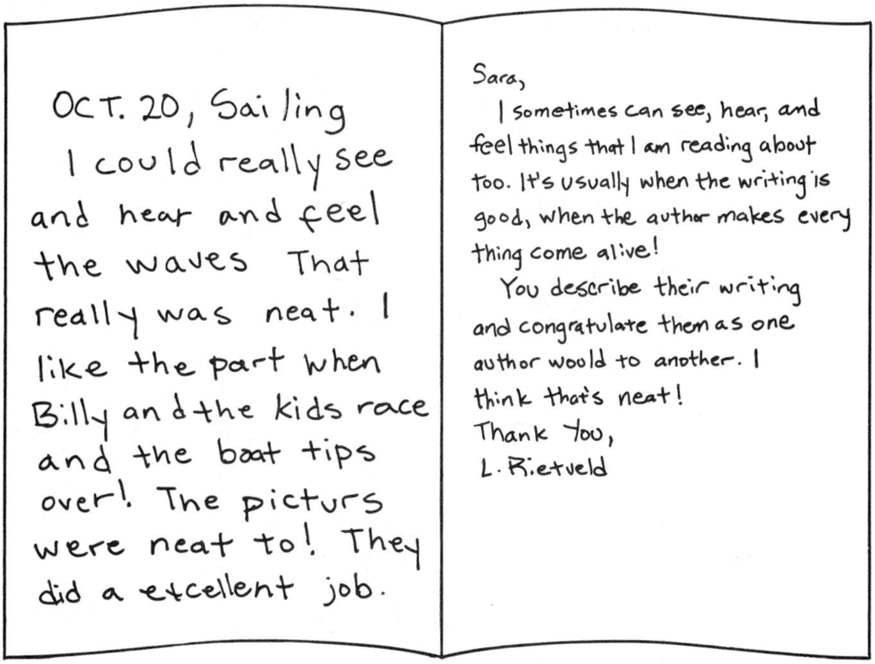

OCT. 20, Sailing
I could really see and hear and feel the waves. That really was neat. I like the part when Billy and the kids race and the boat tips over! The pictures were neat to! They did a extcellent job.

Sara,
I sometimes can see, hear, and feel things that I am reading about too. It's usually when the writing is good, when the author makes every thing come alive!
You describe their writing and congratulate them as one author would to another. I think that's neat!
Thank You,
L. Rietveld

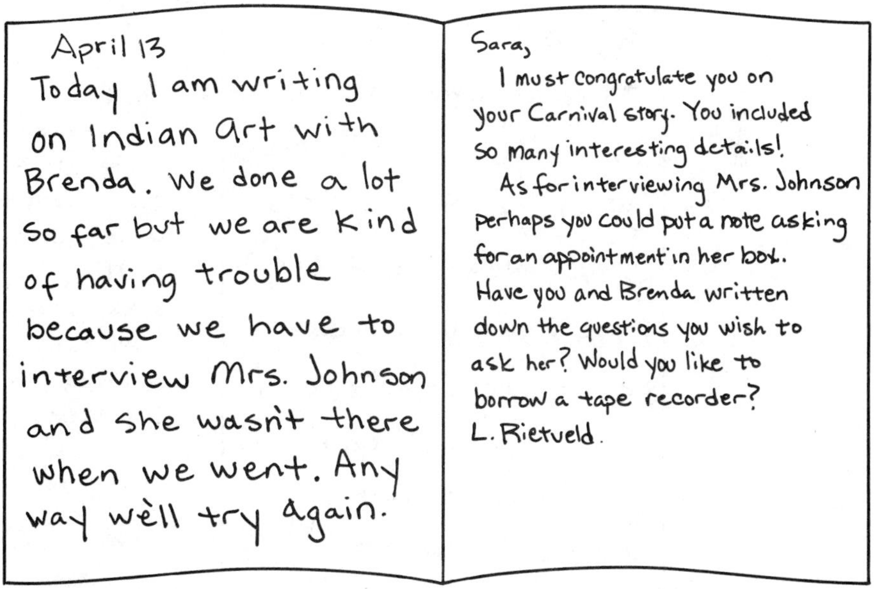

April 13
Today I am writing on Indian Art with Brenda. We done a lot so far but we are kind of having trouble because we have to interview Mrs. Johnson and she wasn't there when we went. Any way we'll try again.

Sara,
I must congratulate you on your Carnival story. You included so many interesting details!
As for interviewing Mrs. Johnson perhaps you could put a note asking for an appointment in her box. Have you and Brenda written down the questions you wish to ask her? Would you like to borrow a tape recorder?
L. Rietveld.

Figure 3–2   Examples of Dialogue Journal Entries

Dear Miss Rietveld

Do We
have to
Do It.
!!!!

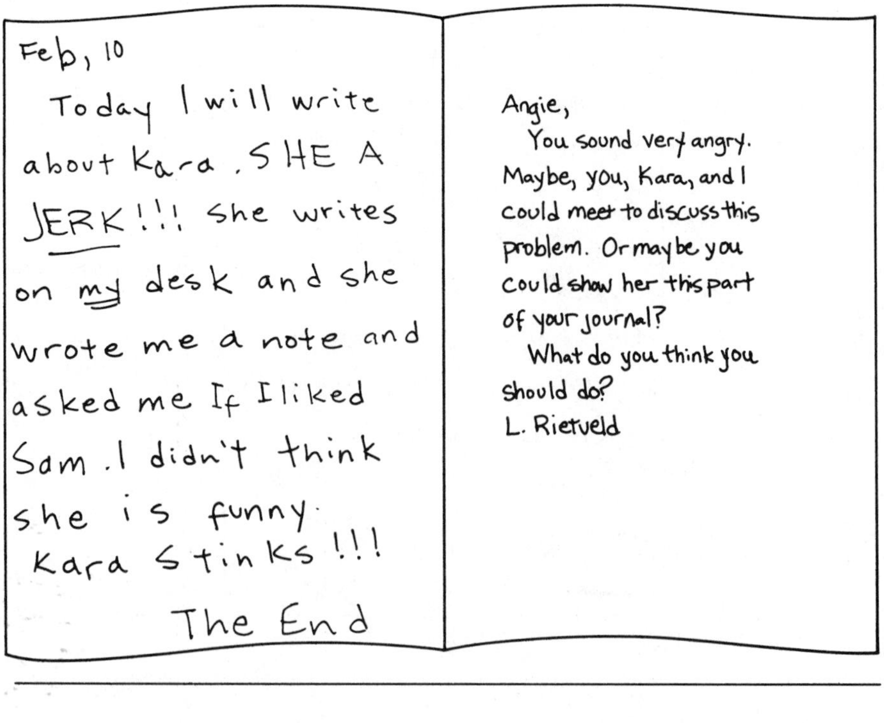

Feb, 10
   Today I will write
about Kara . SHE A
JERK!!! She writes
on my desk and she
wrote me a note and
asked me If I liked
Sam . I didn't think
she is funny.
Kara Stinks !!!
         The End

Angie,
   You sound very angry.
Maybe, you, Kara, and I
could meet to discuss this
problem. Or maybe you
could show her this part
of your journal?
   What do you think you
should do?
L. Rietveld

In your letters to me, talk with me about what you've read. Tell me what you thought and felt and why. Tell me what you liked and didn't like and why. Tell me what these books meant to you and said to you. Ask me questions or for help, and write back to me about my ideas, feelings, and questions.

While there are other ways to begin Dialogue Journals and other types of journals, Atwell's comments describe for students the purpose of the journal and give a very open-ended sense of what might be included. Once initiated, it is important that the journal writing not be shortchanged in terms of time allocation. Unless uninterrupted time is put aside during the school day for everybody to write in their journals, the possibility of obtaining meaningful journal entries diminishes.

Responding to Journals

In many ways suggestions for responding to journals should be rather obvious. Apart from recommending that journal responses by a teacher be sincere, thoughtful and regular, the following represents a compilation of common sense suggestions based upon Kirby and Liner (1981).

1. *Protect the privacy of the journal.* Don't ever read aloud journal entries or share journal entries without the permission of the author.
2. *Be an active reader and sincere respondent.* Write general remarks, share your ideas, make specific suggestions, and react rather than correct.
3. *Be honest with students.* In those situations where students tell you more than what you want to know or include language you would not care to read, tell them to cut it out.
4. *Look for something good.* Don't give up on students; rather encourage them, and avoid sarcasm.
5. *Make journal writing special and interesting.* Don't let it become a chore; respond eagerly and with interest. Take a break from journal writing, if necessary.
6. *Be aware that you cannot be expected to respond every day to each student's journal entry.* Don't make promises to the students about the frequency with which you might respond.

Cautions and Comments

The description of journal writing that has been offered is quite condensed. The present discussion is restricted to Dialogue Journals that were used by elementary students for purposes of responding to reading and writing. Journals can easily be used in other ways—with projects, such as a group investigation of a problem or topic, with field trips, or with any special activity. There are no age restrictions on the use of journals; some educators have even successfully used them with preschoolers. For example, Elliott, Nowasad, and Samuels (1981) have reported involving parents in helping their preschoolers with the transcription.

What is the value of journal writing? There have been very few research studies in which the worth of any type of journal writing has been explored. In terms of evidence of their worth, most of the support comes in statements from those educators who have been involved in the experience. Staton (1980), for example, has commented on the value that was derived from using Dialogue Journals by a teacher, Leslee Reed:

> . . . the openness of the journal as a forum for personal problems as well as for academic ones captures the natural function of language as intentional communication about what matters most to the person. An attitude of trust and interest in everything the writer says characterizes Leslee Reed's attitude toward her students and what they write in their journals. "I learn something new everyday about each one of them. They are fascinating and exciting to get to know." It is no wonder that their willingness to express their own ideas, feelings and experiences in written language improves and creates in them a confidence about writing in general that too few people their age or any age enjoy." (P. 518)

Or, as Nancy Atwell commented when describing how Dialogue Journals and other factors worked together, "It's a dining room table with seventy chairs around it" (p. 251).

REFERENCES

Atwell, N. 1984. Writing and reading literature from the inside out. *Language Arts* 61: 240–52. Describes the use of Dialogue Journals for reading and writing in an eighth grade classroom.

Davis, F. A. 1984. "Why you call me Emigrant?": Dialogue journal writing with migrant youth. *Childhood Education* (November-December). Describes the use of dialogue journals in a migrant education project by New Jersey teachers.

Elliott, S., J. Nowasad, and P. Samuels. 1981. "Me at School," "Me at Home": Using journals with preschoolers. *Language Arts* 58: 688–91. Describes the use of journal writing in a preschool where the teacher and the parents were involved in transcribing entries.

Kirby, D., and T. Liner. 1981. *Inside out*. New York: Boynton-Cook. Presents an overview, guidelines, and suggestions for journal writing.

Kreeft, J. 1984. Dialogue writing—Bridge from talk to essay writing. *Language Arts* 61:141–50. Addresses the question of how dialogue journals help students' writing skills with examples to highlight teacher strategies and student growth.

Markman, M. 1985. Teacher-student dialogue writing in a college composition course: Effects upon writing performance and attitude. Unpublished doctoral diss., University of Missouri. Researches the effectiveness of dialogue journals with college students.

Newkirk, T. 1982. Young writers as critical readers. In *Understanding writing*, edited by T. Newkirk and N. Atwell. Chelmsford, MA: Northeast Regional Exchange. Describes the notion of bringing students inside written language as critics, enthusiasts, and participants.

Staton, J. 1980. Writing and counseling: Using a dialogue journal. *Language Arts* 57: 514–18. Describes the use of dialogue journals and their value.

———. 1984a. Thinking together: The role of language interaction in children's reasoning. In *Speaking and Writing, K–12*, edited by C. Thaiss and C. Suhor. Describes the rationale, purposes, and benefits of dialogue journals.

———. 1984b. The interactional acquisition of practical reasoning in early adolescence: A study of dialogue journals. Unpublished doctoral diss., University of California at Los Angeles. A research study of the use of dialogue journals.

Staton, J., J. Kreeft, and L. Gutstein, eds. *Dialogue*. Washington, D.C.: Center for Applied Linguistics. *Dialogue* is a newsletter about the uses, benefits, and theory of dialogue journals. Dialogue is available through the Center for Applied Linguistics, 3520 Prospect Street, N. W., Washington, D.C. 20007.

Staton, J., R. Shuy, and J. Kreeft. 1982. *Analysis of dialogue journal writing as a communicative event*. Washington, D.C.: National Institute of Education Grant No. G-80-0122, Center for Applied Linguistics. (ERIC No.: vol. 1, ED 214 196; vol 2, ED 214 197). A two-volume description of the use of dialogue journals, including the purposes, structure, and benefits.

ECOLA (Extending Concepts Through Language Activities)

Purpose

ECOLA (Extending Concepts Through Language Activities), which was developed by Smith-Burke (1982), represents an attempt to integrate reading, writing, speaking, and listening for purposes of developing a reader's ability to interpret and monitor his or her own comprehension.

Rationale

As Smith-Burke states, ECOLA is intended to focus "students on the constructive nature of reading and the need to monitor to be sure the interpretation one constructs makes sense" (p. 177). For this purpose, the ECOLA lesson framework places a great deal of importance upon the following learning experiences:

1. *Purposeful reading of text.* Goals for reading a text are thoughtfully developed based upon an understanding of the author's intent and any reason the teacher might have for using the text. Eventually these goals are initiated solely by students.
2. *Written responses.* To crystalize a reader's understanding, students are expected to commit themselves to an interpretation in writing, which they may revise, however, after discussion.
3. *Discussion.* Discussion is viewed as a basis for generating ideas, examining purposes, evaluating interpretations, and considering the efficacy of strategies.
4. *Self-monitoring.* Students are encouraged to verbalize their confusions, commit themselves to an interpretation, and discuss their strategies for understanding text.

Intended Audience

The ECOLA strategy is intended for use with students in upper elementary school through high school. It seems appropriate to use with a variety of texts.

Procedure

Five steps constitute the procedure. The steps are: (1) setting a communicative purpose for reading; (2) silent reading for a purpose and criterion task; (3) crystalizing an interpretation through writing; (4) discussing and clarifying interpretations; and (5) writing and comparing.

Step 1. Setting a communicative purpose. To set a purpose that is communicative requires first a determination of the purposes for which the text might be read. This requires a teacher to determine what he or she would like the students to glean from the text, based upon a consideration of the author's purpose.

Once a determination has been made of the purposes for which the text might be read, two further decisions need to be made. A teacher must decide what type of support the students need; for example, a teacher should examine the text and determine what type of additional preparation for reading a selection (e.g., discussion of key ideas) might be needed. Also, a teacher should determine the actual task to which students are expected to respond. For example, several questions for reading a selection might be subsumed under a general purpose for the assignment.

Step 2. Silent reading for a purpose and a criterion task. Students are reminded of their purpose(s) for reading and made aware that they should be able to support their interpretations with ideas from the text, their background knowledge, or reasoning. Smith-Burke suggests that it is reasonable for different students to read with different goals in mind.

Step 3. Crystalizing comprehension through writing. The purpose of this step is to develop in students the ability to self-monitor and to begin to learn how to verbalize what they don't understand. During this step, each student and the teacher write a response to the overall question or purpose for reading. In writing a response, students are assured that answers will be kept confidential. They are encouraged to both commit themselves to an interpretation, and write about anything that they find confusing. To clarify these problems, they are urged to ask other students. It is then the responsibility of others to explain how they dealt with the same problems.

Step 4. Discussing the lesson. Students are organized into groups no larger than four in size and given a time limit in which they are expected to discuss interpretations, compare responses, and challenge conclusions. Each student is expected to share and explain the basis for his conclusion.

Step 5. Writing and Comparing. The final step is to have students, in small groups or individually, generate a second interpretation. If done as a group, then a consensus must be reached by discussion and resolution. After the revised interpretation has been completed, the students are encouraged to discuss the changes that were made and to talk about the strategies they found helpful in understanding the text.

An example of the ECOLA strategy, applied to a familiar fable, is given on the next page.

Cautions and Comments

Smith-Burke (1982) has offered some guidelines for the use of ECOLA. Since ECOLA is a very intensive process, she has suggested that the approach not be used constantly. Instead, certain steps might be omitted and other approaches occasionally substituted. Also, she has emphasized that the teacher is responsible for leading discussions, giving the students feedback and modeling; students are responsible for deciding how to read and for monitoring what they read.

While Smith-Burke's guidelines are not elaborated and the approach lacks substantiation, the procedure represents a welcome addition to the field. It is among very few strategies that responds to the alarming finding from the National Assessment of Educational Progress that readers have difficulty formulating a written response to text. The procedure distinguishes itself further in terms of meeting obvious needs in its pursuit of argumentation over piecemeal or partial interpretations and its commitment to the refinement and redevelopment of a reader's interpretation following discussion. What distinguishes the strategy even further is the utilization of a child-centered, rather than teacher-directed, consideration of strategies and their efficacy. Self-monitoring is nurtured rather than demanded.

Figure 3-3 Example of ECOLA applied to a Familiar Fable

Story: The Hare and the Tortoise (Aesop's Fables)

The familiar fable describes a foot race between a hare and a tortoise. The hare, thinking he could win the race easily because of his speed, lies down to rest and soon falls to sleep. While the hare was sleeping, the tortoise crosses the finish line and the hare wakes to find he has lost.

1. Setting a communication purpose.

The teacher briefly summarizes the fable and then sets a clear purpose for reading through a discussion with the class.

> Why were fables written?
> Were fable authors trying to communicate a message?
> Has anyone read a fable? Was there a message in that fable for the reader's own life?
> How did you feel about the character(s) in the fable?
> What could a reader (or hearer) of a fable gain from a story of animals?

2. Silent reading for a purpose and a criterial task.

> What is the message of this fable?
> Will everyone agree or could there be many messages?
> Why might someone see (hear?) a different message?

3. Crystalizing comprehension through writing

Students write about the fable particularly in relation to the purpose stated in Step 2 (above).

4. Discussing the lesson.

As students share their ideas and interpretations, their reactions to the fable may change.

5. Writing and Comparing

The teacher reviews purposes for reading and writing.

> Was your second interpretation different from your first?
> What led you to reconsider?
> How did you decide what to change and what not to change?
> Do you think there can ever be one definitive interpretation of fable or story?

REFERENCES

Bartholomae, D., and A. Petrosky. N.d. Facts, artifacts and counterfacts: A basic reading and writing course for the college curriculum. Unpublished manuscript, University of Pittsburgh. Discusses similar endeavors at the University of Pittsburgh.

Brown, A. L. 1980. Metacognitive development and reading. In *Theoretical issues in reading comprehension*, edited by R. J. Spiro, B. Bruce, and W. F. Brewer. Hillsdale, NJ: Erlbaum. Presents a thorough discussion of self-monitoring and its role and development.

Smith-Burke, M. T. 1982. Extending concepts through language activities. In *Reader meets author/bridging the gap*, edited by J. Langer and M. Smith-Burke. Newark, DE: International Reading Association. Presents a description of the steps involved in ECOLA with examples of teacher-student dialogue.

RESPONSE HEURISTIC

Purpose

The Response Heuristic (Bleich, 1978) is designed to promote students' response to literature by helping them independently analyze and interpret literary texts.

Rationale

Answering questions after reading is the most frequently used means to get students to respond to text material, literary or otherwise. Unfortunately, questions rarely provide students with sufficient structure to enable them to evaluate ideas as they are encountered. Additionally, students may become dependent on external prompts in their efforts to react to literature, i.e., they rely on teacher questions to stimulate their thinking. Thus, students do not gain a structure for their own independent analysis of text and may not be able to react beyond a mere literal level parroting of it.

In order to move beyond a literal repetition of text, students need to be able to use their prior knowledge in conjunction with the text information. Thus, comprehension becomes a shared experience between reader and text or, as Petrosky (1982) stated, comprehension occurs "through some kind of structured response that leads to a dialectic which represents the interaction of readers with a text" (p. 21).

A number of reading and language educators (e.g., Tierney and Pearson 1983) currently view reading as a composing process. In other words, comprehending text and composing text are seen as the same process—both are acts of understanding—and language use is viewed holistically rather than as a series of discrete pieces. Writing, therefore, may provide the best means to represent students' understandings of text, if reading is viewed as a composing process and not merely as an act of recall prompted by questions.

One strategy for responding to literature that provides students a structured response format as they interact with text, and that views reading, writing, and responding all as aspects of understanding, is the Response Heuristic (Bleich 1978). Bleich stated that the only way to show understanding is for readers to become writers who express their understandings of the text in their responses. Comprehension, then, means expressing in writing a response to explain the connections that readers make between their reality (prior knowledge) and the texts they create in light of that reality. Thus, unlike recall models of comprehension, the response heuristic provides readers the means to discuss their thoughts and feelings while at the same time making meaning by writing an explanatory response to their reading. Bleich believes this approach to literature response represents comprehension more accurately than the use of questions.

Intended Audience

The response heuristic may be used with all students once they have attained the ability to express themselves in writing. Thus, it is probably most appropriate when used with upper elementary and with older students as a means of getting them to respond to literary texts.

Description of the Procedure

The response heuristic asks students to react in writing in the following three part format: (1) text perceptions, (2) reactions to the text; and (3) associations with the text.

1. Text Perceptions

Since free response to text has a tendency to lack focus and be sketchy, the response heuristic is designed to get students to structure their responses in a more focused manner. The response heuristic begins with references to the text read. It is simply a statement of what a reader sees in the text. For instance, if the response heuristic were being used in conjunction with "Richard Cory" by E. A. Robinson and popularized by Simon and Garfunkel in song, some references to the text might include the following:

> Richard Cory was a gentleman admired by all. He was polite and rich, and everyone wished they were in his place.

2. Reactions to the Text

Once some references to the text are given the next step of the heuristic is for students to react to those references by writing how they felt about them. It is at this point in the response that students begin to make some links to their experiences. To continue with our example of the poem "Richard Cory," some reactions might be:

> I can understand how people look at how things appear on the outside, without bothering to look further, without bothering to find out what's going on inside. It's important to me, though, that people go beyond mere appearances.

3. Associations with the Text

The last part of the response heuristic is where students write about the associations—their feelings and thoughts—that emanate from their perceptions of the text. It is here that the response is further explained by using examples from the students' prior knowledge and beliefs. Associations that might be formulated using our "Richard Cory" example are:

> When I was younger, I was big for my age. People, my friends, and family—especially my father—told me that I'd make a great football player because of my size. They said I was strong and fast enough to be a great back. But nobody—not a single person—bothered to ask me what I wanted. They just told me what I should do. Sure, I was big enough to play, but what good is size if the desire's not there. Besides, I hated football! People were just responding to how I looked and what I had, just as people did with Richard Cory.

Cautions and Comments

Key to the success of the response heuristic, or any other literature response technique, is what happens after students have responded in writing. It is essential that a sharing/discussion of students' individual responses take place. In this way, readers can see how others have interpreted a literary text and can see that a variety of thoughts, feelings, and opinions, and reasons for them can exist about the same text or topic. Readers can begin to treat their responses as critical statements that need to be examined and discussed. Additionally, they can treat their writing as drafts to be refined, revised, and edited. Following such a procedure, students gain experiences in reading, writing about what was read, discussing others' thoughts about reading, critiquing others' writing, and edited and revising.

An additional concern in using the response heuristic is the teacher's role in this process. If an offshoot of this literature response strategy is to create a community of readers and writers, then teachers cannot remain outside observers. They must become part of the context in which the response heuristic is taking place. Teachers also need to read and write and share their unique perspectives with students. Additionally, if the procedure is to work, it will work best with teachers who are alert to the models that students are being provided and either finding appropriate peer models or acting as models themselves for students.

As a final note, not all response to literature strategies need be conducted in writing. The ultimate reason for providing students a structured response format is to get them actively involved in their own learning and to give them a framework for independently analyzing text. The following responses to literature strategies are recommended as viable alternatives to the response heuristic, whether they be used for composing purposes, as with the heuristic, or for strictly verbal discussion purposes:

1. Transactional analysis structures (Readence and Moore 1979) based on the experiences that describe all transactions between individuals as set forth by T. A. Harris. These transactions include withdrawal, rituals, pastimes, activities, games, and intimacy.
2. Stages of moral reasoning (Readence, Moore, and Moore 1982) based on the sequence by which Western cultures develop moral standards as developed by L. Kohlberg. These stages are punishment/obedience, the marketplace, good boy/nice girl, law and order, social contract, and universal ethics.
3. Stages of confronting death (Moore, Moore, and Readence 1983) based on individuals' reactions to death as described by E. Kubler-Ross. These stages include denial, anger, bargaining, depression, and acceptance.

All of the three frameworks mentioned above can provide students an opportunity to analyze literary situations and characters as they interact with text. Together with the response heuristic, they can go far toward moving readers to independence.

REFERENCES

Bleich, D. 1978. *Subjective criticism*. Baltimore: John Hopkins University Press. A discussion of the response heuristic, as well as a critical examination of responses and texts.

Moore, D. W., S. A. Moore, and J. E. Readence. 1983. Understanding characters reactions to death. *Journal of Reading* 26:540–44. Describes how Kubler-Ross' stages of confronting death is used as a means to help students respond to death-related literature.

Petrosky, A. R. 1982. From story to essay: Reading and writing. *College Composition and Communication* 33:19–36. A discussion of the connections between reading, writing, and response to literature, including some examples of the response heuristic.

Readence, J. E., and D. W. Moore. 1979. Responding to literature: An alternative to questioning. *Journal of Reading* 23:107–11. Examines the use of transactional analysis structures as a strategy for students' independently responding to literature.

Readence, J. E., D. W. Moore, and S. A. Moore. 1982. Kohlberg in the classroom: Responding to literature. *Journal of Reading* 26:104–8. Delineates the procedures for using the stages of moral development as a technique for literature response.

Tierney, R. J., and P. D. Pearson. 1983. Toward a composing model of reading. *Language Arts* 60:568–80. Discusses the notion that both reading and writing are composing processes.

READERS THEATRE

Purpose

Readers Theatre is a procedure for integrating the language arts and advancing a student's motivation to read. Additionally, it focuses on improving students' oral reading and interpretation, as well as their composition and comprehension abilities.

Rationale

In a recent book on Readers Theatre, Sloyer (1982) described it in these terms:

> Readers Theatre is an interpretative reading activity for all the children in the classroom. Readers bring characters to life through their voices and gestures. Listeners are captivated by the vitalized stories and complete the activity by imagining the details of scene and action . . . Used in the classroom, Readers Theatre becomes an integrated language event centering upon oral interpretation of literature. The children adapt and present the material of their choice. A story, a poem, a scene from a play, even a song lyric, provide the ingredients for the script. As a thinking, reading, writing, speaking and listening experience, Readers Theatre makes a unique contribution to our language arts curriculum. (P. 3)

Unlike many of the strategies described in this book, Readers Theatre has emerged largely from the hands of teachers as they have crafted its use in the classroom. The rationale for using it stems largely from the enthusiasm with which students are drawn to it. Reading material that was drab and unappealing in normal classroom circumstances becomes alive, exciting, and interpretable when done in conjunction with Readers Theatre. Apart from its motivational value, what contributes to the worth of the procedure are the reading, writing, and listening skills that are refined in conjunction with the development and redevelopment of a script and its performance. What drives Readers Theatre is the performance, rather than some arbitrary determination of what is satisfactory by the teacher.

Intended Audience

Readers Theatre can be used with students at all age levels regardless of their abilities.

Procedures

Readers Theatre involves students in the process from start to finish. Students select their own material, adapt it for presentation to the class, and portray the characters in performances to classmates and others. The steps that might be used in guiding the process are described below. With slight variation these steps are based upon those offered by Sloyer (1982).

1. *Selecting material.* A great deal of care needs to go into the selection of materials. Certainly teachers must judge for themselves the interests of their students. But what seems desirable are tight plots with clear endings and suspense, interesting characters, lively dialogue, and appealing themes. Other than the dramatization of stories, poems, popular songs, advertisements, and other types of text lend themselves to use in Readers Theatre. For variation, sometimes the dramatization can be done in the form of a musical, a TV newscast, or a documentary.

2. *Getting started.* A classroom discussion about theater or a movie is a natural springboard for Readers Theatre. The discussion should be both open-ended and focused on what would it take to change a book into a movie.

3. *A sample to see and read.* Once students have brainstormed about play or moviemaking, they should be introduced to an example of a short story for which there exists a script. The students should be given an opportunity to read both versions and discuss (1) the types of adjustments that were made in changing the text from a story to a play and (2) other issues that need to be considered if the play is to be performed.

4. *Plan for an adaptation.* Using the story for which there already is a script story as a model, the students are encouraged to choose another story from their readers or some other source for them to adapt. A short story or a single scene from a story that students will not find difficult to make into a play is recommended. Before any adaptation takes place, students should read or reread the story and discuss those elements of story that are key to its dramatization. These include the characters and their attributes, the plot, the theme, and the setting.

5. *Adapt the story.* For purposes of adapting the story, use larger poster paper, an overhead, or the chalkboard. Place the title as well as the time, setting, and list of characters on the poster. Then discuss the adaptation.

   a. Depending upon the story the students might discuss:
      (1) the characters in the story and what each says;
      (2) the role of the characters and the narrator (sometimes a character can act as narrator; at other times, an observer who is not part of the action may). In order to give more

students an opportunity to participate, the students may decide on two or more narrators; and
(3) the events, descriptions of feelings or observations and how they might be included in the play as action, sound effects, dialogue, or the narrator's remarks.
b. Following some discussion, write the names of the characters, including the narrator, in bold letters in the margin of the poster. Write the lines assigned to each character next to his or her name. Once the skeleton has begun to develop, encourage the students to make the language more interesting and realistic. If there are characters with no or very few lines, have them suggest revisions so they have more to say.
c. Once the script is completed, reproduce it for performance.

The fable "The Shepherd's Boy and the Wolf" and an adaptation follow.
6. *Preparing for theatrical production.* In preparing for the theatrical production, students need to be introduced to some aspects of stage craft, including working out the positions and actions of the readers on the stage. For this purpose, students can be introduced to the different areas on the stages where action might occur and characters might stand or move. Props and body movements can be discussed and notes made by the students as they discuss what should occur in their play. To assist the students, time might be provided for warm-up exercises in which students experiment with expressing themselves with body actions.

Likewise, students should be given an opportunity to discuss and experiment with their lines. Again warm-up exercises might be used as a means of exploring different voices (angry, friendly, frightened), as well as appropriate pauses and pacing.

With large groups of students, the teacher may wish to organize different casts and production teams. A production team might include a director, a lighting engineer, a sound effects engineer and a stage manager.

Figure 3–4 The Shepherd's Boy and the Wolf

A Shepherd's Boy was tending his flock near a village, and thought it would be great fun to hoax the villagers by pretending that a Wolf was attacking the sheep: so he shouted out, "Wolf! wolf!" and when the people came running up he laughed at them for their pains. He did this more than once, and every time the villagers found they had been hoaxed, for there was no Wolf at all. At last a Wolf really did come, and the Boy cried, "Wolf! wolf!" as loud as he could. But the people were so used to hearing him call that they took no notice of his cries for help. And so the Wolf had it all his own way, and killed off sheep after sheep at his leisure.

You cannot believe a liar
even when he tells the truth.

Figure 3–5   Adaptation

"The Shepherd's Boy and the Wolf"

NARRATOR I: A shepherd's boy was tending his flock near a village, and thought it would be great fun to hoax the villagers by pretending that a wolf was attacking the sheep: so he shouted

BOY: Wolf!

NARRATOR II: And when the villagers came running up . . .

VILLAGERS: Wolf? Where?!

NARRATOR II: he laughed at them for their pains:

BOY: Ha ha . . . I had you fooled!

NARRATOR I: He did this more than once, and every time the villagers found they had been hoaxed, for there was no wolf at all.

BOY: Ha ha . . .

VILLAGERS: (grumbling) That boy! He's fooled us again. Look at him laugh.

NARRATOR II: At last a wolf really did come . . .

WOLF: Yum yum! Look at those tasty lamb chops!

NARRATOR II: and the boy cried . . .

BOY: Wolf! Wolf!

NARRATOR II: as loud as he could.

NARRATOR I: But the people were so used to hearing him call that the took no notice of this cries for help.

VILLAGERS: Ignore him. He only wants to laugh at us. He's a liar.

NARRATOR II: Meanwhile, the wolf had it his own way, and killed off sheep after sheep at his leisure.

ALL: But no one ever came to help, for you cannot believe a liar even when he tells the truth.

Source: V. S. Verson Jones, *Aesop's Fables* (New York: Avenel Books, 1912), p. 41.

Once the students and teacher feel satisfied with issues of staging, students should be given an opportunity to rehearse with their cast. It should be noted that in Readers Theatre students read their lines. *Memorization of a script is not pursued.*

7. *Performing the play and follow-up.* A language event does not end with the performance of the play. Once students perform, the teacher and class discuss how the different characters were portrayed and other aspects of how the play was staged. These discussions serve a variety of functions. Not only do they give the students feedback, they also introduce students to the possibility of revision and further refinement of a play as well as techniques and procedures that might be used in subsequent productions.

8. *Preparing a full-length program.* Now the students have worked through the process of adapting and performing a short story, they are ready to go on to longer productions, adapting other types of text, experimenting with

different types of scripts, and trying out variations in how a play is staged. For this purpose, a number of different teams might be organized. During adaptation of the story, different segments might be parceled out to different work groups. During the planning the performance, different groups can be involved in directing, performing, or being theater critics or reviewers.

Cautions and Comments

For over two decades, Readers Theatre has been used in classrooms by teachers who have reported the benefits of the approach with enthusiasm. In an age of musical videotapes and young moviegoers, students not only enjoy being actors and a member of an audience, they also are attracted to moviemaking and playmaking. Readers Theatre provides students an opportunity to learn about plot, characterization, and some of the less tangible features of stories such as theme, voice, and mood. Furthermore, this learning involves participating rather than observing, is child-centered rather than teacher-directed, and goal-directed rather than arbitrarily required. Certainly it is impossible to incorporate Readers Theatre into a classroom and not enjoy these types of experiences. Care should be taken not to initiate goals that surpass student capabilities. Sometimes a teacher may try to do too much or have overly high expectations for staging a play. Indeed, one of the advantages and disadvantages of Readers Theatre is the extent to which they formalize what in many classrooms occur rather incidentally, and spontaneously. The formality of the procedure extends the use of dramatization of a story to the development of more precise reading, writing, and oral interpretation abilities. At the same time, the formality of the procedure may detract from the frequency with which teachers encourage students to project themselves, dramatize story segments, and explore different voices as they read different stories on a more frequent and incidental basis.

REFERENCES

Busching, B. A. 1981. Readers Theatre: An education for language and life. *Language Arts* 58:330–38. Discusses the value of Readers Theatre and offers suggestions for its implementation in the elementary school.

Coger, L. I., and M. R. White. 1982. *Readers Theatre handbook: A dramatic approach to literature.* Glenview, Ill.: Scott, Foresman. This book presents the rationale, history and principles underlying Readers Theatre. Several scripts and summaries of presentations are included.

Maclay, J. H. 1971. *Readers Theatre: Toward a grammar of practice.* New York: Random House. Discusses the worth of Readers Theatre and makes suggestions on material selection, casting, directing, and staging.

Post, R. M. 1974. Readers Theatre as a method of teaching literature. *English Journal* 64:69–72. Discusses the use of Readers Theatre in high school English classes.

Sloyer, S. 1982. *Readers Theatre: Story dramatization in the classroom*. Urbana, Ill.: NCTE. Presents a comprehensive discussion of Readers Theatre including suggestions for planning and implementing. Represents a rich resource for locating materials appropriate for scripting.

Wertheimer, A. 1974. Story dramatization in the reading center. *English Journal* 64:85–87. Discusses the use of Readers Theatre with reluctant readers at the elementary level.

4

Text-Based Comprehension Strategies

The Unit and Its Theme

In recent years a great deal of attention has been given to how information is presented in narrative and expository text. Researchers have invested considerable effort and devised elaborate systems for analyzing how different texts are structured and whether or not there are certain text features that regularly cause students difficulty. As these characteristics of text have been described, educators have devised strategies and lesson frameworks to prepare students to deal with text features.

The Strategies

The present unit describes seven strategies, which range from procedures for preparing students to read a selection by presenting key concepts to training students in techniques of connecting sentences (for purposes of highlighting complex syntactic structures) *to* teaching students about complex text structures (for purposes of dealing with content area textbooks).

Graphic Organizers

The graphic organizer can be used as a preteaching or postteaching strategy for purposes of introducing or reinforcing the key concepts in a text and how they might be structured.

Concept Attainment Strategy

The Concept Attainment Strategy, also known as the Frayer Model, provides a framework for developing students' understanding of concepts, including the hierarchical structure of these concepts and their attributes.

Idea Mapping

Idea mapping is a method of spatially representing the overall structure of expository text. It provides students a framework for carefully reading expository text, and it provides teachers a tool for examining the nature of text prior to classroom use.

Text Structure Strategy

The Text Structure Strategy is based on the premise that if students are taught different prototypical expository structures, they can use an understanding of these structures as an aid in comprehending texts that have similar structures.

Story Grammars and Story Maps

Story grammars and story maps include a description of two different strategies that are based on the theoretical notions of the structure of stories. Story maps present guidelines to generate questions that accompany short narratives found in basal readers. Story grammars provide students a framework for identifying the plot structure and other key elements of a story.

Sentence Combining

Sentence-combining is aimed at increasing the syntactic knowledge of students. This knowledge serves as a basis for improving writing fluency and reading comprehension.

Cloze Variations

Involving the systematic replacement of words deleted from a passage, the cloze technique—now in widespread use as a teaching and a testing tool—is suggested for use with students at various levels. Various adaptations of this technique are described.

GRAPHIC ORGANIZERS

Purpose

The graphic organizer (Barron 1969), originally called the structured overview, is designed to (1) provide a logical means of preteaching the technical vocabulary of a content chapter, (2) present the students an "idea framework" designed to show important conceptual relationships between content vocabulary, and (3) help content teachers clarify teaching goals.

Rationale

The technical vocabulary of a content subject often proves quite difficult for students. It is Barron's argument that the content teachers must be ever mindful of this fact and should seek ways of making the task less complicated for the students. The graphic organizer provides a systematic approach for doing just that. The subject matter instructor presents a picture, or schematic diagram, of the important words in the chapter and discusses with the students how these words relate one to another. Barron (1969) stated that "words assume the form of 'advance organizers' and provide the students with the cues to the 'structure' of subjects" (p. 29). Thus, the organizer serves as a point of reference as the students begin reading and studying the chapter in more detail.

Intended Audience

Earle (1969) reports the use of the graphic organizer with students in grades seven and above. It is further suggested that teachers in grades four, five, and six could profit from the use of the technique. On occasion, the procedure might be used by the teacher alone in the preparation of a particularly difficult unit.

Description of the Procedure

In order to describe the use of the graphic organizer by the content teacher, the following three stages will be discussed: (1) preparation, (2) presentation, and (3) follow-up.

1. Preparation

Perhaps the most critical stage in the development and use of graphic organizer is this first step. It is at this point that the instructor, by working through this rather simple process, makes some key decisions regarding the major ideas to be stressed during the unit. Four components of the preparation stage summarize the desired sequence.

    a. *Select words.* Rather than moving through the chapter in search of "difficult" words, the teacher proceeds in a more systematic manner (Herber

1978). The first step in this preparation stage, then, is for the instructor to select the major concepts or understandings that are important for the students to know at the conclusion of their study of the topic. By working through the chapter in this manner, the teacher is actually establishing instructional objectives for that particular chapter.

Word selection logically follows selection of major concepts. The teacher can now deal with one major idea at a time and ask the question, "What important words in this chapter help to describe, explain, or communicate this idea?" By asking this question for each of the major concepts, the content teacher has identified those technical terms that the students will need to know. Often a number of difficult words within the chapter are eliminated because they do not tie directly to the major concepts.

To give an example, a social studies teacher may be introducing a chapter on organization of the United States government. The concepts chosen for instruction are: (1) the United States government consists of three governing branches, and (2) a system of checks and balances maintains the powers of each branch of government. The words that might be selected by the teacher as important for understanding these concepts are checks and balances, Senate, legislative, United States government, executive, judiciary, House of Representatives, President, veto, and override, and judicial review.

b. *Arrange words.* The task now is to arrange these words into a diagram form that helps students see the terms and how they interrelate. There is not necessarily a right or a wrong diagram for a given set of terms, but it would appear that some arrangements are better than others. With several pieces of scratch paper available, the teacher might try out several possibilities, then select the one that appears to be the most appropriate.

Continuing the example of the words chosen by the social studies teacher, the words might be arranged in numerous ways. Here is one example:

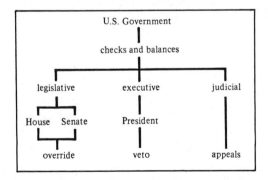

Graphic organizers may be designed for the total chapter. For longer, more complicated chapters, the subject matter instructor may design several organizers, each tied to a major concept. Whatever the decision, the overriding question to be answered is, "Will this organizer assist students to better understand the major concepts and major words of the chapter?" If the answer is "yes," then the teacher has developed a valuable teaching tool.

c. *Add previously learned key words and ideas.* Learning new information is generally easier for students if they can relate the new ideas to previously learned information; therefore, the content instructor is advised to select several important words that the students mastered in previous units and insert these in this new organizer. By completing this step, the teacher is saying to the students that the subject is more than a set of isolated units with little or no relationship to each other. In the example of the words dealing with the United States government, the teacher may decide to add previously learned vocabulary, if that would enhance understanding of the graphic organizer.

d. *Evaluate organizer.* Content instructors by their very training, interest, and experience are experts in their chosen fields; therefore, they may have forgotten what it was like when they first began to pursue information in their major subject. A graphic organizer may be easily interpretable by the content specialist but still be too difficult for a group of high school juniors. This final step in the preparation stage, therefore, is critical. It is advisable to try out the organizer on someone who is not an expert in the field. One could do this with a student or with a fellow teacher in another discipline. Explain the organizer and then ask appropriate questions that tell you whether the person grasps the relationships among the terms used in it. Often people will answer questions in such a manner that they provide the kind of information necessary to suggest some minor revisions that result in a more appropriately constructed design. Once satisfied with the appropriateness of the organizer, the teacher should use it in the context of a total lesson in a regular classroom.

2. Presentation

As a preteaching tool, the organizer is presented on the chalkboard or with an overhead transparency. The instructor actually "talks" the students through the organizer and adds new pieces to it. Students are encouraged to participate. They may add information with which they are already familiar or ask questions regarding the organizer. The teacher may pose questions to check the students' understanding of it. The important thing is that the teacher and the students use the language of the subject matter and simultaneously explore the relationships of these words to each other. It is important to remember that one should not anticipate mastery of terms and relationships at this time.

The entire procedure may take from five to ten minutes, depending on the ability and achievement level of the students and on the complexity of the organizer. At the conclusion of this segment of the preparation stage, the students should have an "idea framework" that should make more detailed learning easier.

3. Follow-up

The graphic organizer may also be used as the students move further into the chapter itself. A student's reaction to an especially difficult idea encountered in the reading might result in the teacher responding, "Do you remember how this idea tied to . . ." as a portion of the organizer is created on the chalkboard. Thus, the organizer becomes a major point of reference throughout the teaching of a particular chapter. New information may be added when the instructor suggests, "Let's see how this new information fits into the organizer that we have been using." For some classes, the organizer might be placed on a large piece of poster paper and placed on the bulletin board. In this way, students may refer to it at any time.

Cautions and Comments

The graphic organizer alone may not teach the technical vocabulary of a chapter as thoroughly as the content instructor may desire. A support system designed to teach the language of the subject more thoroughly is suggested. Earle and Barron (1973) outline a strategy that includes three components: (1) graphic organizer, (2) skills teaching, and (3) extension activities. Graphic organizers are designed and utilized in the manner just described. The skills teaching phase of the strategy occurs in the preparation stage of the instructional framework (see discussion of the instructional framework in Unit 1) and involves the detailed teaching of several of the more important terms used in the organizer. Extension activities give students opportunities to use the words during or following the reading of the chapter. Extension activities are generally paper-and-pencil exercises designed to reinforce the students' understandings of the terms. Matching exercises, word puzzles, and categorizing activities may be used for this purpose. A good source book of such exercises is a book by Herber entitled *Success with Words* (1973). Small group and whole class discussion may follow the completion of the activities.

Several studies cited in the reference section indicate the value of this procedure. However, one wonders whether a strategy that imposes upon students a structure for thinking and reading would be as beneficial as a strategy that might activate students' own ideas. To this end, an organizer might be developed from the student's own ideas prior to, during, or after reading. In this way, the organizer may become more personalized and less abstract.

Barron (1979) has suggested that graphic organizers can be used as a means of post-reading reinforcement and review, if students are given the task of constructing their own organizers. Multiple copies of each word to be used in the organizer are made, using index cards, and passed out to students in small groups. Students are given the task of arranging the words in a diagram to show how they are related. Blank index cards are also provided if students wish to add their own vocabulary terms. The teacher's responsibility in this post-reading graphic organizer strategy is to circulate among the groups, providing support and feedback. The culminating activity is for the class to develop a single graphic organizer under the teacher's direction. By using organizers in this manner, students become more actively involved in their learning.

For those students who may have trouble initially in constructing their own graphic organizers, Readence and Moore (1979) have suggested an interim step between teacher-constructed and student-generated organizers that may serve as an effective transition. The same diagram that was presented to students in the prereading portion of a lesson can be used to help students recall the assigned reading material after reading. Words are deleted from the original organizer and replaced with blanks. Deleted words are listed below the incomplete graphic organizer in random order. The students' task is to complete the diagram using the deleted words, either from recall or by using the text. Individual ditto sheets would be advantageous in this activity.

Finally, in a quantitative and qualitative review of graphic organizer research, Moore and Readence (1984) found that students exposed to postreading graphic organizers learned more than those students exposed to prereading graphic organizers, particularly when vocabulary was the criterion variable. They also found that one of the advantages for using prereading organizers was that the teachers involved in the studies felt that they were better prepared to teach their lessons after having constructed a graphic organizer.

REFERENCES

Barron, R. F. 1969. The use of vocabulary as an advance organizer. In *Research in reading in the content areas: First year report*, edited by H. L. Herber and P. L. Sanders. Syracuse, N.Y.: Reading and Language Arts Center, Syracuse University, 29–39. Presents the basis for the use of structured overviews within the content classroom. Describes how structured overviews may be used in relation to a total vocabulary teaching strategy utilizing preteaching and extension activities.

————. 1979. Research for classroom teachers: Recent developments on the use of the structured overview as an advance organizer. In *Research in reading in the content areas: Fourth report*, edited by H. L. Herber and J. D. Riley. Syracuse, N.Y.: Syracuse University Reading and Language Arts Center, 171–76. Describes the evolution of the graphic organizer strategy and its application in post-reading.

Earle, R. A. 1969. Use of the structured overview in mathematics classes. In *Research in reading in the content areas: First year report*, edited by H. L. Herber and P. L. Sanders. Syracuse, N.Y.: Reading and Language Arts Center, Syracuse University, 49–58. Describes a study in which structured overviews were used in both seventh and ninth grade mathematics classes. Significant differences in favor of the use of structured overviews versus no preteaching were observed when a delayed-relationship test was administered.

Earle, R. A., and R. F. Barron. 1973. An approach for testing vocabulary in content subjects. In *Research in reading in the content areas: Second year report*, edited by H. L. Herber and R. F. Barron. Syracuse, N.Y.: Reading and Language Arts Center, Syracuse University, 84–100. Describes a total vocabulary teaching strategy designed for content teachers. Strategy components include (1) structured overviews, (2) skills teaching, and (3) extension activities.

Herber, H. L. 1973. *Success with words.* New York: Scholastic Book Services. Presents a sourcebook for ideas for dealing with technical vocabulary in social studies, English, science, and math.

————. 1978. *Teaching reading in content areas.* 2d ed. Englewood Cliffs, N.J.: Prentice-Hall, 47–158. Discusses the use of the structured overview with examples.

Moore, D. W., and J. E. Readence. 1984. A quantitative and qualitative review of graphic organizer research. *Journal of Educational Research* 78: 11–17. A synthesis of the research examining the effectiveness of the graphic organizer as a classroom strategy.

Readence, J. E., and D. W. Moore. 1979. Strategies for enhancing readiness and recall in content areas: The encoding specificity principle. *Reading Psychology*:47–54. Examines the use of the graphic organizer as both a prereading and post-reading activity.

CONCEPT ATTAINMENT STRATEGY

Purpose

The Concept Attainment Strategy, also known as the Frayer Model (Frayer, Frederick, and Klausmeier 1969) is designed to (1) develop students' conceptual knowledge about a topic and (2) show the hierarchical relationships of associated concepts.

Rationale

The Concept Attainment Strategy (CAS) is a systematic teaching technique that attempts to develop students' to-be-learned concepts based upon existing conceptual background. As a result, word concepts are taught by the notion of associating the new to the known.

Thelen (1982) has stated that showing students how concepts are hierarchically related is an important step in helping them learn new concepts, but it might not go far enough. It may be that certain concepts to be learned might need more in-depth processing and that they are better understood when students can generalize the concepts to new situations. Thus, it may be that with certain concepts, just providing a graphic organizer (see this Unit) may be insufficient for students to fully grasp a concept. Thelen suggested that CAS was a useful alternative for attaining concepts.

CAS also attempts to clarify concepts by showing how they are hierarchically related. However, it suggests that if examples and nonexamples of new concepts, as well as their relevant and irrelevant attributes, are also provided, the students' learning will be even better. Therefore, CAS examines superordinate, coordinate, and subordinate aspects of concepts, and also stresses those characteristics common to examples of that concept.

Intended Audience

Because of the sophistication involved in the hierarchical arrangement of CAS, the strategy is appropriate only for middle and secondary students. Even then, less able middle school students might have difficulty coping with the strategy.

Description of the Procedure

Thelen (1982) recommended that the Concept Attainment Strategy be implemented using the following seven steps:

1. Develop the target concept;
2. Define the concept;
3. Present the concept;
4. Finish constructing the hierarchy;
5. Guide students to relevant attributes;
6. Guide students to irrelevant attributes; and
7. Complete teaching the concept.

1. Develop the target concept

A hierarchy should be constructed that incorporates the supraordinate, coordinate, and subordinate aspects of the target concept. A supraordinate aspect of a concept is a term that refers to a common, more general concept of which the target concept is a member. Therefore, if our target concept is "reptiles," the supraordinate concept might be "vertebrate." An even more general term would be "animal."

A coordinate aspect of the target concept is a term that denotes other members of the same general, or supraordinate, concept. For instance, a coordinate concept for reptiles is "amphibians." Finally, a subordinate aspect of the target concept is a term that possesses specific features of the target concept and is of a lower classification. In the case of reptiles, subordinate terms might be "alligators," "snakes," and "lizards." Thus, the following hierarchy (Searfoss and Readence 1985) might be constructed for the target concept "reptiles":

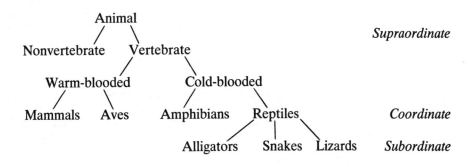

2. Define the concept

Before presenting the concept, be sure to delineate the relevant attributes for later discussion. Relevant attributes may be defined as those characteristics that describe the target concept. Relevant attributes of reptiles, then, might be (a) a vertebrate, (b) breathes air, (c) has scales or bony plates, (d) lays eggs, (e) lack of hair, and (f) is cold-blooded. The examination of relevant attributes of a concept leads students to see not only what an example of it is, but also what is not an example of the concept. For instance, a human being would not be an example of a reptile, since human beings do not have scales or bony plates, do not lay eggs, are hairy, and are warm-blooded. This provides students the opportunity to see the likenesses and differences involved in attempting to define a concept.

3. Present the target concept

At this time students are provided the target concept to be learned and are asked to contribute examples of it. This can be done either individually or in small groups. The examples can be listed on the board as they are offered. Students may challenge one another's examples as to whether or not it is an appropriate example. Thus, "gila monsters, chameleons, snakes, alligators, lizards, and iguanas" can be categorized as appropriate examples of reptiles. On the other hand, if "toads" or "eagles" were offered, they could be challenged as nonexamples and should be properly classified as amphibians and aves, respectively.

4. Finish constructing the hierarchy

Provide students the concept hierarchy that was originally constructed in Step 1. It is essential that the teacher explain why the terms are arranged as they are. The teacher should use questioning techniques to involve the students as much as possible in offering terms that might fit in the resulting diagram to promote fuller understanding.

5. Guide students to relevant attributes

Once all possible examples are given, have students decide what characteristics they have in common (from Step 2). Any misconceptions may be cleared up with regard to what the target concept, in this case, reptiles, is.

6. Guide students to irrelevant attributes

Now have students find differences among the examples offered that do not change the example into a nonexample. In other words, what differences may exist among reptiles that are inconsequential and do not change the example's inclusion as a reptile? Again, this will lead to fuller understanding of the concept. With regard to reptiles, irrelevant attributes might include "whether they walk or slither," "what they eat," or "the size of their eggs."

7. Complete teaching the concept

To complete CAS, provide students with other examples and nonexamples they may not have thought of. These could be concepts they may encounter in their reading; doing so will provide additional reinforcement. When this is completed, students will have offered or been supplied the hierarchy from Step 1 and a list of examples, nonexamples, relevant attributes, and irrelevant attributes. With our reptile example, this list might look like this:

CONCEPT: REPTILES

1. *Examples*

    gila monsters
    chameleons
    snakes
    alligators
    lizards
    iguanas

2. *Nonexamples*

    toads
    eagles
    human beings
    birds
    frogs
    aardvarks

3. *Relevant Attributes*

    vertebrate
    cold-blooded
    lays eggs
    lacks hair
    breathes air
    scales or bony plates

4. *Irrelevant Attributes*

    walk or slither
    what they eat
    size of eggs
    color
    number of eggs
    where they live

Cautions and Comments

The Concept Attainment Strategy provides students with a number of different ways to think about the meaning of word concepts. CAS allows students to discover how new concepts are related to known concepts and to see what a concept represents as well as what it does not represent. As a consequence, CAS should help students generalize the newly learned concept to other learning situations. In past research, the CAS has been used as a basis for developing texts. In a study by Peters (1979) and a study by Moes, Foertsch, Stewart, Dunning, Rogers, Seda-Santana, Benjamin and Pearson (1983) such texts were found to be more comprehendable than texts lacking such a framework.

Key to the success of CAS is student involvement and discovery learning. It is essential that students be involved as much as possible in the creation of the concept hierarchy and in the provision of examples, nonexamples, relevant attributes, and irrelevant attributes. It is a fact that a teacher-created hierarchy and teacher-provided examples and attributes will not be as effective a learning environment as one in which students actively participate.

A final problem with CAS may be the terminology used in conducting the lesson. The terms supraordinate, coordinate, and subordinate may be too complex for some students, particularly those who are less able. Teachers may do well to use another set of terminology, such as "more general, equal, and more specific" to insure that the Concept Attainment Strategy will be effective.

REFERENCES

Frayer, D. A., W. C. Frederick, and H. J. Klausmeier. 1969. A science for testing the level of concept mastery (Working paper No. 16). Madison, WI: University of Wisconsin Research and Development Center for Cognitive Learning. Presents some of the original thinking about the Concept Attainment Strategy.

Moes, M. A., D. J. Foertsch, J. Stewart, D. Dunning, T. Rogers, I. Seda-Santana, L. Benjamin, and P. D. Pearson. 1983. Effects of text structure on children's comprehension of expository text. Paper presented at the National Reading Conference, Austin, Texas. Using the Frayer model as a guide to developing text, these researchers compared the effects upon comprehension of the same information presented using different structures.

Peters, C. 1979. The effect of systematic restructuring of material upon the comprehension process. *Reading Research Quarterly* 11:87−110. Studied the effects of using the Frayer model to structure texts.

Searfoss, L. W., and J. E. Readence. 1985. *Helping children learn to read.* Englewood Cliffs, N.J.: Prentice-Hall. Provides a discussion and examples of CAS.

Thelen, J. 1982. Preparing students for content reading assignments. *Journal of Reading* 25:544−49. Delineates the steps involved in implementing CAS.

IDEA MAPPING

Purpose

Idea mapping (Armbruster and Anderson 1982) was developed for purposes of spatially representing the overall structure of expository text. It is purported to have several instructional uses: to afford teachers a tool for examining the nature of a text prior to classroom use; to direct students to appreciate the structure characteristics of different text; and to provide teachers and students a framework for carefully reading expository text.

Rationale

Based upon the work of Hanf (1971), Merritt, Prior, and Grugeon (1977), and, most notably, Armbruster and Anderson (1982), mapping has emerged as one of the more popular tools for analyzing text. The mapping technique incorporates the visual-spatial conventions for diagramming ideas and the nature of relationships between ideas: concept and example, concept and properties, concept and definition, temporal succession, cause and effect, conditional and comparison. These relationships and their mapping scheme are depicted in Figure 4−1. If extended to a whole text, as depicted in Figure 4−2, the overall pattern provides a spatial representation across the whole text. Armbruster and Anderson (1982) suggest that a variety of "basic text structures" are forthcoming from these overall analyses of text. If the question is asked "Why or how was the text written," then the following description of text types usually emerge: (1) description—a listing of properties, characteristics or attributes, (2) compare/contrast—a description of similarities and differences between two or more things, (3) temporal sequence—relationship between ideas that is largely sequential, (4) explanation—an interaction between at least two ideas or events that is causal or conditional, and (5) definitional/examples—a definition of a concept and examples of the concept. In conjunction with these overall text patterns, Armbruster and Anderson (1982) suggest that there are two types of frameworks or frames of text: static and dynamic. Static refers to text that is largely descriptive or definitional in character; dynamic refers to text that is more explanatory in nature.

Instructionally, Armbruster and Anderson (1982) argue that mapping is a tool by which teachers and students can build a coherent model of the meaning of the text. It serves to involve students with the meaning of the text; it focuses their attention on text structure; and it provides for the transformation of prose into a diagrammatic or visual representation. However, in the one research study in which the worth of mapping was examined, training in the use of mapping did not sustain long-term gains in comprehension (Armbruster and Anderson 1980).

Intended Audience

Mapping has been used extensively with high school students and college-level students as an aid to improving their comprehension of expository text. Simplifications of the procedure (see Cautions and Comments) might be appropriate to use with students at the elementary level.

Procedure

There are countless uses to which mapping can be put, ranging from simply revealing the map of a text to students prior to having them read the text, to having students (or the teacher) create detailed analyses of a text. The present description of mapping is restricted to more recent proposals by Armbruster

Figure 4–1 Types of Mapped Relationships

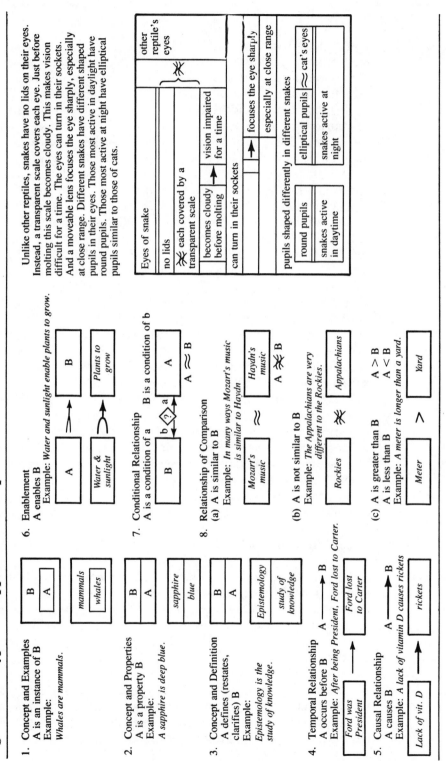

1. Concept and Examples
   A is an instance of B
   Example:
   Whales are mammals.

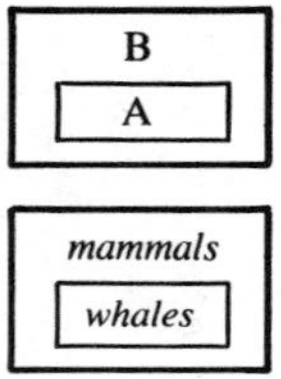

B
A
mammals
whales

2. Concept and Properties
   A is a property B
   Example:
   A sapphire is deep blue.

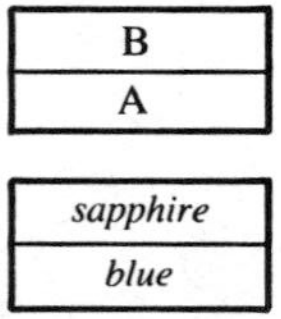

B
A
sapphire
blue

3. Concept and Definition
   A defines (restates, clarifies) B
   Example:
   Epistemology is the study of knowledge.

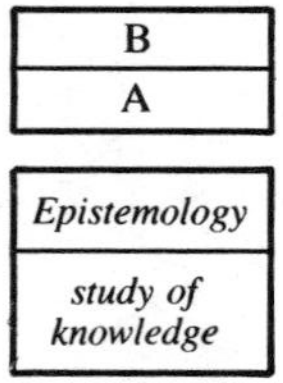

B
A
Epistemology
study of knowledge

4. Temporal Relationship
   A occurs before B   A ——→ B
   Example: *After being President, Ford lost to Carter.*

Ford was President
Ford lost to Carter

5. Causal Relationship
   A causes B   A ——→ B
   Example: *A lack of vitamin D causes rickets*

Lack of vit. D
rickets

6. Enablement
   A enables B
   Example: *Water and sunlight enable plants to grow.*

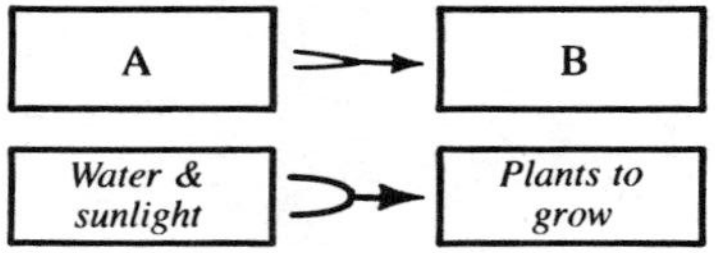

A
B
Water & sunlight
Plants to grow

7. Conditional Relationship
   A is a condition of a   B is a condition of b

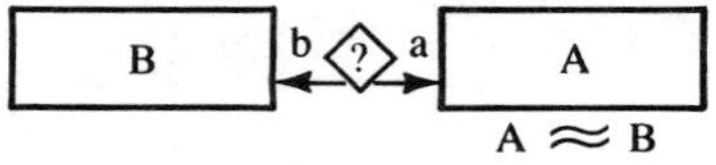

B
b
?
a
A
A ≈ B

8. Relationship of Comparison
   (a) A is similar to B
   Example: *In many ways Mozart's music is similar to Haydn*

Mozart's music
≈
Haydn's music
A ≉ B

   (b) A is not similar to B
   Example: *The Appalachians are very different to the Rockies.*

Rockies
≉
Appalachians

   (c) A is greater than B $A > B$
   A is less than B $A < B$
   Example: *A meter is longer than a yard.*

Meter
>
Yard

Unlike other reptiles, snakes have no lids on their eyes. Instead, a transparent scale covers each eye. Just before molting this scale becomes cloudy. This makes vision difficult for a time. The eyes can turn in their sockets. And a moveable lens focuses the eye sharply, especially at close range. Different snakes have different shaped pupils in their eyes. Those most active in daylight have round pupils. Those most active at night have elliptical pupils similar to those of cats.

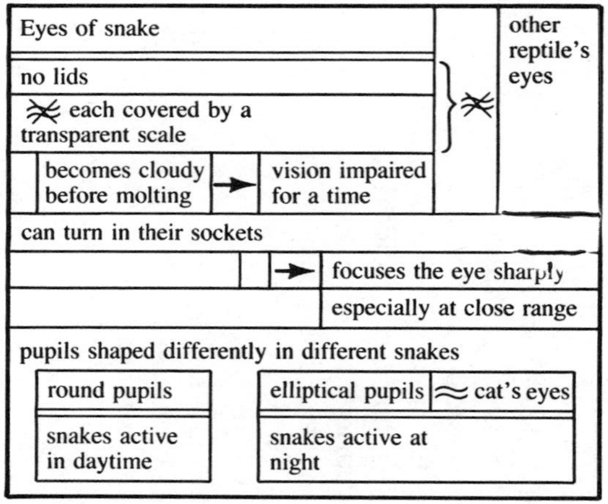

Eyes of snake
other reptile's eyes
no lids
each covered by a transparent scale
becomes cloudy before molting
vision impaired for a time
can turn in their sockets
focuses the eye sharply
especially at close range
pupils shaped differently in different snakes
round pupils
elliptical pupils
cat's eyes
snakes active in daytime
snakes active at night

and Anderson (1982). In the past few years, they have moved away from training students to make their own maps for texts. Instead, they have moved toward having students respond to maps generated by the teacher. In particular, they have pursued the use of maps in two different ways: (1) top-down or starting with the overall framework for a text and refining it or filling in the text and (2) generalizing from some given details to higher order structures.

Using maps top-down

The goal for top-down use of maps is to have students generate higher-order structures or the main-idea and to use this top-level structure to complete written map exercises. For example, a teacher about to assign a chapter on the establishment and growth of cities might begin by giving students a map similar to Figure 4–2.

This frame or map represents the higher order ideas that readers could use to guide their reading of the text. As a written exercise and as a form of evaluation, students could fill out the details of the map. To further constrain the task, the teacher could use the specialized mapping symbols to indicate the exact type of information the reader would be expected to insert. For example, in the map given in Figure 4–3, the form of the map tells the students whether they are provide definitions, examples, attributes, etc.

Sometimes a text is especially difficult to understand. Say the purpose for which the text was written or for which you wish to have your students read it is not congruent with the structure of the text. In these types of situations, it might be useful to introduce the students to the general principle that is overriding. This might be done in the form of introducing students to an additional map that complements, but does not match, the texts assigned to be read.

Figure 4–2   Sample of top-down exercise

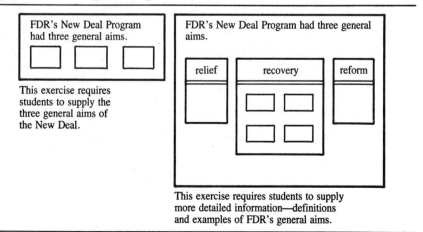

FDR's New Deal Program had three general aims.

This exercise requires students to supply the three general aims of the New Deal.

FDR's New Deal Program had three general aims.

relief   recovery   reform

This exercise requires students to supply more detailed information—definitions and examples of FDR's general aims.

Figure 4-3 Sample of Top-down map

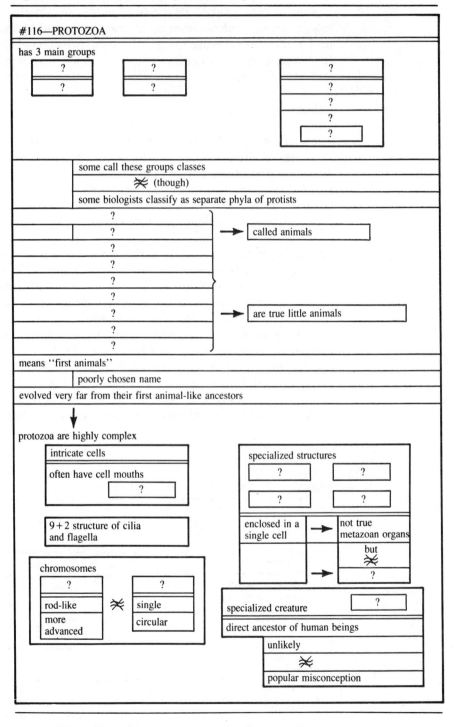

Using maps bottom-up

Using maps bottom-up involves helping students derive higher-order structures by guiding the students to generate principles, superordinate concepts, or main ideas. For example, a bottom-up exercise might have students infer the label for slots from a definition for some attributes. In Figure 4–4, several examples of this type of activity are given. As Armbruster and Anderson (1982) indicate, in many respects these activities represent merely "the converse of the top-down" (p. 16).

Other variations of a bottom-up approach might entail presenting the students a listing of the ideas from a text that they are to organize into a map based upon a reading of the text. Figure 4–5 includes such an exercise.

Obviously there are a variety of different ways students can be involved for moving from the details of a map or text to a coherent representation of that text. Of course, teachers need to have examined the text carefully prior to being able to develop such activities. They need to have developed their own map of the text and considered what they deem as desirable learning outcomes for their students. In choosing mapping as a tool, whether mapping be used in a bottom-up or top-down fashion, they need to consider just what content they wish their students to address, as well as how they would like them to approach the texts. Mapping is not just a vehicle for examining ideas from a text, it is intended to alert students to text features. Indeed, in order to engage in the different activities that have been suggested, students need to be familiar with mapping procedures. They need to know the symbols used to represent different relationships in text, the basic text structures, and the fact that information is presented in different variations of these standard forms.

Figure 4–4   Samples of Bottom-Up Exercises

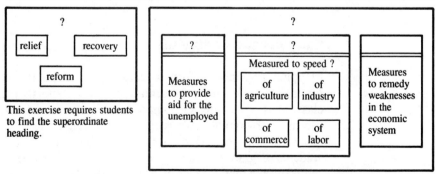

This exercise requires students to find the superordinate heading.

This exercise requires two levels of generalization: (a) superordinate terms for the definitions in the three categories, and (b) a superordinate heading for the terms generated in a.

Figure 4−5a   Sample of Bottom-Up Maps (see model)

Directions to Students:
Make an i-map using the following terms from the chapter on muscle structure.

striations
muscle fibers
striated muscles
elongated cells
sarcolemna
40% of body weight
highly specialized cells

Possible Student Response:

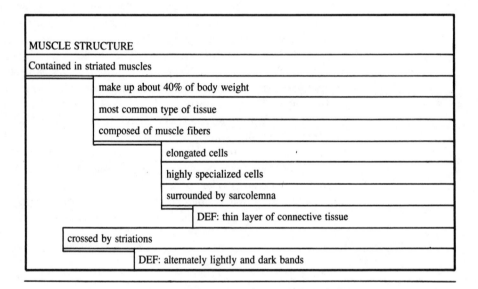

Cautions and Comments

Mapping is not the only form of text analysis, nor is it the only one that provides for the diagrammatic representation of texts and that has been applied to classrooms. Two other such approaches have been developed and adapted for use as instructional tools: networking (Dansereau 1979) and flowcharting (Geva 1983). Networking and flowcharting, like mapping, involve having students diagram or use diagrams to chart the ideas and relationships represented within text. Studies by Bartlett (1978), Dansereau, Holley, and Collins (1980), Geva (1983), Margolis (1982), and Armbruster and Anderson (1980) tend to offer rather mixed results about the benefits of using such techniques. These studies have tended to suggest that most students find the procedures offer very little, and have no obvious or immediate payoff for the investment in time

Figure 4–5b   Sample of Bottom-up Maps

Directions to Students:
Make an i-map listing the chief ideas for and against slavery as presented by Malachy Postlethwayt and Thomas Paine.

Possible Student Response

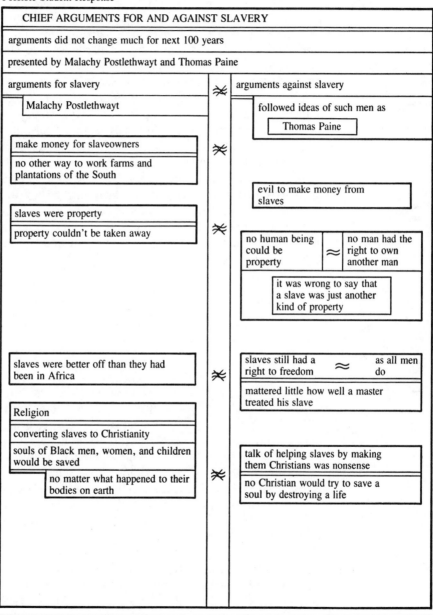

CHIEF ARGUMENTS FOR AND AGAINST SLAVERY

arguments did not change much for next 100 years

presented by Malachy Postlethwayt and Thomas Paine

arguments for slavery	arguments against slavery
Malachy Postlethwayt	followed ideas of such men as Thomas Paine
make money for slaveowners	
no other way to work farms and plantations of the South	
	evil to make money from slaves
slaves were property	
property couldn't be taken away	no human being could be property ≈ no man had the right to own another man
	it was wrong to say that a slave was just another kind of property
slaves were better off than they had been in Africa	slaves still had a right to freedom ≈ as all men do
	mattered little how well a master treated his slave
Religion	
converting slaves to Christianity	
souls of Black men, women, and children would be saved	talk of helping slaves by making them Christians was nonsense
no matter what happened to their bodies on earth	no Christian would try to save a soul by destroying a life

and effort to learn such systems. In all cases, the researchers appear to have been forced to streamline their presentation of the system to students, have gone to great pains to make it interesting, and have tended to avoid making students repeatedly do detailed analyses of texts. As is the case with mapping, most researchers tend to support the use of text analytic procedures by teachers for purposes of creating instructional activities based upon diagrammatic depictions of text and to appreciate the information represented by a text.

Instead of detailed analyses of text, some educators have proposed simplified procedures for interconnecting ideas (see Davidson 1982). Apart from mentioning these developments, there are some other issues. One of the major drawbacks to mapping and these other text analysis procedures is the extent to which they make readers accountable to another author's text. As students read, they should be pursuing their own goals and composing their own text. As presently used, text analysis, specifically mapping, ties the reader to the text they are assigned to read when perhaps it would be more worthwhile to have students generate maps of what they glean from a text and what they might write for themselves. A second drawback to mapping and other text analytic procedures is the extent to which learning how to use a system requires learning the terminology and symbols of that system. Perhaps it would be more appropriate to let students develop their own systems initially and leave the adoption of standardized procedures to later and more extensive uses of the procedure.

REFERENCES

Armbruster, B. B., and T. H. Anderson. 1980. The effect of mapping on the free recall of expository text (Tech. Rep. No. 160). Urbana: University of Illinois, Center for the Study of Reading. Presents a research study in which college-age students were trained in the use of mapping.

———. 1982. Idea mapping: The technique and its use in the classroom (Reading Education Report No. 36). Urbana: University of Illinois, Center for the Study of Reading. Presents various guidelines and examples of how idea mapping might be used in classrooms.

Bartlett, B. J. 1978. Top-level structure as an organizational strategy for recall of classroom text. Unpublished doctoral diss., Arizona State University. Presents a thorough research study that examines the benefits of teaching rhetorical structures.

Dansereau, D. F. 1979. Development and evaluation of a learning strategy training program. *Journal of Educational Psychology* 71:64–73. Discusses the use of networking with college-level structures.

Dansereau, D. F., C. D. Holley, and K. W. Collins. 1980. Effects of learning strategy training on text processing. Paper presented at the annual meeting of the American Educational Research Association, Boston, April.

Presents the findings of a research study in which networking was taught to college-level students.

Davidson, J. L. 1982. The group mapping activity for instruction in reading and thinking. *Journal of Reading* 26:52−56. Describes a simplified version of idea mapping.

Geva, E. 1983. Facilitating reading comprehension through flow-charting. *Reading Research Quarterly* 18: 384−405. Presents the findings of a research study in which flow charting was used to help students deal with expository text.

Hanf, M. B. 1971. Mapping: A technique for translating reading into thinking. *Journal of Reading* 14:225−30. Presents a simplified version of mapping for use by high school students.

Margolis, K. 1982. An instructional study of helping readers identify the gist in expository text. Unpublished diss., University of Illinois. Presents a research study in which high school students were involved in topically defining expository text.

Merritt, J., D. Prior, and D. Grugeon. 1977. *Developing independence in reading*. Milton Keynes, England: Open University Press. Describes the use of mapping and how it might be applied to text.

Tierney, R. J., and J. Mosenthal. 1982. Discourse comprehension and production: Analyzing text structure and cohesion. In *Reader meets author/ bridging the gap*, edited by J. Lange and M. Smith-Burke. Newark, Del.: International Reading Association. Presents an overview of six different text analysis sentences, including mapping, together with implications for classroom use.

TEXT STRUCTURE STRATEGY

Purpose

The text structure strategy is designed to help students recognize and use expository text structures in order to better understand and recall informational type texts.

Rationale

The ability to perceive the organization of text material has long been viewed as a valuable reading strategy (Niles 1974). For example, it has been suggested that knowledge of how the ideas in a text can be bound together to form a logical whole enables students to understand, and later recall, that material better than if the test is perceived as a series of discrete entities. Indeed, recent research (e.g., McGee 1982) has shown that readers who are knowledgeable about text structure have an advantage in comprehension and recall over readers who aren't aware of the organization of text.

There are roughly two types of text material encountered by students in schools: (1) narrative, or story-type, texts such as those found in much of the content of basal readers and literature anthologies; and (2) expository, or informational-type,texts such as those found in science or social studies books. Not surprisingly,students are more familiar with narrative text than expository text. One of the reasons for this is simply that students have more exposure to story-type material both before they start school and in the primary grades, where it predominates instruction.

A second reason is that narrative texts have a consistent structure (setting, initiating event, internal response, attempt, consequence, and reaction), while expository texts may take a variety of structures. Meyer and Freedle (1984) list five different types of expository text structures: (1) description, (2) collection, (3) causation, (4) problem/solution, and (5) comparison. Additionally, they found that text structures that are better organized (causation, problem/solution, comparison) are more easily recalled than text structures that display less organization (description, collection). The following teaching strategy focuses primarily on the first three types of expository text structures.

Intended Audience

Expository text structure is mainly encountered in content area textbooks that are usually associated with middle and secondary schools. However, content area texts are frequently used in the primary grades, and samples of expository passages are increasingly finding their way into basal readers. Therefore, teaching students to use expository text structure is appropriate for students at all grade levels.

Description of the Procedure

Prerequisite to any strategy to teach text structure successfully are three factors suggested by McGee and Richgels (1985). First, teachers must be knowledgeable about structure, i.e. they have thoroughly analyzed text so they can focus students' attention on the specific aspects that let one recognize and use text structure. Second, the passages used for instruction are well-organized and consist of a predominant structure. Third, the students must become actively involved in using the strategy while they read and after they read.

Before we present a teaching strategy for expository text structure, the three main text structures mentioned earlier will be defined. A causative text structure is one in which a relationship is specified between reasons and results in a time sequence. A problem/solution structure is similar to a causative structure except that solution is added to the structure that is designed to break the causative link. Finally, a comparative structure organizes elements on the basis of their similarities and differences and implies no causality or time sequence. (For an in-depth examination of text structure in general, see Pearson and Camperell 1981.)

The following general strategy for teaching expository structure is recommended by Readence, Bean, and Baldwin (1985) and consists of (1) modeling, (2) recognition, and (3) production.

1. Modeling

Before expecting students to use text structure, it is necessary to demonstrate exactly what it is. This can be done by having teachers model their thought processes for students as they (the teachers) use text structure. In essence, teachers think aloud for students. Passages that students will encounter in their reading should be used, since those are most relevant for students. During modeling, it is essential to show students a particular text structure and point out *why* it is a certain type and *how* that structure type is organized. Additionally, it is necessary to point out any words that signal, or cue, the reader into what the text structure is. It has been found that signal words such as "however," "because," "therefore," assist students in becoming aware of text structure and improving their recall (Meyer, Brandt, and Bluth 1980).

2. Recognition

This part of the teaching sequence amounts to "walking" students through a particular text structure. This can be accomplished by asking judicious questions that focus students' attention on selected aspects of the structure. Teachers may wish to start the recognition step on a listening level first. By doing so students can attend directly to the structure, particularly when a difficult text might cause students to divide their attention between reading the text and perceiving the structure. Additionally, teachers may also choose to begin with sentences or paragraphs before moving on to lengthier passages. The essential part of this step, however, is that the students verbalize the *why* and *how* of the text structure. In this way teachers begin to shift responsibility for learning text structure from themselves to the students. As a guide to helping students recognize text structure, Bartlett (1978) offers the following checklist:

CHECKLIST FOR TEACHING
TEXT PATTERNS

1. Did you pick out the organization as *problem-solution*?
   If so, _____ great!
   If not, _____ did you ask the two questions before reading?
   or,

(Continued)

_____ did you find the main idea? ("The problem is . . .
sugar and starch?")

_____ did you find how this main idea was organized?
(one part about a *problem*, another part about a *solution*)

2. Did you write the name of the top-level organization at the top of
the recall page?

If so, _____ so far, so good!

If not, _____ mmmmm!

3. Did you write down the main idea as the first sentence?

If so, _____ keep it up!

If not, _____ oh no!

4. Did you have *two* parts in arranging your sentences?

If so, _____ not far to go now!

If not, _____ tut tut!

5. Were the *two* parts: one for the problem, one for the solution?

If so, _____ I bet you remembered a lot!

If not, _____ Oh cripes!

6. Did you check?

If so, _____ double halo!

If not, _____ don't be overconfident!

---

3. Production

Once students have gained some facility in perceiving text structure, they
should now be ready to produce a text structure on their own. Just as recognition precedes production, a logical extension of perceiving text structure
through reading is producing it through writing. Using a graphic organizer or
some other form of skeletal outline based upon a text passage, students are
directed to compose their own version of the passage. They are told to write
using a particular text structure and whatever signal words are appropriate
to cue that structure. In this way, writing is used as a means to reinforce
students' knowledge of text structure; and writing with a particular structure in
mind should also reinforce the logical organization necessary in effectively
communicating through writing.

Cautions and Comments

In a recent study, Taylor and Beach (1984) were able to be successful at
improving the reading comprehension abilities of middle graders by instruction
in certain text structures. Despite the success of this work, we would question
whether text structure can or should be taught isolated from content and
purpose. Teaching text structure by itself, without any emphasis on what is
being written and why, would seem likely to detract from meaningful negotia-
tions between authors and readers.

Another problem relates to reality. It is cautioned that not all text that students encounter will be well-organized. In reality, often text is not organized in a straightforward manner. To cope with this dilemma, Alvermann (1981) has suggested that the text be "reorganized" into more useful relationships by employing a graphic organizer, which places the important ideas in a format that depicts a well-organized text structure. By doing so, she found that both the quantity and quality of recall by students was facilitated.

McGee and Richgels (1985) go one step further in their suggestions for dealing with poorly formed text. They recommend that, instead of graphic organizers, a discussion of the text in comparison to what an idealized, or well-organized, text on that topic would look like should take place. Following that the text should be revised, creating a well-formed text with an apparent structure and explicit links. Thus, writing is again used as a means to reinforce students' knowledge of text structure. Along this line of reasoning, Harrison (1982) has had a great deal of success in having high school students rewrite their textbook material for each other.

REFERENCES

Alvermann, D. E. 1981. The compensatory effect of graphic organizers on descriptive text. *Journal of Educational Research* 75:44–48. Research study showing positive effects on comprehension for the use of graphic organizers with poorly organized text.

Bartlett, B. J. 1978. Top-level structure as an organizational strategy for recall of classroom text. Unpublished doctoral diss., Arizona State University. A study that yielded very positive results due to the teaching of four commonly found structures to ninth graders.

Harrison, C. 1982. The nature and effect of children's rewriting school textbook prose. Paper presented at the Ninth World Congress of Reading, Dublin. Describes a study in which high school students rewrote texts and their rewritten versions were compared with the original texts for comprehensibility.

McGee, L. M. 1982. Awareness of text structure: Effects on children's recall of expository text. *Reading Research Quarterly* 17:581–90. Study that found that those students who were aware of text structure comprehended better than those who were not aware of structure.

McGee, L. M., and D. J. Richgels. 1985. Attending to text structure: A comprehension strategy. In *Reading in the content areas: Improving classroom instruction*, edited by E. K. Dishner, T. W. Bean, J. E. Readence, and D. W. Moore. 2d ed. Dubuque, IA: Kendall/Hunt. Discusses the use of writing as a means to teach text structure.

Meyer, B. J. F., and R. O. Freedle. 1984. Effects of discourse type on recall. *American Educational Research Journal* 21:121–43. Study that found that certain types of expository text were comprehended better than others.

Meyer, B. J. F., D. Brandt, and G. J. Bluth. 1980. Use of top-level structure in text: Key for reading comprehension of ninth-grade students. *Reading Research Quarterly* 16:72−103. Study that found an advantage for using signal words to assist students in perceiving text structure and improving recall.

Niles, O. S. 1974. Organization perceived. In *Perspectives in reading: Developing study skills in secondary schools*, edited by H. L. Herber. Newark, DE: International Reading Association. Review emphasizing the practical aspects of teaching text structure.

Pearson, P. D., and K. Camperell. 1981. Comprehension of text structures. In *Comprehension and teaching: Research reviews*, edited by J. T. Guthrie. Newark, DE: International Reading Association. Review of the research on text structure with recommendations for research and instruction.

Readence, J. E., T. W. Bean, and R. S. Baldwin. 1985. *Content area reading: An integrated approach*. 2d ed. Dubuque, IA: Kendall/Hunt. Describes a strategy for teaching text structure that includes modeling, recognition, and production.

Taylor, B., and R. W. Beach. 1984. The effects of text structure instruction on middle grade students' comprehension and production of expository work. *Reading Research Quarterly* 19:134−46. Describes a research study in which the authors studied the effects on comprehension of writing texts with structures.

STORY GRAMMARS AND STORY MAPS

Purpose

Story grammars and story maps have become teaching tools to aid readers in their development and use of a sense of story. During reading comprehension, they direct the questions that teachers use in conjunction with the guided reading of a story.

Rationale

In 1947, Gates advocated the importance of a sense of story in the reader's comprehension of narrative. Now several decades later, a number of educators are proponents of procedures for developing in readers a sense of story and ensuring that the guidance they receive is true to the story line. What has spurred this recent interest in stories is the propagation of a number of different

Figure 4−6   Example of a story grammar analysis of a simple text

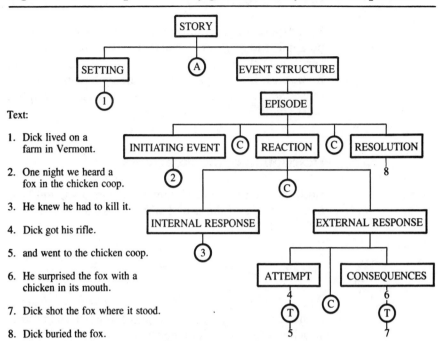

Text:

1. Dick lived on a farm in Vermont.

2. One night we heard a fox in the chicken coop.

3. He knew he had to kill it.

4. Dick got his rifle.

5. and went to the chicken coop.

6. He surprised the fox with a chicken in its mouth.

7. Dick shot the fox where it stood.

8. Dick buried the fox.

procedures for analyzing stories—for defining what some researchers have labeled as a grammar for stories. In this vein, the efforts of Kintsch (1977), Mandler and Johnson (1977), Rumelhart (1975), Stein and Glenn (1979), Thorndyke (1977), and Warren, Nicholas, and Trabasso (1979) are most notable. One of the major theses in this work is that stories have a somewhat predictable grammar that readers can sense and use in comprehending them. Consider the following story and its depiction in Figure 4−6.

While there are various ways a story might be depicted graphically, this figure illustrates some features of attempts to define what constitutes a story in terms of these grammars. As the figure suggests, a story can be organized into several categories of events, such as setting and event sequences, which in turn can be broken down into subseries of initiating events, reactions (internal and external responses), and resolutions.

With these methods, educators have generated two types of strategies for improving readers' comprehension of stories. Beck and McKeown (1981) developed the notion of a story map for use in preparing the questions to guide a reader through a narrative selection. Cunningham and Foster (1978) and Dreher and Singer (1980) generated guidelines for developing in students a sense of story, which the students themselves can apply to narratives.

Intended Audience

For purposes of generating questions for a story, the story map procedures can be applied to any story—whether it be a narrative intended for adults or for very young children. If developing a sense of stories by using a story grammar framework is your goal, most students beyond the sixth grade have such a sense. Some researchers have suggested that even at the fourth grade level, most children have a sense of story.

Description of the Procedures

Both the use of a story grammar (Cunningham and Foster 1978; Dreher and Singer 1980) and the use of story maps (Beck and McKeown 1981; Pearson 1982) will be described.

Story Grammars

Apart from their use in text analysis research, story grammars have been used in instructional settings for purposes of heightening student awareness of the structure of stories. Cunningham and Foster (1978) describe procedures they developed and used with sixth grade students. Their intent was to generate a study guide framework that they might be able to use with not just one, but most, of the stories the students are assigned. The framework that was developed is presented in Figure 4–7.

What follows is a description of what occurred as the procedure was introduced to the class:

> Ms. Foster noted the group's resistance to something new, then told them that it would be clearer once she gave them an example. She proceeded to tell them a story of the knight rescuing the lady and filled in the diagram on the board as she went along. Several students commented that they understood a little better, and Ms. Foster proceeded to do the first story in the short story book. All of the students read along silently as Ms. Foster read the story aloud. As she read a page, she filled in the diagram on the board.
>
> By the time she reached the third page of the first story, some students were joining her in choosing answers. She then shifted the procedure by saying, "Okay, who are the characters in this part of the story? . . . "Has the location changed?" (P. 368)

The lesson continued in this fashion through the remainder of the story. Once the story was complete the teacher explained that the diagram when completed included the important parts of the story.

In a similar attempt, Dreher and Singer (1980) had students fill out the

Figure 4–7 Simplified diagram of a story's structure

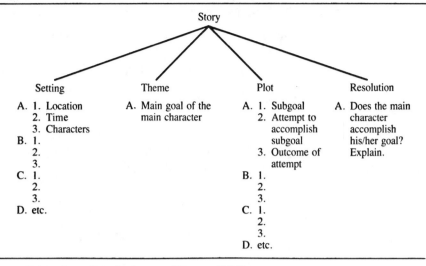

Taken from Cunningham and Foster (1978).

chart given in Figure 4–8. The first step in their procedure was to explain the chart and its components and then distribute a story and copies of the chart for the students to complete with the help of the teacher. After discussing the chart with students and the reasons for responding as they did, a second story and chart were distributed for them to complete in groups of three. This was followed with a third story and chart, which were to be completed independently by each student.

Story Maps

Story maps are used to generate questions for the guided reading of any narrative. The design of questions around a story map involves a rather simple procedure. Based upon an intuitive sense of what the premise or starting point of a story is, the teacher lists major events and ideas that make up the story. This list includes explicit and implicit events, as well as any links between these events. This framework serves as the basis for generating questions for the story. It ensures questions that, as Beck and McKeown (1981, 915) point out, "match the progression of ideas and events in the story." They feel it is more appropriate to keep to addressing a story's progression in terms of events and ideas, before dealing with ideas out of sequence or extending the reader's interpretation of the story. As they stated: "The extension of text ideas can enhance comprehension if a map of the story has already been developed" (p. 915).

Figure 4–9 is an example of a story map generated for a story and the questions derived from the map.

Figure 4–8   Story structure chart

Fill in the sentences from the story that fit each part of this chart.

1. Setting
  Where does the story take place?
  Who are the main characters of
  the story?
  When does the story take place?

  _____

  _____

  Is there any other information
  that helps us get the picture of
  what things are like at the beginning of the story?

  _____

  _____

2. Goal
  What is the main *goal* or purpose
  of the main character?

  _____

  _____

  Is there any other information
  about the main character's goal?
  Maybe the story explains the
  reason the main character wants
  the goal.

  _____

  _____

3. Plot
  How does the main character try to get the goal?

A. First try
  Something happens.

  _____

  What does the main character do?

  _____

  _____

  How did it turn out?

  _____

  Is there any other information
  about the *first try?*

  _____

  _____

B. Second try
  Main character makes a new plan
  to get the goal.

  _____

  Main character tries new plan.

  _____

  _____

  How did it turn out?

  _____

  Is there any other information
  about the *second try?*

  _____

  _____

4. Ending
Did the main character get the goal?

  _____

Is there any other information about the
way the story ended?

  _____

  _____

Taken from Dreher and Singer (1980).

Figure 4–9   Story and Story Map

Ring Story (By Julia DeVoss)
  "You'd better not lose this ring, Pam" Pam's sister advised as Pam slid

the shining ring onto her middle finger. "It's my favorite ring and I'm letting you wear it only because of the dance."

Pam looked at the golden ring glittering in the sun. The tiny red stone shone like a light and sent an oblong red shadow across Pam's hands. Tonight was the dance and now everything was perfect—her dress, her shoes, and the ring.

Putting the finishing touches on her dress, Pam heard her father's voice. "Let's go, Pam," he called, "it's time to go to the dance!" Pam ran excitedly down the stairs, glancing at her image reflected in the hall mirror. All was in place . . . everything except the ring. Pam stared at her empty finger in disbelief. Where had it gone?

Quickly Pam raced back upstairs. In a panic she looked everywhere she had been since she placed the precious ring on her finger. She tore through her dresser drawers, through her closet, back through the hallway. Her eyes scanned every inch of the floor. There was no ring.

"Daddy!" Pam yelled downstairs, "Wait a minute more, I'm coming!" Pam ran into the bathroom. She had just washed her hands. Perhaps the ring had slipped off her finger and had fallen into the sink. Pam stared down into the empty bowl. The ring was gone. Slowly she raised her eyes to her face now streaked with tears.

"I'll tell Daddy I can't go to the dance until I find the ring," she said to herself.

Sadly Pam raised her hands to wipe her eyes—and there on her finger twinkled the golden ring. It had been there all the time, on her other hand.

"Next time," Pam said as she smiled at her reflection, "I'll stop and think before I look so hard for something that isn't lost!"

STORY MAP
THE SETTING
Character(s): Pam, Pam's sister and father
Place: Pam's home
↓
THE PROBLEM
Pam cannot find her sister's ring.
↓
THE GOAL
Pam must find the ring.

→ EVENT 1   Pam looks everywhere she had been in her bedroom.

→ EVENT 2   Pam looks in the bathroom sink.

→ EVENT 3   Pam looks at her hands.

THE RESOLUTION
Pam finds the ring on her own hand.

Question 1. Where and when did the story occur? (The first question always deals with the setting. Leave the question out only if it does not seem important to the story.)

Question 2. Who is the hero or heroine? (Usually a question about the protagonists will follow.)

Question 3. What is Pam's problem? What did Pam need? Why is Pam in trouble? (This question can take various forms, but it deals with the protagonist's problem and leads into the next question, which is a goal question.)

Question 4. What does Pam need to do? (This is the first of a series of questions that follow the events of the story.)

Question 5. What was the first thing Pam tried to do to get out of her predicament?

Question 6. What did she do when that didn't work?

Question 7. Why did she become depressed?

Question 8. How did Pam finally solve her problem?

Question 9. What lesson did she learn?

The last few questions deal with the resolution and, while there is no fixed number of questions that might be asked, the key is to have addressed the main story elements based on the story map. Other questions that might be more provocative (If you were . . . ?) or allow for more intrepetative responses (What might the ring symbolize . . . ?) might be introduced at this time.

Cautions and Comments

The use of story grammars as a tool to sensitize students to stories, and the application of story maps for the purpose of developing questions to guide the treatment of story selections, represent sincere attempts to apply research to practice. What is debatable is whether they have taken all factors into consideration. For instance, Cunningham and Foster (1978) reported that the bottom students liked reading stories using story grammar frameworks; and they believed these students improved in their ability to comprehend stories. In contrast, in a similar study Dreher and Singer (1980) were not as impressed with the results they acquired with fourth graders. Subsequently, they criticized Cunningham and Foster (1978) for their claims and argued that students did not appear to need story grammar instruction because they already have a well developed sense of story. More recently, a study by Fitzgerald and Spiegel (1983) seems to have, at least, temporarily put an end to the disagreement. In their study, 20 fourth graders who were identified as lacking a keen sense of story profited from instruction directed at developing their sense of stories. The fact that they were able to identify such students and that these students showed gains due to instruction supports the use of such frameworks with selected students.

What about story maps? Are Beck and McKeown's claims reasonable? Beck and McKeown (1981) claim that an integrated and sequential line of questioning will lead to better story understanding than either a random barrage of questions or a mix of provocative questions, opportunities for interpretative response, and story line questions. Unfortunately, we do not have the data to substantiate their claims. Intuitively, a well-ordered set of questions would seem to be better than a random set, but less intuitively reasonable is the suggestion that provocative questions and interpretative probes may detract from story understanding. Often such probes may be what engages the reader; indeed, they may fuel the reader's interest to read more thoughtfully and diligently.

There are some issues that cut across the use of both story maps and grammars. As Brewer and Lichtenstein (1982) argued, a story grammar framework does not make a story a story. In fact, their research points to the fact that what distinguishes a story are more aesthetic aspects of a reader's response, such as suspense. Perhaps an argument can be made for facilitating emotional response to a story over or in conjunction with dealing with the story elements. Maybe readers should be encouraged to enjoy rather than dissect a story. These are questions that, due to lack of data, have to be answered subjectively.

REFERENCES

Beck, J., and M. G. McKeown. 1981. Developing questions that promote comprehension: The story map. *Language Arts* 58: 913–18. Provides an overview of the story map and reasons for its use.

Beck, J., M. G. McKeown, E. S. McCaslin, and A. M. Burke. 1979. *Instructional dimensions that may affect comprehension.* Pittsburgh: Learning, Research and Development Center. Presents the notion of story map and compares it with strengths and weaknesses of the guided reading in basals.

Brewer, W. F., and E. H. Lichtenstein. 1982. Stories are to entertain: A structural-affect theory of stories (Tech. Rep. No. 265). Urbana-Champaign, Ill.: University of Illinois, Center for the Study of Reading. Presents an argument against the value of story grammars and for the role of suspense in story understanding.

Cunningham, J., and E. O. Foster. 1978. The ivory tower connection: A case study. *The Reading Teacher* 31:365–69. Discusses a teacher's attempt to use story grammars as a way of sensitizing sixth graders to story structures.

Dreher, M. J., and H. Singer. 1980. Story grammar instruction is unnecessary for intermediate grade students. *The Reading Teacher* 34:261–68. In conjunction with a partial replication of the Cunningham and Foster (1978) study, this article questions whether story grammar instruction is necessary.

Fitzgerald, J., and D. L. Spiegel. 1983. Enhancing children's reading comprehension through instruction in narrative structure. *Journal of Reading Behavior* 15:1–17. Reports a research study involving training 20 students who were found lacking in story structure awareness.

Gates, A. I. 1947. *The improvement of reading.* 3d ed. New York: Macmillan. A classic among college texts with some discussion of the importance of developing a sense of story.

Kintsch, W. 1977. On comprehending stories. In *Cognitive processes in comprehension*, edited by M. Just and P. Carpenter. Hillsdale, N.J.:

Erlbaum. Offers a description of the processes involved in story comprehension.

Mandler, J. M., and N. S. Johnson. 1977. Remembrance of things parsed: Story structure and recall. *Cognitive Psychology* 9:111–51. Presents justification for the use of story grammars.

Pearson, P. D. 1982. *Asking questions about stories*. Boston: Ginn. Discusses and demonstrates the use of story maps with basal story selections.

Rumelhart, D. E. 1975. Notes on a schema for stories. In *Representation and understanding: Studies in cognitive science*, edited by D. G. Bobrow and A. M. Collins. New York: Academic Press. Presents one of the seminal theoretical discussions of story grammars.

Stein, N. L., and C. G. Glenn. 1979. An analysis of story comprehension in elementary school children. In *New directions in discourse processing*, edited by R. O. Freedle. Norwood, N.J.: Ablex. Discusses story grammars and the research pertaining to children's story understanding.

Thorndyke, P. W. 1977. Cognitive structures in comprehension and memory of narrative discourse. *Cognitive Psychology* 9:77–110. Presents research and theory related to story grammars.

Warren, W. H., D. W. Nicholas, and T. Trabasso. 1979. Event chains and inferences in understanding narratives. In *New directions in discourse processing*, edited by R. O. Freedle. Norwood, N.J.: Ablex. Presents a method for analyzing stories based upon event chains which can be applied to all stories and used as a basis for generating questions.

SENTENCE COMBINING

Purpose

Sentence combining is an instructional procedure aimed at increasing syntactic knowledge and thereby increasing both writing performance and reading achievement.

Rationale

Disenchanted with the methodology associated with teaching writing using analytic procedures and formal grammar, but at the same time encouraged by the interrelationships shown to exist between syntax and language processing, many have come to acclaim sentence combining as a means of improving both writing fluency and reading comprehension (Combs 1975; Mellon 1967; Stotsky 1975; Straw and Schreiner 1982). Sentence-combining instruction teaches students to read two or more short, simple sentences and combine them into one sentence. The thinking underlying sentence combining and its more recent counterpart, sentence reduction (Ney 1976), is based on the assumption that sensitizing students to the methods by which ideas are expressed and related in text will develop their ability to compose and comprehend.

In past research, sentence combining has been found to have a positive effect upon writing fluency with elementary students (Green 1972; Perron 1974), with secondary students (Combs 1975; O'Hare 1973), and college-level students. In reading research, attempts to validate the claims regarding sentence combining are less substantial. A study by Crews (1971) showed that sentence combining did not improve the reading comprehension abilities of fourth graders. In a study with ninth graders by Howie (1979), sentence combining and sentence reduction had no impact upon either a cloze test or the *Gray Oral Reading Test*. On the other hand, Machie (1982), as well as Straw and Schreiner (1982) and Obenchain (1971), reported positive results for sentence combining.

In recent years, sentence-combining activities have extended beyond small sets of sentence pairs to what has been termed "rhetorical sentence combining," in which students must combine several sentences from a text.

Intended Audience

Sentence-combining activities in their simplest form can be used with students in the primary grades. Most frequently, the activities have been applied to students in the upper elementary school through college.

Procedures

Sentence combining can be traced back to textbook activities in which students were expected to join together sentences with coordinating conjunctions (and, at the same time, as well as), conditionals (if, since, although), relative pronouns (which, that), and causal temporal connectives (when, because, as, before, during). The most widely used method stems from the work of O'Hare (1973), who replicated an earlier curriculum by Mellon (1967). What made O'Hare's approach distinctive was the elimination of grammatical terminology. O'Hare devised a method of providing written cue words for each sentence-combining transformation that disposed of the need for technical terminology to complete the operation.

Introducing students to sentence combining

Initially students are introduced to the notion of sentence combining through examples offered by the teacher of sentences that demonstrate the use of a connective or another method of combining sentences. During these demonstrations, students are directed to notice how sentences are combined, based upon the meaning they imply and "how they sound" rather than any set rule. In an attempt to direct students to determine the worth of a certain combination (based upon meaning and not a rule), students are asked to share their combinations and to judge as a group which combinations of the same sentences are acceptable and which should be rejected. From those that are acceptable, they determine (by consensus) the sentence combination they prefer. Throughout these deliberations, students are encouraged to discuss the bases for their rejections, acceptances, and preferences.

Sentence combining activities: Sequencing

Sentence combining is usually done by units dealing with separate and somewhat distinct skills. A unit might address the use of "and" between clauses; another unit might deal with "appositives." For each unit there are examples that are modeled and application activities that are discussed and evaluated. Most teachers usually adopt sentence combining as an approach in which these various skills are sequenced across one or more semesters. Some teachers prefer to use sentence combining for selected skills only. In the latter cases, the sentence-combining activities often are integrated into the writing or reading program, based on the curriculum in place or on diagnosis by the teacher.

As students develop confidence in combining groups of sentences, theoretical sentence-combining activities may be used to extend, supplement, or apply these skills. Examples of selected sentence combining activities are given in Figures 4−10 and 4−11.

Figure 4−10   Grammatical Sentences Combining (Appositives)

Combine each sequence of sentences below into a single sentence with at least one appositive.

Example:

1. One of the most controversial public school issues is "mainstreaming."
2. "Mainstreaming" is the growing practice of integrating physically and mentally handicapped children into regular classes.

One of the most controversial public school issues is "mainstreaming," *the growing practice of integrating physically and mentally handicapped children into regular classes.*

OR

"Mainstreaming," *one of the most controversial public school issues*, is the growing practice of integrating physically and mentally handicapped children into regular classes.

A. 1. Pet owners upset by soaring veterinary costs can now register for Medipet.
   2. Medipet is a prepaid insurance plan for dogs and cats.

B. 1. The Parthenon is an ancient temple in Athens.
   2. The Parthenon was dedicated to the goddess Pallas Athena.
   3. Pallas Athena was the special patroness of the city.

C. 1. Murphy's Law is that if anything can go wrong, it will.
   2. Murphy's Law is known to schoolchildren the world over as "Jellybread always falls jelly-side down.

D. 1. When a victim suffers a major burn, damage usually extends far beyond the burn site.

2. A major burn is one in which at least 20 percent of the skin is lost.

E. 1. Herbert Hoover was a civil engineer before becoming President.
   2. Herbert Hoover helped to precipitate the Great Depression.
   3. The Great Depression was the most serious economic upheaval in United States history.

Figure 4–11   Rhetorical—Sentence Combining Appositives

Combine the following sentences into an effective essay that includes several appositives.

Example:

1. The Pentagon is our nation's military headquarters.
2. The Pentagon is a maze of corridors and offices.
3. The Pentagon is a labyrinth confusing and intimidating to outsiders.

The Pentagon, our nation's military headquarters, is a maze of corridors and offices, a labyrinth confusing and initimidating to outsiders.

THE LIFE AND DEATH OF A CELL

1. The bacteria cell is like a fortress.
2. The fortress is self-contained.
3. The cell is an organism.
4. The organism has parts.
5. The parts function for protection.
6. The parts function for nourishment and waste disposal.
7. The parts function for reproduction.
8. Outside the wall of the bacteria cell is a capsule.
9. The capsule is a layer.
10. The layer is slimy.
11. The layer is jellylike.
12. The layer helps protect the cell from chemicals.
13. The chemicals are in its surroundings.
14. The cell wall is another layer.
15. The layer is protective.
16. The layer encloses the organism.
17. The layer keeps food molecules out.
18. The food molecules are large.
19. A bacteria cell secretes enzymes.
20. Enzymes are chemicals.
21. The chemicals break down the molecules so that they can enter the cell.
22. The molecules are large.
23. The molecules are of starches.
24. The molecules are of proteins.

Examples for both figures taken from D. Dikaer, A. Kerek, and M. Morenburg. *The writer's action: Sentence combining activites.* New York: Harper & Row, 1979.

Cautions and Comments

In the rationale section, selected research studies offer mixed support for the influence of sentence-combining instruction on reading comprehension. Unfortunately, there are problems interpreting such results, since each study included different subjects, different tests and a different approach to sentence combining. In Obenchain's study, for example, sentence-combining instruction was extended to having students respond to essay questions in the literature units; in other studies, sentence-combining instruction was more isolated. Intuitively, Obenchain's approach seems more reasonable.

It would seem that if we are to understand and use sentence combining, we need more information on what students are deriving from instruction. As Stotsky (1975) argued, any gains due to sentence combining are more indirect than direct. It is possible that sentence combining forces students to attend to sentences; and this attention, rather than increases in syntactic knowledge, accounts for any changes in writing fluency or reading comprehension.

Since its inception, sentence combining has become differentiated as different advocates have developed their own approaches. For example, not all methods include the same sequence of skills. Some methods teach sentence combining as an isolated curriculum strand; others support a more integrated approach; for example, some sentence-combining approaches have students apply these skills to their reading and writing of essays. The basis for selecting O'Hare's sentence-combining approach for description in this book was based upon its widespread use and on some of its features. Specifically, among the features that seem impressive are the avoidance of grammatical terminology and the emphasis O'Hare gives to having students develop a criteria for judging the acceptability and preference of some combinations over others. Such judgments by students would seem to have benefits that extend to developing an attitude that texts are never perfect.

Regardless of the method that a teacher might use, what seems problematic is the possibility for sentence combining to become an end in itself. Sentence-combining activities that are done mindlessly seem to offer very little that is worthwhile.

REFERENCES

Combs, W. E. 1975. Some further effects and implications of sentence-combining exercises for the secondary language arts curriculum. Unpublished doctoral diss., University of Minnesota. Presents research that examines carefully the worth of sentence combining.

Crews, R. 1971. A linguistic versus a traditional grammar program—the effects on written sentence structure and comprehension. *Educational Leadership* 29:145–49. Presents research in which the effects of sentence combining upon reading and writing are explored.

Green, E. 1972. An experimental study of sentence-combining to improve written syntactic fluency in fifth grade children. Unpublished doctoral diss., Northern Illinois University. Presents research on the effects of sentence combining.

Howie, S. M. 1979. A study of the effects of sentence combining and writing ability and reading level of ninth grade students. Unpublished doctoral diss., University of Colorado. Presents research on the effects of sentence combining.

Machie, B. C. 1982. The effects of a sentence-combining program on the reading comprehension and written composition of fourth grade students. Unpublished doctoral diss., Hofstra University. Presents research on the effects of sentence combining.

Mellon, J. C. 1967. Transformational sentence-combining: A method for enhancing the development of syntactic fluency in English composition. Washington, D.C.: U.S. Office of Education Cooperative Research Project 5-8418. Provides an extended report of the rationale and uses of sentence combining, including research data.

Ney, J. W. 1976. The hazards of the course: Sentence combining in freshman English. *English Record* 27:70−77. Presents a research-based discussion of the use of sentence combining.

Obenchain, A. 1971.Effectiveness of the precise essay question in programming the sequential development of written composition skills and the simultaneous development of critical reading skills. Unpublished masters thesis, George Washington University. Presents research on the influence of sentence combining upon reading and writing improvement.

O'Hare, F. 1973. Sentence combining: Improving student writing without formal grammar instruction. Urbana, Ill.: National Council for Teachers of English. Presents a primary source for the use of sentence combining.

Perron, J. D. 1974. An explanatory approach to extending the syntactic development of fourth grade students through the use of sentence-combining methods. Unpublished doctoral diss., Indiana University. Presents research on the use of sentence combining.

Stotsky, S. L. 1975. Sentence-combining as a curricular activity: Its effect on written language development and reading comprehension. *Research in the Teaching of English* 9:30−71. Represents a most substantial review of sentence-combining methods, research and its utility.

Straw, S. B., and R. Schreiner. 1982. The effect of sentence manipulation on subsequent measures of reading and listening. *Reading Research Quarterly* 17:339−52. Presents research on the influence of sentence combining on reading performance.

CLOZE VARIATIONS

Purpose

When used as a teaching strategy, the cloze technique contributes to the readers' use of syntactic information with sentences. More specifically, the technique forces students to use the context of a sentence to suggest replacements for deleted words.

Rationale

Taylor (1953) described the cloze procedure as: . . . a method of intercepting a message from a "transmitter" (writer or speaker), mutilating its language patterns by deleting parts, and so administering it to "receivers" (readers and listeners) that their attempts to make the patterns whole again potentially yield a considerable number of cloze units. (P. 416)

Since Taylor made such a statement, cloze has been widely advocated as a method for assessing whether or not students can comprehend text, and as a procedure for improving reading comprehension. Unfortunately, there is a growing body of research that suggests cloze should *not* be assumed to be directly associated with reading comprehension. Most notable among these studies is the work of Shanahan, Kamil, and Tobin (1982) and Shanahan and Kamil (1983), which has shown that cloze is neither sensitive to intersentential aspects of text nor to prior knowledge. Indeed, it seems questionable just what the relationship of cloze to reading comprehension is. At best, cloze appears to measure—and maybe heighten—a student's use of the syntax of and information presented with individual sentences. For this reason, we have incorporated cloze variations in this unit with other text-based strategies.

Intended Audience

The cloze procedure has been recommended for use with readers at all levels. Its use has been referenced at the first grade level (Gove 1975) through college level (Bloomer 1962; Friedman 1964; Blumenfield and Miller 1966; Martin 1968; Guice 1969).

Description of the Procedure

For those who have used the cloze procedure as a measure of the comprehensibility of printed material, it would be best to note some differences between the use of the technique in those settings and the use of the strategy as an instructional device. These essential differences are summarized in the following table:

CLOZE PROCEDURE

Characteristic	As a measuring device	As a teaching tool
Length	(1) 250−350 word selections.	(1) Initially, may use single sentences.

Characteristic	As a measuring device	As a teaching tool
		Later, passages of no more than 150 words
Deletions	(2) Delete every *n*th word with approximately 50 for the total word passage	(2) Make deletions selectively and systematically in accordance with proposed use
Evaluation	(3) With this procedure, only exact word replacement is correct. Sometimes a teacher may analyze student responses in terms of their syntactic and semantic characteristics	(3) Synonyms or other replacements are appropriate
Follow-ups	(4) Usually none	(4) Student and teacher discussion of the exercise helps comprehension

Several individuals have attempted to outline systematic procedures for using the cloze technique as a comprehension-building strategy (Bloomer 1962; Schell 1972; Bortnick and Lopardo 1973; Gove 1975). The following procedural outline incorporates the thoughts of each of those individuals.

1. Teacher Preparation

a. *Selecting materials.* Schell (1972) suggests that, in the early stages, materials should be at the students' independent reading level. Teachers can extract written selections from stories and poems in basal readers, from selections in subject matter texts, or from language experience stories the students themselves generate. There are some cloze-type materials available through several publishers. It is important to note that teachers themselves produce some of the most effective materials.

As we mentioned earlier, passages should be shorter than those passages generally used when cloze is a testing device. For example, teachers may use single sentences initially with first graders, gradually moving to selections in which ten to fifteen deletions have been made (Gove 1975).

b. *Designing the cloze exercise.* There appears to be a logical progression in the format for presenting cloze exercises. Consider the examples that follow only as a guideline for developing cloze exercises. We present them in order of difficulty and suggest that the teacher follow this order in using the exercises with students.

1. Sentences in which the teacher deletes one word; a multiple choice format with two choices. Notice in the following example that the two choices include the correct item and a foil, or an incorrect item, that is quite different graphically and is a different part of speech.

1. monkey
"We saw a   at the zoo . . .
2. soon

2. The same format as above, but with the foil somewhat graphically similar to the correct item and a different part of speech.

1. mostly
"We saw a   at the zoo . . .
2. monkey

3. Two choices, both the same part of speech.

1. monkey
"We saw a   at the zoo . . .
2. money

4. Three choices that include the correct item, a word of the same part of speech, and a word that represents a different part of speech.[1]

1. money
"We saw a 2. mostly at the zoo . . .
3. monkey

From these highly structured examples, one can move to less structured items. Again, in terms of difficulty, one could progress with exercises of this type:

1. A single graphophonic clue in a sentence where only one word could reasonably fit.

---

1. This example is similar to a testing strategy, the maze technique, described by Guthrie et al. (1974).

"I think the square t_____ will look better in the dining room than the round one you considered buying."

2. A single graphophonic clue in a sentence where several choices are possible.

"We bought a bag of p_____ at the grocery store."

Finally, the teacher could use sentences and passages similar to these, but without the graphophonic rule.

Again, we suggest this sequence simply to provide a guideline for the development of cloze activities. Obviously, the teacher must consider the difficulty of the printed materials and the reading sophistication of the students when developing exercises of this type.

The reader may have noticed that each of the examples above contains a noun deletion. Schell (1972) suggests that in the early stages of instruction, the teacher should delete only nouns and verbs. Later, he or she may emphasize categories such as adjectives or adverbs.

2. Instruction

In many kindergarten and first grade classrooms, the instructional program might include oral cloze activities. The following is an example of one such activity:

> I am going to say some sentences, but I will leave off the last word of each sentence. See if you can tell me what word I left out. Let's try this one: "At Joe's birthday party on Saturday, we had some ice cream and _____." What word(s) make(s) sense there?

Discussion then could center on why students have various answers. This type of activity provides a logical introduction to the use of written cloze activities.

When initiating written cloze activities, the teacher might begin with a whole class activity focused on material presented on an overhead projector. The teacher should direct students to read through the entire sentence or passage before attempting to supply the deleted word(s). A student volunteer could read the material and supply the missing word(s). One other student who has responded differently could read and provide his responses. Class discussion would center on such questions as:

> Why did you choose this word? What word or group of words indicate to you "building" should be placed in the blank? How does your word contribute to the meaning of the passage? When your word is in the sentence, what does the sentence (or passage) mean? How does your word contribute to the meaning in a different way? When your word is in the sentence, does the sentence (or passage) have a different meaning? (Gove 1975, 38)

Other students could add their suggestions with continued discussion centered on these questions.

Later, the teacher could give the mimeographed cloze passages to complete individually. In small group discussions, the teacher asks each student to explain why he or she used a particular word. The small group discussions would then lead to large group discussion of some of the more interesting or controversial items.

An exercise such as the following might be used with a group of intermediate level readers. Obviously, the teacher would not type the deleted words on the students' mimeographed copies, but we include the words here for discussion purposes.

Would you like to find a rich (*gold*) mine? There's one in the Superstition Mountains of Arizona. Jacob Walz, an (*old*) prospector from Germany, was one of the last known persons to (*visit*) the mine. Before Walz died in 1891, he gave (*simple*) directions to the mine. There is also supposed to be a map. But no one has ever been able to find what is now (*called*) "The Lost Dutchman Mine."[2]

Each of the words in parentheses offers students the opportunity to supply a variety of other words. For example, in place of the word "old," students might offer replacements such as "elderly," "adventurous," "interesting," "ugly," or "eccentric." Discussion then could center on why these choices are feasible, and why words like "young," "robust," and so on, are not acceptable.

Jongsma (1971) and others have suggested that this discussion procedure may be the key to the successful use of cloze as a teaching strategy. There is very little evidence to suggest that cloze exercises alone will produce better comprehenders.

Cautions and Comments

There appear to be an endless number of ways that teachers can use the cloze procedure to improve the comprehension skills of readers. For example, Rankin (1959) proposed the use of cloze exercises to assist readers who have difficulty with text in their content classrooms. More recently, Blachowicz (1977) proposed using the cloze technique with primary grade students.

Furthermore, there seem to be a number of alternative cloze formats. Two additional cloze formats have appeared in recent research studies and may present possibilities for use in teaching. A limited cloze technique (Cunningham and Cunningham 1978) employs the traditional deletion pattern of every fifth word with the deleted words randomly ordered and placed in columns on a separate sheet.

2. R. G. Smith and R. J. Tierney, *Fins and Tales*, Scott, Foresman Basics in Reading. (Glenview, Ill.: Scott, Foresman, 1978), 72.

EXAMPLE OF LIMITED CLOZE

Money that people choose to save rather than spend is very important. Here is the reason. The _____ and machinery a worker _____ have a great deal _____ to do with how much _____ can get done. You _____ know this. But tools _____ machinery cost money. Someone _____ get together enough money _____ build the factory and _____ machinery to help workers _____ more.

List of Deletions for Limited Cloze:

to	tools
he	must
has	already
and	to
buy	produce

Another format, the least-major-constituent limited-cloze (Cunningham and Tierney 1977), deletes every fifth least-major-constituent (syntactic unit sometimes larger than words) and randomly orders them in columns on a separate sheet. The following example provides the same selection as above, but deletes syntactic units.

EXAMPLE OF LEAST-MAJOR-CONSTITUENT LIMITED-CLOZE

Money that people choose to save rather than spend is very important. _____ is the reason. The tools and machinery a worker _____ have a great deal to do with _____ he can get done. You already know _____ . But tools and machinery cost money. _____ must get together enough money to build _____ and buy machinery to help _____ produce more.

Deleted Units:

how much	has
the factory	workers
here	someone
this	

With the widespread use of cloze, however, comes the need for caution. As was suggested in the Rationale, cloze should not be assumed to be directly associated with comprehension. Indeed, it seems that some people are using cloze haphazardly. The reader should note that merely completing cloze activities will not result in students' improved comprehension. Rather, comprehension improvement using cloze depends upon the reader's purpose, the text's demands, and the teacher's follow-up during and after a cloze activity. To this end, teachers should use cloze selectively with passages and purposes where students' ability to produce replacement words or phrases is a worthwhile activity. For example, cloze might be inappropriate with text for which a more reader-based understanding is appropriate. Finally, we need to stress the fact that there is very little research that supports the use of cloze as a procedure either for testing or for developing comprehension.

REFERENCES

Blachowicz, C. L. Z. 1977. Cloze activities for primary readers. *The Reading Teacher* 31:300−302. Describes how teachers can use variations of cloze successfully with primary readers.

Bloomer, R. H. 1962. The cloze procedure as a remedial reading exercise. *Journal of Developmental Reading* 5: 173−81. Describes the use of the cloze procedure as a remedial technique for college students.

Blumenfield, J. P., and G. R. Miller. 1966. Improving reading through teaching grammatical constraints. *Elementary English* 43: 752−55. Presents a description of a study in which twenty college English students completed a variety of cloze exercises.

Bortnick, R., and G. S. Lopardo. 1973. An instructional application of the cloze procedure. *Journal of Reading* 16: 296−300. Provides specific direction for using cloze procedure to improve comprehension. Emphasis is placed on the important of teacher direction.

Cunningham, J. W., and P. M. Cunningham. 1978. Validating a limited-cloze procedure. *Journal of Reading Behavior*, 10: 211−13. Presents a variation of the traditional cloze format.

Cunningham, J. W., and R. J. Tierney. 1977. Comparative analysis of cloze and modified cloze procedures. Paper presented at National Reading Conference, New Orleans. Provides a comparison of the traditional cloze format with two modified versions.

Friedman, M. 1964. The use of the cloze procedure for improving the reading of foreign students at the University of Florida. Unpublished doctoral diss., University of Florida. Describes an experimental study in which one group received cloze passages constructed from *McCall-Crabbs Standard Test Lessons in Reading.*

Goodman, K. S. 1967. Reading: A psycholinguistic guessing game. *Journal of the Reading Specialist* 4: 126−35.

Gove, M. K. 1975. Using the cloze procedure in a first grade classroom. *The Reading Teacher* 29: 36−38. Describes how the teacher can use cloze procedure in conjunction with basal readers and with the language experience approach.

Guice, B. M. 1969. The use of the cloze procedure for improving reading comprehension of college students. *Journal of Reading Behavior* 1: 81−

92. Provides a description of four groups of college students who received instruction using cloze passages.

Guthrie, J. T., N. A. Burnham, R. I. Caplan, and M. Seifert. 1974. The maze technique to assess, monitor reading comprehension. *The Reading Teacher* 28: 161–68. Presents a multiple-choice-type variation of the cloze procedure.

Henk, W. 1977–78. A response to Shanahan, Kamil, and Tobin: The case is not yet clozed. *Reading Research Quarterly* 13:508–37. Presents a response to the first study of Shanahan, Kamil, and Tobin, which resulted in a second study by them.

Jongsma, E. 1971. *The cloze procedure as a teaching technique*. Newark, Del.: International Reading Association. Presents descriptions of past research that used cloze procedure as a teaching tool; offers suggestions for future cloze research.

Martin, R. W. 1968. Transformational grammar, cloze, and performance in college freshmen. Unpublished doctoral diss., Syracuse University. Describes a study in which researchers gave three groups of college students passages to improve their reading comprehension.

Rankin, E. 1959. Uses of the cloze procedure in the reading clinic. *Proceedings of the International Reading Association* 4:228–32. Suggests ways of using cloze procedure to bridge the gap between clinical instruction and instruction in the content classroom.

Sampson, M. R., W. J. Valmont, and R. V. Allen. 1982. The effects of instructional cloze on the comprehension, vocabulary and divergent production of third grade students. *Reading Research Quarterly* 17:389–99. Presents positive results from a study in which students who received instruction in cloze with selected deletions outperformed a control group.

Schell, L. M. 1972. Promising possibilities for improving comprehension. *Journal of Reading* 5: 415–24. Presents detailed information on the use of cloze as a teaching technique.

Shanahan, T., and M. Kamil. 1983. A further investigation of sensitivity of cloze and recall to passage organization. In *Searches for Meaning in Reading/Language Processing and Instruction*, edited by J. A. Niles and L. A. Harris. Thirty-second Yearbook of the National Reading Conference, Rochester, N.Y., National Reading Conference. In response to Henk's critique, presents a study that further disputes cloze as a method of improving comprehension.

Shanahan, T., M. Kamil, and A. Tobin. 1982. Cloze as a measure of intersentential comprehension. *Reading Research Quarterly* 17:229–55. Presents a research study that raised serious questions about the use of cloze as a measure of text comprehension.

Taylor, W. L. 1953. Cloze procedure: A new tool for measuring readability. *Journalism Quarterly* 30: 415–33. Provides the first description of the cloze technique.

Weaver, G. C. 1979. Using the cloze procedure as a teaching technique. *The Reading Teacher* 32: 632–36. Presents a comprehensive review of the use of cloze as an instructional tool.

5

Meaning Vocabulary Strategies

The Unit and Its Theme

Without a doubt there is a direct relationship between vocabulary knowledge and reading comprehension. As Anderson and Freebody (1981) suggested in conjunction with an extensive review of research: "Word knowledge is a requisite for reading comprehension: people who do not know the meanings of words are most probably poor readers" (p. 110). Conversely, if students are introduced to relevant vocabulary before they encounter them in text, their ability to construct meaning from text likely will be enhanced. This is particularly true of informational or content area text. Additionally, new vocabulary words are more easily retained when students are given an opportunity to explore those words in depth conceptually through a variety of language modes.

The Strategies

Our rationale is that teachers who have access to a repertoire of strategies that will introduce and reinforce relevant vocabulary words are in a better position to help students learn and retain words. Thus, five strategies are described in this unit that teachers can use in various aspects of the instructional lesson to promote students' vocabulary development.

Possible Sentences

Possible Sentences is designed to help students determine the meanings of unknown words by pairing them with known words in sentences they think

172

might "possibly" be found in a text. Thus, the strategy enables students to predict word meanings and verify their accuracy as they read.

List-Group-Label

Based upon a strategy originally developed by Taba, List-Group-Label asks students to free associate terms related to a stimulus topic, and then to group and label these terms. Thus, the strategy serves as a means to activate students' prior knowledge about related concepts or to review concepts gleaned from reading.

Contextual Redefinition

Contextual Redefinition is designed to enable students to use context to make an informed guess about a word's meaning. Additionally, it attempts to provide students with a strategy for using context in independent reading situations.

Preview in Context

Using the notion of classroom discussion, Preview in Context is designed to help students discover the meaning of unknown words that they encounter in their reading. Thus, the strategy can be readily applied in all classroom situations.

Feature Analysis

Feature Analysis is an attempt to expand and refine students' vocabulary and related concepts after they read. In essence, it uses categorization as a systematic means to reinforce word meaning.

REFERENCE

Anderson, R. C. and P. Freebody. 1981. Vocabulary knowledge. In *Comprehension and teaching: Research reviews*, edited by J. T. Guthrie. Newark, DE: International Reading Association.

POSSIBLE SENTENCES

Purpose

Possible Sentences (Moore and Arthur 1981) is designed to help students to

1. Learn new vocabulary to be encountered in a reading assignment;
2. Make predictions about sentences to be found in their reading;
3. Provide purpose for reading; and
4. Arouse their curiosity concerning the text to be read.

Rationale

Possible Sentences (PS) was designed as a means to enable students to determine independently the meanings and relationships of unfamiliar words in text reading assignments. Students make predictions about the relationships between the unknown words, read to verify the accuracy of the predicted relationships, and use the text to evaluate and refine their predictions. Thus, prediction is used to create interest and to focus students' attention on the meanings and concepts to be acquired.

Intended Audience

Moore and Arthur (1981) specified that PS could be used whenever students encounter unfamiliar vocabulary during reading assignments in subject matter classrooms. Therefore, it is implied that PS can be used with middle and secondary students in content areas. However, the strategy is probably appropriate for all levels of students reading and learning from expository text.

Description of the Procedure

Possible Sentences is a five-part lesson and consists of the following steps: (1) list key vocabulary, (2) elicit sentences, (3) read and verify sentences, (4) evaluate sentences, and (5) generate new sentences.

1. List key vocabulary

To begin a PS lesson, the teacher lists the essential vocabulary of a text selection on the board and pronounces the words for the students. The teacher has determined beforehand that the words are central to the major concepts to be encountered in the text and that they can be adequately defined by their context. For instance, from a text on skin disorders, the following terms might be listed:

Skin Disorders

moles	warts
acne	freckles
boils	athlete's foot
virus	infection
fungus	congenital

2. Elicit sentences

Students are then asked to use at least two words from the list and make a sentence, one they think might possibly be in the text. The sentences are recorded, one at a time, on the board and the words used from the list should be underlined. It is important that the sentences be recorded exactly as given, even if students provide incorrect information. This is necessary for the evaluation phase that follows. Students may use words already in previous sentences so long as a new context is created. Continue eliciting sentences until students can produce no more or until a specified length of time has elapsed. However, encourage students to use every word from the list at least once.

Below are some possible sentences students might offer with the list of words related to skin disorders:

1. *Warts* are caused by an *infection.*
2. *Moles* can be a *congenital infection.*
3. You shouldn't squeeze *boils* or *acne.*
4. *Moles* and *freckles* are harmless.
5. Either *fungus* or a *virus* causes *athlete's foot.*

3. Read and verify sentences

Students are asked to read the text to check the accuracy of the sentences generated.

4. Evaluate sentences

With the text available for reference, a discussion ensues as each sentence is evaluated. Those sentences that are not accurate are either omitted or refined, according to what the text states. The discussion of the sentences calls for careful reading, since judgments as to the accuracy of sentences must be defended by students.

Examining the possible sentences related to skin disorders, sentence C is accurate as stands. Sentence A will have to be refined. Warts are not caused by infections; they are viral in nature. Sentence B also needs refinement. Moles can be congenital, but they are not infections. Sentence D is technically correct; however, it is more accurate to state that "*Moles* and *freckles* are harmless unless irritated." Finally, sentence E needs to be modified to state that athlete's foot is caused by a fungal infection.

5. Generate new sentences

After the original sentences have been evaluated, the teacher asks for additional sentences. This step is taken to further extend students' understanding of the meanings and relationships of the vocabulary terms. As new sentences are generated, they are checked against the text for accuracy. All final sentences should be recorded in their notebooks by the students.

Cautions and Comments

Possible Sentence is a structured language activity that requires students both to recognize the contextual setting of words and to produce their own contextual settings. However, there are some concerns that teachers need to be aware of before implementing a PS lesson. Care needs to be taken to insure that vocabulary can be defined by the context. Authors do not always provide explicit contexts in their writing, and PS requires that the context be one in which the meaning of a word is at least directly implied. Additionally, the choice of vocabulary terms needs to be considered to conduct a successful PS lesson. If only unfamiliar words are chosen from a text, students will have difficulty generating sentences. Particularly with passages of a highly technical nature, it is essential also to list some words that will be familiar to students. Otherwise, students will not be able to use their prior knowledge to make connections between what they know and the unfamiliar words they are to learn. Finally, if too many technical words are found in a text or if an absence of defining contexts is noted, then it may behoove the teacher to choose a different strategy or, even more appropriately, a different text.

Possible Sentences provides students an opportunity to use all language processes as they learn new word meanings. Using their prior knowledge, students are asked to make connections between new and known vocabulary words and evaluate them. Students use speaking to express these connections; they use listening to hear other students' ideas and connections. They read to verify the possible sentences generated and the refined versions are written in their notebooks. Thus, students become actively involved in their new learning.

There is an additional benefit in using PS. Teachers are able to assess what knowledge students bring to the learning task, how they rectify their misconceptions about a topic, and whether or not students have actually learned the word meanings and their related concepts. As a result, teachers can get an idea of how much additional reinforcement may be needed for students to learn the material. Finally, it should be emphasized that very little research on the use of possible sentences exists to date.

REFERENCE

Moore, D. W., and S. V. Arthur. 1981. Possible sentences. In *Reading in the content areas: Improving classroom instruction*, edited by E. K. Dishner,

T. W. Bean, and J. E. Readence. Dubuque, IA: Kendall/Hunt, 138−43. Describes the rationale, procedures, and suggestions for using Possible Sentences.

LIST-GROUP-LABEL

Purpose

List-Group-Label (Taba 1967) is designed to encourage students to (1) improve their vocabulary and categorization skills, (2) organize their verbal concepts, and (3) aid them in remembering and reinforcing new vocabulary.

Rationale

The List-Group-Label (LGL) lesson was originally conceived by Taba as a means to help students deal with the technical vocabulary in science and social studies classes. It is based on the notion that categorizing words can help students organize new concepts and experiences in relation to previously learned concepts. In essence, LGL attempts to improve upon the way in which students learn and remember new concepts.

Intended Audience

List-Group-Label was originally used by Taba with elementary school students. However, the strategy seems appropriate for students at all grade levels.

Description of the Procedure

List-Group-Label is an easy-to-implement three-part strategy that uses (1) listing, (2) grouping/labeling, and (3) follow-up.

1. Listing

The teacher begins the LGL lesson by selecting a one- or two-word topic to serve as a stimulus for listing words. Using a chalkboard, an overhead transparency, or any other means appropriate for recording students' responses, the stimulus topic is written at the top of the board or paper. Topics should be drawn from the materials that students are reading and learning from. For example, if students are about to start a unit on volcanos, volcanos might be used as the topic to begin a LGL lesson. On the other hand, almost any topic of which the students have some prior knowledge might be suitable.

Students are asked to brainstorm related to the topic, i.e., to think of any word or expression related to the topic. Using our volcano example, the teacher might say, "Think of any word or words that reminds you of the topic 'volcano.'" Responses are recorded and the teacher should accept all word associations given by the students, unless the response cannot be justified by the student.

The list of words should be kept manageable. Depending on the topic itself and the grade level of the students, approximately 25 responses should be adequate. When most children have had an opportunity to offer a response, the listing portion of the lesson can be terminated by stating, "I'll take only two more words." Below is a list of responses students might generate using 'volcano' as a stimulus topic:

Volcano

lava	Mt. St. Helens	eruption
explosion	ash	rocks
destruction	magma	Pompeii
fire	death	earthquake
dust	smoke	heat
Krakatoa	cinders	molten

2. Grouping/labeling

To begin this portion of the lesson, the teacher should read the list orally, pointing to each word as it is pronounced. For older students this step may not be necessary, but it is cautioned that even older readers, particularly those of lesser ability, may benefit from this. The students are then instructed to make smaller lists of words related to (in this case) the topic of volcanoes, using only words from the large list that the class generated. These smaller groupings should consist of words that have something in common with one another; and each grouping should have at least three words in them. Words from the large list may be used in more than one smaller group, so long as the groupings are different. Students are also told that they must give their group of words a label or title that indicates the shared relationship they possess.

3. Follow-up

Using another part of the chalkboard or piece of paper, the teacher solicits and records categories of words and their labels from the students, one grouping at a time. After a category is recorded, the student offering the group must state verbally why the words have been categorized in the particular way stated. In this way, all students can see category possibilities that may not have occurred to them.

The following are possible groupings that may be generated from the large list of 'volcano' words:

1. lava, ash, rocks, dust, smoke = things emitted from a volcano
2. Mt. St. Helens, Krakatoa, Pompeii = famous volcanoes

3. explosion, destruction, death, earthquake = results of a volcanic eruption
4. lava, fire, cinders, molten, magma = hot volcanic parts

Cautions and Comments

Perhaps the most beneficial aspects of List-Group-Label are the modeling and sharing that are built into the strategy. It is through this sharing that students are exposed to ideas and concepts that may be beyond their experiential background and, thus, enable learning to occur. Therefore, it is most important that modeling and sharing be emphasized as part of the lesson.

Modeling may also occur as part of the instruction that the teacher provides. For younger or poorer students for whom categorization might prove to be a problem, the teacher should "walk" students through the "how" and "why" of LGL. This might include (1) constructing the first category and providing a title for it to show students the process of categorization; (2) providing an initial list of words for students to group and label; (3) making the categories yourself and having students label them; and (4) providing the labels and having students find words to fit the category.

Other suggestions for using List-Group-Label include the use of small groups of students to categorize and label rather than just having individual students accomplish this task on their own. This increases the interaction and sharing among individuals, as well as streamlines the whole group discussion that follows grouping and labeling; i.e., instead of individuals reporting their groupings, only a spokesperson for each small group does the talking. For younger students or groups of students, LGL may also be personalized by recording the individual's or group's name by the category that has been offered.

It must also be mentioned that LGL is based on the notion that some prior knowledge is essential for the lesson to be successful. If a teacher assumes prior knowledge on the part of students where little or none exists, LGL stands little chance for success. For instance, using 'volcano' as a stimulus topic for students who are too young will probably result in very few word associations being given. Similarly, using an unfamiliar topic such as "parts of the brain," even with older students, will usually result in failure, too.

Obviously, prior knowledge plays much less of a role in LGL if the strategy is used as a means of reinforcement in the post-reading portion of an instructional lesson. In such a case, knowledge gained from the text is going to take precedence over prior knowledge. Therefore, LGL can be an excellent strategy for review purposes, even if the topic was originally unfamiliar. Indeed, Bean, Inabinette, and Ryan (1983) found that high school subjects produced significantly higher vocabulary retention scores when LGL was used as a post-reading review strategy.

Other problems that may occur with LGL involve aspects of categorization. It is cautioned that semantic, meaning-oriented groupings be emphasized rather than those that focus on surface commonalities of words chosen for a grouping. For example, the following category is perfectly legitimate, though not what is called for in LGL:

explosion, destruction, eruption = three syllable words

If such a category would occur, teachers are cautioned that they must accept the category but point out that meaningful, rather than surface, associations are desired. Another categorization problem that might occur is the propensity of some students to try to make the largest grouping they possibly can. This can be dealt with by simply limiting the number of words that may be used in one group to five or, at the most to, seven words. Finally, some words defy classification. To deal with this, Readence and Searfoss (1980) suggested creating a "misfit" list of all those words that do not fit a category. Exploring why certain words do not fit a category can also prove instructionally beneficial for students.

As a closing note, the diagnostic value of LGL should be mentioned. In a prereading situation, teachers can find out what it is that students know and what it is that will require teacher instruction. In a post-reading situation, teachers can find out what students have learned and what will require reteaching. Finally, as a straight vocabulary development lesson, teachers can find a source of words from students' experiences that might require clarification.

REFERENCES

Bean, T. W., N. B. Inabinette, and R. Ryan. 1983. The effect of a categorization strategy on secondary students' retention of literacy vocabulary. *Reading Psychology* 4:247–52. Research study that reports positive effects for the use of List-Group-Label as a post-reading strategy.

Readence, J. E., and L. W. Searfoss. 1980. Teaching strategies for vocabulary development. *English Journal* 69:43–46. Discusses the use of categorization in general and List-Group-Label in particular as a means to develop vocabulary.

Taba, H. 1967. *Teacher's handbook for elementary social studies*. Reading, Mass.: Addison-Wesley. Describes the original uses of the List-Group-Label strategy.

CONTEXTUAL REDEFINITION

Purpose

Contextual Redefinition (Cunningham, Cunningham, and Arthur 1981; Readence, Bean, and Baldwin 1981) is designed to help students: (1) use context to unlock the meaning of unknown words, (2) make informed, rather than haphazard, guesses about word meanings using context, and (3) learn a general decoding strategy that may be applied in independent reading situations.

Rationale

Contextual Redefinition is a decoding strategy that stresses the importance of context in predicting and verifying word meanings. Context enables students to make more informed guesses about the meaning of words in print and to monitor those predictions by checking them for syntactic/semantic appropriateness as reading progresses. Since authors frequently provide clues to the meanings of words in sentences, it is essential that students be able to use those clues as an aid in deriving meaning from print. Contextual Redefinition provides a format for decoding unknown words that capitalizes on the use of context and endeavors to give students a strategy that can be used in their own independent reading.

Intended Audience

Contextual Redefinition is appropriate for students of all grade levels who may encounter in their reading a few difficult words that may be defined in the context in which they occur.

Description of the Procedure

Contextual Redefinition may be implemented using a five-step procedure: (1) select unfamiliar words, (2) write a sentence, (3) present the words in isolation, (4) present the words in context, and (5) use a dictionary for verification.

1. Select unfamiliar words

Words to be used with this strategy are not randomly chosen; rather, they are identified in conjunction with the reading assignment at hand. Teachers should examine the text to be read to select those words (1) whose meaning may be necessary to understand the important ideas of the text and (2) whose meaning or use may present trouble to students as they read. For the sake of demonstrating this strategy, the following words will be used: (a) hippophagy, (b) carapace, and (c) arachibutyrophobia.

2. Write a sentence

At least a sentence context needs to be provided so students have appropriate clues to each word's meaning. If the text already has such a context, use it; otherwise, one will have to be created. If a context is created, it is recommended that various types of clues (e.g., synonyms, comparison/contrast, definition, etc.) should be used. In this way students are able to experience the variety of ways authors may provide help in conveying meaning.

With our example the following sentences might be used:

(a) The drought had been so long and severe that the cattle had died. Only the horses had survived. Yet, the natives were so hungry that they had to resort to *hippophagy* to avoid starvation.

(b) Without its *carapace*, a turtle is subject to certain death from its enemies or the elements.

(c) Because Waldo was born with a cleft palate, he would never eat peanut butter. Though he was told by the doctors that he was totally healed, Waldo had developed *arachibutyrophobia*. Because of that, peanut butter was out of the question.

3. Present the words in isolation

Using an overhead transparency or a chalkboard, ask students to provide definitions for each word. It is suggested that the teacher pronounce each word as it is introduced so students at least know how the word sounds. When offering their individual guesses, students must provide a rationale for them. As a group, students should try to come to some consensus as to what they believe the best meaning is. Obviously, some predictions may be "off-the-wall" or even humorous. However, this is part of the process of learning—focusing on associations with recognizable parts of the word when it is in isolation robs the reader of the clues provided by a surrounding context. In other words, guesses offered when a word is presented in isolation are usually haphazard and uninformed.

With our example words, it is easy to see that some students could say that "hippophagy" has something to do with hippos, that "carapace" has something to do with a pace car at a race, and that "arachibutyrophobia" has something to do with a fear of spiders.

4. Present the words in context

At this point in the lesson, students are presented each word in its appropriate context, using the sentence or sentences from the text or those developed by the teacher. Again, students are asked to offer guesses about the meaning of each word and provide a rationale for each definition. In doing this, less able students are able to experience the thinking processes involved in using context to derive a meaning. In other words, students are able to act as models of appropriate reading behavior for one another. As before, students should try to come to some consensus as to the best meaning of the word offered.

In this part of the strategy, students should learn that context provides much information about the meaning of words and allows for quite informed predictions. Additionally, students should learn that simply guessing at a word in isolation to get its meaning is not very accurate and can be frustrating.

5. Use a dictionary for verification

In this step, a student or students are asked to consult a dictionary to verify the guesses offered. The dictionary definition is shared with the rest of the class and a discussion ensues concerning the quality of the predictions given when the words are presented (1) in isolation and (2) in context. It is now that teachers should point out or, even better, have students discover, the differences involved in guessing during these two steps of Contextual Redefinition.

Cautions and Comments

Contextual Redefinition provides teachers a format to help students learn the use of context in ascertaining the meanings of unfamiliar words. It is easy to implement, requires little extra teacher preparation to use, and does have the potential for transfer to students' other reading situations. Additionally, the strategy allows students to become actively involved in the discovery of new word meanings rather than just passive receivers of teacher-provided meanings.

It must be remembered, however, that Contextual Redefinition is a strategy to introduce new vocabulary words, not a strategy to teach and reinforce vocabulary words.Therefore, teachers must provide the necessary extension activities for students in order to insure that the words are retained. Additionally, another concern about this strategy is one that Gipe (1978–79) stated in her research on teaching word meanings. Teachers should try to assure that the words used in explaining a new word are familiar; one cannot expect a student to learn a new word when it is first introduced in a sentence that has other unknown entities in it.

A final mention must be given to the importance of modeling behavior. Built into the strategy is the reading behavior of fluent readers; fluent readers use all available clues (graphophonic, syntactic, semantic) to derive the meaning of an unknown word. Contextual Redefinition tries to demonstrate to students that this is the proper way to cope with unknown words in text reading assignments. Modeling behavior is also used when students explain their thought processes to others in the class. It must not be assumed that all students will deal equally well with the various contexts that can be encountered. As students share their thoughts and ideas with one another, this presents an opportunity for others to pick up on and understand what happens in deriving meaning from print. Finally, it should be stressed that very little research on the use of contextual redefinition exists to date.

REFERENCES

Cunningham, J. W., P. M. Cunningham, and S. V. Arthur. 1981. *Middle and secondary school reading.* New York: Longman. Presents Contextual Redefinition as a strategy to help middle/secondary students deal with new vocabulary.

Gipe, J. P. 1978–79. Investigating techniques for teaching word meanings. *Reading Research Quarterly* 14:624–44. Research study that found that a vocabulary teaching method emphasizing context proved effective.

Readence, J. E., T. W. Bean, and R. S. Baldwin. 1981. *Content area reading: An integrated approach*. Dubuque, IA: Kendall/Hunt. Presents the steps involved in conducting a Contextual Redefinition lesson in the content areas.

PREVIEW IN CONTEXT

Purpose

Preview in Context (Readence, Bean, and Baldwin, 1981) helps students to (1) discover the meanings of new vocabulary words and (2) analyze context for word meaning clues.

Rationale

Students need to develop a habit of trying to use their own experiences and the knowledge they can gain from context in discovering the meaning of unknown words they encounter in their reading. Teachers, on the other hand, need access to a strategy that shows students how to use context, yet lends itself readily to normal classroom situations. Preview in Context is a strategy that seems to suit both of those needs.

Intended Audience

Preview in Context is designed to present new vocabulary words to students by using the materials normally employed in classroom instruction. Therefore, the strategy is probably appropriate for students at all grade levels.

Description of the Procedure

Preview in Context can be implemented using the four-step procedure: (1) preparation, (2) establishing context, (3) specifying word meaning, and (4) expanding word meaning.

1. Preparation

Words are selected from the text or other reading material that are to be learned by the students. These words should be both important to the major ideas presented in the text and likely to be unfamiliar to the students. Only a few words at a time should be presented in order to prevent the lesson from becoming boring. For purposes of illustrating the strategy, we use the example word "insipid" as used in the following short paragraph:

> His teaching lacked spirit. He had presented his lesson in a dull manner, failing to challenge or stimulate his students. The teacher knew he had made an *insipid* presentation.

2. Establishing context

The words are now presented to the students, and they are directed to its surrounding context. The word and its context are first read aloud to the students as they follow along in the text. Then the students are asked to reread the material silently.

3. Specifying word meaning

It is here that students are asked to use their prior knowledge as the teacher asks questions of the students to enable them to discover the meaning of the word. In essence, through questioning and discussion, the teacher "talks" the students toward the identification of the word's probable meaning in its existing context. Using our example of the word "insipid," the questioning might go as follows:

> **Q:** What does the sentence tell you about the word "insipid?"
> **A:** I guess the teacher didn't do so well.
> **Q:** Why didn't he do so well?
> **A:** It sounds like he was dull and uninteresting. He probably had a bad day!
> **Q:** Then what might an insipid presentation be?
> **A:** A dull and uninteresting one!

4. Expanding word meaning

When students have an understanding of the meaning of the word in its existing context, try to extend this understanding by conducting brief discussions of other possible contexts, synonyms, or antonyms for the word. If they have access to them, students might use a dictionary, thesaurus, or a book of synonyms and antonyms as reference for the discussion. Obviously, the purpose of these discussions is to reinforce the word's meaning as an aid to retaining it. An example discussion for "insipid" is given below:

> **Q:** Who else might make an insipid presentation?
> **A:** The President; any politician; a minister; a college professor.
> **Q:** How could you avoid an insipid presentation?

A: Be better prepared; tell some jokes; show that you're interested in what you're saying; use hand gestures.

Q: What words do you know that mean the same as insipid?

A: Dull; uninteresting; lifeless; flat; inane.

Q: What words do you know that mean the opposite of insipid?

A: Interesting; animated; forceful; zesty.

Further expansion of the word's meaning can be accomplished by having the
students record the word in their notebooks for later review and study. Each
word entry should contain a short definition, some synonyms, and a student-
generated context.

Cautions and Comments

Preview in Context is a very informal technique to introduce new vocabulary
words to students. It is spontaneous and requires little in the way of extra
teacher preparation. Preview in Context is easily implemented, gets students
actively involved in the learning, and is relevant to instruction. Best of all, it fits
in readily with what already goes on in many classrooms rather than presents a
novel procedure that students have to adjust to.

It must be remembered that Preview in Context should only be used when
the existing context provides students sufficient clues to venture a probable
guess as to the word's meaning. Otherwise, a better context might need to be
written, and a strategy such as Contextual Redefinition could be used. Additionally, this is a strategy to "preview" words only. Though the words to be
learned are expanded somewhat in the last step of the procedure, other forms
of vocabulary reinforcement are needed. Finally, much of the success of this
strategy is due to skillful questioning and discussion by the teacher. This must
be kept in mind if Preview in Context is to be implemented successfully.

REFERENCE

Readence, J. E., T. W. Bean and R. S. Baldwin. 1981. *Content area reading:
An integrated approach*. Dubuque, IA: Kendall/Hunt. Discusses Preview in Context and provides examples of its use.

FEATURE ANALYSIS

Purpose

Feature Analysis (also called Semantic Feature Analysis by Johnson and
Pearson 1978) is designed to help students to:

1. Improve their vocabulary and categorization skills;
2. Understand the similarities and differences in related words; and
3. Expand and retain content area vocabulary and concepts.

Rationale

Feature Analysis (FA) is a categorization strategy derived from the theoretical construct of the cognitive structure as the way in which individuals organize knowledge. Briefly, as human beings process information, categories are established in the cognitive structure based largely on cultural and experiential patterns. Rules (feature analysis) are formulated to allocate objects (words or concepts) into these categories. In this way, category interrelationships are established in the cognitive structure so individuals can search their category systems (knowledge) efficiently to make sense of their experiences. Of practical relevance, FA is intended to provide a systematic procedure for exploring and reinforcing vocabulary concepts through the use of categorization.

Intended Audience

Johnson and Pearson (1978) described Feature Analysis as a strategy that could be used with elementary students to develop their vocabulary. However, FA can also be used to refine and reinforce vocabulary and related concepts in a post-reading situation in content area classrooms.

Description of the Procedure

Feature analysis may be implemented using the following six steps:

1. Category selection;
2. List words in category;
3. List features;
4. Indicate feature possession;
5. Add words/features; and
6. Complete and explore matrix.

1. Category selection

The key to FA is to start slowly and to begin with something familiar to students. A category topic (e.g., pets) is selected by the teacher. Once students are familiar with the strategy, the kinds and the abstractness of the category topics (e.g., freedom, climate) may increase. For illustration purposes, we use a rather simplistic example with the category of "pets."

2. List words in category

Once the category topic has been introduced, the teacher provides words that name concepts or objects related to the category. As students become accustomed to the strategy, they should provide these words. In the case of our example of "pets," the following words might be introduced initially: (a) dog, (b) fish, (c) hamster, (d) frog, and (e) duck.

3. List features

The teacher must now decide what features (traits, characteristics) are to be explored in the category "pets." As before, students should provide these features once they become familiar with the strategy. Since some category topics would have many features that could be explored, as is the case with our example, start with only a few features and build on them later in the lesson. For our example, features to be examined are whether the pet (a) lives on land, (b) lives in the water, (c) has wings, (d) has fins, (e) has legs, and (f) has fur.

After the first three steps of the strategy have been completed, we should have a feature matrix that looks like the following:

CATEGORY: PETS

	land	water	wings	fins	legs	fur
dog						
fish						
hamster						
frog						
duck						

4. Indicate feature possession

Students are guided through the feature matrix for the purpose of deciding whether or not a particular pet possesses each of the features. When beginning FA, it is recommended that a simple plus/minus (+/−) system be used to indicate feature possession. A more sophisticated system, such as a form of the Likert scale (1 = never; 2 = some; 3 = always), may be substituted once students are familiar with the strategy, and a system that explores the relative degree of feature possession is desired. Feature possession should be based on typical patterns, i.e., though some dogs may not have fur, this is not typical of them. The feature matrix for "pets" should look as follows using a +/− system:

CATEGORY: PETS

	land	water	wings	fins	legs	fur
dog	+	−	−	−	+	+
fish	−	+	−	+	−	−
hamster	+	−	−	−	+	+
frog	+	+	−	−	+	−
duck	+	−	+	−	+	−

5. Add words/features

At this point in the strategy, it is time to expand the matrix. The teacher, or preferably the students, should generate new words to be added, followed by new features to be analyzed. Depending on the familiarity of the category or time limitations, the teacher may wish to set a limit on the number of words or features that can be added. This will typically be done automatically as categories become more abstract and begin to rely less on the prior knowledge that students may possess.

In our example, words such as (a) turtle, (b) rabbit, and (c) snake might be added. Features to be added might include (a) has feathers, (b) swims, and (c) flies. Adding words and features to the matrix is an attempt to further expand students' vocabulary and to develop concepts through categorization. The next and final step completes the FA strategy.

6. Complete and explore matrix

Students proceed now to complete the feature matrix by using the identical feature possession system as before with the added words and features. Our final example matrix might look like this:

CATEGORY: PETS

	land	water	wings	fins	legs	fur	feathers	swims	flies
dog	+	−	−	−	+	+	−	−	−
fish	−	+	−	+	−	−	−	+	−
hamster	+	−	−	−	+	+	−	−	−

	land	water	wings	fins	legs	fur	feathers	swims	flies
frog	+	+	−	−	+	−	−	+	−
duck	+	−	+	−	+	−	+	+	+
turtle	+	−	−	−	+	−	−	+	−
rabbit	+	−	−	−	+	+	−	−	−
snake	+	−	−	−	−	−	−	+	−

The final part of this step is the exploration of the feature matrix. Students are asked to examine how words in the matrix relate, yet how they are still unique. For instance, it can be noted that even though the dog, the hamster, and the rabbit are different pets, they still have many similar traits. At the same time, they are also different from all the other pets listed and compared. Additionally, it can be seen that only certain pets have wings or typically swim.

Exploring the feature matrix is best accomplished when the students, rather than the teacher, note these similarities and differences. Further expansion of the matrix may continue at this point, if the students so desire or the teacher assigns it.

Cautions and Comments

On the positive side, Feature Analysis has been shown to be effective with selected students (Johnson, Toms-Bronowski, and Pittelman 1983) and is relatively easy to implement and can be fun. On the negative side, it does present some concerns that teachers need to be aware of. Categorization, as espoused in this strategy, is more sophisticated than it normally is. Some students may find FA to be difficult at first. If such is the case, Readence and Searfoss (1980) suggest that simple categorization excercises and strategies such as List-Group-Label be used as a means to introduce the concept of categorization and to act as a way into Feature Analysis. A second concern revolves around the plus/minus feature possession system. The strategy looks at *typical* patterns related to feature possessions, yet there are many exceptions to what is typical. Looking at our example, it can be argued that there are flying fish and that turtles and ducks "live," at least part of the time, in the water. It is recommended that if Feature Analysis is to be used frequently in the classroom, then teaching students to use a more sophisticated analysis system is warranted. This may lessen the amount of haggling students do in the analysis process. Finally, as with any strategy, the more actively involved the students become in category selection and in the selection of words and features to be explored, the better the strategy will work.

Categorizing Feature Analysis as strictly a vocabulary development technique for elementary students presents a very narrow view of this strategy. FA has great potential in other aspects of vocabulary development, as well as in becoming an integral part of both elementary and secondary reading and content area lessons. Baldwin, Ford, and Readence (1981) have shown how Feature Analysis can be used as an alternative approach to teaching students word connotations. Perhaps the best use, however, of this strategy is when it is used as a means to reinforce the vocabulary and related concepts of text in a content area reading lesson (Readence and Searfoss 1980; Stieglitz and Stieglitz 1981). For example, if students were involved in a health unit on drugs, FA would be an excellent means to reinforce and review the likenesses and differences of the various drugs. After all, not all drugs are habit forming, create physical dependence, or are hallucinogens! Feature Analysis provides an effective means for examining these characteristics.

REFERENCES

Baldwin, R. S., J. C. Ford, and J. E. Readence. 1981. Teaching word connotations: An alternative strategy. *Reading World* 21:103–8. Describes and provides examples of Feature Analysis as a means to help students learn word connotations.

Johnson, D. D., and P. D. Pearson. 1978. *Teaching reading vocabulary*. New York: Holt, Rinehart & Winston. A text that explores vocabulary development in general and Feature Analysis in particular.

———. 1984. *Teaching reading vocabulary*. 2d ed. New York: Holt, Rinehart & Winston. An updated version of the aforementioned text.

Johnson, D. D., S. Toms-Bronowski, and S. D. Pittelman. 1983. An investigation of the effectiveness of semantic mapping and semantic feature analysis with intermediate grade level children. Program Report 83–3. Madison: Wisconsin Center for Education Research, University of Wisconsin. Presents the findings of a carefully conducted study of the use of the technique.

Readence, J. E., and L. W. Searfoss. 1980. Teaching strategies for vocabulary development. *English Journal* 69:43–46. Discusses the use of Feature Analysis as a means to extend vocabulary concepts in the post-reading portion of an instruction lesson.

Stieglitz, E. L., and V. S. Stieglitz. 1981. SAVOR the word to reinforce vocabulary in the content areas. *Journal of Reading* 25:46–51. Discusses Feature Analysis as a means to reinforce vocabulary in the content areas.

6

Study Skills Strategies

The Unit and Its Theme

One special form of reading is studying. Study-type reading is an attempt to organize text material in such a way as to enhance later attempts to review and retain it. Thus, students need to have access to strategies that will focus their attention on selected aspects of text, provide a format for organizing the text, and facilitate students' attempts to practice and utilize that material. Such strategies should include those techniques that enable students to deal both with information gleaned from text and with information received via the lecture method.

The Strategies

The five strategies discussed in this unit present various ways to help students study and retain text and text-related information. They range from a strategy that incorporates the use of annotations, to one that helps students independently set purpose for reading, to one that enables students systematically to take lecture notes.

REAP Technique

Designed to improve students' analytical reading skills, REAP also results in improved writing and study skills. The strategy consists of four basic steps: *R*ead, *E*ncode, *A*nnotate, *P*onder; thus, resulting acronym—REAP.

A Notetaking System for Learning

Much of what students learn in secondary and college classrooms comes from the instructor via the lecture method. Effective notetaking procedures can do much to aid students in learning and retaining a vast amount of information. Although the literature describes several notetaking methods, the authors have selected one technique for inclusion in this unit.

Herringbone Technique

A strategy best suited for the history classroom, the herringbone technique provides the students a logical means of outlining and thus remembering the events of history. Appropriate for students in the middle grades and above, the technique would be useful to all students initially, but it appears most beneficial to students who experience difficulty with organizing material.

Survey Technique

Designed as a spinoff of the SQ3R method of study, the survey technique is a strategy that could be a substitute for the preparation stage of the Instructional Framework or for the readiness stage of a Directed Reading Activity. The technique offers the teacher and students an opportunity to "walk through" the chapter together. Most useful with students who might find the material especially difficult, the Survey Technique also furnishes the teacher an opportunity to show the students a model of good study behavior.

SQ3R Method of Study

The reading literature describes a variety of study methods. Some techniques appear to be useful across all subject areas; others are specifically for individual content subjects. This unit discusses the SQ3R procedure and refers to several other study techniques.

REAP TECHNIQUE

Purpose

The REAP technique (Eanet and Manzo 1976) is designed to (1) improve the comprehension skills of readers by helping them synthesize an author's ideas into their own words and (2) develop students' writing ability as an aid for future study and recall of ideas they acquire through reading.

Rationale

The REAP (*R*ead, *E*ncode, *A*nnotate, *P*onder) technique starts from the premise that readers comprehend best when asked to communicate the ideas gleaned from a passage they have read. REAP is conceived as an alternative to the Directed Reading Activity and the Guided Reading Procedure, described earlier in this text.

Specifically, the REAP technique actively involves readers in processing the ideas an author has set down in print. The purpose is for readers to communicate in their own words an understanding of the text and discuss those ideas with others. In this way the readers internalize a text-based understanding. It is perceived that this internalization enhances the meaningful processing of those ideas, thus crystalizing the readers' own thinking concerning the author's message.

REAP uses writing as a vehicle to translate an author's ideas into the readers' own words, so this strategy also serves to enhance the writing skills of students. Additionally, these written translations may serve as the basis for continued study or for review of an author's ideas. Thus REAP, requiring active involvement with print, can encourage students' maturity and independence in reading.

Intended Audience

The REAP technique is intended for use from junior high through college. It may provide the basis for group instruction or may be adapted for individual use as a study method.

Description of the Procedure

The REAP technique consists of four stages:

R—*Reading* to discover the author's ideas;
E—*Encoding* the author's ideas into one's own language;
A—*Annotating* those ideas in writing for oneself or for sharing with others; and
P—*Pondering* the significance of the annotation.

Central to the REAP technique is developing students' ability to write annotations. Therefore, the discussion of the REAP strategy follows these steps: (1) writing annotations, (2) teaching students to write annotations, and (3) pondering the annotations.

1. Writing annotations

Writing annotations requires readers to interact with the ideas of the author, to synthesize them into their own language, and to set them down in writing. Eanet and Manzo (1976) and Manzo (1973) described several different types of annotations that students might use. Types include the heuristic annotation, summary annotation, thesis annotation, question annotation, critical annotation, intention annotation, and motivation annotation.

To serve as examples, annotations have been constructed for the following selection:

> We encourage children to act stupidly, not only by scaring and confusing them, but by boring them, by filling up their days with dull, repetitive tasks that make little or no claim on their attention or demands on their intelligence. Our hearts leap for joy at the sight of a roomful of children all slogging away at some imposed task, and we are all the more pleased and satisfied if someone tells us that the children don't really like what they are doing. We tell ourselves that this drudgery is good preparation for life, and we fear that without it children would be hard to "control." But why must this busywork be so dull? Why not give tasks that are interesting and demanding? Because, in schools where every task must be completed and every answer must be right, if we give children more demanding tasks they will be fearful and will instantly insist that we show them how to do the job. When you have acres of paper to fill up with pencil marks, you have no time to waste on the luxury of thinking. By such means children are firmly established in the habit of using only a small part of their thinking capacity. They feel that school is a place where they must spend most of their time doing dull tasks in a dull way.[1]

a. *Heuristic annotation*

> We encourage children to act stupidly, not only by scaring and confusing them, but by boring them . . .

The heuristic annotation depicts the essence of the author's message through the selection of the author's words. Like the above quotation, it should stimulate a reaction.

b. *Summary annotation*

> Schools may become more interesting places for children if they are provided with meaningful activities designed to promote thinking rather than dull, repetitive busywork.

1. J. Holt, *How Children Fail.* (New York: Pitman, 1964), 210−11.

The above annotation provides a summary of the selection by condensing the author's ideas on the type of activities children should face in school. The summary annotation omits examples, descriptions of presently used activities, and explanations of recommended school tasks. It presents only a synopsis of the author's main ideas.

c. *Thesis annotation*

If schools became places to think, they would challenge and threaten the status quo.

A thesis annotation is a precise statement of the selection's theme, the author's point of view. Use of this type entails detailing what the author is saying. The above statement attempts to do this briefly and incisively.

d. *Question annotation*

What do teachers consider good preparation for life? Why is there no time to work on "the luxury of thinking?" How do students react to school?

A question annotation involves addressing the germane ideas of a selection in question form. In the above annotation, the questions address the points in the passage by Holt.

e. *Intention annotation*

As Holt tries in his other writing, he attempts to convince his reader of his thesis by painting a negative picture of the status quo.

An intention annotation entails specifying the author's reasons for writing. The annotator considers what is given by the author and what is known of the author. It is obvious that the annotator has read other material by Holt.

f. *Motivation annotation*

Holt is trying to suggest what is wrong with schools and give a solution to the problem. It is his argument that schools are monotonous when they should be challenging students to think.

A motivation annotation is a statement in which the author's motives, biases, and perceptions are addressed. The above annotation speculates as to Holt's motives for writing the selection.

g. *Critical annotation*

Holt is right. Schools may become more interesting places for children if they provide experiences which challenge them to think.

> Clearly, school is more learning the system than learning to solve problems. Clearly, schooling is largely irrelevant.

The critical annotation details the author's point of view, the annotator's reaction to this position, and the basis for the annotator's reaction. In the above annotation, the annotator reacts positively to Holt and defines some reasons.

The different annotations may or may not be suitable for different selections. As Eanet and Manzo suggested ". . . some annotations are more suitable to some types of writing than are others" (p. 648). The teacher or annotator needs to address this possibility prior to proceeding with annotations.

2. Teaching strategies to write annotations

It is suggested that students cannot be expected to write annotations cogently without prior exposure to the process. That is, students must learn this skill and practice it before a teacher can expect them to use it successfully.

Eanet and Manzo (1976) recommended the following paradigm in teaching students to write annotations:

> Step One: Recognizing and defining.
> Step Two: Discriminating.
> Step Three: Modeling the process.
> Step Four: Practicing.

A Summary annotation illustrates the paradigm.

a. Step One: *Recognizing and defining.* The teacher asks students to read a short selection and then furnishes them with a Summary annotation. Using questioning techniques and discussion, the teacher should elicit from the students how the furnished annotation relates to the selection read. In lieu of whole-group instruction, the teacher may choose to have small groups of students attempt to work jointly at this task. In either case, the goal of the teacher is to aid students in formulating the concept of the Summary annotation.

b. Step Two: *Discriminating.* As in the previous step, the teacher asks the students to read another short selection. However, the teacher now presents them with multiple annotations. The recommended number is three annotations, one of which constitutes a good Summary annotation. The other two should be erroneous in some fashion—either too broad, too narrow, or too divergent from the ideas in the selection. Again through class discussion, students should choose the best annotation. They should justify their choice and explain why the other choices are unsatisfactory. Small groups are also a recommended alternative to the whole-group instructional situation. The task of discriminating between good and poor annotations will further refine students' skill with annotations.

c. Step Three: *Modeling the Process.* Students now read a third selection. The teacher demonstrates to the students how to write the Summary annotation effectively. It is most crucial that the teacher "walk" the students through this step by telling them the thought processes undertaken in writing the annotation. The teacher should demonstrate to the students the relationships between the major ideas so students will be able to write a cogent annotation, or rewrite it as necessary. This modeling process is essential in communicating what a good Summary annotation is, and what students should do to arrive at a good one.

d. Step Four: *Practicing.* The practicing step has two parts. First, the students read a new passage and individually write an annotation. Then, forming groups of three or four, students develop the best Summary annotation possible, using their individual attempts as the basis for this interaction. Students also may refer to the passage, if necessary. The total group then compares, discusses, and evaluates the final group products.

3. Pondering the annotations

This part of the annotation process corresponds to the "ponder" stage of the REAP strategy. The students "ponder," or process it, for personal study or for classroom activities. The annotation has now become a powerful tool for comprehension and study, limited only by teachers' imagination and students' needs.

Specifically, Eanet and Manzo (1976) recommend four uses of annotations. First, this technique may be useful in a reading class, either developmental or remedial, that uses individualized instruction. As the teacher works with individuals, the other students read individually from materials of their choice. Before the end of class, each student writes a Summary annotation on the material read that day. This process serves the students as a short review when they begin reading the next day. It also provides the basis for both an individual conference with the teacher and a progress check. When the students have read the whole book, they write a new, more comprehensive annotation that includes a critical evaluation and attach it to the book. This annotation will serve as an aid for other readers who choose to read the book.

Second, the instructor may adapt this annotation procedure for the school library. As students finish reading a book, they write an annotation, and the library keeps it on file. When new readers select a book, they can consult the annotations file in making their decision. The annotations can provide other students with information about a book before they read it.

Third, annotations may be used to prepare secondary or college English students in classes for writing projects. The annotations can serve as a foundation for more extensive critique writing. For example, students may read and annotate two or three articles that offer varied opinions on a topic of interest. Next, students would write a comparative essay or research paper on the topic, using the annotations as the basis.

Finally, the teacher may use the annotations as required readings to enhance students' study efforts on materials of importance in the curricula. This assignment promotes in-depth study and provides the basis for classroom discussion and review. These required annotations may also serve to improve the writing skills of students.

Cautions and Comments

Too often students approach their textbook reading and notetaking with a vague overall purpose such as "pull out main ideas." The REAP technique affords a systematic procedure by which teachers can guide their students' interactions with author's ideas. Specifically, this technique can serve to direct and record purposeful interactions between a reader and a text. REAP can guide the reader to use alternative annotations as a way to select appropriate procedures for gleaning, recording, and using textual information.

The strategy appears to have some major shortcomings. Specifically, many students may find the task of writing annotations both difficult and painstaking. Students who lack the ability to adequately derive main ideas from reading selections may find the task of writing certain annotations particularly arduous. Teachers desiring to use the REAP technique may wish to teach main idea skills to such students before proceeding. To this end, Moore and Readence (1980) provide a systematic procedure that may be useful for teaching students main idea skills. Obviously, the teacher should use the strategy selectively, with students for whom it is appropriate and with text for which it is relevant. If teachers use REAP in a lock-step fashion with all students, they may find the strategy either inappropriate or more difficult than the task they intended to teach.

REFERENCES

Eanet, M. 1978. An investigation of the REAP reading/study procedure: Its rationale and efficacy. In *Reading: Discipline Inquiry in Process and Practice*, edited by P. D. Pearson and J. Hansen. Twenty-seventh Yearbook of the National Reading Conference, Clemson: National Reading Conference, 229–32. Reports a study in which the efficacy of REAP is explored.

Eanet, M. G., and A. V. Manzo. 1976. REAP—A strategy for improving reading/writing study skills. *Journal of Reading* 19:647–52. Presents a detailed discussion of how to use the REAP technique in the classroom.

Manzo, A. V. 1973. CONPASS: English—A demonstration project. *Journal of Reading* 6:539–45. Describes the use of annotations as an aid to improving reading comprehension.

Moore, D. W., and J. E. Readence. 1980. Processing main ideas through parallel lesson transfer. *Journal of Reading* 23:589–93. Describes a procedure for teaching students of process main ideas.

A NOTETAKING SYSTEM FOR LEARNING

Purpose

The Notetaking System for Learning (Palmatier 1973) is designed to (1) provide students with a systematic means of organizing class notes and (2) provide a sound means for reviewing content information.

Rationale

Although there are certainly exceptions, many content classrooms at the secondary and college levels are structured around class lectures, supplemented by textbook assignments. Most traditional notetaking techniques consider only one portion of the class at a time; i.e., they deal with taking notes in lectures *or* with notetaking procedures for specific reading assignments. Palmatier's Notetaking System for Learning (NSL) is a flexible system that encourages the student to combine the two approaches.

Intended Audience

Although it is believed that some simplified notetaking procedures should be taught at an earlier point, the Notetaking System for Learning appears best suited for students in the ninth grade through college. It also would seem appropriate for above-average students in grades seven and eight.

Description of the Procedure

Obviously, in order for students to use any type of notetaking procedure, they need to have available the basic notetaking materials—paper and pencils. As many classroom teachers know, this is the point at which many notetaking strategies can and do break down.

It is suggested that students use only one side of 8½ × 11-inch loose-leaf notebook paper with a three-inch margin on the left side of the page. If this legal-line paper cannot be purchased, students can add their own margins to standard notebook paper. The following discussion of procedure will focus on these three major components of the system: (1) recording, (2) organizing, and (3) studying.

1. Recording

Notes generally are first recorded from the lecture, with reading notes added at a later time. The lecture notes are placed to the right of the three-inch marginal line. The specific format is best left to the individual student, but Palmatier (1973) does suggest the use of a format that utilizes both (a) subordination—a modified outlining procedure—and (b) space. Space will vary depending upon the degree of change between items presented. If the lecture information appears to flow easily from one idea to another, then little space is left between the noted ideas; however, at the point when the topic obviously changes course or when there is some confusion as to how the ideas tie together, the student would be advised to leave a larger space so that more information may be added later.

Again, the student should not use the back of the notebook paper. This will only cause confusion when the student later tries to organize or study the notes. The completed notetaking procedure should result in a format similar to the one shown in Figure 6−1. Note that each page should be numbered as the notes are recorded. This will avoid some confusion during the study portion of the procedure.

Figure 6−1

2. Organizing

If time is available, immediately following the lecture session the student should organize his or her notes while the ideas and details are fresh. The student has two tasks during this portion of the NSL procedure:

   a. *Labeling.* By examining separately each informational unit within the recorded notes, the student should be able to provide labels that briefly describe the information presented. Labels should be placed to the left side of the marginal line and directly in line with the appropriate recorded notes.
   b. *Adding.* Following the labeling process, Palmatier (1973) suggests that the student now insert important information from the text directly into the lecture notes. If adequate space has been provided between important ideas, the reading notes may be easily added to the lecture note page; if more space is needed, the back of the notebook paper can now be used in this integration process.

Following the above procedure, a page of notes now could resemble the example in Figure 6−2.

Figure 6-2

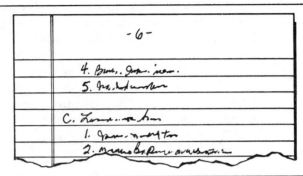

3. Studying

The Notetaking System for Learning not only provides a simple means for recording ideas, but also provides a systematic approach to the study of the notes. Since both lecture and reading notes are recorded within the system, the student will have no need to return to the text material or to shuffle back and forth between two sets of notes.

For study purposes, the notes are removed from the loose-leaf binder and spread out so that only the left hand margin of each page is visible. The labels now become the focal point for the study session.

The type of exam for which the student is studying can dictate the manner in which the notes are approached. For an objective test, the student might approach the labels at random, thus approximating the multiple choice, true-false, and matching questions on this type of exam. For an essay test, the student might approach the study task in a more organized manner, usually starting at the beginning of the notes and moving through them in the order in which they were presented. The labels in the left hand margin become the question stems for the purpose of study. A label is transformed into a question, which the student proceeds to answer. Verification is obtained by lifting the next page of notes and reading the information written to the right of the label. This procedure is followed throughout the study period. As the information on a page is learned, it can be returned to the loose-leaf notebook. Study concludes when all of the pages are back in their proper place in the notebook.

Cautions and Comments

Secondary teachers and college professors often complain about the inability of their students to take adequate notes. Yet it is rare indeed to find the word "notetaking" in a secondary text or in a school district's curriculum guide. Very simply, the skill is not taught; rather it is "assumed" the student will develop it.

Teachers at the secondary level who rely heavily upon the lecture method may want to spend a portion of their instructional time teaching the students how to take notes efficiently. The time investment should pay off in students more completely understanding the subject. Teachers will also be developing an important survival skill that their students will be sure to need in other course work.

In teaching a strategy such as the Notetaking System for Learning, it is important that it be presented early in the school year. To determine if the class as a whole needs such instruction, the teacher might conclude a lecture near the beginning of the first unit by asking the students to turn in their day's notes for the purpose of an informal evaluation. Two questions should be asked as each individual's notes are skimmed: (1) Has this student noted the essential concepts and supporting detail emphasized in the unit? (2) Is the material organized in a way that will lead to successful study of the material for testing purposes?

If the answer to either question is "no" for the majority of the students, then the decision to teach the process must be made. It is also cautioned that knowledge of main ideas and/or outlining may be prerequisite skills to the Notetaking System for Learning. Therefore, effective implementation of NSL may not be accomplished before such abilities are developed. In conclusion, it must be emphasized that better notetaking practices do not necessarily result simply by urging students to do a better job. Anderson and Armbruster (1984) have also cautioned that for any notetaking strategy to be effective, attention focusing and purposeful information processing are required.

REFERENCES

Anderson, T. H., and B. B. Armbruster. 1984. Studying. In *Handbook of reading research*, edited by P. D. Pearson. New York: Longman. Discusses the efficacy of notetaking as a study strategy.

Palmatier, R. A. 1971. Comparison of four notetaking procedures. *Journal of Reading* 14:235–40, 258. Compares four notetaking procedures for relative effectiveness and efficiency.

———. 1973. A Notetaking System for Learning. *Journal of Reading* 17: 36–39. Presents a detailed explanation for a notetaking procedure that has proved useful to secondary and college students.

HERRINGBONE TECHNIQUE

Purpose

The Herringbone technique is a structured outlining procedure designed to help students organize important information in a text chapter.

Rationale

For many students, the quantity of information contained within a twenty-page content chapter can be overwhelming. By providing structure, a content teacher can assist students in remembering the important information within the chapter. The Herringbone strategy suggests that the important information can be obtained by asking six very basic comprehension questions—Who? What? When? Where? How? and Why? By providing an outline to record this information, the teacher provides the structure for notetaking and for future study of the recorded information.

Intended Audience

The Herringbone technique is intended for use with students in the fourth through twelve grade levels. As with several strategies within this unit, the procedures appears most appropriate for those students whose reading levels are below the difficulty level of the adopted text.

Description of the Procedure

The classroom teacher must first prepare for instruction. The important preparation questions (Herber 1978) include the following: (1) What are the major concepts that I want my students to understand at the conclusion of this chapter? (2) What are the important vocabulary terms that relate directly to these major concepts? (3) How will my students learn this information? and (4) As I consider the major concepts I have identified (see Question 1), and as I consider the ability and performance level of my class, which of the identified concepts do I expect all of my students to master and which do I expect only my better students to achieve?

Completing this preparation step gives the teacher a perspective as to what information will be important as the students are guided in the use of the Herringbone procedure.

Students may be prepared for the assignment by following the suggestions outlined in the preparation stage of the Instructional Framework or in the readiness stage of the Directed Reading Activity discussed in Unit 1. Once this has been accomplished, the students are introduced to the Herringbone form and its use.

Introduction of form

The Herringbone form, which can be mimeographed in large quantities on standard 8½ × 11-inch paper, appears in Figure 6–3.

The students are instructed that they will be seeking the answers to these questions and will be recording their answers on the Herringbone form as they read the chapter.

Initially, the classroom teacher could put the Herringbone form on a transparency and display it on a screen for all students to see. As the whole class "walks through" the strategy, the teacher writes in the information on the transparency as the students fill in their forms. With some groups or with whole classes, this "walk-through" procedure may involve only the first couple of

Figure 6–3

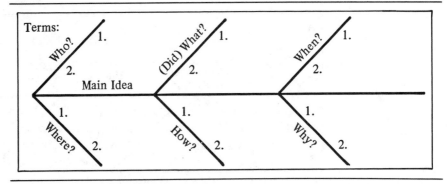

chapter subtopics, while with other groups the teacher and students may complete the whole chapter together.

Using the form

After the students have been sufficiently prepared for learning the information within the chapter and after they understand the structure of the form, they are ready to begin the reading and recording process. The students are advised to read the information seeking answers to the following expanded questions:

1. Who was involved? (Answer should yield the name of one or more persons or groups.)
2. What did this person or group do?
3. When was it done (the event discovered in Question 2)?
4. Where was it done?
5. How was it accomplished?
6. Why did it happen?

As students work through this procedure and record their answers, they should discover the important relationships within this information.

EXAMPLE

For a chapter on "The War against Germany" in a United States history text, students were advised to read the first main topic and record their answers to the six key questions. Thus, the first main topic, "The United States Enters the War," resulted in the recorded information in Figure 6–4.

Some subtopics will yield more than one important set of facts, as Figure 6–4 illustrates. Others may provide only one important piece of information.

Note also in the example that two terms that might cause some prob-

Figure 6-4

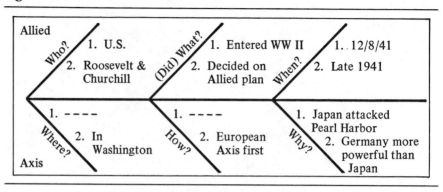

lems with some students were noted on the left-hand column of the form. By instructing students to record unfamiliar terms, the teacher discovers those terms that, even though they may have been pretaught, are confusing to the students and thus need to be taught, retaught, emphasized, and/or reinforced.

Follow-up

In addition to traditional follow-up activities, the Herringbone strategy appears to present some unique possibilities. In the chapter on "The War against Germany," students recorded the following information on their forms:

Who?   Germany
What?   Invaded USSR
When?   June 1941
Where? Leningrad, Moscow, Stalingrad
How?   ——
Why?   Thought could capture Russia

As with this example, textbook authors often do not provide all the information necessary to answer all the questions. In some instances the particular bit of information may not be important; in other instances, it may be very significant. The Herringbone form provides students and teachers alike with a visible display of information "gaps." If the teacher deems the missing information important, then students may be asked to infer the missing information and to pursue the answers through the formation of research teams.

Other answers provided by the text authors would be pursued in the same way. For example, the text authors' answer to the question, "*Why* did Germany invade the USSR?" might be considered rather superficial. The authors simply state that Germany invaded the USSR because Germany thought it could capture Russia. The classroom teacher might want to extend the search for understanding by asking, "But why did Germany think it could capture

Russia?" Predictions could be made by students, followed by attempts to search out information in other sources.

Finally, the Herringbone form contains the term "Main Idea" on its midline (see Figure 6–3). After the students have completed the chapter and their outline, they are asked to make a statement that would represent the main idea of the chapter. This step is similar to the final step in the Survey Technique described next. Using the history book example, the teacher might ask, "What one statement can you make that would tell what the authors are saying about the war against Germany?" One student's response: "The war was long and costly in terms of money and lives, but eventually resulted in the defeat of Germany by the Allied Forces."

Cautions and Comments

As described above, the Herringbone technique provides students with a structure for taking notes from a textbook chapter, for observing relationships, and for studying and remembering information. This high amount of structure appears valid only in situations where students might profit from such assistance. In particular, it would appear to be most effective when used alternatively with a number of techniques described in this unit and some described in Unit 1. Otherwise, where students need to develop their own strategies or where the text material is not "meaty," this technique may be inappropriate.

Again, in the initial stage of teaching this strategy, the teacher may need to "walk through" part or all of a chapter so that the students gain a sense of the type of information they should be seeking. With some groups or with whole classes, this form may become the structure for class learning; i.e., it is possible that the teacher will use the "walk-through" approach each time the Herringbone technique is used.

REFERENCES

Herber, H. L. 1978. *Teaching reading in content areas.* 2d ed. Englewood Cliffs, N.J.: Prentice-Hall. Provides specific suggestions for preparing a content lesson.

SURVEY TECHNIQUE

Purpose

The survey technique (Aukerman 1972) is intended to (1) provide the students with a systematic approach for previewing a content chapter and (2) provide the classroom teacher with an additional approach to use in preparing students to read the text.

Rationale

The acquisition of effective study skills is recognized as one of the major goals of upper-level reading instruction. The survey technique described by Aukerman (1972) provides the content teacher with a systematic means of walking the students through the first step of Robinson's (1961) SQ3R method of study. Specifically, the survey technique is designed to prepare the students for the reading of a text by arranging a whole-class overview of the textual material. By using the technique on numerous occasions throughout the school year, the teacher attempts to lead the student to understand the importance of previewing prior to reading.

Intended Audience

Although probably more useful at the secondary level, the survey technique may also be used at the upper elementary level. It could certainly be useful at this level when the students are scheduled to tackle an especially difficult chapter. As with most highly structured procedures, the technique would appear most valuable for those students who have difficulty with the text material.

Description of the Procedure

The survey technique serves as a substitute for the readiness stage of the Directed Reading Activity or the preparation stage of the Instructional Framework. The objective is to prepare the students for the actual reading of the text by arranging a whole-class overview procedure that results in an understanding of the total chapter content.

As with other instructional strategies discussed in this book, decisions must be made by the teacher as to what particular information to emphasize. By identifying the major understandings the students are to acquire in a given chapter, the content instructor becomes aware of those portions of the chapter to emphasize during the class survey.

Aukerman (1972) outlined a six-step procedure that may be used with any traditionally designed content textbook. The technique follows easily when the text chapter contains the following format: chapter title, introduction, main headings with subtopics, summary, review questions, and exercises.

With that format in mind, the teacher may adapt Aukerman's six-step procedure in this way.

1. Analysis of chapter title

After reading the title with the students, the instructor might ask questions such as "What do you think this chapter is going to be about?" "What do you already know about this topic?" "How do you see this chapter relating to the unit we just completed?" Regardless of reading ability, all students can participate in this type of activity.

2. Analysis of subtitles

The teacher will note each of the subtitles so that each student will understand the overall outline for the chapter topic. This preview may also involve the second step in Robinson's (1961) SQ3R method—the question step. Students could be asked to turn each of the headings into a question. The resulting questions provide the students with specific purposes for reading the text under each of the headings. For example, the subtitle "Advantages of Cotton Production" result in the question "What were the advantages of cotton production?"

Questions may be developed by the class as a whole and placed on the chalkboard or on an overhead projector. After using the survey technique on several occasions, the content instructor might request that each student develop his or her own set of questions. Whether as a whole-class or as an individual activity, the development of questions results in a student-produced guide that should be extremely valuable when students are later asked to read and study the chapter in more detail.

3. Analysis of visuals

Often some of the most important information in a chapter may be found in the visuals of the chapter. Many students ignore these aids, while others may not possess the necessary skills to interpret the pictorial information. This third step in the survey technique gives the content teacher an opportunity to stress the importance of these visual aids and, if necessary, to teach the students how to obtain information from them. The following bar graph example, Figure 6–5, might appear in a seventh grade geography book.

The teacher would ask questions to determine if the students were able to glean information from the bar graph. Two questions might be: "What is the major cotton producing state in the United States?" "What do you suppose the authors of our text meant by the term 'Expressed in 1,000-Bale Units?' " If the students have difficulty with these two questions, the teacher could take a brief period of time to describe the major features of a bar graph and to show students how much information may be obtained from such a simple figure. With the graph shown in the particular example, it would probably be necessary to explain the numerical system so that students would understand that they would need to multiply the number of units depicted on the graph times 1,000 to determine the actual number of bales produced by each state; i.e., in 1974, California actually produced $1,000 \times 2,595 = 2,595,000$ bales of cotton. Other questions might include the following: "Where are the majority of the

Figure 6−5

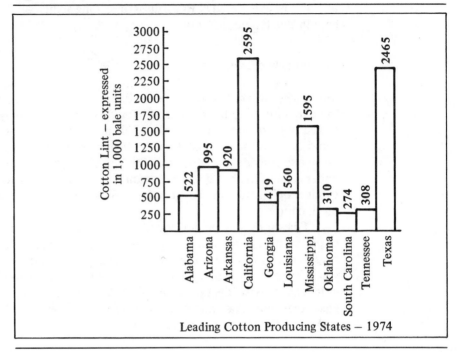

Leading Cotton Producing States − 1974

leading cotton producing states located?" "Why do you think Kentucky is not one of the major cotton producing states?"

4. Introductory paragraph(s)

Many textbook authors use one or more introductory paragraphs to set forth the important ideas within the chapter. Students might be asked to read this information silently. The discussion that follows should concentrate on how the information in the introduction fits with the information discovered in the first three steps of the procedure. A question like the following might be used: "Now that we have read this introductory material, can you see how this information supports some of the things we discovered as we surveyed the chapter?"

5. Concluding paragraph(s)

Generally, the final paragraphs of a content text chapter provide a summary of the chapter content. By reading the summary *before* reading the total chapter in detail, students receive additional confirmation of what they discovered in all the previous steps of their survey.

6. Deriving the main idea

Aukerman suggests that out of Steps 4 and 5, reading and discussing the introductory and concluding paragraphs, the class as a whole should develop a concise statement that could stand as the main idea of the chapter. The statement should be written out on the board or put on a transparency for all to see. Students should now be ready to pursue a more detailed study of the chapter content.

Cautions and Comments

The survey technique appears to be worthwhile in its own right as well as an excellent means of introducing students to the initial phases of the SQ3R method of study and of demonstrating the value of this technique for studying content material. In addition, as instructors observe students using the Survey Technique more effectively, instructors could gradually withdraw this structure, thus allowing the students to take more responsibility for their own learning.

A minor shortcoming of the procedure is the exclusion of review questions at the end of a chapter. Assuming they are worthwhile, they could be used as a check of the efficacy of surveying other facets of a chapter prior to reading the text. For example, one effective way of using end-of-chapter questions within Aukerman's survey technique would be to deal with these questions immediately after a discussion of the chapter title. The teacher or a student could read aloud each question to the class and ask the students to note briefly what they think the answer to that question might be. If students have no idea of the answer to a particular question, they are advised to leave it blank. After each question has been considered individually by each student, and possibly after a small group discussion, the instructor can deal with the questions in a whole-class discussion. By using the chapter questions in this manner, the teacher is saying to the students, "Let's find out what the author thinks is important in this chapter and let's see how much of this information we already know." Thus, students have an opportunity to review their previous knowledge of the topic before they move on to more detailed study of the unit.

Following this procedure, the remaining five steps of the survey technique could be used to gain further information on the topic. After the main idea has been derived, the class could return to the questions at the end of the chapter to discover how many new answers resulted from the survey procedure. It is not unusual for students to answer correctly 20 to 30 percent of the questions during their initial attempt at them and answer another 20 to 30 percent after surveying the chapter.

REFERENCES

Aukerman, R. C. 1972. *Reading in the secondary school classroom*. New York; McGraw-Hill, 47−62. Presents a detailed discussion of how the survey technique might be used by the content teacher.

Robinson, F. P. 1961. *Effective study*. Rev. ed. New York: Harper & Row.
Provides a detailed description of the SQ3R method of study.

SQ3R METHOD OF STUDY

Purpose

The purpose of the SQ3R method of study as developed by Robinson (1946) is to (1) provide students with a systematic approach to study type reading and (2) promote more efficient learning of assigned reading materials.

Rationale

High school and college instructors have for years lamented the fact that the majority of their students lack an efficient, systematic method for studying a textbook assignment. It would appear that some general method of study would be better than no method at all. One of the first, and by far the most popular, study methods described in the professional literature was developed by Robinson (1946). The SQ3R method of study is designed to lead students systematically through the study of an assigned text chapter by taking advantage of the format of most textual material and using reading techniques assumed to be efficient and effective for these purposes.

Intended Audience

As a viable study procedure, the SQ3R method of study appears best suited for those students who are studying content chapters in a self-contained classroom or in a departmentalized situation in the upper grades. Although the survey portion of the procedure can be presented in the earlier grades, the total technique appears most suitable for students in grades four and above.

Description of the Procedure

As stated in the Rationale section, the SQ3R method of study was designed to take advantage of the consistent format in most traditional content textbooks. Each chapter generally contains a title, an introduction, a number of headings and subheadings, a concluding or summary statement, and some questions or problems posed by the textbook author(s) at the end of the chapter. This format leads naturally to the five steps that make up the SQ3R procedure: (1) survey, (2) question, (3) read, (4) recite, and (5) review.

1. Survey

Perhaps the most important single element in the procedure is the initial survey or preview step. The survey should provide each student with an overview of the chapter content. The survey step should take the students logically through the chapter, seeking to answer these questions: "What is this chapter about?" "What kind of information does the author tell us about this subject?"

The survey step then requires the student to read and think about the chapter title, the introductory paragraph(s), the headings and subheadings, the concluding paragraph, and the end-of-chapter questions. In addition, students are encouraged to survey the pictorial information within the chapter.

At the conclusion of this step, the students should have a general understanding of the chapter content. The amount of time devoted to the survey of a particular chapter depends on the length and complexity of the topic and on the reader's own skill. Something in the range of five to fifteen minutes generally appears appropriate.

2. Question

Students now should be ready for a more detailed study of the chapter. The question step provides a purpose for reading the material in more detail. Very simply, the student selects the first boldface topic in the chapter, reads it, and proceeds to restate it in the form of a question. An example may help to illustrate this procedure. The subtopic "Causes of World War I" would become in question form, "What were the causes of World War I?" The student now is ready to move to the third step.

3. Read

The first of the three "R" steps is to read the material immediately following the first subtopic. The purpose of this reading is to find the answer to the question posed in Step 2. With this very specific question in mind, students will tend to move fairly rapidly through the material in pursuit of the answer. Once they have finished reading the material under the first heading, students are ready to move to Step 4 of the procedure.

4. Recite

In Steps 2 and 3 above, each student formulated a question using the first subtopic in the chapter and then read to find the answer to the question. At this point, students are asked to pause and reflect on the answer. Students are encouraged to answer their question in their own words. This recitation is also the point at which students may record brief notes in their notebook for later review and study. Students then would repeat Steps 2–4 as they work through the remainder of the chapter.

5. Review

Immediately upon the completion of Steps 2, 3, and 4 for the final subtopic of the chapter, the student should spend approximately five minutes reviewing the notes and attempt to recall the main points of the chapter. The student then reads each main heading and tries to remember the supporting or explanatory information. Later reviews will also be helpful aids for long-term remembering.

Cautions and Comments

Two of the major difficulties associated with the SQ3R method of study have been (1) the shortage of instructional procedures for ensuring appropriate use and (2) the teacher's inability to convince students of the value of such a procedure (Adams, Carnine, and Gersten 1982). Although a number of upper-level teachers have taught the method to their students, the question remains, "How many students regularly use the procedure?" or "How many effectively use it?" Possibly, students may find the procedure tedious. Possibly, the procedure may become an end to itself rather than serve as a useful tool that is to be fitted to the reading task at hand.

Indeed, the use of SQ3R must be developed in relevant situations. As the need arises, one approach might be to begin by using the Survey Technique (discussed in this unit) with the whole class, then add the question and read steps when the students have seen the value of the survey step and are using it on their own.

Finally, it should be mentioned that there are numerous alternatives to the SQ3R method. Some of these may be more appropriate than SQ3R for a particular subject area. Among the alternative study procedures are: (1) OK4R (Pauk 1974); (2) Panorama (Edwards 1973); (3) PQRST (Spache and Berg 1966); and (4) PQ4R (Thomas and Robinson 1977).

REFERENCES

Adams, A., D. Carnine, and R. Gersten. 1982. Instructional strategies for studying context area texts in the intermediate grades. *Reading Research Quarterly* 18:27−55. Study investigating the effectiveness of SQ3R in middle school classrooms.

Edwards, P. 1973. Panorama: A study technique. *Journal of Reading* 17: 132−35. Source for Panorama (Purpose, Adaptability, Need to Question, Overview, Read, Annotate, Memorize, Assess) study technique.

Pauk, W. 1974. *How to study in college*. 2d ed. Boston: Houghton Mifflin. Source for OK4R (Overview, Key Ideas, Read, Recite, Reflect, Review) study technique.

Robinson, F. P. 1946. *Effective study*. New York: Harper and Bros. Introduces the use of the SQ3R method to aid students in their study.

———. 1961. *Effective study*. Rev. ed. New York: Harper and Bros. Revised edition of the previously cited text with examples of diagnostic tests and practice exercises.

————. 1962. *Effective reading*. New York: Harper and Bros. Describes a wide range of study skills, including SQ3R, to enhance the reading ability in subject matter areas.

Spache, G. D., and P. C. Berg. 1966. *The art of efficient reading*. New York: Macmillan. Source for PQRST (Preview, Question, Read, Summarize, Text) study techniques.

Thomas, E. L., and H. A. Robinson. 1977. *Improving reading in every class*. 2d ed. Boston: Allyn and Bacon. Source for PQ4R (Preview, Question, Read, Reflect, Recite, Review) study technique.

APPENDIX

DIAGNOSTIC USE OF A STUDY SKILLS STRATEGY

Illustration: Informal assessment of study skills

A student, Thomas, was given an assignment to read pages 301 to 305 in his history textbook. He was given a paper and pencil and told that he would be given a test on the material.

Thomas read to page 303, but did not read pages 304 and 305. Thomas failed to use a provided overview for the selection, survey technique, the questions at the end of the section, or the notes; but he did refer to the picture and graphic aids. When given a test on the material, Thomas failed to read the test directions; he proceeded to circle an answer rather than underline possible answers. His performance seemed mediocre. When Thomas was halfway through the test, he was permitted to return to his textbook to help him find the answers and to recheck other answers. He did not use the book until he had started the next-to-the-last question. This was a question about Orville Wright. Thomas scanned the selection and the went to the index to look up "Orville." He then was instructed to look for "Wright." He found the page number but still could not find the answer. Next, Thomas was directed to suggest and use selected references to learn more about the topic. He offered to use these: the dictionary to learn more about the meaning of a word; encyclopedias to learn more about the topic; and an atlas to locate places mentioned in the text. When told to describe and refer to these reference sources, it was apparent that he was familiar with them and could use them profitably. When asked how often he used this material, he said, "Rarely."

From an analysis of his performance, it seems Thomas makes limited and ineffective use of study skills. He scans, uses visual aids, and knows about the use of an index; however, he does not preview, vary reading rate, take notes, outline, or follow written directions. To help Thomas study more efficiently and effectively, the SQ3R method of study or a modification might be used. The five steps of SQ3R should result in Thomas' fixing important points in his memory. A modification of SQ3R might emphasize the value of prereading material—skimming through the pages to be read, reading headings and sub-heading, summarizing paragraphs, or formulating questions to guide reading. In addition, Thomas should be shown and given opportunities to improve his organizing, outlining, summarizing, note-taking, and test-taking skills. To guide his reading, he might be encouraged to ask himself the following question. Prior to reading, he might ask: What do I already know about this subject? After and during reading, he might ask: What do I now know about this subject? What else do I want or need to know? How might I use this information?

7

Strategies and Practices for Teaching Reading as a Language Experience and with Shared Books

UNIT OVERVIEW

The Unit and Its Theme

For many years teachers have recognized the worth of the child's own oral language and experiences as basic ingredients in beginning reading instruction. As far back as 1908, Edmund Huey reported the use of a sentence method that drew on the child's language and experiences to describe pictures. Through the first half of this century, numerous educators cited and recommended an experience-based approach to teaching reading (e.g., Storm and Smith 1930; Gans 1941; Lamoreaux and Lee 1943). In recent years, interest in using the language and experience of children has continued to grow. Researchers and educators in their search for the *one* best method for teaching reading have turned their attention to language acquisition and the psycholinguistic nature of the reading process. In the middle of the 1960s, the resulting approach became widely recognized and identified by its now familiar label, "the language experience approach." In the 1970s and early 1980s, the approach has become widely used throughout the world. For example, Breakthrough to Literacy developed for use in Great Britain became widely used throughout the British Commonwealth (Mackay, Thompson, and Schaub 1970). Various offshoots of the approach that appeared as developments in other areas have dove-tailed with the approach. For example, the procedure has been accepted for use with adolescents (e.g., McWilliams and Smith 1981), used in conjunction with word processors (e.g., Barber 1982), and specific strategies developed for extending comprehension abilities with the procedure (Sulzby 1980).

217

As these developments occurred with the language experience approach, researchers began exploring more intensely infant encounter with print in the environment and during shared reading experiences with parents. What has emerged in conjunction with these developments are approaches that further capitalize on the language experiences of young children.

The rationale of these approaches is based on the notion that children are born with a prowess for language acquisition and that this prowess can and should be directed toward the acquisition of reading abilities. To this end, proponents of the language experience approach, shared book experiences, and the role of environmental print advocate taking advantage of the experiences that children bring to reading. By conveying these experiences through language, children can move back and forth from oral to written expression. From this foundation, children develop quite naturally the ability and interest to read widely, deeply, and fluently.

The implementation of the language experience approach, shared book experience, and environmental print require teacher understanding of students' experiences and abilities with language. The language experience approach involves facilitating—rather than teaching—children "how to learn to read" or "how to read." In other words, to teach reading as a language experience requires that the teacher respond to students as they teach themselves about reading. Teacher-directed activities should neither hinder learning nor distort appropriate reading behavior. With these ideas in mind, teachers might review the suggestions of Allen, Ashton-Warner, Holdaway, and Stauffer, and then possibly generate their own strategies.

The Strategies

The present unit describes five strategies for teaching reading as a language experience. These strategies represent several of the major variations of this approach.

Allen's Language Experiences in Communication

The Language Experiences in Communication represent an attempt by Roach Van Allen to develop a comprehensive language-based approach to reading. Most people credit Allen with nurturing the evolution of the language experience approach. Allen's intent has been to develop an approach that provides the language competencies essential to promote reading. In comparison with others, this approach provides the most comprehensive and detailed suggestions for teaching reading as a language experience.

Ashton-Warner's Organic Reading

Organic Reading is an experience-centered approach to reading instruction based upon Sylvia Ashton-Warner's teaching experiences with Maori children in New Zealand. It is designed to bridge the gap between the language world of the child and the language world of books through the use of each child's key vocabulary.

Stauffer's Language-Experience Approach

The Language-Experience Approach represents Russell Stauffer's conceptualization of the language experience approach for teaching beginning reading. His approach focuses on the use of individual- and group-dictated stories, the use of word banks and the use of creative writing activities. As a beginning reading approach, it can serve either to supplement or to substitute for traditional basal reading programs.

Shared Book Experience

Shared Book Experience adopts the principles of prebook experiences between young children and their parents to the classroom. As described by Doake (1985) and Holdaway (1979), Shared Book Experience is intended as a means of establishing early reading experiences that capitalize on the children's natural prowess with stories and that dovetail story experiences with other language activities.

Patterned Language Approach

Patterned Language Approach by Bridge adopts the use of predictable story material and a structured language experience approach to provide teachers with a whole-part procedure for introducing students to reading. The procedure is intended for use with beginning readers to develop an initial vocabulary, as well as readers' use of meaning cues, syntactical cues, and graphophonic features of words.

REFERENCES

Barber, B. 1982. Creating BYTES of language. *Language Arts* 59:472–75.

Gans, R. 1941. *Guiding children's reading through experiences*. New York: Teachers College.

Huey, E. G. 1908. *The psychology and pedagogy of reading*. New York: Macmillan.

Lamoreaux, L., and D. M. Lee. 1943. *Learning to read through experiences*. New York: Appleton-Century-Crofts.

McKay, D., B. Thompson, and P. Schaub. 1970. *Breakthrough to literacy: Programme in linguistics and English teaching*. London: Schools Council (Longman).

McWilliams, L., and D. Smith. 1981. Decision stories. *Journal of Reading* 25: 142–45.

Storm, G. E., and N. B. Smith. 1930. *Reading activities in primary grades*. Boston: Ginn.

Sulzby, E. 1980. Using children's dictated stories to aid comprehension. *Reading Teacher 33*: 772–78.

ALLEN'S LANGUAGE EXPERIENCE APPROACH IN COMMUNICATION

Purpose

The Language Experience in Communication represents the language experience approach as advocated by Roach Van Allen (1976). It is designed to develop the language competencies essential for the promotion of reading. To this end, it provides each child with opportunities to (1) experience communication in various situations, (2) study aspects of communication, and (3) relate the ideas of others to self.

Rationale

Historically, the writings and material of Roach Van Allen have been largely responsible for this approach's recognition and evolution. Allen's rationale for the language experience approach stems largely from a project sponsored by the Department of Education, San Diego County, California, where researchers pursued the question, "Of all the language experiences available for study in the elementary school years, which ones have the greatest contribution to make to reading?" This work served to identify twenty essential language experiences and give the approach its now familiar label, "language experience."

With the approach's evolution, these twenty experiences have been organized into a design for a total language arts/communication curriculum. Figure 7–1 shows its design (Allen 1976, 13). Within the design, the twenty language experiences fall within a framework of three strands and occur through the development of four types of activities. The three strands are experiencing communication, studying communication, and relating communication of others to self. The four types of activities integral to the development of these experiences are language acquisition, language prediction, language recognition, and language production.[1]

1. Language acquisition is directed toward increasing students' inventory of words, knowledge of ways to express themselves, and ability to explain the unfamiliar. Language prediction

Figure 7-1

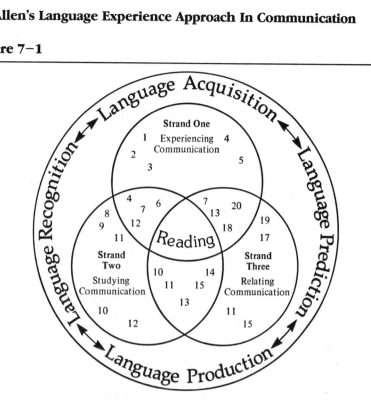

Reading in a Language Experience Approach

I. Experiencing Communication

1. Oral sharing of ideas
2. Visual portrayal of experiences
3. Dramatization of experiences
4. Responding rhythmically
5. Discussing and conversing
6. Exploring writing
7. Authoring individual books

II. Studying Communication

8. Recognizing high-frequency words
9. Exploring spelling
10. Studying style and words
11. Studying language structure
12. Extending vocabularies
13. Reading non-alphabetic symbols

III. Relating Communication of Others to Self

14. Listening to and reading language of others
15. Comprehending what is heard and read
16. Organizing ideas
17. Assimilating and integrating ideas
18. Searching out and researching multiple sources
19. Evaluating communication of others
20. Responding in personal ways

entails developing students' abilities to anticipate aspects of language and language patterns in their reading and listening. Language recognition is directed toward having students see the relationship between their language and the printed language of others. It includes developing their awareness of the characteristics of print and certain word identification skills. Language production involves having the student communicate through a variety of different media, associating most communications with speaking and writing, and realizing that ideas can be expressed, written, and read.

The implementation of Allen's curriculum design is guided by certain principles and assumptions about language and the learner, and the interactive nature of the two. The assumption is that students acquire reading and writing skills in the same way they acquire oral language skills. It is suggested that teachers recognize that students vary in language and language acquisition in accordance with their habits, age, socioeconomic group, and geographic region; teachers should further recognize that language changes slowly, continuously, creatively, and personally. To this end, it is Allen's premise that the "one big responsibility of a teacher at any level of instruction is to help each child to habituate, and to internalize certain truths about self and language" (Allen 1976, 52). The conceptualization of these truths became the approach's trademark. This conceptualization was:

What I can think about, I can talk about.

What I can say, I can write (or someone can write about).

What I can write, I can read.

I can read what others write for me to read.

(Allen and Allen 1966, Level 1, 6)

In more recent years this conceptualization has evolved into the following:

I can think about what I have experienced and imagined.

I can talk about what I think about.

What I can talk about I can express in some other form.

Anything I can record I can tell through speaking or reading.

I can read what I can write by myself and what other people write for me to read.

As I talk and write, I use some words over and over and some not so often.

As I talk and write, I use some words and clusters of words to express my meanings.

As I write to represent the sounds I make through speech, I use the same symbols over and over.

Each letter of the alphabet stands for one or more sounds that I make when I talk.

As I read, I must add to what an author has written if I am to get full meaning and inherent pleasure from print.

From: Roach Van Allen, *Language Experiences in Communication*. Copyright © 1976 by Houghton Mifflin Company. Reprinted by permission.

Intended Audience

Allen's language experience approach can be used with students of all ages and abilities. It provides for a total language arts curriculum that can be implemented within a single group, a whole classroom, or across a whole school. The approach works with whole-class, group, or individual instruction.

Description of the Procedure

According to Allen, it is not his intention to suggest exactly how to develop a language experience approach, but to suggest ways it might be implemented. In so doing, he assumes that teachers understand the philosophy of this approach, its curriculum rationale, learning center organization, and the use of multiple materials.

The language classroom proposed by Allen can be characterized by direct and indirect teaching activities within the framework of an instructional schedule. The direct and indirect teaching procedures entail the use of (1) patterns of teacher-pupil interaction, (2) learning centers, and (3) planned programming. These provide the skeleton or organizational framework on which the instructional schedule clings. For purposes of discussion, the organizational framework is presented, and a presentation of specific teaching suggestions follows.

Organizational framework

1. *Patterns of Teacher-Pupil Interactions*.

Depending upon the nature of the activity, Allen suggests whole-class, group, or individual organizational patterns. Whole-class activities are suggested for the following:

a. Reading aloud to or by children,
b. Oral discussion of topics of interest,
c. Oral composition of stories,
d. Films, filmstrips, and other audiovisual presentations,
e. Introduction and demonstrations of games or learning centers,
f. Seminars on various skills, and
g. Singing, rhymes, choral reading, or unison reading.

Group activities are suggested for the following:

a. Teacher taking dictation for one child,
b. Children working, reading, or playing games with each other,
c. Teacher reading with individuals or groups,
d. Meeting a group's skill needs,
e. Completing work initiated with class,
f. Editing manuscripts for publication, and
g. Planning and rehearsing dramatizations.

Individual activities are suggested for the following:

a. Conferring with students about writing individual books,
b. Conferring with students concerning their progress,

    c. Helping with spelling or word recognition, and

    d. Taking dictation from individuals for whom sharing would be inappropriate.

2. *Learning Centers.*

To meet the specific needs of the approach, Allen suggests and describes a variety of permanent and temporary learning centers for the language classroom. Several of his suggestions are described below.

    a. *Strand learning centers.* Once children have internalized the curriculum rationale, large centers made up of subcenters are suggested for each strand. For example, within a larger center for self expression (Strand One), there might be various subcenters for directing art expression, creative writing, and creative dramatics. Within a center for language study (Strand Two), there might be subcenters for editing manuscripts, review of language skills, and dictation experiences. Within a third, larger center for reflection (Strand Three), there might be subcenters for leisure reading, puppets, listening, and reading instruction.

    b. *The discussion center.* Allen sees the discussion center as the hub of the language classroom. It is where the teacher introduces activities, stimulates interest, shares stories, establishes classroom procedures, and evaluates the program. It is where the students share and present ideas to other classmates.

    c. *The arts and crafts center.* An arts and crafts center is suggested to provide the students a "treasure house" of creative materials and to serve as a "launching pad" for expression. This center is where children express themselves through various media within a recreational setting. Allen sees this expression as furnishing the raw materials essential for speaking, listening, reading, and writing.

    d. *The discovery center.* A discovery center serves to highlight the language of science and encourages children to discover new things or look at familiar things with new perspectives. Toward these ends, it is equipped with microscopes, magnifying glasses, and collections of plants, insects, and minerals.

    e. *The dramatization center.* A dramatization center serves to encourage children to discover themselves and relate to others through dramatization. The center is equipped with masks, puppets, and clothing.

    f. *The language study center.* A language study center provides students a variety of different activities by which to acquire aspects of language, such as word study, language anticipation, grammar, and sight words.

    g. *Reading research center.* A reading research center provides the students a place to browse, research, and read a variety of material. Intended for relaxation reading and research, it contains reference material, recreational reading materials, books written by the children, and magazines.

h. *Writing/publishing center.* A writing/publishing center is a place where children find both resources and motivation. Here children are stimulated to write, edit, review, and publish manuscripts. Here, newspapers, magazines, and previously published books of other children might be located.

Allen provides a number of other suggestions for learning centers that might be activated with program planning. Among his major suggestions are a music center, a cooking center, a viewing/listening center and, for relaxation and contemplation, a quiet place.

3. *Program Planning.*

Program planning is another essential aspect of Allen's organizational framework for teaching reading as a language experience. Program planning serves to structure learning experiences; for this purpose, Allen provides guidelines for recording, charting, and implementing the language experience program. His specific guidelines include the following suggestions.

a. Major language goals should be selected and implemented regularly and systematically. For example, language goals should be selected from each of the three strands and emphasized for no less than one week. Over a month or six weeks, each of the twenty language experience substrands should be emphasized by the teacher.
b. To serve the language concepts being emphasized, the teacher should develop learning centers to meet the students' needs and adjust the class grouping plans to afford maximum benefits.
c. Teacher-pupil interactions should be suited to the activities and needs of the students.
d. Evaluation procedures should be selected that can assess the program in terms of its objectives.

The chart in Figure 7–2 is suggested by Allen to guide program planning (Allen 1976, 88).

Specific teaching suggestions

In addition to the organizational framework, Allen makes several specific teaching suggestions for establishing certain learning experiences. In an effort to provide a representative and detailed examination of some essential aspects of Allen's approach, his suggestions for dictated stories are presented.

Suggestions for dictated stories. Dictated stories are an integral part of Allen's language experience approach. They afford students the opportunity to learn about language through experiencing, studying, and reflecting on oral communications.

Figure 7−2

Name_____ Class_____ Dates_____ to_____

Theme or language emphasis: _____

Activities from the Three Strands	Classroom Organization*			Learning Centers Activated† (with materials and equipment needed)	Evaluation‡			
	TC	SG	I		In	CR	St	PC
Experiencing communication								
Studying communication								
Relating communication of others to self								
Other activities								

*TC – total class   †Learning centers available: Discussion, Arts   ‡In – informal inventory
 SG – small group   and Crafts, Cooking, Dramatization, Game,   CR – criterion reference
   I – individuals   Reading/Research, Viewing/Listening,   St – standardized test
                      Writing/Publishing, A Quiet Place   PC – personal conference

From: Roach Van Allen, *Language Experiences in Communication.*
Copyright © 1976 by Houghton Mifflin Company. Reprinted by permission.

Allen breaks his suggestions for dictated stories into thirteen basic steps. They are:

1. Visit with the student for the purpose of discussing a topic of interest. Have students tell the names for things and describe their color, size, shape, function, parts, feelings, taste, smell, quantity, and related actions or events.
2. Decide whether the goal is for the student to provide description or to tell a story of some kind. If telling a story is the goal, have the student tell the whole story; then decide whether to write all of the student's ideas or some of them. Allen points out that often the goals for the dictation can be served by writing only one or two of the student's ideas. As the stories or labels are written, the teacher and student should talk about the

letters, their names, their formation, the sounds they represent, and their structure. As Allen (1973) suggests:

Talk about alphabet symbols you are using to represent the sounds the child made. (Let other children listen.) Let it be known that the letters have names, that some words begin with capital letters, that the same letters are used over and over as the first letters of words, that the same words appear over and over, that some ending sounds appear over and over, and they may tell us "how many" or "when." (P. 1)

3. After writing the story or the student's ideas, read the text back to the student and ask if the text is what the students said. The student might be asked to read along or to read some words or sentences alone.
4. Display the students' ideas or stories in the room and invite the students either to tell about their ideas or stories or to read them to the group. Some sentences might be read in unison to show the proper phrasing during reading. Have students compare their stories for word study. For example, students might study two or three characteristics of words, such as words that are the same, words the rhyme, words that begin or end the same, words with similar meanings, and words that are names. Allen suggests that teachers and students might identify these characteristics by underlining with different colored pens.
5. Students might be invited either to read words, phrases or sentences, or to read along in unison. Allen points out that involvement is more important at this point than correctness or the identification of poor readers.
6. The teacher or students might identify words that appear five or more times in students' stories and place them on a chart entitled "Words We All Use." Allen suggests this chart can be used as an aid for developing a reading vocabulary, as a source for word games, as a resource for the correct spelling of words, and as a way to determine if the student is ready for book reading. In terms of the latter purpose, Allen suggests a student is ready for book reading only when the vocabulary on this chart matches the vocabulary of books.
7. The students' dictated stories are copied onto ditto masters, duplicated, bound, and distributed to each student. Eight or ten stories are suggested for each book.
8. When students become interested in writing, Allen suggests they trace their recorded story.
9. After tracing, students might be encouraged to copy stories on spaces left between each line.
10. The students move from copying below each line to copying on a separate sheet of paper.
11. The students write their own stories on the chalkboard.
12. A group or the whole class listens to the stories and makes suggestions for editing. The edited story is written on a story strip and displayed.

13. Students involve themselves in writing and refining their own stories at the Writing Center. The Writing Center can include for those students who cannot write, independent tracing, copying, and other activities.

Cautions and Comments

Allen (1976) suggests that there are certain features about the language experience approach to teaching communication that distinguish it from traditional approaches to reading and from other aspects of language experience approaches. These include:

1. Students' oral language grows and is used to develop language acquisition, production, recognition, and prediction abilities;
2. Vocabulary control occurs naturally rather than artificially through the students' natural use and acquisition of the vocabulary they use;
3. Students' vocabulary acquisition is accelerated through developing an understanding of words and language, rather than through drills;
4. Individualization, grouping, and teaching patterns vary with students' individual and group needs and not solely with their abilities;
5. In comparison with other language experience approaches, the language experience approach to teaching communication affords a comprehensive curriculum design for creating learning environments and for screening activities;
6. Word identification skills are taught directly and in relationship with writing and spelling;
7. Students initially read familiar rather than unfamiliar story material. This provides them with a basis and the confidence for reading other material;
8. Students read initially within the context of their own linguistic environment, rather than within a language environment that is unfamiliar to them;
9. Students learn about language through expression and through exposure to the various language media. These experiences afford them an understanding of language patterns and the writing system;
10. Students gain exposure to a wide variety of reading material, including newspapers, magazines, recreational reading material, reference material, and stories written by their peers;
11. The use of a variety of multimedia materials stimulates the students' interests and expression;
12. Students are afforded opportunities to become fully involved in personalized learning experiences. Their ideas are valued and used as the basis for these experiences;
13. Students internalize a pattern of thinking about reading. This pattern suggests that ideas can be spoken, written, or read; and
14. Students learn to read as a result of their increased sensitivity to

their environment, their language, and their discovery of how reading meets their personal needs.

The approach does distinguish itself from other traditional approaches to teaching reading and from other language experience approaches. It does, as Allen suggests, provide teachers a wealth of suggestions for implementing a comprehensive language-arts-based approach to teaching reading. But there are certain of these suggestions that might be questioned. For example, Allen states that reading, writing, speaking, and listening are closely interrelated. However, he assumes that in practice these activities can be taught concurrently and interchangeably. During the dictation of a story, the teacher would refer students to a study of how letters are formed and how they sound. As Smith (1973) suggests, reading, writing, speaking, and listening should not be taught concurrently when the interchange detracts from meaningful and purposeful communication. The emphasis upon the mechanics of writing would tend to do just that.

Other examples of questionable practices include Allen's suggestions for direct rather than indirect word identification skills instruction, his emphasis upon words and the acquisition of a sight vocabulary, and his suggested use of choral and unison reading. Again, advocates of a psycholinguistic notion of reading (Smith 1973) would claim this approach over-emphasizes the mechanics of word-perfect reading.

Research evidence to support Allen's approach is rather limited, and that which is available tends to be negative (Kendrick and Bennett 1966). In defense of Allen, the research that has been implemented has seemed rather insensitive to the subtleties of the goals he outlined. Measurement procedures and analysis techniques have seemed inadequate to truly evaluate the effectiveness of this approach.

Allen did not invent the language experience approach, but he should be given a great deal of credit for its emergence, popularity, and evolution. His language experience approach to teaching communication represents his most recent efforts and his response to demands for a more comprehensive and structured language experience approach. The enigma of the approach may be that while it is not sufficiently prescriptive for some teachers, it may be too prescriptive for others.

REFERENCES

Allen, R. V. 1968. How a language experience program works. In *A Decade of innovations: Approaches to beginning reading*, edited by E. C. Vilscek. Newark: International Reading Association, 1968. Provides a brief overview of the approach's rationale and guiding principles.

———. 1973. Suggestions for taking dictation. Unpublished paper, University of Arizona. Describes his suggestions for taking students' dictation.

———. 1976. *Language experiences in communication*. Boston: Houghton Mifflin. Provides a detailed discussion of the approach's rationale and methods of implementation.

Allen, R. V., and C. Allen. 1966–68. *Language experiences in reading, Levels I, II, and III.* Chicago: Encyclopedia Brittanica. Provides extensive resource material, including suggestions for lessons, teaching methods, materials and activities, for use with elementary school students.

———. 1969. *Language experiences in early childhood.* Chicago: Encyclopedia Brittanica. Provides extensive resource material, including suggestions for lessons, teaching methods, materials and activities for use in first grade or early childhood programs.

———. 1976. *Language experience activities.* Boston: Houghton Mifflin. Contains more than 250 activities for use with the approach and in learning centers.

Aukerman, R. C. 1984. *Approaches to beginning reading.* 2d ed. New York: John Wiley and Sons, 331–38. Provides a detailed discussion of the approach's development, rationale, methods, and materials.

Hoover, I. W. 1971. Historical and theoretical development of a language experience approach to teaching reading in selected teacher education institutions. Ed.D. thesis, College of Education, University of Arizona, Tucson. Presents a survey of the language experience approach's historical development and its introduction in teacher education institutions.

Kendrick, W. M., and C. L. Bennett. 1966. A comparative study of two first-grade language arts programs. *Reading Research Quarterly* 2:83–118. Reports a research study comparing the language experience approach with a traditional basal method.

Lee, D. M., and R. V. Allen. 1963. *Learning to read through experience.* New York: Appleton-Century-Crofts. Presents a 146-page overview of the language experience approach.

Smith, F. 1973. Twelve easy ways to make reading difficult. In *Psycholinguistics and reading*, edited by F. Smith. New York: Holt, Rinehart & Winston. 183–96. Discusses the problems associated with selected instructional principles and practices.

ASHTON-WARNER'S ORGANIC READING

Purpose

Organic reading (Ashton-Warner 1958) is an experience-centered approach to reading instruction based upon Sylvia Ashton-Warner's twenty-four years of teaching experiences with New Zealand Maori children. It is designed to provide a bridge from the known to the unknown, a bridge that can help students move from their own experiences to sharing the written experiences of others.

Rationale

In her various books, *Spinster* (1958), *Teacher* (1963), and *Spearpoint* (1972), Ashton-Warner presents the rationale and details of her procedure. She states that organic reading is derived from the notion that learning experiences should begin with the "intrinsic" rather than with the "extrinsic"; she suggests that students should relate to their own innermost thoughts before relating to the thoughts of others. Her goal as a teacher is to "release the native imagery and use it for working material" (Ashton-Warner 1972, 17).

Along this line of reasoning, the student's initial exposure to reading should afford an organic, instinctive reaction to reading. As Ashton-Warner suggests:

> First words must mean something to a child. First words must have intense meaning for a child. They must be a part of his being.
> How much hangs on the love of reading, the instinctive inclination to hold a book! Instinctive. That's what it must be. The reaching out for a book needs to become an organic action, which can happen at this yet formative age. Pleasant words won't do. Respectable words won't do. They must be words organically tied up, organically born from the dynamic life itself. They must be words that are already part of the child's being. (Ashton-Warner 1963, 30)

Aston-Warner claims that the longer the student's reading is organic, the stronger it will become. She suggests that teachers should reach into the minds of students to touch this key vocabulary; when a number of words are acquired, students should be given opportunities to write and read stories based upon this vocabulary. Ashton-Warner suggests that in so doing the foundation to a lifetime of reading can be laid.

Intended Audience

Organic reading is suited for use on either an individual, a group, or a classroom basis with any student. It was proposed as a beginning reading method with children from divergent cultures, specifically New Zealand Maori children, but has also been used in the United States.

Description of the Procedure

Sylvia Ashton-Warner describes the organic reading approach as integral to the total curriculum. Organic reading would be one aspect of the organic teaching program. During a school day, students would be scheduled to do "organic work" and "standard work." Both these aspects of the school program would involve what Ashton-Warner refers to as "input" and "output" periods. As suggested by Ashton-Warner, the typical school day would entail the following activities (1963, 101):

TYPICAL DAY'S ACTIVITIES

Morning
   Organic Work

Output period (approximately 1 hour 45 minutes)
- conversation, art activities, craft activities, singing, creative dance, key vocabulary, organic vocabulary, etc.

Input period (approximately 1 hour)
- key vocabulary (for little ones), organic vocabulary, organic discussion, stories, pictures, etc.

Afternoon
Standard work
Output period (approximately 1 hour)
- nature study and numbers

Input period (approximately 50 minutes)
- standard vocabulary, standard reading, Maori book vocabulary and reading, supplementary reading, stories, songs, poems, letters (for little ones)

Organic reading involves four movements or periods in the student's development. The first movement begins with the students generating words they wish to learn. The latter movements involve the students in writing and reading stories.

First movement

The first movement entails, as Ashton-Warner puts it, reaching into the child's "inner mind" to discover the child's key vocabulary. Ashton-Warner suggests that each student has a key vocabulary, which, if it is to be reached, requires a great deal of teacher sensitivity and patience. It is probed during the morning output period when the teacher holds personal conferences with each student. The teacher elicits these key words from the student and writes each on a 12 × 5-inch card as it is spoken. The student then takes the work, traces it, studies it, and, when ready to move on to other activities, places in in the teacher's word box.

Later that same morning, each student is given further experiences with these same words. Namely a check is made to see if the words are remembered. An opportunity is given for the student to use them in organic writing and spelling activities. In the latter activities, the student will (a) write either a sentence or a story using the key vocabulary words and (b) be presented with the words for either naming or spelling. The chalkboard rather than paper is used extensively for these activities.

Several other techniques are used to learn and check each student's key vocabulary. At the beginning of each school day, students receive their cards mixed together and emptied on the classroom floor. When the students enter, they have to scramble to find their own word cards. Ashton-Warner suggests that the recalled cards represent the student's "living" key vocabulary. Following this line of reasoning, words that are not recalled are removed and destroyed. To facilitate further learning, each student then sits with a partner, and they hear and help each other say their words.

According to Ashton-Warner, each student's key vocabulary reflects the student's inner self. The words in this key vocabulary center upon the student's primitive instincts. Specifically, they reflect ideas related to fear and sex. Among the fear words often suggested were *ghost*, *frightened*, *cry*, and *wild*. Among the sex words often suggested were *kiss*, *love*, *dance*, and *together*.

Second movement

As the students' vocabulary develops, they progress through the other movements. By the time the second movement has been reached, the student has acquired a sizeable key vocabulary and has begun suggesting words from "outside" rather than "inside," such as *happy days* and *snowy mountains*. In this movement, the use of two words replaces the use of single words; longer, yellow cards replace the white word cards. The student again traces the words written on the card, puts them in a story, and, during the morning input period, writes them on the chalkboard and spells them. Early every morning, the students will once again arrive to find their new cards piled on the floor and will begin a search for them. During this movement, the students begin to read either homemade or teacher-made books that use key vocabulary words. These are the students' stories, made from their own words by their teacher or their parents. The students read these books to themselves and each other.

Third and fourth movements

As the students continue to progress, they move through Ashton-Warner's third and fourth movements. During these movements, the student progresses from writing his or her own small stories with teacher assistance to writing small stories without teacher assistance to writing rather sophisticated stories.

During these movements the student's vocabulary is ever changing; Ashton-Warner suggests words appear and disappear with their changing appeal. Whenever the student adds a new word, the teacher writes it in the back of the student's own story book. These back pages assume the role of a personal dictionary for the student.

During these movements, time is also alloted to vocabulary building, reading, sharing, and discussing stories. During vocabulary periods, students write their words on the chalkboard and spell them aloud. During organic reading and sharing, students not only read and master their own stories, but also share them with others. Following organic reading and sharing, the students discuss each other's stories, then proceed to use the Maori readers. These readers contain stories collected from the work of previous children. They are intended as an introduction to reading published books.

During the afternoon input and output periods, the students are presented with standard school experiences in accordance with their level of development. These experiences purport to introduce the students to the culture at large. Experiences would include nature study, numbers, standard vocabulary, standard reading, listening experiences, songs, and poems. For students at the key vocabulary level, they would also include letter writing activities.

Cautions and Comments

There have been a number of evaluations of Ashton-Warner's ideas (Packer 1970; Duquette 1972). These evaluations have yielded mixed results in terms of the carry-over of the approach to published reading programs, but they do support Ashton-Warner's claim that her approach affords a more enjoyable and meaningful approach to developing beginning readers' attitudes and abilities. As she suggests in her own evaluation of the use of the approach with American children (*Spearpoint* 1973), organic reading may have differential success in accordance with the general attitude and desire of children for learning.

Teachers should recognize that the approach necessitates a great deal of daily preparation. Teachers would have to be aware of and record each student's developmental level and scheduled activities, and, in particular, to teach the student's key vocabulary. Teachers would need to be able to provide the mechanisms for generating stories based upon the students' vocabularies and for having students write their own stories.

Finally, it should be noted that certain aspects of Ashton-Warner's approach lack adequate development. For example, while her suggestions for using and generating key vocabulary seem reasonable, some of her proposed methods are ill-defined and poorly reasoned. In places her approach lacks sufficient definition to be understood or implemented, and some of her suggestions lack a base either in theory or in research, e.g., her procedures for spelling and writing words.

REFERENCES

Ashton-Warner, S. 1958. *Spinster*. New York: Simon and Schuster. Describes aspects of her life as a teacher of New Zealand Maori children and refers to her organic teaching methods.

――――. 1963. *Teacher*. New York: Simon and Schuster. Provides a detailed description of her organic teaching methods, their rationale and their use with New Zealand children.

――――. 1972. *Spearpoint*. New York: Alfred A. Knopf. Describes Ashton-Warner's experiences with her method while teaching in Colorado.

Aukerman, R. C. 1984. *Approaches to beginning reading*. 2d ed. New York: John Wiley and Sons, 368−71. Provides a summary description and discussion of the organic teaching methods.

Duquette, R. J. 1972. Research summary of Barnette-Duquette study. *Childhood Education* 48:438−40. Presents a summary of a research study in which Ashton-Warner's key vocabulary concept was used with students of varying reading ability in different United States cities.

Packer, A. B. 1970. Ashton-Warner's key vocabulary for the disadvantaged. *Reading Teacher* 23:559−64. Presents the findings of a United States study in which words in students' key vocabulary were compared with basal word lists.

Veatch, J. 1978. *Reading in the elementary school*. 2d ed. New York: John Wiley and Sons, 343−57. Discusses key words and its relation to beginning reading.

Veatch, J., F. Sawicki, G. Elliot, E. Barnette, and J. Blakey. 1979. *Key words to reading: The language experience approach begins*. 2d ed. Columbus: Charles E. Merrill. Provides a description of how key vocabulary can be integrated into an individualized reading program.

Wasserman, S. 1972. Aspen mornings with Sylvia Ashton-Warner. *Childhood Education* 48:348−53. Describes a teacher's exposure to organic teaching through a workshop run by Ashton-Warner.

STAUFFER'S LANGUAGE-EXPERIENCE APPROACH

Purpose

The purpose of the Language-Experience Approach advocated by Russell Stauffer (1970) is to take advantage of the linguistic, intellectual, social, and cultural wealth a student brings to school so that the transfer from oral language to written language can be made.

Rationale

In the preface to his book, *The Language-Experience Approach to the Teaching of Reading* (1970), Stauffer makes the following statement:

> The best label that can be applied to the Language-Experience Approach is "The Eclectic Approach to Reading Instruction." It embraces the best practices regardless of their sources and does so in a functional communication-oriented way.

He suggests that essential to the Language-Experience Approach are the relationships that exist among language, thought, and experience, and among the communicative skills of reading, writing, speaking, and listening. More specifically, he suggests:

1. Reading, writing, speaking, and listening occur within the context of purposeful communication;
2. The interests, curiosities, creativity, culture, capacity, percepts, and concepts of each individual are used;
3. The use of word recognition and word identification is developed in a meaningful context ensuring the use of meaning clues;

4. Reading skills which are taught are assimilated and used;
5. Individual interests and understandings are extended and refined; and
6. An appreciation of the value and uses of reading is afforded.

To these ends, the Language-Experience Approach is a total language arts approach that relies heavily upon dictated stories, word banks, and creative writing.

Intended Audience

The Language-Experience Approach is designed for use as a beginning reading approach with students of various ages and abilities. It is appropriate for use either on a one-to-one, a group, or a whole-class basis.

Description of Procedure

The following description of Stauffer's Language-Experience Approach is not intended to be exhaustive, but instead to represent its major characteristics. The interested reader is directed to Stauffer's book, *The Language-Experience Approach to the Teaching of Reading* (1970), for further details. Those aspects we will discuss include (1) dictated experience stories, (2) word banks, and (3) creative writing.

1. Dictated experience stories

Dictated experience stories are the core of Stauffer's Language-Experience Approach. They provide students with the opportunity to learn to read much as they learn to talk. They also provide a means of getting started with reading and for developing, refining, and extending reading skills.

As a way of getting started, Stauffer suggests the use of whole-class dictated stories. During the first few weeks, the whole-class dictated stories provide the students an opportunity to become familiar with the procedure and to get acquainted with each other linguistically, culturally, and socially. Once familiar with the procedure, the students engage in group-dictated stories and, ideally, individual-dictated stories.

Across whole-class-, group-, and individual-dictated experience stories, the procedures used by the teacher are quite similar. For this reason, they will be discussed together.

a. *Generating the dictated experience story.* To generate the dictated experience story requires that the teacher locate a stimulus with which the student can associate and through which, Stauffer suggests, students can "examine more carefully the world about them, to see new horizons, to view the past and the future, and to act upon it intellectually" (Stauffer 1970, 55). The stimulus might be an event, an idea, or a concrete object. It might involve something the students can see, touch, or feel, and, with the help of teacher questioning, discuss.

When the teacher feels the students are able and willing to generate some dictation, the stimulus is put aside and the students gather around a chart set up for dictation. For class-dictated stories, a lined chart approximately 2 × 3 feet is suggested; for group-dictated stories a chart approximately 12 × 15 inches. For individual-dictated stories, letter-sized paper is suggested.

The teacher now asks the students to tell about the stimulus; as the students offer ideas, these are recorded by the teacher. In a whole-class or a group situation, only selected students would be given an opportunity to dictate sentences. Once the several sentences are recorded, the teacher might terminate the generation activity and reread the sentences to check if the recorded ideas are stated appropriately.

b. *Reading the story and follow-up activities.* Once the students' dictated story is completed, it is read. First the teacher reads the story; then the teacher and students read the story in unison. As the story is read and read again, the teacher points to each word. The teacher may then direct the students to draw a picture depicting their story, to identify known words in the story, or to begin other activities.

On the second day, the students are again referred to their dictated experience story. If the story is a class effort, the class is first divided into groups, with at least one child who contributes to the story in each group. Typically, the activities of the second day are sequenced in this way:

1. Each student follows along, either individually or in groups, as the teacher reads their individual, group or class stories.
2. As the teacher points to each word, the story is read by the teacher and student in unison.
3. The whole story or portions of the story are read by selected individuals or by the author of the story.
4. The students match, name, or locate selected words.
5. The students locate and underline words they know or the whole group knows.
6. To check on known words, the teacher has the student(s) reread the dictated story orally. If the student fails to recognize a word previously underlined, the underlining is crossed, e.g., donkey. This marking indicates "donkey" is no longer a known word.

On the third day, students in the class are given the opportunity to do more intense study of their stories. When stories were dictated with the whole class, the teacher reproduces the story and distributes it to each student. Individually, students read over the story and underline known words. Stories are then placed in class and personal folders. The students whose stories are generated individually or in a group are given an opportunity to reread their stories and check (after a reasonable "forgetting period") whether they still remember their words from the previous day. For the purpose of providing a schedule for group dictation, Stauffer (1970) suggests the following activities across a week:

GROUP DICTATING SCHEDULE

	Group I (least mature)	Group II	Group III	Group IV (most mature)
Monday	dictating	other activities	other activities	dictating
Tuesday	re-reading and word study	dictating	dictating	re-reading and word study
Wednesday	re-reading and word study	re-reading and word study	re-reading and word study	other activities
Thursday	dictating	re-reading and word study	other activities	dictating
Friday	re-reading and word study	dictating	dictating	re-reading and word study

2. Word banks

As Stauffer describes the word-bank file, it is "a personalized record of words a pupil has learned to read or recognize at sight" (Stauffer 1970, 74). The file of words emanates from the dictated stories generated by the student. It includes only words that the student has identified as being known across successive days. These are words that have been underlined at least twice. As a check on the students' recognition of these words, the teacher has them identify their words. For this purpose, a small window card is suggested. (See diagram) The window frame is placed over each underlined word in random order. The random ordering of presentation prevents the student's use of context.

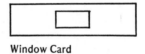

Window Card

Henry

Henry is my very best friend.
He is an ant that I keep in an
ant house beside my bed. He has
six legs and is brown and red.

The students' known words form the deposits and reserves of their individual word banks. Each known word is written or typed on a card (approximately 3/8 × 1 1/2 inches) and filed. As the word bank expands beyond thirty cards, an alphabetic filing system is introduced. Thus, each student gains a personalized file of known words, which acts both as a resource and as a dictionary. To use the word bank cards as a resource, Stauffer suggests a variety of activities: composing stories, word attack activities, discrimination activities, categorization activities, and finding other occurrences of the words in print.

3. Creative writing

Another facet of Stauffer's Language-Experience Approach grows out of the students' word banks—creative writing. Stauffer defines creative writing as "a composition that reflects a child's own choice of words, ideas, order, spelling, and punctuation" (Stauffer 1970, 78).

The students' first encounter with writing is expected to occur with the writing of names and recognition of words. But creative word usage begins with the construction of sentences from words in the word banks. Using their word cards, students' first creative writing experiences occur when they lay out simple sentences and stories with their cards. When a word not in their card bank is required, they begin to learn to write and spell, using their new word recognition skills.

To begin creative writing experiences, Stauffer suggests the use of 12 × 18-inch paper. To provide a space for illustration, he suggests leaving the top half unlined. To guide lettering and to afford ample spacing between lines, he suggests ruling five lines with 3/4-inch spacing, and lines 3/8-inch wide between each two of these lines across the bottom of the page.

As described by Stauffer (1970, 82−83), the following guidelines may help the teacher in developing creative writing abilities from these beginnings:

a. Students should want to write rather than be coerced into writing;
b. Instructions to students should be simple and direct;
c. Creative writing topics may be suggested, but students should be encouraged to write about anything they wish;
d. Students should be encouraged to write legibly and spell accurately, but not at the expense of interferring with the flow of their ideas;
e. Students' ideas should be encouraged to flow freely through teacher assistance and questioning when needed; and
f. Students' writing should be evaluated in terms of quality of expression and not purely by "adult standards."

Cautions and Comments

Stauffer's language-experience approach provides the teacher with a comprehensive, well-articulated, and experience-based language arts program for initial reading. The approach seems suitable for use with students of varying ages and capabilities. It provides for a variety of language-experience activities in all four facets of the language arts. It may be used either to eventually supplement or to substitute for a total reading program. Stauffer's approach affords incidental instruction for the development, extension, and refinement of word identification skills, spelling skills, writing skills, concept development skills, and general comprehension.

As evidence of the approach's use and value, Stauffer provides a wealth of actual examples taken from teachers in different settings and also cites theory and research. Several related research studies are abstracted in the appendices to his book (Stauffer 1970).

However, the approach does seem to have at least one major shortcoming. Namely, it appears that the approach places an undue emphasis upon the recognition of isolated words. This emphasis occurs in the pointing to words during reading, in the identification and mastery of single words, and in the word banks composed of single, known words. Students with whom the approach is used are in danger of becoming non-fluent readers and word callers, if they give each word the power these activities suggest. If reading for meaning is our goal, the approach should place less emphasis upon word-perfect reading and the acquisition of single known words and give more emphasis to reading with understanding.

REFERENCES

Stauffer, R. G. 1965. The language-experience approach. In *First grade reading programs*. Edited by J. Kerfoot. Newark: International Reading Association. Provides additional information concerning Stauffer's language-experience approach.

———. 1969. *Directing reading maturity as a cognitive process*. New York: Harper & Row, 186–238. Presents a detailed discussion of aspects of Stauffer's language-experience approach.

———. 1970. *The language-experience approach to the teaching of reading*. New York: Harper & Row. Presents a detailed account, with examples, of the rationale and procedures of this approach.

Stauffer, R. G., and W. D. Hammond. 1967. The effectiveness of language arts and basic reader approaches to first grade reading instruction—extended into second grade. *Reading Teacher* 20:740–46. Presents research findings in which Stauffer's approach is compared favorably with basic reading program instruction.

———. 1969. The effectiveness of language arts and basic reader approach to first grade reading instruction–extended into third grade. *Reading Research Quarterly* 4:468–99. Presents an extension of previous research findings concerning the Stauffer approach.

SHARED BOOK EXPERIENCE

Purpose

Shared Book Experience is an attempt to adapt the principles of preschool book experience to the classroom and to refine the procedures to be a very powerful system of learning. As described by David Doake and Donald Holdaway, shared book experience is intended as a means of affording early reading experiences to groups of students that are intimate and dovetail with other language activities.

Rationale

Shared Book Experience began in New Zealand in an attempt to unite the language learning experiences of students by shifting to the center of early reading experiences "the enjoyment of a rich, open literature of favorite stories, poems and songs" (Park 1982). Holdaway (1979), who has been one of the major advocates of this approach, has suggested that the model underlying the Shared Book Experience has its roots in the same developmental tenets of learning spoken language and acquiring other learnings. He suggests, for example, that Shared Book Experience has its bases in learning experiences similar to the bedtime story situation. Just as it is important for a bedtime story to be enjoyable, interesting, and presented in relaxed circumstances, so Holdaway argues that stories should be introduced to classes in a relaxed, nonthreatening, and motivating setting. Similarly, the read-it-again phenomena, which is a characteristic of bedtime stories, is integral to maximizing the utility of stories. In particular, stories that students look forward to rereading can be a used as (1) independent reading material, even if children roleplay as readers and (2) to focus the reader's attention on certain aspects of the text, for example, words and predictable features of language.

The major tools of the Shared Book Experience are what might be considered oversized books. These books are intended to be at the center of the reading and writing program. They serve two basic functions: they take advantage of good literature, and they capitalize upon the social dynamics of a classroom. Indeed, the initial name for Shared Book Experience was "cooperative reading." The rationale behind the enlarged text is as the New Zealand Department of Education has suggested:

> When a teacher is working with an enlarged text . . . the right climate and the right auditory and visual conditions exist for effective skills teaching. The enlargement of print enables precise, accurate attention to be focussed on word and every letter detail. (P. 3)

As the above comments suggest, Shared Book Experience is not seen as separate from other aspects of the reading and writing program. Doake (1985) and Holdaway (1979) have viewed the use of Shared Book Experience as working hand in hand with a language experience approach and as a precursor to individualized reading. Holdaway has depicted how the Shared Book Experience might work in conjunction with other activities in Figure 7–3. Apart from this general depiction of the interrelationships, Holdaway has discussed at length a number of reading and writing activities that might use the raw material of the books as their base.

Holdaway has claimed that there are innumerable benefits that might be

Figure 7–3   The cycle of success in Shared Book Experience

accrued from the use of the Shared Book Experience. His suggestion of the benefits and their cyclic nature are presented in Figure 7–4. At the heart of his advocacy of the Shared Book Experience is his belief, as he has stated:

> Gathered around a book as a natural, sharing community children learn more from participation than from direct instruction: they learn from the teacher's model, from their own sensible involvement, and from each other, without any sense of competition or pressure. They also learn from judicious instruction which is more intelligible because of its real and obvious purposes. (Park 1982, 819).

Intended Audience

A Shared Book Experience approach can be used in almost any situation when you wish to focus a group's attention on a single text. As described by Holdaway (1979), it is most suited to use in preschools or the first grade.

Figure 7-4   Balancing approaches and materials

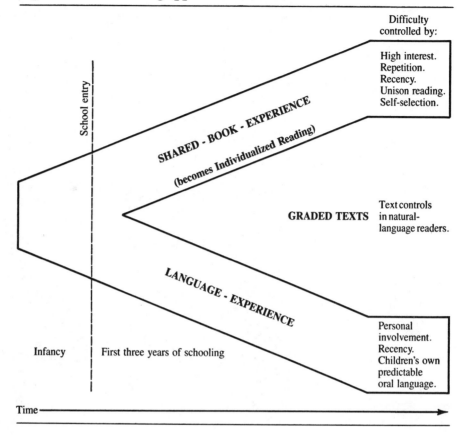

Procedure

The Shared Book Experience centers around the use of enlarged books or overheads of good quality that are predictable stories that can be presented to a class or group of students. These enlarged copies of different books are intended to be sufficiently interesting and predictable to engage young readers in anticipating what will happen in the story and in participating whenever selected words or phrases are repeated. As the story is read aloud to the children, the teacher will enlist the use of a pointer to ensure the children follow along. After reading, students are given functional skills activities, language extension experiences, and time to read independently either the new story or one of their previous favorites.

For instance, a class which has been involved in reading a big book copy of "The Three Billy Goats Gruff" might be involved in dramatizing the story and in choral reading. Also they might choose to learn about goats or write their own story based upon this tale. The stories that the class generate might be published and used as further reading material for the class. In essence, the

Figure 7-5   Children enjoying Shared Book Experience during Independent Time

story serves as the stimulus for other literacy learnings. A typical Shared Book Experience involves the following activities:

1. Tuning-in: The enjoyment of poetry and song. Here the students are given opportunities to participate in and enjoy singing or reading along with the class.
2. Rereading of a favorite story: If possible students are encouraged to make predicts and read along with the story. Sometimes children may direct the reading.
3. Learning about print and about language. This entails what is termed functional skills teaching and innovation. Functional skills teaching includes developing comprehension skills, listening skills, learning conventions such as left to right and reference labels, prediction, confirmation and self-correction, sight vocabulary, auditory discrimination, letter sound associations, letter names, punctuation and intonation patterns. For this purpose,

Figure 7–6   Follow-up activity involving word masking

masks might be used to cover parts of words, phrases, sentences or lines from a story as a way of focusing students attention on elements of the print. At other times, it might entail using windows to highlight words or other activities.

Innovation is the creation of a new statement based upon a familiar pattern or theme. At the simplest level, it might involve changing the name of a character in a story. At other times, it might involve changing a number of different words in the context of sentences. For example, it might involve an activity similar to the following:

If I had a hammer, I'd hammer in the morning . . .
      bike   ride   afternoon . . .
      pencil   write   sunshine . . .

Additional activities that can be part of a shared book experience are:

1. Introduction of a new story;
2. Independent reading of favorite stories; and
3. Expressive activities arising from the literature such as writing, dramatization, art, creative movement, etc.

As Holdaway (Park 1982) says, the choice of material, especially the material that is enlarged, must be very carefully selected. It must be able to grip students, have a good plot, be predictable, include interesting pictures, and, if possible, have repetitive elements, patterns, and maybe rhyme.

After students develop some security with these materials, Holdaway suggests that teachers might include among the independent reading materials some of the graded readers, assuming they are not overly stilted.

Cautions and Comments

The Shared Book Experience has met with a great deal of success in New Zealand, Australia, Canada, and parts of the United States. Holdaway warns, however, that the Big Books that are such an integral part of the approach are not panaceas and can be easily misused. He emphasizes that the essential feature of Shared Book Experience is the union of the Big Book with other learning experiences, including extension activities and functional skills learning. He also warns that the Shared Book Experience should not be viewed as a license to enlarge all of any story. He emphasizes, as do others, that careful selection of interesting and predictable story material is essential.

There are other problems that may emerge with the use of the Shared Book Experience, which may be inherent to the approach itself. First, there are at this stage very few published Big Books and few sets of functional activities that might be used in conjunction with the stories. Obviously, any teacher using Big Books would need to do a lot of preparation or have the help of colleagues. Second, the guidelines for functional skill work and extensions, especially writing extensions are sketchy at best. Third, sometimes the suggestions offered seem inconsistent with the psycholinguistic thinking that is cited as the theoretical basis for the approach. For example, the suggestions for improving use of syntactic and semantic clues are sentence-bound, the phonics instruction verge on the piecemeal, and the guidelines for developing comprehension abilities, as well as literary appreciations, are not substantial. Finally, as Holdaway (1979) suggested, there has been very little in the way of research that has examined the use of the approach.

REFERENCES

Doake, D. B. 1979. Book experience and emergent reading behavior. Paper presented at the International Reading Association, Atlanta. Describes study of Shared Book Experience.

————. 1985. Reading-like behavior: Its role in learning to read. In *Observing the language learner*, edited by A. M. Jaggar and M. T. Smith-Burke. Newark: Del.: International Reading Association/NCTE. Describes how Shared Book Experiences contribute to learning to read.

Holdaway, D. 1979. *Foundations of literacy*. Sydney: Ashton-Scholastic. Presents a thorough discussion of the Shared Book Experience, including theoretical rationale, examples from classrooms, and information pertaining to how the approach relates to the total school literacy program.

New Zealand Department of Education. 1978. *Shared book experience procedures, Unit 6, Early reading inservice course*. Wellington: E. C. Keating, Government Printer. Provides an overview of the approach, including suggestions for activities, material, and slides demonstrating the approach.

———. 1978. *Suggestions for making enlarged books, Early reading inservice course*. Wellington: Department of Education. Presents graphically procedures for enlarging books including illustrations, print, choice of paper, assemblying and storage.

Park, B. 1982. The big book trend—A discussion with Don Holdaway. *Language Arts* 59: 815–21. Presents an interview with Donald Holdaway in which the Shared Book Experience is thoroughly discussed.

PATTERNED LANGUAGE APPROACH

Purpose

The Patterned Language Approach (Bridge 1979; Bridge and Burton 1982; Bridge, Winograd, and Haley 1983) is intended to provide students success in their initial encounters with books through the use of a combination of a structured language experience approach with patterned or predictable stories. The strategy has been shown to be useful for purposes of developing an initial vocabulary, a positive attitude to reading, and the use of context.

Rationale

The Patterned Language Approach represents an adaptation of three proposals: (1) the notions of Bridge and Burton (1982) on the use of predictable stories (2) the suggestions by Cunningham (1979) for using structured language experience stories, and (3) some of Martin and Brogan's (1971) guidelines for using patterned books. The authors of the approach claim that the approach represents a response to Frank Smith's (1978) belief that students learn to read by reading and a suggestion by K. Goodman (1976) that predictability is an essential ingredient for early reading material. The question the Patterned Language approach addresses is: How are beginning readers to practice reading when they cannot yet read?

They respond to this question with the claim (and data supporting this claim) that patterned books, if used appropriately, are a most effective way for beginning reading. As they stated:

Patterned books contain repetitive structures that enable readers to predict the next word or line or episode. After hearing such material read aloud, children can join in and "read" along even though at that point they are probably not able to recognize the individual words. However, repeated opportunities to recognize high frequency words in dependable contexts help them develop a sight vocabulary that can soon be recognized in other contexts. (1983, 884)

Sentence matching activities and dictated stories are used to avoid the possibility that children just memorize the story "and are not really reading" (p. 887).

Intended Audience

The Patterned Language Approach is intended for use in the first grade or kindergarten. With suitable material, the approach seems suited to use with students at any age level.

Description of the Procedures

The procedure is based on the careful selection of appropriate "patterned stories," which are used in a whole-to-part fashion. Students begin with what Martin and Brogan (1971) refer to as "whole book success" in which they role play successful readers, as well as develop a trust of print. Their attention is then focused on sentences and words for purposes of developing flexible reading strategies and an initial vocabulary.

To aid in the selection of appropriate material, Bridge (1979) and Bridge, Winograd, and Haley (1983) offer sources and guidelines for using and selecting predictable stories, as well as generating dictated stories. In terms of "predictable" stories, they offer several lists similar to the following:

Figure 7-7   Predictable Books

Adams, Pam. *This Old Man.* New York: Grossett and Dunlap, 1974.

Alain. *One, Two, Three, Going to Sea.* New York: Scholastic Press. 1964.

Aliki. *Go Tell Aunt Rhody.* New York: Macmillan, 1974.

Aliki. *Hush Little Baby.* Englewood Cliffs, N.J.: Prentice-Hall, 1968.

Aliki. *My Five Senses.* New York: Thomas Y. Crowell, 1962.

Allen, Roach V. *Language Experiences in Communication.* Boston: Houghton Mifflin, 1976.

Allen, Roach V., and Claryce Allen. *Language Experience Activities.* Boston: Houghton Mifflin, 1982.

Asch, Frank. *Monkey Face.* New York: Parents' Magazine Press, 1977.

Balian, Lorna. *The Animal.* Nashville: Abingdon, 1972.

Figure 7-7 *(Continued)*

Balian, Lorna. *Where in the World is Henry?* Scarsdale, N.Y.: Bradbury Press, 1972.

Barohas, Sarah E. *I Was Walking Down the Road*. New York: Scholastic Press, 1975.

Barrett, Judi. *Animals Should Definitely Not Wear Clothes*. New York: Atheneum, 1970.

Barton, Byron. *Buzz, Buzz, Buzz*. New York: Scholastic Press, 1973.

Baskin, Leonard. *Hosie's Alphabet*. New York: The Viking Press, 1972.

Battaglia, Aurelius. *Old Mother Hubbard*. Racine, Wis.: Golden Press, 1972.

Baum, Arline, and Joseph Baum. *One Bright Monday Morning*. New York: Random House, 1962.

Becker, John. *Seven Little Rabbits*. New York: Scholastic Press, 1973.

Beckman, Kaj. *Lisa Cannot Sleep*. New York: Franklin Watts, 1969.

Bellah, Melanie. *A First Book of Sounds*. Racine, Wis.: Golden Press, 1963.

Berenstain, Stanley, and Janice Berenstain. *The B Book*. New York: Random House, 1971.

Bonne, Rose. *I Know an Old Lady*. New York: Scholastic Press, 1961.

Brand, Oscar. *When I First Came to This Land*. New York: Putnam's Sons, 1974.

Brandenberg, Franz. *I Once Knew a Man*. New York: Macmillan, 1970.

Brooke, Leslie. *Johnny Crow's Garden*. New York: Frederick Warne, 1968.

Brown, Marcia. *The Three Billy Goats Gruff*. New York: Harcourt Brace Jovanovich, 1957.

Brown, Margaret Wise. *The Friendly Book*. Racine, Wis.: Golden Press, 1954.

Brown, Margaret Wise. *Four Fur Feet*. New York: William R. Scott, 1961.

Brown, Margaret Wise. *Goodnight Moon*. New York: Harper & Row, 1947.

Brown, Margaret Wise. *Home for a Bunny*. Racine, Wis.: Golden Press, 1956.

Brown, Margaret Wise. *The Important Book*. New York: Harper & Row, 1949.

Brown, Margaret Wise. *Where Have You Been?* New York: Scholastic Press, 1952.

Burningham, John. *Mr. Gumpy's Outing*. New York: Scholastic Press. 1970.

The Bus Ride. Glenview, Ill.: Scott, Foresman, 1971.

Cameron, Polly. *I Can't Said the Ant*. New York: Coward, McCann, and Geoghegan, 1961.

Carle, Eric. *Do You Want to Be My Friend?* New York: Thomas Y. Crowell, 1971.

Carle, Eric. *The Grouchy Ladybug*. New York: Thomas Y. Crowell, 1977.

Carle, Eric. *The Mixed Up Chameleon*. New York: Thomas Y. Crowell, 1975.

Carle, Eric. *The Very Hungry Caterpillar*. Cleveland, Ohio: Collins World, 1969.

Charlip, Remy. *Fortunately*. New York: Parents' Magazine Press, 1971.

Figure 7−7   *(Continued)*

Charlip, Remy. *What Good Luck, What Bad Luck*. New York: Scholastic Press, 1964.

Considine, Kate, and Ruby Schuler. *One, Two, Three, Four*. New York: Holt, Rinehart & Winston, 1965.

Cook, Bernadine. *The Little Fish that Got Away*, Reading, Mass.: Addison-Wesley, 1976.

Crews, Donald. *Freight Train*. New York: Greenwillow, 1978. (Incorporates position words and follows as sequence.)

de Paola, Tomie. *Pancakes for Breakfast*. New York: Harcourt Brace Jovanovich, 1978.

de Regniers, Beatrice Schenk. *Catch a Little Fox*. New York: Seabury Press, 1970.

de Regniers, Beatrice Schenk. *The Day Everybody Cried*. New York: The Viking Press, 1967.

de Regniers, Beatrice Schenk. *How Joe the Bear and Sam the Mouse Got Together*. New York: Parents' Magazine Press, 1965.

de Regniers, Beatrice Schenk. *The Little Book*. New York: Henry Z. Walck, 1961.

de Regniers, Beatrice Schenk. *May I Bring a Friend?* New York: Atheneum, 1972.

de Regniers, Beatrice Schenk. *Willy O'Dwyer Jumped in the Fire*. New York: Atheneum, 1968.

Domanska, Janina. *If All the Seas Were One Sea*. New York: Macmillan, 1971.

Duff, Maggie. *Johnny and His Drum*. New York: Henry Z. Walck, 1972.

Duff, Maggie. *Rum Pum Pum*. New York: Macmillan, 1978.

Einsel, Walter. *Did You Ever See?* New York: Scholastic Press, 1962.

Emberly, Barbara. *Drummer Hoff*. Englewood Cliffs, N.J.: Prentice-Hall, 1967.

Emberly, Barbara. *Simon's Song*. Englewood Cliffs, N.J.: Prentice-Hall, 1969.

Emberly, Barbara, and Ed Emberly. *One Wide River to Cross*. New York: Scholastic Press. 1966.

Emberly, Ed. *Klippity Klop*. Boston: Little, Brown, 1974.

Ets, Marie Hall. *Elephant in a Well*. New York: Viking, 1972.

Ets, Marie Hall. *Play with Me*. New York: Viking, 1955.

Flack, Marjorie. *Ask Mr. Bear*. New York: Macmillan, 1932.

Florian, Douglas. *A Bird Can Fly*. New York: Greenwillow, 1980. (Pattern: 3 pages state what an animal or bird can do; a 4th what it cannot do, and introduces another that can.)

Galdone, Paul. *The Gingerbread Boy*. Boston: Houghton Mifflin, 1975.

Galdone, Paul. *Henny Penny*. New York: Scholastic Press, 1968.

Galdone, Paul. *The Little Red Hen*. New York: Schoalstic Press, 1973.

Figure 7-7 *(Continued)*

Galdone, Paul. *The Three Bears*. New York: Scholastic Press, 1972.

Galdone, Paul. *The Three Billy Goats Gruff*. New York: Seabury Press, 1973.

Galdone, Paul. *The Three Little Pigs*, New York: Seabury Press, 1970.

Ginsburg, Mirra. *The Chick and the Duckling*. New York: Macmillan, 1972.

Greenberg, Polly. *Oh Lord, I Wish I Was a Buzzard*. New York: Macmillan, 1972.

Guilfoile, Elizabeth. *Nobody Listens to Andrew*. New York: Scholastic Press, 1957.

Higgins, Doin. *Papa's Going to Buy Me a Mockingbird*. New York: Seabury Press, 1968.

Hoban, Tana. *Count and See*. New York: Macmillan, 1972.

Hoffman, Hilde. *The Green Grass Grows All Around*. New York: Macmillan, 1968.

The House That Jack Built. New York: Holt, Rinehart & Winston, 1962.

Hutchins, Pat. *Good-Night Owl*. New York: Macmillan, 1972.

Hutchins, Pat. *Rosie's Walk*. New York: Macmillan, 1968.

Hutchins, Pat. *Titch*. New York: Collier Books, 1971.

Joslin, Sesyle. *What Do You Say Dear?* New York: Scholastic Press, 1958.

Joyce, Irma. *Never Talk to Strangers*. Racine, Wis.: Golden Press, 1967.

Kalan, Robert. *Rain*. New York: Greenwillow, 1978.

Keats, Ezra Jack. *Over in the Meadow*. New York: Scholastic Press, 1971.

Kent, Jack. *The Fat Cat*. New York: Scholastic Press, 1971.

Kesselman, Wendy. Illustrated by Tony Chen. *There's a Train Going by My Window*. Garden City: Doubleday, 1982. (Rhythmic verse and refrain.)

Klein, Leonore. *Brave Daniel*. New York: Scholastic Press, 1958.

Kraus, Robert. *Good Night Little ABC*. New York: Scholastic Press, 1972.

Kraus, Robert. *Whose Mouse Are You?* New York: Collier Books, 1970.

Krauss, Ruth. *Bears*. New York: Scholastic Press, 1948.

Krauss, Ruth. *A Hole is to Dig*. New York: Harper & Row, 1952.

Langstaff, John. *Gather My Gold Together: Four Songs for Four Seasons*, Garden City: Doubleday, 1971.

Langstaff, John. *Oh, A-Hunting We Will Go*. New York: Atheneum, 1974.

Langstaff, John. *Over in the Meadow*. New York: Harcourt Brace Jovanovich, 1957.

Laurence, Ester. *We're off to Catch a Dragon*. Nashville: Abingdon, 1969.

Le Tora, Bijow. *Nice and Cozy*. New York: Four Winds, 1980. (Rhyming text and refrain.)

Lexau, Joan. *Crocodile and Hen*. New York: Harper and Row, 1969.

The Lion's Tail. Glenview, Ill.: Scott, Foresman, 1971.

Lobel, Anita. *King Rooster, Queen Hen*. New York: Greenwillow, 1975.

Figure 7–7 *(Continued)*

Lobel, Arnold. *A Treeful of Pigs*. New York: Greenwillow, 1979.

Mack, Stan. *10 Bears in My Bed*. New York: Pantheon, 1974.

Mars, W. T. *The Old Woman and Her Pig*. Racine, Wis.: Western Publishing Company, 1964.

Martin, Bill. *Brown Bear, Brown Bear, What Do You See?* New York: Holt, Rinehart & Winston. 1967.

Martin, Bill. *Fire! Fire! Said Mrs. McGuire*. New York: Holt, Rinehart & Winston, 1970.

Martin, Bill. *Freedom Books*. Los Angeles: Bowmar, 1965.

Martin, Bill. *A Ghost Story*. New York: Holt, Rinehart & Winston, 1970.

Martin, Bill. *The Haunted House*. New York: Holt, Rinehart & Winston, 1970.

Martin, Bill. *Instant Readers*. New York: Holt, Rinehart & Winston, 1970.

Martin, Bill. *Little Owl Series*. New York: Holt, Rinehart & Winston, 1965.

Martin, Bill. *Monday, Monday, I Like Monday*. New York: Holt, Rinehart & Winston, 1970.

Martin, Bill. *Sounds of Language*. New York: Holt, Rinehart & Winston, 1966.

Martin, Bill. *Spoiled Tomatoes*. Los Angeles: Bowmar, 1967.

Martin, Bill. *Teacher's Edition to the Sounds of Language Readers*. New York: Holt, Rinehart & Winston, 1966.

Martin, Bill. *Teacher's Guide to the Instant Readers*. New York: Holt, Rinehart & Winston, 1971.

Martin, Bill. *Wise Owl Series*, New York: Holt, Rinehart & Winston, 1967.

Mayer, Mercer. *If I Had . . .* New York: Dial, 1968.

Mayer, Mercer. *Just for You*. Racine, Wis.: Golden Press, 1975.

McGovern, Ann. *Too Much Noise*. New York: Scholastic Press, 1967.

Memling, Carl. *Riddles, Riddles form A to Z*. Racine, Wis.: Golden Press, 1972.

Memling, Carl. *Ten Little Animals*. Racine, Wis.: Golden Press, 1961.

Moffett, Martha. *A Flower Pot is Not a Hat*. New York: E. P. Dutton, 1972.

Nodset, Joan. *Who Took the Farmer's Hat?* New York: Scholastic Press, 1963.

O'Neill, Mary. *Hailstones and Halibut Bones*. Garden City: Doubleday, 1961.

Palmer, Janet. *Ten Days of School*. New York: Bank Street College of Education, Macmillan, 1969.

Patrick, Gloria. *A Bug in a Jug*. New York: Scholastic Press, 1970.

Peek, Merle. *Roll Over!* Boston: Houghton Mifflin, 1981.

Peppe, Rodney. *The House that Jack Built*. New York: Delacorte, 1970.

Petersham, Maud, and Miska Petersham. *The Rooster Crows: A Book of American Rhymes and Jingles*. New York: Scholastic Press, 1971.

Polushkin, Maria. *Mother, Mother, I Want Another*. New York: Crown, 1978.

Figure 7-7   *(Continued)*

Preston, Edna M. *The Temper Tantrum Book*. New York: Viking, 1969.

Preston, Edna Mitchell. *Where Did My Mother Go?* New York: Four Winds, 1978.

Quackenbush, Robert M. *Poems for Counting*. New York: Holt, Rinehart & Winston, 1965.

Quackenbush, Robert. *She'll Be Comin' Round the Mountain*. Philadelphia: Lippincott, 1973.

Quackenbush, Robert. *Skip to My Lou*. Philadelphia: Lippincott, 1975.

Regniers, Beatrice. *Willy O'Dwyer Jumped in the Fire*. New York: Atheneum, 1968.

Rokoff, Sandra. *Here is a Cat*. Singapore: Hallmark Children's Editions, no date.

Rossetti, Christina. *What is Pink?* New York: Holt, Rinehart & Winston, 1965.

Scheer, Jullian, and Marvin Bileck. *Rain Makes Applesauce*. New York: Holiday House, 1964.

Scheer, Jullian, and Marvin Bileck. *Upside Down Day*. New York: Holiday House, 1968.

Sendak, Maurice. *Chicken Soup with Rice*. New York: Scholastic Press, 1962.

Sendak, Maurice. *Where the Wild Things Are*. New York: Scholastic Press, 1963.

Dr. Seuss. *Dr. Seuss's ABC*. New York: Random House, 1963.

Shaw, Charles B. *It Looked Like Spilt Milk*. New York: Harper & Row, 1947.

Shulevitz, Uri. *One Monday Morning*. New York: Scribner's, 1967.

Skaar, Grace. *What Do the Animals Say?* New York: Scholastic Press, 1972.

Sonneborn, Ruth A. *Someone Is Eating the Sun*. New York: Random House, 1974.

Spier, Peter. *The Fox Went Out on a Chilly Night*. Garden City: Doubleday, 1961.

Stover, JoAnn. *If Everybody Did*. New York: David McKay, 1960.

Thomas, Patricia. Illustrated by Mordicai Gerstein. *"There are Rocks in My Socks!" Said the Ox to the Fox*. New York: Lothrop, 1979. (Repetition and rhyme.)

Tolstoy, Alexei. *The Great Big Enormous Turnip*, New York: Franklin Watts, 1968.

Wahl, Jan. *Drakestail*. Illustrated by Byron Barton. New York: Greenwillow, 1978. (Refrain and cumulative plot.)

Watson, Clyde. *Father Ox's Pennyrhymes*. New York: Scholastic Press, 1971.

Welber, Robert. *Goodbye, Hello*. New York: Pantheon, 1974.

Westcott, Nadine Bernard. *I Known an Old Lady Who Swallowed a Fly*. Boston: Little, Brown, 1980.

Figure 7–7   *(Continued)*

Wildsmith, Brian. *Brian Wildsmith's ABC*. New York: Franklin Watts, 1962.

Wildsmith, Brian. *The Twelve Days of Christmas*. New York: Franklin Watts, 1972.

Withers, Carl. *A Rocket in My Pocket*. New York: Scholastic Press, 1967.

Wolkstein, Diane. *The Visit*. New York: Knopf, 1977.

Wondriska, William. *All the Animals Were Angry*. New York: Holt, Rinehart & Winston, 1970.

Wright, H. R. *A Maker of Boxes*. New York: Holt, Rinehart & Winston, 1965.

Zaid, Barry. *Chicken Little*. New York: Random House, no date.

Zemach, Harve. *The Judge*. New York: Farrar, Straus and Giroux, 1969.

Zemach, Margot. *Hush, Little Baby*. New York: E. P. Dutton, 1976.

Zemach, Margot. *The Teeny Tiny Woman*. New York: Scholastic Press, 1965.

Zolotow, Charlotte. *Do You Know What I'll Do?* New York: Harper & Row, 1958.

The sequence of lessons to be followed with any single book or the children's own dictated story is as follows:

1. The teacher reads the book to the group and then reads it again inviting the students to join in when they are able to predict what is coming. The group may then be divided into subgroups for various choral readings in which they change parts. When dictated stories are used, the lesson is the same, except the first lesson is preceded with a discussion and the generation of a story is dictated by the students.
2. The teacher and students read the story from the book together. Then the story is read from a chart without the picture clues or, if a "Big Book" (see Shared Book Approach in this unit) is being used, with the pictures covered.
3. The teacher and students read the story from the chart. The students are given sentence strips containing lines of the story. They match the steps with the corresponding line in the story by placing the strip under the line.
4. The students as a group read the story from the chart. They are then given word cards to match with words on the chart.
5. The students as a group read the story from the chart. In random order, the teacher places word cards from the story at the bottom of the chart. The students locate each of these words on the story and place them in the order with which they occurred in the story. The procedure is requested for each section of the story.

Cautions and Comments

In two studies, a Patterned Language Approach has been shown to be equal or superior to a "typical" basal approach with first graders. Bridge, Winograd, and Haley (1983) have reported that the use of a Patterned Language Approach—in contrast to a typical basal approach—spurred the acquisition of sight vocabulary, induced students to use context clues, and created more positive feelings about reading. In a second study, Bridge and Burton (1982) were not able to show significant differences, but suggested similar trends were evidence in their data.

As a method for beginning formal reading instruction, the Patterned Language Approach shares a great deal in common with Holdaway's procedure for using a Shared Book Approach and R. V. Allen's Language Experience Approach for Reading. What the Patterned Approach offers that these other approaches do not are straightforward procedures for having students simultaneously attend to meaning, the flow of a text, the syntax, and graphophonic features. What also distinguishes the approach from others is the examination of its efficacy by Bridge. Too few strategies are subjected to the scrutiny that systematic research examinations can provide.

What may be a limitation of the procedure is the routine itself. If followed repetitively, the specific steps suggested may become more tedious than educative. Otherwise, a great deal of care needs to go into the presentation of the material or varying the word and sentence matching procedures. What is also a limitation of the procedure is the failure of Bridge and her colleagues to spell out how predictable story material should be selected or produced by the teacher. When suggesting that teachers direct students' attention to words, Bridge and her colleagues never indicate which words or how many should be identified and matched.

Despite these limitations, the approach does serve the purposes for which it was intended. It represents an approach that allows students to learn to read by reading.

REFERENCES

Bridge, C. 1979. Predictable materials for beginning readers. *Language Arts* 50:503–07. Describes the use of predictable or pattern stories and how they might be used by teachers.

Bridge, C., and B. Burton. 1982. Teaching sight vocabulary through patterned language materials. In *New inquiries in reading research and instruction*, edited by J. A. Niles and L. A. Harris. Washington, D.C.: National Reading Conference, 119–23. Presents a research study in which "patterned" stories were used.

Bridge, C., P. Winograd, and D. Haley. 1983. Using predictable materials vs. preprimers to teach beginning sight words. *The Reading Teacher* 36: 884–91. Represents the primary source for a Patterned Language Approach.

Cunningham, P. 1979. Beginning reading without readiness: Structured language experience. *Reading Horizons* 19:222–27. Describes a structured approach for using students' dictated stories.

Goodman, K. S. 1976. *Reading: A conversation with Kenneth Goodman.* Glenview, Ill.: Scott, Foresman. Discusses how psycholinguistic thinking applies to beginning reading.

Martin, B., and P. Brogan. 1971. *Teachers guide to the instant readers.* New York: Holt, Rinehart & Winston. Provides guidelines and suggestions for using predictable stories.

Rhodes, L. K. 1979. Comprehension and predictability: An analysis of beginning reading materials. In *New perspectives on comprehension*, edited by J. C. Hartse and R. Carey. Bloomington, Ind.: Indiana University, School of Education. Presents a research study in which the worth of patterned stories was examined.

Rhodes, L. K. 1981. I can read! Predictable books as resources for reading and writing instruction. *The Reading Teacher* 34:511–18. Discusses the use of patterned or predictable stories in a classroom.

Smith, F. 1978. *Understanding reading.* 2d ed. New York: Holt, Rinehart & Winston. Presents a theoretical discussion of reading and learning to read based upon psycholinguistic thinking.

APPENDIX

DIAGNOSTIC USE OF STRATEGIES FOR TEACHING READING AS A LANGUAGE EXPERIENCE

Strategies for teaching reading as a language experience were described in Unit 7. This description of diagnostic use of these strategies is intended to be relevant to each of them and to the general use of the language experience approach. Of necessity, therefore, this section is nonspecific to the different strategies. Its main focus is upon the kind of activity necessary to meet and expand the student's language capabilities. It focuses upon four aspects involved in the dictated-story strategy for teaching reading as a language experience. These aspects are language generation, language expression, language production, and language study.

Language generation refers to the motivation or stimulus activity used to create student interest in sharing and describing experiences. Student responsiveness varies with interest in a topic and students' motivation for sharing. The question arises: What is needed to stimulate expression? Expression may be stimulated through the use of a picture, a concrete object, dramatization, puppets, manipulative activity, a field experience, or a discussion. Activities can range from the concrete to the vicarious, depending upon the motivation and background of the student for a particular topic.

Language expression refers to the nature and structure of the expression rendered by the student. Based upon the students' capabilities and the topic under consideration, it may be appropriate to expect students to describe and relate their ideas in either words, phrases, a sentence, sentences, or a story. A decision will need to be made as to which should be sought and expected.

Language production refers to producing a record of the student's expression. After the student's ideas have been expressed, a decision must be made about recording these ideas. This should be based upon the student's capabilities, and the purpose which the language activities and the record will serve. Language production can range from a record of part of the student's dictation to a record of the student's entire dictation. To avoid the potential tedium of this activity, both the teacher and student might record segments of a single dictated story. In some cases, the student's purposes can be best served with the task of writing one or two words.

Language study refers to the activities that follow the student's generation and expression of ideas. Usually these activities involve rereading the student's written record and other reading-related actions. For the purpose of rereading, a decision must be made as to when and how much a student is capable of reading. It is possible that students may be able to read a record of their ideas with little or no assistance. In other cases, the teacher may need to read it to the student several times or along with the student before the student is ready to read even a few sentences or even a few words. In terms of reading-related activities, a student's needs may be best met through comprehension, or through vocabulary-related or other activities.

Illustration

To illustrate the diagnostic use of strategies to teach reading as a language experience, the following example with a single student is offered. The strategy would need to be modified slightly for use with a group.

Scott was a seven-year-old with limited interest and ability in reading. He seemed unable to read material at a low first-grade level and was reported to be unable to recognize many words. To assess Scott's reading and reading-related abilities, his responsiveness to various activities was examined. Specifically, Scott's responsiveness in language generation, language expression, language production, and language study activities was examined. In addition, his differential responsiveness to selected print awareness activities and book-handling abilities was determined.

Task One: Language Generation, Language Expression, Language Production, and Language Study

As a language generation activity, Scott was asked to describe a caterpillar presented to him in a jar. During this activity, Scott seemed most attentive and interested. He described the caterpillar in rich detail. He was then asked to tell a story about the caterpillar; he did so with enthusiasm. He gave complete sentences and a cohesive story. The story was then written for Scott while he watched. At this point, his interest seemed to dwindle. He even seemed distracted when asked to write selected words. He gave his story a title but seemed uninterested in rereading the story. The story was read to Scott; then Scott was asked to read along. When asked to read the story by himself, Scott faltered on approximately ten percent of the words. He seemed overly concerned about "sounding out" the words, rather than reading for meaning. Through follow-up activities, Scott's comprehension and use of context were further assessed. Scott accurately answered questions dealing with main idea and supporting details, with cause-effect, and with predicting outcomes. When given an oral cloze activity, he could accurately fill in the blanks. His responses are scored on the following scale.

LANGUAGE EXPERIENCE
ACTIVITY NEEDS

Language generation

Concrete   Vicarious
experience   experience
//_____X_____//

Describe: Concrete activities and directed discussion needed

Language expression

words   phrases   sentence   sentences   story
//_____X_____//

Describe: Capable of generating connected sentences and a story

Language production

teacher writes   teacher and pupil write   pupil writes
//_____X_____//

Describe: Inattentive, needs teacher direction

Language study

teacher reads   teacher and pupil read   pupil reads
//_____X_____//

Describe: After teacher reads, can read along

Related Activities: (Comprehension, identifying important words, context clues) Specify: good comprehension, asked and answered questions, good oral cloze

Specific language abilities

	Many	Some	Little	None
Spontaneous ideas	X			
Variety of ideas		X		
Originality of ideas		X		
Specificity of ideas	X			
Completeness of sentences		X		
Connections between sentences		X		
Variety of sentences				X
Richness of sentences				X
Variety of phrases				X
Variety of vocabulary				X

Conclusions: The language experience lesson suggested that with appropriate adaptations the strategy could be used effectively with Scott. In terms of language generation and expression activities, Scott responded with interest to concrete experiences. He was able to express his thoughts orally, to observe details such as likenesses and differences, and to express his thoughts in a logical manner. In terms of language production, Scott tended to be inattentive. For this reason and based upon his present abilities, Scott might profit from language production activities in which a portion of his dictation was recorded by the teacher and a portion by the student. In terms of language study, he should be afforded an opportunity to have the story or sentences read back to him several times prior to his own reading of these materials. Related word and language study, including oral cloze and comprehension, would seem appropriate to help extend and reinforce Scott's acquisition of reading skills. Given his general inattentiveness, sessions should be brief and free of distractions, and should afford varied teacher-pupil interactions.

Task Two: Print Awareness

To determine Scott's general awareness of print, he was given two sets of print awareness activities.

In the first set of activities, Scott was asked to identify words "in" and "out of" a familiar context. Product labels or trademarks supplied the familiar context, such as "Coca Cola" and "Kentucky Fried Chicken." To assess whether Scott recognized the purpose of the labels, he was shown the products and asked to identify the portion of the labels which named the product. The labels were then presented for identification apart from their packages. Scott performed well on all of these tasks. He seemed aware of the function and meaning of print. Next, he was shown the words isolated from the label for identification purposes, both in the commercial and the standard printed forms of the labels. Scott would recognize most of these words when they were presented in the commercial print form, but not when presented in the standard print form. It was obvious that Scott had not transferred his knowledge of print in his environment to the more standard form of print as commonly seen in books. His level of responses are shown on the following scale.

	Many	Some	Little	None
Recognizes purposes of labels on packets	x			
Recognizes purposes of print on labels	x			
Recognizes meaning of print detached from label		x		
Recognizes print in standard label form				x

In the second print awareness activity, Scott worked with a simple recipe. He was shown four directions with identical three-word stems. "Put in the _____." Only the ingredient word for each direction differed. In the context of the recipe, Scott learned the three-word stem and the ingredients. He could read the directions by himself and read the label on each ingredient.

Conclusions: It was apparent that Scott was familiar with print in his environment, but had yet to transfer this knowledge to reading standard print. When given a reason to read, such as following a recipe, Scott quickly became familiar with the print, regardless of its graphic form. If he is given meaningful print experiences, it would seem that Scott can and will read. This fact should be capitalized upon for improving Scott's general and specific reading ability.

Task Three: Bookhandling Knowledge

To determine bookhandling behavior, Scott was given the following tasks. He was asked to identify a book on display and to tell what might be done with it. He was asked to describe what was inside a book and then told to show where the book actually began. To assess Scott's knowledge about pages, he was asked to show a page, and to indicate the first and last page in a book as well as the top and bottom of the page. To assess Scott's knowledge of the purpose of print, he was asked to explain what the print on the page tells and to identify where the print began and ended on the page. He was then asked to identify the first and last word on the page and to show how the page would be read. To assess his knowledge of words, he was asked to point to any word, to look for matching words, to find words that began the same way, to locate words that ended the same way, and to tell what was indicated by words beginning with capitals. Finally, he was asked to show and to explain the purposes of the pictures in the book.

Conclusions: Scott's responses to these tasks indicated familiarity with the purpose of a book and with the function of pages and print, and an understanding of the left-to-right and top-to-bottom conventions of the printed page. Scott was able to identify a word and match words but did have difficulty understanding the function of capitals and letters. It seems likely that as Scott dictates, reads, and writes his own experience stories, a better understanding of books will be gained.

8

Practices for Individualization and Recreational Reading

UNIT OVERVIEW

The Unit and Its Theme

Individualized reading, which centers on the child and not on the material, seeks to counteract some of the disadvantages of those approaches that do not account for individual differences in each learner. It is a major premise of practices for individualizing reading that the development of the individual is more important than the materials, the sequence of skills or activities, or any other mandates that might homogenize students. The teacher's task becomes to work with each student in an intensive one-to-one situation and to tailor reading programs to the specific needs of those individuals. The task demands that teachers have the knowledge and skill required to plan, implement, direct, and evaluate reading programs.

In addition to the cognitive aspects of developing competent readers, a major goal of reading instruction should be the development of life-time readers—individuals who not only can read, but who do read. Children and adults discover the joy of reading not by being told that reading is exciting and stimulating, but by being given the opportunity to read materials of their own choosing in a quiet, nonpressured environment.

The Practices

Four practices designed to aid classroom teachers in individualizing their reading program and promoting recreational reading are discussed in this unit. Unlike many of the practices discussed in previous units, which are very specific in design, the practices discussed here are global in nature.

To provide a preview of this unit, a brief summary of the practices follows.

Individualized Reading

Individualized reading is a reading system based upon self-interest, self-selection, and self-pacing. It is appropriate for use at all levels, and it attempts to capitalize on the notion that students should assume some responsibility for their own learning.

Learning Stations and Centers

Learning centers are designed to create an alternative classroom environment, one which combines the structure of traditional classrooms and the personalization of open education. Learning centers, which may be used throughout the grades for reading instruction, provide opportunities for increased self-direction and interaction by students.

Criterion-Referenced Management Systems

Used to focus instruction on specific skill behaviors, criterion-referenced management systems provide the means for teachers to begin to individualize instruction. Criterion-referenced management systems provide the teacher with specific information concerning students' skill mastery at various stages of reading acquisition.

Uninterrupted Sustained Silent Reading

The Uninterrupted Sustained Silent Reading period could be one of the major components of a successful reading program. Very simply, time is set aside during the school day to provide students with an opportunity to read. Students, as well as their teacher, read materials of their own choosing in a quiet, relaxed atmosphere.

INDIVIDUALIZED READING

Purpose

Based upon the notion of seeking, self-selection, and self-pacing, individualized reading is designed to (1) focus reading instruction on the individual needs of each child and (2) aid teachers in guiding children toward assuming responsibility and initiative for their own growth in reading.

Rationale

As with any reading method, individualized reading is designed to develop a reader's abilities and interests. However, the basic premise in individualized reading differs greatly from that in other methods. Olson (1949) suggested three major principles that have become the foundation of individualized reading—seeking, self-selection, and self-pacing. Olson explained that students are continually exploring their own environment in search of experiences that fit with their growth and needs. Applied to reading, this means that the most conducive environment for reading growth would be one in which students are surrounded by materials to explore and select from and to read at their own pace. Such exploration is done in accordance with students' own needs and interests. In terms of actual reading instruction, the procedure that has evolved from this point of view was summarized briefly by Smith (1963) as follows:

> Each child selects a book that he wants to read. During the individual conference period, the teacher sits in some particular spot in the room as each child comes and reads to her. As he does so, she notes his individual needs and gives him appropriate help. Finally, she writes what the child is reading, his needs, and strengths on his record card. Then another individual conference is held and so on. If several children need help on the same skills, they may be called together in a group for such help. (P. 142)

Intended Audience

Although individualized reading has been more widely used in the elementary grades, the technique readily lends itself to teaching in the content areas, particularly where a multiple-textbook approach is employed to expose students to various ideas and opinions.

Description of the Procedure

An individualized reading program is heavily dependent on (1) self-selection, (2) ample supply of reading material, (3) student-teacher conference, (4) flexible needs grouping, and (5) sharing books.

1. Self-selection

Possibly the most basic ingredient in the individualized reading program is that every student be taught reading with materials that the student chooses. As

Veatch (1978) suggested, the student is taught to select reading material based on two criteria:

a. I like it.
b. I can read it.

Obviously, an important teacher function is to expose students constantly to the variety of material available for reading. Through brief, enticing descriptions of these materials, the teacher can encourage the student to select the most desirable and motivating material. This, in essence, is the first responsibility of the teacher in planning—to make sure each student is given suitable material during the reading program.

2. Ample supply of reading material

Essential to a program of self-selection is an ample supply of reading material for the student. A variety of material is needed if a student is to select a book he or she can handle with comfort. Veatch (1978) recommended that in order to maintain an adequate supply of reading material in the classroom, there should be available at least three to five titles per student.

Books are needed on many grade levels, since the range of ability in a classroom is wide. Typically, the range of difficulty should extend from one or two grade levels below the slowest reader to one or two grades above the best reader in the class. Thus, for example, in a typical first grade class, the teacher selects books for students ranging from picture books of the earliest prereading level to those books of at least fifth-grade difficulty.

Additionally, even though bright readers can effectively deal with materials of greater difficulty than average readers, their interests may be similar. Hence, a variety of books dealing with the same topic on different levels of difficulty is necessary.

There are many possible sources available for a teacher who is trying to gather three to five titles for each student in the class. The school librarian can be an invaluable aid and a tremendous source of information concerning books. Public libraries and bookmobiles provide other sources of reading material for the classroom. Book fairs also can be a means of securing additional materials for the students.

Paperback books are another source for stocking the classroom library, since they are relatively inexpensive when compared to the price of hardbacks. Book clubs, such as those of Scholastic Book Services, often provide discount rates for paperbacks. Often neglected, but still excellent sources of reading materials, are magazines and newspapers. Again, they are relatively inexpensive, and a teacher can request that the students bring in old magazines or newspapers from home to maintain an adequate supply.

Finally, abandoned or old sets of basal readers can be used to supplement the book supply. Basal readers do have stories that attract children; the individual story selections can be separated into small books for distribution as "mini-books." Teachers of different grade levels can exchange a certain number of basal readers among themselves.

3. Student-teacher conference

Central to the individualized reading program are the individual sessions a student has with the teacher. These individual conferences essentially determine the character of the reading program, since it is during these conferences that the student receives important personal direction in reading activity. The teacher needs to have specific purposes in mind and the ability to analyze and understand the reading performance of each student. This is essential in order to conduct a speedy, but thorough, conference and in order to insure that each student gets the necessary amount of individual attention and instruction that will provide for optimum growth.

A teacher does not check on everything a child reads, but rather concentrates on what the child has selected and prepared for presentation. Veatch (1978) described four areas that should be explored in the conference session:

1. The mechanical aspects of the student's reading ability;
2. The student's ability to read critically;
3. The student's personal involvement; and
4. The ability to hold an audience while reading aloud.

In the area of mechanical skills, the teacher might ascertain the student's ability to use word attack skills when encountering words that present difficulty. When reading critically, the student should be able to get the overall sense of the story, as well as be able to delve into the author's purposes. Knowing why a certain book is chosen is considered important for the student, not only for the student's own personal development, but also for gaining the ability to recommend the book to others in the class. Personal involvement with characters in the book also should be explored. Finally, the area of oral reading with expression should be explored.

Essential to the individual conference are the records the teacher keeps on each student. It is with these annotations that the teacher can guide the student in reading and also plan for grouping activities. The following is an example of such a record:

Juan	8.5 Age	2.5 Rdg. Ach.
9/5 Horton Hatches the Egg (p. 21, oral)		
Saw value of commitment.		
Group: checking organization of details		
Ind. Assign.: Vocabulary exercises		

From such an annotative record, the teacher can plan the next day's reading activities for the student. For example, the student Juan might work in a group to improve his skill in reading for details. Additionally, he will work on his own with vocabulary activities or the teacher can wait until several children have the same skill need and group them together to work on that area.

4. Flexible-needs grouping

Groups are formed based upon the observations and diagnoses teachers have made during individual conferences and other observations made during school day. When the teacher sees that at least two students have the same need, a group can be formed.

It is to be emphasized that groups be formed in an individualized program when at least two students need to know something or do something that the others in class do not need to know or do. These groups are flexible in the sense that they are formed only temporarily to fill a need and then are disbanded.

This is contrary to the usual practice of grouping, which is organized on the basis of low, middle, and high reading abilities. This conventional grouping plan is usually indefinite and allows for little flexibility in instruction. Additionally, such grouping allows for the negative aspects of peer pressure and labeling—the low group (e.g., "the Buzzards") become "dummies," and everyone knows it!

Groups may be formed easily when the teacher keeps good records of the individual conferences. By looking over these records, the teacher can readily see those students who are having common difficulties. For instance, the teacher can see that Juan, the student mentioned in the sample record, is only one of five students who are having difficulty with organizing their ideas. Thus, the teacher can save valuable time by grouping the five together. Instead of spending time teaching each student individually, time is efficiently used by helping all of them with the same thing at the same time.

Groups may also be formed for other purposes, some of which may be highly specific. Interest groups may be organized around a common concern. On the other hand, a few students can be grouped together for the specific purposes of finding more challenging reading material or for help in selecting a book at their reading level.

5. Sharing books

Individualized reading provides students with an opportunity to share their reading experiences. In common practice, the sharing of books is accomplished through written reports that, unless creatively used, become tedious. As an alternative, teachers might give students a variety of ways to share books. These sharing activities might range from simple reflection on the content of the book to a dramatic presentation of an inspiring part of the book. Role playing, pantomiming, movie scripts, advertisements, radio scripts, posters, and puppetry are suggested alternatives from which the children might select.

Cautions and Comments

Individualized reading presents the teacher with a viable alternative to other approaches, by emphasizing personal involvement and decision making on the part of the student. However, there are some major deterrents to its use.

Since individualized reading is predicated upon the idea of self-selection, and self-selection from an ample supply of books, these two factors may militate against the success of the program. For example, the lack of a large number of appropriate titles from which to choose may limit the self-selective process, and students may not find a title that matches both their interests and their reading abilities.

A problem that seems to arise is the pressure to complete as many individual conferences as possible in each day. Ideally, the teacher will not neglect anyone, even the brightest of readers. In reality, overly long conferences with some students will result in less available time for the other students. Thus, some students may not get the individual attention necessary to progress adequately in reading.

Similarly, the success of an individualized reading program is in part dependent upon the vitality of the teacher-student conferences and sharing experiences. To ensure student involvement, both student conferences and sharing experiences will need to be meaningful and varied according to individual reading experiences.

Finally, individualized reading represents a viable alternative for the classroom teacher. Like most approaches, it demands that teachers possess an adequate understanding of the reading process and the reading curriculum. Like an individualized reading practice, it demands extensive teacher preparation and recordkeeping.

REFERENCES

Blakely, W. P., and B. McKay. 1972. Individualized reading as part of an eclectic reading program. In *Elementary reading today: Selected articles*, edited by W. H. Miller. New York: Holt, Rinehart & Winston, 111–20. Presents the results of an investigation that lends credibility to individualized reading procedures.

Fader, D. N., J. Duggins, T. Finn, and E. B. McNeil. 1976. *The new hooked on books*. New York: Berkeley. Updates a discussion of a saturated book program.

Groff, P. 1972. Helping teachers begin individualized reading. In *Elementary reading today: Selected articles*, edited by W. H. Miller. New York: Holt, Rinehart & Winston, 101–6. Reviews twelve basic questions and points of concern when planning and initiating a program of individualized reading.

Hunt, L. 1970. Effect of self-selection, interest, and motivation upon independent, instructional, and frustration levels. *The Reading Teacher* 24:

146–51. Examines the effect of major tenets of individualized reading on the traditional concepts of reading levels.

Olson, W. C. 1949. *Child development*. Boston: D. C. Heath. Presents the basic principles of individualized reading.

Sartain, H. W. 1972. Advantages and disadvantages of individualized reading. In *Individualizing reading instruction: A reader*, edited by L. A. Harris, and C. B. Smith. New York: Holt, Rinehart & Winston, 86–96. Provides the pros and cons of an individualized reading program.

Smith, N. B. 1963. *Reading instruction for today's children*. Englewood Cliffs, N.J.: Prentice-Hall, 129–62. Traces the historical development of individualized reading and presents examples of its use.

Veatch, J. 1978. *Reading in the elementary school*. 2d ed. New York: John Wiley and Sons. Provides the basic plans from which to establish an individualized reading program with particular emphasis on classroom management.

LEARNING STATIONS AND CENTERS

Purpose

The purpose of learning stations and centers is to (1) create a classroom environment conducive to individualizing reading instruction and (2) increase the opportunities for students to be involved in self-directed learning activities.

Rationale

Learning stations and centers represents an attempt at individualizing instruction, reflecting a compromise between the rigidity of the traditionally structured classroom and the disenchantment resulting from noisy and undirected open classrooms. They also reflect certain political and social pressures that prompted their advent. As Gilstrap and Martin (1975) suggested:

> Although the learning center strategy appears to be a natural outgrowth of the continued search for ways to individualize instruction, which has been supported through research and practice, the search has been intensified by the recent social and economic pressures on public school educators to be more accountable for their work with students. (P. 77)

The term "learning center" is a rather loose term for an area in either the classroom or the school where students may have access to learning materials and activities. These materials and activities are directed toward providing specific learning opportunities with defined objectives and self-management procedures.

Typically, the classroom employing learning centers differs in a number of ways from the conventional classroom. The classroom becomes a decentralized learning laboratory, physically divided into various areas or centers, instead of having the chalkboard and teacher's desk at the front serve as the focal point of learning. The students, working independently or in small groups, carry out their own learning activities with the aid and guidance of the teacher. The time involved in whole-group instruction also is significantly reduced (Hanson 1972).

Intended Audience

Learning centers may be used throughout the grades for reading instruction. Although they are commonly associated with the elementary and middle schools, they are also appropriate for reading instruction in secondary schools.

Description of the Procedure

Learning centers can play a significant role in helping students learn to read. They can be used effectively with almost any reading system, by providing both the incentive and the materials to practice reading and the developmental skill activities necessary for independence in reading.

A discussion of learning centers and how to employ that strategy in the classroom revolves around three areas: (1) classroom organization, (2) student and teacher responsibilities, and (3) integrating centers into the reading program.

1. Classroom organization

Major differences can exist in the way a classroom is organized and in which centers are used. Central to the organization are the goals of instruction and the needs of the students. Once these areas have been considered, decisions can be made to obtain maximum effectiveness from the centers.

One decision that must be considered is whether the centers are to be used as the primary vehicle of instruction or as a supplement to the regular instruction program. The mode of instruction has a bearing on how the classroom is arranged. For example, if centers are used as supplementary, then they probably will be limited in number and are best placed around the classroom, leaving the central area of the classroom open for whole-group instruction. On the other hand, if centers are the primary mode of instruction, the number of centers will be larger and the need for a central area for whole-group instruction is not as imperative.

Another decision concerning classroom organization that must be considered is the type, number, and arrangement of learning centers. Once the teacher has decided whether centers will be primary or supplementary in scope, the variety of centers used in the classroom is limited only by the imagination of that teacher.

Figure 8-1

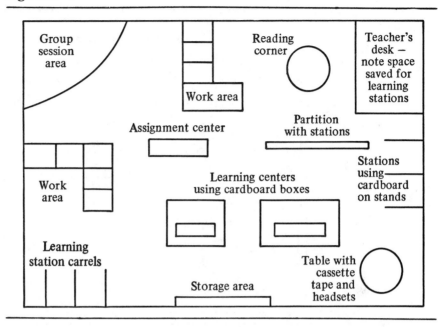

Obviously, the total room arrangement needs careful examination. The use of centers requires that the classroom be arranged into areas. These areas might include an area for teacher-directed group activities and areas for independent and follow-up work. Around the classroom, independent centers might be located on bulletin boards, chalkboards, connected desks, tops of cabinets, even the floor. A possible room arrangement that might be used and several examples of learning center structure are shown in Figures 8-1 and 8-2.

Allen (1976) recommended that centers be organized around three major themes:

a. *Self-expression* activities for personal communication,
b. *Language study* activities for comprehending how language works, particularly for reading and writing, and
c. *Language-influence* activities, which bring learners in contact with the ideas and language of others.

Centers organized around self-expression activities include opportunities for oral expression, creative writing and dramatics, art expression, and musical expression. Language study centers would be organized to include games for reviewing language skills, dictation experiences, writing mechanics, and study skills. Finally, centers organized around language-influence activities provide opportunities for students to view films and filmstrips, to use puppets as story

Figure 8-2

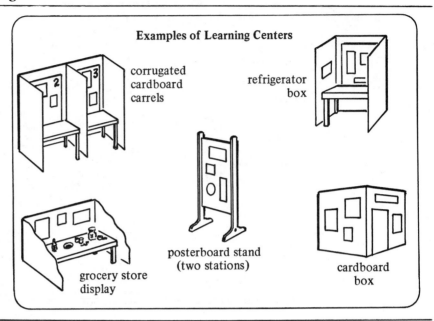

Examples of Learning Centers

corrugated cardboard carrels

refrigerator box

posterboard stand (two stations)

grocery store display

cardboard box

characters, to listen to stories and music, to browse through books, and to have reading instruction.

2. Student and teacher responsibilities

Students may work in individual, paired, or small-group instructional situations at the centers. They are responsible for getting involved in their work, planning their time accordingly, and asking for help when needed. Students are permitted to talk or work with their friends and to enjoy some free time when their work is finished.

Although they are out of the constant supervision of the teacher, students in the learning centers are responsible for maintaining harmonious relations with others. Disruptions and distractions are to be avoided. This may seem a formidable task, but the motivating factors and the freedom inherent in the center approach militate against most disruptions. Additionally, the teacher can employ the use of class meetings and individual conferences to deal with problems of that type.

The responsibilities of the teacher include being a learning facilitator and a diagnostician. To facilitate learning, the teacher sets the psychological climate in which students become motivated to pursue learning activities and offers suggestions or raises questions as the students work. Through interaction and observation, the teacher diagnoses the needs and abilities of the students. Activities can then be designed which will be of more interest and value for them.

A learning center concept does not completely eliminate the need for teacher-directed activities; rather, it shifts the emphasis. A teacher may find that certain class activities are more effective when delivered in a whole-group situation. Centers then act as reinforcing agents of that activity, by supplementing and complementing the teacher-directed initiative.

Another major responsibility for the teacher is to develop and maintain the learning centers. New and additional activities need to be added continually to the centers. Additionally, some centers need to be replaced or rotated to provide a wide variety of experiences for the students. Although it will take considerable effort and creativity by the teacher, the richer the learning environment is in opportunities and materials, the better the students will learn.

Before initiating learning centers, the teacher is also responsible for communicating the intent of the learning center approach and for maintaining a stable, calm environment conducive to learning. Students must be made aware of their responsibilities to themselves as learners and to others in the class attempting to learn. The ground rules can be laid in group meetings and reinforced in individual conferences. Upon beginning this approach, teachers need to start slowly and build slowly, as children become accustomed to working on their own.

Finally, the teacher is responsible for establishing methods of scheduling and assigning learning center activities. Work should be scheduled at the centers in accordance with their intended purposes. For example, if learning centers were to be used mainly for reinforcement, this schedule might be used.

8:30–8:45	Following whole class discussions, students are assigned either to a teacher-directed group activity or to independent learning center activities.
8:45–9:15	Teacher guides the reading of a selection with one group. At learning centers, other students proceed with follow-up activities from work of the previous day.
9:15–10:00	Upon completion of the selection, groups are assigned to centers to extend and reinforce understandings from the selection. Teacher supervises the work at all centers.

For purposes of assigning and organizing activities at the learning centers, teachers need a mechanism for distributing and gathering the students' learning center work. To initiate learning center activities, students might be given schedule sheets and/or assigned "mailboxes," such as milk cartons, in which they may both locate and return their assignments. A numbering system could be used to assign students to specific learning center sites; these assignment sheets could serve as a record or to evaluate the work done at the centers.

3. Integrating centers into the reading program

In the classroom organized around learning centers, centers can be integrated or organized around some presently or previously existing programs. For example, centers can be integrated with the basal reader series by providing opportunities for individualized practice. Using their diagnostic abilities, teachers can identify areas where additional practice is warranted and prescribe activities for students to do in the center. To augment the basal approach, extension enrichment or follow-up activities can be developed and situated in the centers.

Formatively, the language experience approach can readily work concurrently with a learning center approach. For example, a reading center could expose students to what others have written, while a writing center could provide students with the opportunity for self-expression by creating their own story. A listening center could expose the student to the thoughts and words of others.

To these several ends, learning centers should be self-administrative. They should provide a purpose, good directions, and evaluation to ensure that students are involved not only in learning, but in learning about learning. Sometimes, especially with poorer readers, the use of tape recorders and visuals may substitute for written directions. The following example may illustrate this idea.

Purpose: As we continue with our unit on "The World of Sports," we need to become aware of the equipment used in various sports. The stories you have read mention different equipment. Match the sports equipment words correctly with the sports of baseball, hockey, golf, and basketball.

Directions

1. Take word cards from the pocket.
2. Read the words and place them in the large pocket that best describes the sport.
3. If some words are new to you, check the stories you have just read on this sport and maybe a dictionary.

Evaluation

1. Check your products with the key.
2. Put all word cards and key cards back in right pockets.

Follow-up Activity

Write up an advertisement about the equipment from one of the sports, using as many of the

Follow-up Activity (Continued)
products as possible. Compare
your advertisement with others
in the local newspaper.

Cautions and Comments

Learning centers can aid a teacher in individualizing the classroom by providing opportunities for students to work in an informal atmosphere on specific activities designed to meet their needs and interests. Additionally, learning centers provide opportunities for the development of self-direction and self-awareness, and for the enhancement of students' self concepts.

However, the decentralization of the classroom under the centers approach does present the teacher with a few management problems. Foremost among these problems is the noise level of the classroom. The busy hum natural to learning centers can become an incessant clamor. On the other hand, trying to enforce a rule of silence in the centers may stifle interaction and informality in learning.

Management problems could also arise from the constant movement from center to center as students endeavor to complete their activities. It is essential for the teacher to communicate to students the necessity of settling into groups to do their work. Centers must be well stocked and constantly replenished with new learning activities designed to involve students in the work. To be meaningful, learning activities should not just be "busy work." Students should understand why they are doing what they are doing.

Another management problem may result from not providing help to students when they need it. If more than one student needs help at a time, grumbling, or, even worse, disruption, could result while they await the teacher's help. Students are many times impatient when they seek assistance; yet they must learn to wait their turn and, perhaps, be taught to go on to an alternate task while waiting. Also, if too many students are demanding assistance, the assigned work may not be at the right level of difficulty or in the correct amount. Better materials may be the answer.

Since learning centers aid in individualizing instruction, it becomes incumbent upon teachers to develop and maintain efficient methods of record keeping. Without such a system, it will become impossible to prescribe the kinds of meaningful activities necessary for students to develop in reading.

REFERENCES

Allen, R. V. 1976. *Language experiences in communication*. Boston: Houghton Mifflin, 66–74. Discusses the role of learning centers as part of an overall language laboratory organization designed to promote language learning in all curricular areas.

Allen, R. V., and C. Allen. 1976. *Language experience activities*. Boston:

Houghton Mifflin. Presents various learning centers that can be used as part of an overall language laboratory organization.

Gilstrap, L. R., and W. R. Martin. 1975. *Current strategies for teachers*. Pacific Palisades, Calif.: Goodyear, 77–84. Provides suggestions and checklists for setting up learning centers.

Hanson, R. A. 1972. Creating a responsive classroom reading environment with learning centers. In *Individualizing reading instruction: A reader*, edited by L. A. Harris and C. B. Smith. New York: Holt, Rinehart & Winston, 122–29. Concerns the role of learning centers in the classroom environment with specific emphasis on the reading program.

Kaplan, S. 1973. *Change for children*. Pacific Palisades, Calif.: Goodyear. Ideas, illustrations, and activities for learning centers and room arrangements.

Marshall, K. 1975. *Opening your class with learning stations*. Palo Alto, Calif.: Education Today. Presents practical suggestions for developing and implementing a learning stations approach in the classroom.

Vacca, R. T., and Vacca, J. L. 1974. Consider a stations approach to middle school reading instruction. *The Reading Teacher* 28:18–21. Offers a rationale and suggestions for the use and implementation of learning centers in a middle-school reading class.

Veatch, J. 1978. *Reading in the elementary school*. 2d ed. New York: John Wiley, 98–141. Discusses the use of a variety of learning centers to augment independent work during the reading period in an individualized program.

CRITERION-REFERENCED MANAGEMENT SYSTEMS

Purpose

The purpose of criterion-referenced management systems is to (1) provide focused instruction on specific skill behaviors by describing and prescribing an individual's mastery of specific skills, and (2) aid teachers in individualizing their reading programs by providing the means by which to differentiate those students who have mastered program objectives from those who have not.

Rationale

The term criterion-referenced management systems is used to describe the plethora of commercially-made and teacher-made systems that share (1) a sequentially ordered set of objectives for reading skills monitored by such systems, (2) tests composed of items or subtests designed to measure these objectives, (3) prescribed mastery levels for determining either adequate or inadequate skill attainment, (4) a cross-referenced file of exercises that teachers can use with students toward the attainment of skill mastery, and (5) reports that specify individual and group performance by skills and mastery levels. The terms "skill management systems," "objective-based reading instruction," and "subskills approach" are often used interchangeably to describe what has been deemed criterion-referenced management systems.

Advocates of criterion-referenced management systems argue that there is both pragmatic and theoretical support for their hierarchical skills management position. As Samuels (1976) suggested:

> The subskill approach . . . attempts to reduce the number of students who will experience difficulty in reading by teaching skills before the problem appears. (Pp. 173–74)

As Smith, Otto, and Hansen (1978) suggested:

> We need skills. Teachers need them to systematize instruction and to teach efficiently. Readers need them to approach the complex task of reading efficiently and effectively. (P. 44)

It seems that among advocates of such approaches, criterion-referenced management systems afford both useful and efficient individualized learning experiences. In an era of accountability, criterion-referenced management systems are viewed as a procedure by which instruction can be systematized and progress toward goals monitored by parents, administrators, and legislators.

Intended Audience

Although criterion-referenced instruction has been used more extensively in the elementary grades, it is also used throughout the grades to provide evaluation and instruction for students purported to need specific skill reinforcement.

Description of the Procedure

The key to individualizing instruction using criterion-referenced systems lies in an effective management system. Typically, a management system for a criterion-referenced system consists of (1) program objectives, (2) record-keeping system, and (3) cross-referencing of materials.

1. Program objectives

A basic ingredient of criterion-referenced instruction is the program objectives, usually stated in behavioral terms. Such behavioral objectives define performance standards, the basis of criterion-referenced instruction. It is against these performance standards, or criteria, that an individual's performance, or mastery, is evaluated. It is toward these performance level standards that instruction is prescribed.

In organizing for instruction in the individualized program, behavioral objectives function to break the broad content of reading into manageable parts or skill areas. Behavioral objectives purportedly help set clear purposes for both the student and the teacher as to why a particular task is being performed.

2. Record-keeping system

Essential to criterion-referenced instruction is keeping accurate records of the objectives that have and have not been mastered by the students. Such information is used for sorting students into flexible skills groups based on common instructional needs.

From this basic information, the teacher can construct individual folders and classroom charts as aids for individualizing instruction. The individual folders are simply file folders keyed to the program objectives stated for that particular grade level of the total school reading program. Next to each objective, space might be provided to indicate criterion-level performance and to specify whether mastery has been attained. Constructed in this way, the folders often follow a student through the elementary school years to provide a continuous record of progress.

Classroom charts are sometimes used to ascertain the progress of a total class of students in their attainment of particular objectives. Student names might be listed on one side of the chart and program objectives listed across the top. In this way, a grid is obtained for checking off students who have attained each objective. Figure 8–3 provides an example of a classroom chart.

3. Cross-referencing of materials

Within the framework of criterion-referenced instruction, the teacher's task is to fit the specifics of the materials into the specific exercises that students need to do in order to reach mastery of their program objectives. Once the objective has been specified, the teacher must gather and identify reading passages, workbook exercises, games, and activities that will aid the student in attaining

Figure 8–3

Comprehension Objectives – Grade One						
NAME	1	2	3	4	5	6

mastery of that objective. To this end, criterion-referenced systems usually provide cross-indexes of published reading.

Cautions and Comments

As Duffy (1978) pointed out:

> A controversy surrounds the use of objective-based reading instruction. Proponents point to promising research results and to the help teachers receive from its focus on task analysis, subskills, specific pretesting for diagnosis, and systematic monitoring for pupil progress. Critics, on the other hand, point to the weaknesses that result when objective-based instruction is carried to extremes, to the abuses evident in hasty or poorly conceived implementation. (P.519)

The advantages of criterion-referenced management systems are obvious. They afford a systematic procedure for monitoring, prescribing, and measuring mastery of reading skills and subskills. They allow teachers, administrators, legislators, and parents to operate with clearly established guidelines.

To the layperson, the shortcomings of criterion-referenced management systems are less obvious, but substantial. Johnson and Pearson (1975), for example, suggested six major shortcomings. As they stated:

> There are at least six things that bother us about skill monitoring systems: 1) their psycholinguistic naivete, 2) their "assembly-line" underpinnings, 3) their concern for skill at the expense of interest, 4) their advocacy of sequencing separable reading skills, 5) the validity of their assessment instruments, and 6) the very notion of mastery itself. (P. 758)

It is their argument that criterion-referenced management systems are theoretically naive, practically inappropriate, and minimally beneficial. They argue that criterion-referenced management systems inappropriately and inaccurately purport to define, measure, and monitor educational accountability in reading. Furthermore, in so doing criterion-referenced systems often misdirect attention away from the goal of learning to read for meaning and enjoyment.

REFERENCES

Coulson, J., and J. F. Cogswell. 1965. Effects of individualized instruction on testing. *Journal of Educational Measurement* 2:59–64. Presents some initial research on the effects of criterion-referenced testing in an attempt to individualize instruction.

Duffy, G. G. 1978. Maintaining a balance in objective-based reading instruction. *The Reading Teacher* 31:519–23. Discusses some of the pitfalls and solutions involved in implementing a skills management system.

Guszak, F. J. 1978. *Diagnostic reading instruction in the elementary school.* New York: Harper & Row. Presents the concept of the diagnostic reading teacher—one who uses criterion-referenced instruction as the basis for the teaching of reading.

Johnson, D. D. and P. D. Pearson. 1975. Skills management systems: A critique. *The Reading Teacher* 28:757–64. Critically reviews the use of skills management systems in the teaching of reading.

Lawrence, P. S., and B. M. Simmons. 1978. Criteria for reading management systems. *The Reading Teacher* 32:332–36. Reviews factors to be considered in the initiation of a criterion-referenced management system.

Mager, R. F. 1962. *Preparing instructional objectives.* Palo Alto, Calif.: Fearon. Provides a basic programmed handbook for the preparation and construction of behavioral objectives.

Otto, W. 1973. Evaluating instruments for assessing needs and growth in reading. In *Assessment problems in reading*, edited by W. H. MacGinitie. Newark: International Reading Association, 14–20. Reviews the basic approaches of assessment and their limitations in measuring student growth.

Otto, W., R. Chester, J. McNeil, and S. Meyers. 1974. *Focused reading instruction.* Reading, Mass.: Addison-Wesley. Presents a basic approach to focusing reading instruction through the use of behavioral objectives and criterion-referenced instruction.

Otto, W., R. Rude, and D. L. Spiegel. 1979. *How to teach reading.* Reading, Mass.: Addison-Wesley. Describes skills-management systems: their characteristics and application.

Rude, R. T. 1974. Objective-based reading systems: An evaluation. *The Reading Teacher* 28:169–75. Reviews six published criterion-referenced programs and suggests a format for evaluating other programs.

Samuels, S. J. 1976. Hierarchical subskills in the reading acquisition process. In *Aspects of reading acquisition*, edited by J. T. Guthrie. Baltimore: Johns Hopkins University Press, 162–79. Discusses the advantages, disadvantages, and problems associated with skill hierarchies.

Smith, R. J., W. Otto, and L. Hansen. 1978. *The school reading program.* Boston: Houghton Mifflin, 38–63. Provides a discussion of skills management systems, including a response to criticisms.

Thompson, R. A., and C. D. Dziuban. 1973. Criterion-referenced reading tests in perspective. *The Reading Teacher* 27:292–94. Concerns the nature of criterion-referenced testing and the cautions inherent in such an approach.

Wormer, F. B. 1974. What is criterion-referenced measurement? In *Measuring reading performance*, edited by W. E. Blanton, R. Farr, and J. J. Tuinman. Newark: International Reading Association, 34–43. Provides a definition of criterion-referenced measurement and compares it to standardized testing.

UNINTERRUPTED SUSTAINED
SILENT READING

Purpose

Generally recognized objectives of Uninterrupted Sustained Silent Reading (USSR) are (1) to provide students with a quiet time to practice their silent reading, (2) to provide students with models of good silent reading behavior, and (3) to increase students' abilities to sustain silent reading for longer periods of time.

Rationale

Much time is spent teaching students *how* to read; however, it is here argued that few classroom teachers provide students either a model for reading or the opportunity to read materials for pleasure. USSR is intended to provide students the opportunity to practice the art of reading—an opportunity to become actively involved in the reading act with materials of their own choosing. Just as playing golf and seeing others play golf gives a neophyte golfer the opportunity to learn to play, USSR is intended to provide the reader with the opportunity to become a better reader by reading and seeing others read. McCracken and McCracken (1978) suggested USSR provides students with the following messages:

> Reading books is important.
> Reading is something anyone can do.
> Reading is communicating with an author.
> Children are capable of sustained thoughts.
> Books are meant to be read in large sections.
> The teacher believes that the pupils are comprehending (because he or she doesn't bother to check).

> The teacher trusts the children to decide when something is well written, when something important has been read (because the teacher expects pupils to share after USSR). (P. 408)

Intended Audience

Uninterrupted Sustained Silent Reading is appropriate for students at kindergarten levels through senior high school. College and adult reading programs also could profit from the use of the technique. The technique may be used by an elementary teacher with a self-contained classroom, by a content teacher in a departmentalized program, or by a total school staff during a predetermined period of the school day (Ganz and Theofield 1974).

Description of the Procedure

USSR contains three vital elements: (1) preparation, (2) the reading period, and (3) follow-up.

1. Preparation

Perhaps the key to the success of a USSR program is this vital first step. Students should understand what they are going to be doing during the activity, why it is important, and how it will be carried out.

The idea of USSR should be discussed with students several days in advance of the first reading session. The emphasis at this stage should be on the fact that the students will be allowed to select whatever reading material they desire to read during this period. Although students should be encouraged to bring their favorite reading material to class for USSR sessions, several students predictably will forget on occasion; therefore, the teacher should collect a variety of reading materials that will remain in the classroom and can be used during USSR sessions. The collection should be changed occasionally to provide a variety of offerings.

Teachers also should be sure to inform their administrator(s) and colleagues of what they are doing and should inform them not to interrupt unless an emergency arises.

It is essential that all students in the class understand the rules of USSR. Presentation of the rules a day or two before the start of USSR allows students and teachers to discuss why these particular regulations are necessary. It is suggested that the rules be reviewed just prior to the first USSR session. The three cardinal rules of USSR are:

  a. *Everybody reads.* Both students and teacher will read something of their own choosing. Completing homework assignments, grading papers, and similar activities are discouraged. The reading should be for the pleasure of the reader.
  b. *There are to be no interruptions during USSR.* The word "uninterrupted" is an essential part of the technique. Interruptions result in loss of comprehension and loss of interest by many students; therefore, questions and comments should be held until the silent reading period has concluded.
  c. *No one will be asked to report what they have read.* It is essential that students feel that this is a period of free reading with the emphasis on reading for enjoyment.

2. The reading period

The USSR period begins as soon as the students have been given a sufficient amount of time to select their reading materials and the teacher has reviewed the rules briefly. Following the first session, it may be only necessary occasionally to remind the students of the rules.

a. *Setting the time.* The time length of the very first USSR session should be such that the majority of the students within the class can easily sustain their silent reading. For the lower grades, this may mean three to five minutes; for upper elementary grades, five to ten minutes; and for secondary classrooms, ten to fifteen minutes. It is probably better initially to underestimate students' ability to sustain silent reading, since one of the goals of USSR is to increase gradually the time devoted to the activity. Depending upon the ability and interest level of the students, reasonable goals might be fifteen to twenty minutes for primary level classrooms; twenty to thirty minutes for the middle grades; and thirty minutes for high school classes. These times should be considered as only guidelines.

b. *Timing USSR.* Most teachers have found that a kitchen timer or an alarm clock works best as the timing device for USSR sessions. The timer should be set for the agreed-upon time and then placed in such a position that students are unable to see the face of the device. This procedure solves the problem of the "clock watchers" within a classroom. For this same reason, a large classroom clock should not be used as the timing device. Another advantage of the alarm clock or kitchen timer is that it provides a definite end to the USSR session. The sound of an alarm clock leaves no doubt that the reading period has come to an end, and that it is time to move on to other activities.

c. *The role of the teacher.* During the USSR period, the teacher is doing exactly what all the students in the class are doing—reading for pleasure. The teacher has the very important role of showing good, sustained silent reading behavior. For some students in the classroom, this may be the first opportunity to observe an adult who is reading for pure enjoyment.

It is important to keep this one activity in mind. There are a number of things that a teacher should *not* do during USSR. The class instructor should not correct papers, plan lessons, take attendance, or perform similar school-related activities. By doing this type of activity, teachers are, in effect, saying to students, "Reading is an important activity for you, but not for me." Likewise, the teacher should not move around the classroom to seek out those students who are not reading or those students who are potential trouble makers. Besides not serving as an adequate model, a teacher in the monitoring role becomes a potential "interrupter" of the reading process.

d. *Interruptions during USSR.* It is not unusual for interruptions to occur occasionally, especially in the initial phase of using the procedure in the classroom. Interruptions that cause the classroom teacher and a large number of students to look up from their reading should generally result in an end to the reading period for that day. However, persons guilty of interrupting should not be reprimanded; rather, the classroom teacher may simply say, "I'm sorry, but that concludes our USSR session for today. Please put your reading material away and we will proceed with our next lesson." The instructor should be prepared to move quickly to the next scheduled activity without providing the individual who interrupted with the attention that the student might be seeking. The activity immediately following the USSR also should not appear to be arranged as a means of punishment, i.e., tests and other equally unpopular activities are best scheduled at other times.

After the habit of silent reading has been firmly established, minor and unintentional interruptions may be handled smoothly without resulting in an end to the reading session. In these situations, the teacher might respond in this manner: "I hope that the interruption did not cause you to completely lose your train of thought. Do you think you can return to your reading without any problems?" If most students respond affirmatively, then the teacher provides a model by returning immediately to reading. Very minor disturbances that cause the instructors and only one or two students to look up from their reading should be ignored. After quickly evaluating the situation, the teacher should return immediately to the reading. This action has the effect of saying, "No problem. Let's continue our reading."

e. *Concluding the reading period.* USSR ends with the sound of the timer. The instructor should be prepared to move to the next scheduled activity. Occasionally, teachers may provide students a few additional minutes of reading time. This "buffer" period allows students an opportunity to read until a more appropriate stopping point is reached.

3. Follow-up

McCracken (1971) suggested that after the first week of USSR, the teacher may begin to think of ways to encourage sharing what has been read during the silent reading sessions. The teacher can set an example by making a brief comment about interesting ideas the students have read, by keeping a log of the books and the number of pages read, and by similar actions that show a sincere interest in the reading act. These sharing activities can result in greater student interest in reading.

It must be emphasized that such sharing activities should not begin until after the USSR activity has been firmly established. If the teacher begins to prompt students to share too early in the beginning sessions, USSR might deteriorate into something other than reading for enjoyment.

Cautions and Comments

To reiterate, the key to success of USSR is the role of the teacher. The teacher, by the very act of reading, is communicating the *value* of reading to the students. Conversely, any lack of interest or enthusiasm by the teacher can result in a similar reaction by the students.

In the beginning stages of implementation of this activity, it is probably best to proceed slowly and to take small steps. USSR should be undertaken at the classroom level before any consideration is given to a school-wide program. Even though there have been some successful school-wide USSR programs, there are also reservations regarding programs that insist that everyone read at the same time of day and for the same amount of time. Certainly, differences in the amount of time allocated for the lower primary grades versus time allocated for the upper intermediate grades are one consideration.

Finally, though USSR is a simple technique and can easily be implemented in the classrooms at any level, it is very difficult to evaluate. It should not be surprising that research studies, in which the influence of USSR upon achievement and attitude has been studied, have yielded quite mixed results. In some studies, students involved in USSR have exhibited improvements in reading achievement and attitude beyond the norm or what students not involved in USSR attain. In most studies, however, there has been no measurable advantage for USSR. Perhaps other measures of the influence of USSR are needed, for example, the extent to which students are able to sustain their reading or have acquired a reading habit or use what they read (during USSR times) in their writing or other work. Despite the lack of definitive support for the procedure, its usefulness should not be forgotten. The strategy provides teachers a manageable procedure for increasing reading time.

REFERENCES

Berglund, R. L., and J. L. Johns. 1983. Primer on uninterrupted sustained silent reading. *The Reading Teacher* 36:534–39. Discusses in "ins" and "outs" of implementing USSR.

Evans, H. M., and J. C. Towner. 1975. Sustained silent reading: Does it increase skills? *The Reading Teacher* 29:155–56. Describes a study comparing the use of USSR with the use of basal supplements.

Gambrell, L. B. 1978. Getting started with sustained silent reading and keeping it going. *The Reading Teacher* 32:328–31. Discusses preparation for and management of the USSR.

Ganz, P., and M. B. Theofield. 1974. Suggestions for starting USSR. *Journal of Reading* 17:614–16. Provides recommendations for initiating a USSR program on a school-wide basis.

Hunt, L. C. 1971. Six steps to the individualized reading program (IRP). *Elementary English* 48:27–32. Describes the intent and procedures for implementing USSR.

McCracken, R. A. 1971. Initiating sustained silent reading. *Journal of Reading* 14:521–24, 582–83. Recommends six rules teachers must follow to implement USSR successfully.

McCracken, R. A., and M. J. McCracken. 1978. Modeling is the key to sustained silent reading. *The Reading Teacher* 31:406–8. Describes how and what a teacher does during and after silent reading; also defines what students do.

————. 1972. *Reading is only the tiger's tail*. San Rafael, Calif.: Leswing Press. Provides recommendations for initiating a USSR program.

Moore, J. C., C. J. Jones, and D. C. Miller. 1980. What we know after a decade of sustained silent reading. *The Reading Teacher* 33:455–450. Reviews the research on USSR.

Schaudt, B. A. 1983. Another look at sustained silent reading. *The Reading Teacher* 36:934–36. Reviews research studies and guidelines suggested for implementation of USSR.

APPENDIX A

DIAGNOSTIC USE OF RECREATIONAL READING

Diagnostic use of a recreational reading strategy involves studying the students' recreational reading behavior and preferences. On an informal basis, studying recreational reading behavior can afford information on how students locate material; on what students read; on how students read; and on why students read what they read. Formally, recreational reading behavior can be studied for these same purposes, in addition to the purpose of answers to the following questions: What other materials might students read? How might students improve their ability to locate material? How might students increase their reading enjoyment?

Illustration

The following two examples illustrate a slightly formal assessment of recreational reading behavior. The first example describes an assessment of the recreational reading behavior of an advanced high school student. The second illustration describes behavior of several fifth graders.

Illustration One

Ralph was an advanced high school student who claimed that he read some magazines and scanned the newspaper, but did not do much recreational reading.

In order to assess Ralph's recreational reading behavior, a somewhat formal assessment was planned. Three types of material were selected for this purpose: fictional material, periodicals (magazines and newspapers), and nonfictional material. Twenty to thirty items on a broad range of subjects in each area were presented to Ralph. He was asked to choose the item he preferred; to explain why he chose it; to make two other choices in each area; and to identify what he would definitely not choose to read. In all three areas, he had read some books and was familiar with others. For those that were unfamiliar to him, he was given a brief description.

Fictional books were presented first. Ralph quickly selected a book containing Mark Twain stories, choosing the book because, "I know he's entertaining." Ralph suggested that he enjoyed Twain's characters and stories. His next selection was *The Choirboys* by Joseph Wambaugh because someone had recommended it. *Siddhartha* was Ralph's third choice because it was "thin." *In One Car*, a book containing "1,000 funny stories," Ralph suggested he would not read.

Next, Ralph was presented a variety of periodicals. From the magazines presented, he selected *Réalitiés*, a French magazine translated into English that he had never seen before. He claimed he enjoyed magazines with interesting and different articles. His other choices were an engineering journal and *Smithsonian*. He showed no interest whatsoever in any of the popular magazines, such as *Sports Illustrated*.

Of the nonfictional books presented, Ralph chose *The Essential Lenny Bruce* because of a strong interest in Lenny Bruce's humor. He had read and enjoyed *Bury My Heart at Wounded Knee* and said he would like to read *Passages*, but suggested that he did not usually like self-awareness books. In terms of reference material, he showed no interest in the *Guinness Book of World Records*, in *The World Almanac*, or in encyclopedias. Ralph said that he had access to these materials but rarely used them unless it was required. He did show an interest in one specific reference book dealing with opera; Ralph stated that he wished he owned such a book.

Conclusions: Ralph based his selection of books on several things: his familiarity with the style of the author, the book's novelty, personal interest in the book, the recommendations of others, and the book's size. Ralph expressed strong likes and dislikes, spontaneously explaining the reasons for his choices. His choices reflected well-developed interests in selected areas, such as opera. Given appropriate material, Ralph's recreational reading could be extended within his areas of interest and perhaps to other areas. To this end, Ralph should be given regular opportunities to review and select reading material. The teacher might suggest that Ralph read published book reviews, join a book club, visit bookstores, or join a library. Ralph should adopt a daily recreational reading schedule, plan regular library visits, and subscribe to one or two magazines.

Illustration Two

Except for some occasional newspaper reading, Pat, Sandon, Monique, and Nadine were ten-year-olds who did very little reading apart from what was required.

An informal assessment of their recreational reading was conducted to assess their interests, their methods of selecting books, and their behavior while reading for pleasure. To this end, they were presented three tasks. The first was to select from a variety of books and magazines those they would prefer to read and those they would prefer not to read. The second task was to go through a basal reader and select stories or poems that interested them. The final task was to go through the newspaper in the same manner that they did at home.

In the first task, that of choosing books and magazines that they liked or disliked, they seemed reasonably sure of what they did not care to read: they immediately rejected two books on football and one about a dog. They mentioned an interest in *Black Beauty*, due to a recent television viewing of this story. Individually, they chose books on automobiles, gymnastics, mystery stories, cartoon-type paperbacks, and comics. When asked to read orally short segments of their choice from these selections, each read with obvious interest and understanding. In the second task, they each browsed through a basal reader and chose a story they would enjoy. Again, they could read this without any difficulty. Throughout this session, they talked enthusiastically about their interests, especially of cars, horses, and gymnastics.

In the final task, the students were asked to recreate their normal newspaper-reading habits with the morning paper. The students looked through the newspaper from front to back, skimming headlines, stopping once to read about a truck crash. Sandon explained he collected interesting articles from the paper, especially any dealing with cars. Sandon, Nadine, and Pat expressed interest in the comic section and listed as favorites those comics with a minimum of print. In terms of other sections of the paper, all students said that they referred to the weather forecast, the television schedule, and sometimes the advertisements. The students could answer questions about what they had read in the various sections of the newspaper.

Conclusions: The students' reading interests seem restricted to selected topics and to certain types of stories. They expressed an interest in fiction and nonfiction dealing with automobiles, horses, and gymnastics. To foster their enjoyment of reading, they might be given an opportunity to select from several books and magazines dealing with these topics. A librarian might be consulted for these purposes. To encourage the students to read this and other material, they might be introduced to new books through posters, discussions, listening experiences, films, or filmstrips. Sandon's interest in newspaper reading should continue to be encouraged and might be extended to other magazines. To this end, he might sample magazines and books from bookstores and the library. The other children should be encouraged to follow up their interests in similar ways.

APPENDIX B

SUGGESTIONS FOR INDIVIDUALIZED READING CONTRACTS

Contract	*Book Contract*
I, agree to read for 30 minutes each day.	Name

	PAGES	TIME
M		
T		
W		
Th		
F		
Comments:		

Book title and author	*Dates*	*Opinion*

| | CONTRACT | |
Checklist	Indicate Minutes	Comments
Area:	M T W Th F	
Silent reading		
Comprehension		
Vocabulary		
Study skills		
Research		
Listening		
Story writing		
Bookmaking		
Other; specify		

DAILY ASSIGNED ACTIVITIES

Date   Name

Completion of three tasks in each area is required. More can be completed.

A. Reading   Checked by Teacher

   a. Read silently <u>(book title)</u>   _____

        Pages read: _____   _____

   b. Book report, poster, review   _____

   c. Comprehension activities   _____

        Exercise no. _____   _____

   d. Vocabulary activities   _____

        Exercise no. _____   _____

   e. Other _____   _____

B. Writing   _____

   a. Write a story.   _____

   b. Write a letter to a friend.   _____

   c. Write a postcard.   _____

   d. Other _____   _____

C. Research   _____

   a. Plan a trip to California.   _____

   b. Learn more abut California's
      history.   _____

   c. Develop a schedule for
      preparing and traveling to
      California.   _____

   d. Other _____   _____

Evaluation:

TIMED AREA CONTRACT

1. Reading: 30 minutes minimum
   Book title:
   Pages read:
   Time _____ to _____ = _____

2. Social Studies: 45 minutes minimum
   Research area:
   Work done:
   Time _____ to _____ = _____

3. Math: 20 minutes minimum
   Exercises done:
   Time _____ to _____ = _____

DAILY LOG

Name   Date

	Activity	*Evaluation*
9:00–9:30	_____	_____
9:30–10:00	_____	_____
10:00–10:30	_____	_____
Recess		
11:00–11:30	_____	_____
11:30–12:00	_____	_____
Lunch		
1:00–1:30	_____	_____
1:30–1:45	_____	
Recess		
2:00–2:30	_____	_____
2:30–3:00	_____	_____

AN EXAMPLE OF AN
INDIVIDUALIZED THEME
CONTRACT DEALING WITH
VALUES AND MEDIA

Some commercials state that if you use their product, you will be more beautiful, your work will become easier, your life will be more enjoyable, and so on.

Watch 10 commercials. List the product being advertised. Check the "benefits" of using each product.

Product	Increases Beauty	Saves Time	Helps Make Friends	Lessens Work	Makes Life More Comfortable	Relieves Pain
1.						
2.						
3.						
4.						
5.						
6.						
7.						
8.						
9.						
10.						

List three "benefits" stated above that are most often mentioned in T.V. commercials.

_____

_____

_____

Can you tell what a person cares about by the bumper sticker on his or her car?

Sticker	*Value*
Save the Whales	_____
If you can read this you are too close	_____
Back the Farmers	_____
Add others.	_____
_____	_____
_____	_____
_____	_____
_____	_____

Design a bumper sticker with an important message. Make the bumper sticker and put it on your car.

Add a newspaper headline, story heading, or picture to the *Good News Collage.* Do the same for the *Bad News Collage.* For which collage was it easier to find pictures?

_____

Why do you think newspapers print more bad news than good news?

_____

_____

_____

Write a letter to the editor stating why you think the *Star* or *Citizen* should report more *Good News* to the people of Tucson.

Listen to the top tunes on records or radio. Name your favorite song among the top ten hits.

Title: _____

What is the message of the song?

_____

_____

_____

_____

Do you agree with the message? _____

_____ I like the song because of its lyrics (words).

_____ I like the song because of its melody (tune).

What are some of the things the following groups choose to do repeatedly and, therefore, seem to value?

1. Teenagers: _____

_____

2. Elderly People: _____

_____

3. Teachers: _____

_____

4. Musicians: _____

_____

Some people use billboards to advertise their message.

Does Kino have a message worth advertising? _____

Investigate the possibility or renting billboard space for one month to advertise our message. Where should our billboard be located? _____

(Maybe we should ask a business with a similar message to sponsor this project.)

CONTRACT COMPLETION
REQUIREMENTS

State why you like or dislike a specific sculpture, painting, architecture, and so on.

Write critiques on several T.V., radio, billboard, newspaper, or magazine advertisements.

Find three eamples of recorded music that generate three different feelings or emotions.Describe your feelings.

Create something of personal value in at least one of the following:

> photography
> music
> art
> dance

Find an object that represents these values: beauty, love, friendship, truth, peace, and equality. State your reasons for choosing each object.

9

Oral Reading Strategies and Practices

The Unit and Its Theme

Current practices seem to indicate that much instructional time in our elementary classrooms is devoted to oral reading. Although there is value in oral reading for beginning reading instruction, there is some question as to the effectiveness of the way the activity may be conducted in the classroom.

The most frequent oral reading activity is that of "round-robin" or "circle" reading. In this activity, each student in turn reads a small portion aloud to his or her reading group or to the class as a whole, while the other students follow along silently. This practice is used primarily in conjunction with the basal reading program.

Despite its widespread use, research does not support this practice. Recent research by Anderson, Mason, and Shirey (1984) and research reviews by Allington (1984) and Brulnsma (1981) suggest the practice of round-robin reading is suspect. They conclude that its use in classrooms is not defensible if comprehension is the goal.

Oral reading is a communication skill. It is a way of delivering information or providing entertainment to listeners. If used in this way, oral reading would seem best done for a specific purpose, and a student's performance would seem best evaluated in terms of its communicative value.

Strategies

The four strategies discussed in this unit are designed to aid the teacher in planning oral reading activities that have specific purposes. Three of the strategies are mainly developmental in nature and focus on the communicative aspects of oral reading. The other strategy tends to be used with students who may be having difficulty in reading. As a preview of this unit, a brief summary of the strategies follows.

Choral and Repeated Reading

Choral and repeated reading is a strategy designed to give students practice in reading with the proper expression. Useful as a whole-class reading activity, this strategy provides students with active involvement in print and puts prime emphasis on interpreting meaning.

Radio Reading

Providing practice for students in both reading and listening, radio reading focuses instruction on the ultimate goal of oral reading—communicating a message. It is useful throughout the grades wherever oral reading is one of the teaching methods, particularly as a substitute for "round-robin" reading.

Paired Reading

Paired reading accomplishes a dual purpose: it provides practice for students in reading for meaning, and it aids the teacher in grouping for instruction. Along with peer tutoring, paired reading is suited for use with students in the elementary grades.

Echo Reading

Echo reading is designed to foster the acquisition of vocabulary and oral fluency. It is most effective in a one-to-one instructional situation and primarily with students in the elementary grades.

REFERENCES

Allington, R. L. 1984. Oral reading. In *Handbook of reading research*, edited by P. D. Pearson, R. Barr, M. L. Kamil and P. Mosenthal. New York: Longman.

Anderson, R. C., J. Mason, and L. Shirey. 1984. The reading group: An experimental investigation of a labyrinth. *Reading Research Quarterly* 20:6–39.

Brulnsma, R. 1981. A critique of "round-robin" oral reading in the elementary classroom. *Reading-Canada-Lecture* 1:78–81.

CHORAL AND REPEATED READING

Purpose

The purpose of choral and repeated reading is to

1. Provide practice for students in reading with the expression necessary to add to meaning;
2. Develop self-assurance by giving every student a chance to function as part of a group; and
3. Aid students in developing an appreciation for oral expression.

Rationale

Artificial barriers are sometimes created by students and between students when oral reading occurs. For example, poorer readers may not like to read orally, and the shy student who rarely volunteers in any class activity will often be hesitant about oral reading. On the other hand, the overly-confident student, if given the opportunity, might dominate an oral reading exercise.

Choral and repeated reading provides the teacher with a socialization tool. Poor readers as well as shy ones can use the whole-group format to avoid humiliating corrections while they gain confidence in themselves. The obtrusive student may be tempered through the same whole-group format, which discourages that student from showing off.

Additionally, choral and repeated reading can develop students' interest in the creative forms of language such as poetry, where as previously students might have had negative feelings toward poetry.

Finally, choral and repeated reading provides students with the opportunity to become actively involved with print, placing the prime emphasis on interpreting and expressing meaning. Many times, words and not meaning are emphasized in reading activities. Choral and repeated reading develops students' abilities to read for meaning—the eventual goal of the act of reading.

Intended Audience

Choral and repeated reading is suitable for any school population. Grade level and achievement level are inconsequential, because of the group approach of this strategy. Class size also matters little, as the teacher can divide any large group into smaller, more manageable, choral groups.

Description of the Procedure

As a substitute for oral reading as commonly practiced, choral and repeated reading presents the teacher with a unique instructional activity that can unite all readers, regardless of ability, in a common reading experience. At the same time, this strategy can provide students with entertainment, group involvement, and practice in reading with self-expression.

In order for choral reading be carried out effectively, the teacher must be prepared to deal with (1) developing rhythmic sensitivity and (2) casting.

1. Developing rhythmic sensitivity

Before choral and repeated reading can be accomplished successfully, the students should be guided by the teacher through progressive steps to develop their sensitivity for rhythm. The teacher should not make any assumptions concerning students' ability in choral and repeated reading. By guiding them through the activity first, the teacher is assured that students have the framework to establish eventual independence in that activity.

The concept of modeling is very appropriate with this activity. One way to impress young children is for the teacher to be an example. By showing students that poetry and other creative forms are enjoyable, by sharing these things with the class, and by demonstrating the desired self-expression, the teacher should find students experience little difficulty in beginning choral and repeated reading.

A variety of selections should be used to aid students in acquiring a sensitivity for rhythm, mood, and voice modulation. The teacher should demonstrate proper phrasing, tempo, and enunciation with the selections for choral reading and, through discussion, emphasize the importance of proper expression in conveying a poem's mood and meaning.

Choral and repeated reading might begin with short selections, preferably memorized. Eventually, longer selections, possibly with the rhythm marked, may be introduced.

To provide additional reinforcement for students, a tape recorder may be used for evaluative purposes. Students may also participate as critical listeners by separating themselves from the choral groups and providing feedback. After a few successful experiences, students may begin, and be encouraged, to suggest other ways selections might be interpreted and read. Sound effects and pantomiming may also be used.

Finally, when selecting material for choral and repeated reading, care should be taken to ensure selections have an easily understandable theme and a distinct rhythm.

2. Casting

Casting is a term used in choral and repeated reading to refer to the way a selection is divided into parts and assigned to members of the class for reading. Once the rhythm and tempo of a particular selection are understood, the teacher and students should choose from the following methods of organization for choral and repeated reading:

a. Refrain;
b. Dialogue;
c. Line-a-child or line-a-choir;
d. Cumulative; and
e. Unison.

a. *Refrain.* With certain poems that have a chorus, either the teacher or a designated group can recite the narrative, with the rest of the class responding in the chorus. The refrain provides a good beginning for choral and repeated reading.

b. *Dialogue.* Poems with considerable dialogue (often a question-and-answer format) readily lend themselves to a two-part casting. Alternate responses can be made between boys and girls or between high and low voices.

c. *Line-a-child or line-a-choir.* This arrangement engages three or more individuals or choirs in rhythmic response. Some lines also may be spoken in unison by all participants. This type of choral and repeated reading has variety and provides a challenge for students to respond in the exact tempo.

d. *Cumulative.* In this form of choral and repeated reading, the intent is to create a crescendo effect. Unlike the line-a-choir method, the introduction of a new group to the presentation is permanent, not temporary. This is a more difficult form of choral and repeated reading because voice quality, rather than volume, is necessary to attain a significant climax.

e. *Unison.* This is the most difficult type of choral and repeated reading, even though it has the simplest structure. An entire group or class reads every line together. The potential for problems in blending and timing is very great in unison reading. Monotonous reading often results if the children are inexperienced and insufficient direction has been given by the teacher. This method is best suited for intermediate level students.

The following verse from a poem provides an example of how one type of casting may be used in a choral and repeated reading exercise.

The Triantiwontigongolope[1]

1st child:	There's a funny insect that you do not often spy,
2nd child:	And it isn't quite a spider, and it isn't quite a fly;
1st child:	It is something like a beetle, and a little like a bee,
2nd child:	But nothing like a woolly grub that climbs upon a tree.
1st child:	Its name is quite a hard one, but you'll learn it soon, I hope.
1st child:	So, try:
Chorus:	Tri-
All:	Tri——anti——wonti——
Children:	Triantiwontigongolope

---

1. "The Triantiwontigongolope" from *A Book for Kids* by C. J. Dennis is reprinted by permission of Angus & Robertson Publishers.

The refrain in this selection can be used with one group of students reciting the narrative while the other recites the chorus. Individual lines or stanzas of the poem may also be assigned to groups of students and the line-a-choir, cumulative, or unison casting may be implemented, depending on the sophistication of the students.

Cautions and Comments

Choral and repeated reading provides students with a unique and valuable language experience, since it integrates reading with two other linguistic skills: listening and speaking. Additionally, choral and repeated reading builds positive attitudes toward participation in groups and develops students' imaginative abilities.

However, choral and repeated reading can contribute little to the reading and language development of students if it is not used properly. A common practice with choral and repeated reading has been for the teacher to select a passage for choral reading, teach it to students who either read it well or memorize it, assign parts of it to groups, and then "drill" the students until the passage sounds good according to the teacher's conception of "good" choral reading.

This practice negates the instructional objectives of (a) making the selection meaningful to the students, (b) developing creativity, and (c) developing self-expression. Strict, tense drill directed by the teacher does not set the proper learning conditions, but active involvement on the part of the students does.

Another area of concern in choral and repeated reading is maintaining the students' focus on the meaning being conveyed. Students have a tendency to focus attention on their delivery of the selection and sometimes lapse into overdramatics. It must be emphasized that it is the choral and repeated reading that is on display, and not the students themselves.

A further meaning-related concern in choral and repeated reading is that all students should have a similar understanding of the selection. This is essential in order to convey effectively, as a group, a depth of feeling and sensitivity to words.

A last area of concern is voice quality. Each word must be enunciated at the same time by the whole group—a difficult task to accomplish for some students. Finally, students must also learn that it is not necessary to read loudly when expressing themselves; rather, they should read with warm but firm voices, the choral reading itself will take care of the volume.

REFERENCES

Allen, R. V. 1976. *Language experiences in communication.* Boston: Houghton Mifflin, 150–54. Discusses the value of choral reading in the language arts program.

Burns, P. C. and B. L. Broman. 1983. *The language arts in childhood education*. 5th ed. Boston: Houghton Mifflin. Describes a number of choral reading activities.

Lapardo, G., and M. Sadow. 1982. Criteria and procedures for the method of repeated readings. *Journal of Reading* 26:156–60. Describes how to use repeated reading in the classroom.

Petty, W. T., D. C. Petty, and M. F. Becking. 1976. *Experiences in language: Tools and techniques for language arts methods*. Boston: Allyn and Bacon, 119–23. Explores the use of choral reading as an enjoyable way to interpret literature.

Spache, G. D., and E. B. Spache. 1977. *Reading in the elementary school*. Boston: Allyn and Bacon, 244–54. Examines the use of oral reading in the primary program and cites claims for and against its use.

Temple, C. A., and J. W. Gillett. 1984. *Language arts: Learning processes and teaching practices*. Boston: Little, Brown. Provides examples of using choral reading in the language arts program.

RADIO READING

Purpose

The purpose of radio reading (Greene 1979) is to provide for students in

1. Accurately communicating a message through oral reading;
2. Comprehending at the listening level; and
3. Summarizing and restating an orally read message.

Rationale

Radio reading provides the teacher with a viable alternative to the common practice of "round-robin" reading. Too often, oral reading situations deteriorate into word-attack sessions. Unlike "round-robin" reading, radio reading does not allow for prompting or correction. Rather, it focuses instruction on the ultimate goal of oral reading—to comprehend and communicate a message.

Radio learning derives its name from the analogy between a radio announcer talking to a listening audience and the oral reading situation. The reader functions as the radio announcer with a script, and the listeners serve as the audience listening to a radio program. It is the purpose of the reader to communicate accurately a message in oral reading. The listeners respond by discussing and restating the message and evaluating whether the passage was clearly rendered.

Intended Audience

Radio reading is appropriate throughout the grades, whenever oral reading is used in instruction. It is particularly suitable in the elementary grades as a substitute for "round-robin" reading; however, it is also useful in the content areas, especially where interpretive reading is done. Radio learning may be used in either a one-to-one or a group setting.

Description of the Procedure

Radio reading creates a "safe," nonthreatening atmosphere for the reader, in which comprehension, not word-perfect reading, is the primary instructional goal. In order to implement a radio reading lesson properly. Searfoss (1975) recommended that four steps be followed:

1. Getting started;
2. Communicating the message;
3. Checking for understanding; and
4. Clarifying an unclear message.

1. Getting started

In this step of the lesson, the teacher sets the tone for the proper atmosphere by explaining the procedure to the students. The simple ground rules of radio reading are these: the reader reads and the listeners listen.

The teacher leads the activity by explaining the remaining three steps of the strategy to the students. Emphasis is placed on the responsibility of the reader to communicate a message to the listeners, just as a radio announcer communicates to his audience. Since the audience (listeners) will not have a copy of the material, the teacher instructs them to attend closely to the oral reading.

It is also the job of the teacher to select materials for radio reading that are appropriate in difficulty and length. The materials should be challenging, though not frustrating, and should be narrative or expository in nature. For example, short stories or selections from basal-type readers would be appropriate. The material should be of reasonable length so as not to overwhelm the listener. As a guideline, Searfoss (1975) recommended that each reader should orally read only a paragraph or two in the lower grades, progressing up to as much as a page in the intermediate grades.

2. Communicating the message

Since the job of the reader is to convey a clear message, the reader is permitted to change words, insert new words, or omit words where warranted. The role of the reader in this activity is similar to that of the fluent, silent reader; both are attending to meaning rather than to individual words. The reader is responsible, however, for deciding when he or she needs help with an unknown word. Greene (1979) stated that when giving directions for radio reading, the teacher should say, "If you come to a word you need and you cannot figure it out, put your finger beside it and ask, 'What is that word?'"

Again, since radio reading is comprehension-oriented, and further delay on a word would increase the probability of short-term memory interference, the teacher or other listeners should refrain from prompting or beginning a word-attack lesson. The reader should be given the word immediately so he or she can continue, with as little interruption as possible, to process meaning.

3. Checking for understanding

The listening audience has control over the student's oral reading and, if necessary, over rereading. If an accurate message has been communicated by the reader, the check for understanding will be brief. The discussion of what was heard, whether teacher-led or student-initiated, will move quickly. After a quick summary has been volunteered, other listeners can confirm the message. Allowances are made for inferences and rewording, as long as accuracy is maintained.

Thus, the reader earns the right to continue reading by communicating a clear message. In a group situation, the role of the radio reader may rotate to give every reader an opportunity to read; the same procedure is followed.

4. Clarifying an unclear message

If the listeners give conflicting information or are able to detect errors during the discussion, the reader has not communicated a clear message. It is the radio readers' responsibility to clear up the confusion by returning to the story and rereading the portions of concern.

It is still the reader's job to achieve clarity in the passage. The listener may decide that the reader needs assistance to achieve that goal. However, as before, prompting must be avoided to maintain the necessary atmosphere for radio reading.

Cautions and Comments

Since radio reading differs greatly from current oral reading practices, the teacher should be certain the four steps outlined are followed. Two areas of caution warrant discussion to enable the teacher to maintain the proper instructional climate for radio reading.

One area of caution concerns the students' response to the procedural steps of radio reading. Ideally, the students will quickly understand the rules and follow them. Radio reading will then be performed smoothly, i.e., the students will read as well as they can, requesting help when necessary. In reality, students may manifest other types of responses to this instructional format, causing possible difficulties for the teacher in its implementation.

One possible difficulty is for the reader to request help at an inappropriate time. Such an occasion arises when it is apparent that the reader already knows the word or has adequate word-attack skills to decode the word. The only recourse the listener has in this situation is to tell the reader the requested word.

It is most likely correct to assume that the reader is testing the rules concerning the reader's and the listener's responsibilities for unknown words, rather than simply displaying deficiencies in reading. Thus, not responding to a request for help, or prompting the reader, violates the contract between the reader and the listener and makes the rules of radio reading worthless. If the reader requests help, it must be immediately supplied.

An additional response that a student may manifest is not to request help when he or she does need it. The reader then will be redirected to render a clear message after the oral reading. On the other hand, failure to respond at all presents the listener with an entirely different situation. In either an individual or a group situation, the appropriate response for the listener, after waiting a reasonable length of time, is simply to say, "What's the rule?"

In an individual situation, it may be necessary for the listener to restate the rule concerning unknown words. If a response is still not elicited, then radio reading should be ended for the day. A clarification of the procedural steps is then in order. In a group setting, a no-response situation is much easier to deal with. Anytime the radio announcer (reader) ceases to broadcast, the listeners will tune to a new "station," i.e., the first reader's right to continue reading ceases, and a new radio reader takes over.

A second caution concerning the instructional climate for radio reading is the tendency of teachers to prompt, to correct, or to initiate a word-attack lesson when a reader encounters difficulty or requests help. Such tactics are inappropriate with this strategy. It disrupts the process of reading and converts the activity into a word-attack lesson.

If the reader makes an error and the teacher corrects it, the responsibility for "correctness" shifts to the teacher and deprives the reader of the responsibility for meaningful reading. Prompting also removes from the reader the responsibility for relaying the message.

There is clearly no place for prompting or for correcting in radio reading. If an error is made in an oral rendering, the burden of dealing with it rests with the listener, who must be skillful enough to pick it out and remember it until the passage has been read. It is the reader's responsibility alone to render a clear, comprehensible message from the assigned passage.

REFERENCES

Greene, F. P. 1979. Radio reading. In *Reading comprehension at four linguistic levels*, edited by C. Pennock. Newark, Del.: International Reading Association, 104–7. Discusses the concept of radio reading and describes the procedure.

Searfoss, L. W. 1975. Radio reading. *The Reading Teacher* 29:295–96. Outlines four basic steps in implementing radio reading.

PAIRED READING

Purpose

The purpose of paired reading (Greene 1970) is to

1. Give students practice in meaningful oral reading;
2. Aid teachers in individualizing instruction; and
3. Create a nonthreatening instructional atmosphere conducive to learning.

Rationale

Paired reading is intended to provide an opportunity to increase the amount of oral reading activity in a group situation, within the structure provided by the teacher. Based upon ideas used in peer tutoring, paired reading involves the pairing of two children of differing reading fluency. Its purpose in the context of oral reading is to entertain and teach. Paired reading uses students as peer-models for other students of lesser reading competence, within a relaxed, nonthreatening atmosphere.

Intended Audience

Paired reading activities would be appropriate as a grouping aid in most reading situations throughout the elementary grades. This strategy also lends itself well to situations where peer, rather than teacher, instruction would enhance the confidence of the reader.

Description of the Procedure

Paired reading is a method of instruction in oral reading that allows the teacher to use an educational tool of great potential—the student. This technique requires that the teacher pair two students of different reading competence in an oral reading situation. The students may be of the same chronological age, or one of the readers may be slightly older. A pairing that involves a more competent younger student and a less competent older one is not advised. Each student in the pair reads from materials suited to his or her own reading ability.

To provide for maximum effectiveness, the two students sit side by side, so that one can follow while the other reads. When the less competent one reads, it is suggested that the more competent student refrain from any premature prompting. If the less competent student does encounter a word that proves difficult to decode, this student should ask the more competent reader to pronounce the word.

Another difficulty that may arise when the less competent student is reading is the failure to communicate a message accurately. Through a combination of self-monitoring and retelling, the paired readers can focus on comprehending and communicating the message. Both readers should be taught to ask themselves continually as they read, "Does that make sense?" Additionally, at the finish of the oral reading, the reader is asked to retell what has just been read. Retelling is an appropriate means to monitor comprehension; it lacks the pressure and anxiety usually associated with answering questions at the end of a passage.

At a point halfway through this activity, the more competent student begins to read. Suggested times for changing readers are ten to fifteen minutes in the primary grades and twenty to thirty minutes in the intermediate grades.

While the more fluent one is reading, the role of the less competent student becomes that of a listener following along in the text. That student is thus continually exposed to new vocabulary, seeing and hearing the new word and, perhaps, assimilating it into his or her sight word vocabulary. The more fluent reader acts as a model of meaningful oral reading for the other student, using the proper rhythm and phrasing.

Cautions and Comments

If implemented properly, paired reading will be a worthwhile activity for both readers in the pair and a boon for the teacher, since the method provides for more responsive instruction in oral reading. Perhaps the key to its successful implementation is careful pairing of the students and preparation of the more competent reader.

The psychological and emotional benefits of paired reading are clear. The more competent reader gains prestige from becoming a "teacher"; this student's self-esteem is boosted. The less fluent reader profits from the relaxed atmosphere of the situation and gains more confidence in reading through working with a more knowledgeable reader.

Almost every student can contribute something to a tutoring situation; however, the teacher must be careful to select students who will be compatible in a paired situation. In addition to knowing the reading capabilities of the students, the teacher also has information available concerning their behavioral and emotional make-up. Using this information, the teacher can match the needs of the less competent reader to the cognitive and affective strengths of the more fluent reader.

Regardless of native strengths and abilities, the more competent reader needs guidelines from the teacher. The student needs to know the overall goals and purpose of paired reading, as well as his or her role in the strategy. In particular, the more fluent reader needs to be aware that prompting and correcting the less competent reader are not appropriate in paired reading. Emphasis should also be placed on the more fluent reader's role as a model. The teacher will have to monitor each pair occasionally to ensure that proper working relationships are being established and maintained.

Finally, teachers are cautioned that having a reader follow visually as well as aurally may present a situation where a conflict arises between the rate information is received visually and is received aurally. This conflict may cause unnecessary difficulties, especially for the nonfluent reader.

REFERENCES

Boraks, N., and A. R. Allen. 1977. A program to enhance peer tutoring. *The Reading Teacher* 30:479–84. Describes a training program for peer tutoring with emphasis on effective teaching interaction and positive interpersonal relations.

Ehly, S., and S. C. Larsen. 1975–76. Peer tutoring in the regular classroom. *Academic Therapy* 11:205–8. Provides a rationale and guidelines for implementing a general peer tutoring program.

———. 1976. Peer tutoring to individualize instruction. *Elementary School Journal* 76:475–80. Offers a variety of suggestions for designing a tutoring program as an aid in individualizing instruction.

Greene, F. P. 1970. Paired reading. Unpublished paper, Syracuse University. Discusses the rationale and implementation of paired reading.

Nevi, C. N. 1983. Cross-age tutoring: Why does it help the tutor? *The Reading Teacher* 36:892–98. Reviews a number of theories advanced on the effectiveness of peer tutoring.

ECHO READING

Purpose

The purpose of echo reading is to increase the reading fluency of students who have had difficulty in reading.

Rationale

Echo reading was originally conceived by Heckelman (1969) and is also known as the "neurological impress method," or the "impress method." Heckelman hypothesized that current reading methods allow a student to commit many mistakes, which become very deeply imprinted and are not easily corrected. Because of the time and difficulty involved in correcting these mistakes, students do not make any progress in reading.

Heckelman believed that implementing a new learning procedure could suppress the older methods of learning and thus enable children to read. As a result of this thinking, the impress—or echo—method was used. Its intent was to expose readers only to accurate, fluid reading patterns. After a certain length of time for instruction, the correct reading patterns would become deeply "impressed" and would replace previously learned patterns.

Intended Audience

Echo reading has been used almost exclusively with readers who have had difficulty progressing in reading. The procedure should be employed in a one-to-one instructional situation.

Description of the Procedure

The echo method is a technique that involves the student's visual, aural, oral, and tactile abilities in the process of learning to read. It is recommended that the procedure be used for fifteen minutes a day in consecutive daily sessions. After a total instructional time of seven to twelve hours, there is often a significant rise in achievement by the reader.

At the start of echo reading, the reading material used should be at a level slightly lower than the reader can handle adequately. By using material on which the reader has already experienced success, the teacher increases the probability that the echo method will get off to a successful beginning. Material to be used with the procedure should be varied to maintain the student's interest. Newspapers, magazines, and fiction and nonfiction books might be used.

Before echo reading starts, some preliminary instructions are given to the student. The student is told to disregard accompanying pictures in the story. The teacher also indicates to the student not to be concerned with reading at all; rather, the student is asked to do as well as possible in terms of just saying the words. The student is told only to slide his or her eyes smoothly across the line of print without stopping or going back. At no time does the teacher attempt to correct any mistakes the student may make.

As echo reading begins, the reader is seated slightly in front of the teacher with both participants jointly holding the reading material. Both read in unison; the voice of the teacher is directed into the reader's ear at this close range. In beginning sessions, the teacher is supposed to read slightly louder and faster than the student. This aspect allows the reader to make maximum use of the aural and visual senses involved in this strategy.

As the student beings to master the material and gains confidence in saying the words, the teacher may choose to read with a softer voice or even lag slightly behind the student. If the student falters, the teacher should resort to immediate reinforcement by increasing loudness and speed.

In the beginning sessions, the goal is to establish a fluent reading pattern. Therefore, it is often necessary for the teacher and student to repeat sentences and paragraphs several times until that goal is reached. Once this is accomplished, the teacher and student may move on to more difficult materials. Usually no more than two or three minutes of repetitive reading is required before a fluent reading pattern is established. It is recommended that the teacher regularly reinforce any success the student meets.

To accompany their voices, the teacher's finger simultaneously moves along the line of print. The finger is placed directly under the word as it is spoken, in a smooth, continual fashion. It is emphasized that the flow of the teacher's finger must coincide with the speed and flow of the oral reading.

Once accustomed to the echo method, the student can begin to take over this function from the teacher. At first, the teacher may need to help the student by guiding the student's finger until a smooth, continuous movement is established.

The coordination of the movement of the finger with the flow of the oral rendition is essential. It is argued that if the teacher's finger is not placed under the word as it is spoken, the aural and oral sensory modes will not be operating in conjunction with the visual and tactile modes (Heckelman 1969).

The major concern of the echo method is the style, not the accuracy, of the oral rendition. At no time during the reading is the student questioned on the material, either for word recognition or comprehension. However, if the student volunteers any information, the teacher permits it.

If success with the method has not been achieved by the fourth hour of its use, the procedure should be terminated. A changeover to another method is then suggested.

Cautions and Comments

Particularly in the beginning stages of echo reading, a student may experience some difficulty, due to the novelty of the situation or to the conflict that can arise between aural and visual input. A teacher might counter student complaints of not being able to keep up by urging the student to disregard mistakes and to continue reading. Slowing down slightly to a more comfortable speed or rereading some initial lines may eliminate student discomfort with the technique. However, forcing students to process visual and auditory information concurrently may require them to change their natural processing procedures for these types of input. This change may cause undue difficulty and warrant termination of this time-consuming procedure.

Echo reading seems to place an undue emphasis upon the psychomotor skills involved in reading, rather than upon the reading-thinking process that direct those skills. If reading-thinking processes direct the use of aural and visual skills, then, logically, reading improvement should begin with these reading-thinking processes. In other words, the emphasis given psychomotor skills within echo reading seems misplaced and in danger of detracting from meaningful reading experiences by which the student might acquire visual and aural skills both naturally and incidentally.

REFERENCES

Heckelman, R. G. 1969. A neurological-impress method of remedial-reading instruction. *Academic Therapy* 4:277−82. Introduces and describes the concept of the impress method.

Hollingsworth, P. M. 1970. An experiment with the impress method of teaching reading. *The Reading Teacher* 24:112−14, 187. Reports the results of a study designed to overcome some limiting factors of the impress method.

———. 1978. An experimental approach to the impress method of teaching reading. *The Reading Teacher* 31:624−26. Describes results from the use of the impress method.

Memory, D. M. 1981. The impress method: A status report of a new remedial reading technique. *Journal of Research and Development in Education* 14:102−14. A review of the literature of the impress method.

Trela, T. M. 1967. *Fourteen remedial reading methods*. Belmont, Calif.: Lear/ Siegler Feron, 1967, 6−8. Reviews the procedures and rationale of the impress method.

10

Word Identification Strategies

The Unit and Its Theme

No aspect of reading instruction has been the subject of more debate than that dealing with word identification instruction. These debates suggest that instruction in word identification, particularly in phonics, is the single most important ingredient in the entire reading program. Such arguments seem to disregard the notion that word identification includes skills other than phonic skills. These arguments ignore the notion that word identification and phonics are only a means to an end; reading for understanding. The issue addressed in this unit is not *whether* to teach, but *how* to teach, word identification skills. This unit addresses the problem of preparing readers to deal with unknown words they encounter as they read.

    The unit presents the theoretical bases and procedures for some of the alternative ways to teach word identification. In so doing, it provides a backdrop for examining alternatives.

The Strategies

Four strategies designed to improve the reader's word identification skills are presented in this unit. The strategies represent both traditional and contemporary suggestions for developing word identification abilities. A brief summary of the strategies provides a preview of the unit.

Analytic Method

The analytic method is among the most widely used of the traditional methods for teaching phonics. This method is designed to have readers use known words to discover strategies for decoding unknown words.

Synthetic Word Families

The synthetic word families approach is another widely used traditional method for developing phonic and word identification abilities. It is designed to serve three purposes: (1) to help readers learn the sounds represented by letters and some methods of blending these sounds into words; (2) to increase the student's sight vocabulary through the use of consonant substitution; and (3) to aid students in word identification skills through the use of blending and minimally contrasting word elements.

Syllabaries

The syllabaries strategy has evolved in recent years. This approach is designed to improve word identification skills through the use of the syllable as the unit of pronunciation.

Goodman's Reading Strategy Lessons

Reading strategy lessons represent an attempt to translate the theories of Kenneth Goodman (1967–75) into practice. Advocates of Goodman's psycholinguistic perspective on reading have designed these lessons to help readers focus on and strengthen their use of the syntactic or grammatic, the semantic or meaning, and the graphophonic or sound-symbol cueing systems involved in reading.

ANALYTIC METHOD

Purpose

The analytic method of phonics instruction is designed to provide students with strategies for decoding unfamiliar words; in this method, students are encouraged to employ their knowledge of the phonic elements within familiar words.

Rationale

The analytic method of phonic instruction is based on the premise that words can be analyzed into their common phonic elements. The student is introduced to a number of "common" words, from which an analysis of component parts can follow. That is, when the student has a bank of words with the same phonic features, phonics instruction begins. For example, students might be asked to "discover'" this generalization: common sound of the letter *b* as in *bat*, *ball*, and *boy*.

In essence, this method places stress on meaning and on the importance of building a bank of known words as the basis for acquiring certain phonic understandings. Letter sounds are never learned in isolation, thus avoiding the distorted notion that isolated letters have sounds. Phonic elements are learned through discovery, rather than through rote memorization.

Intended Audience

The analytic method of phonics instruction is suggested for use with beginning readers, where the emphasis is placed on learning sound/symbol relationships. The method may be used in conjunction with existing classroom materials or as a substitute for them, either in a group or in an individual situation.

Description of the Procedure

The discussion of the actual teaching of an analytic phonics lesson focuses on the following steps:

1. Auditory and visual discrimination;
2. Auditory discrimination;
3. Word blending; and
4. Contextual application.

1. Auditory and visual discrimination

Hearing and seeing the likeness and differences in sound and letters are essential parts of phonics instruction. It is from this base that an analytic phonics lesson begins. If a teacher were to present a phonics lesson concerning the single consonant *d*, the first thing to do would be to put a sentence on the board, underlining the word containing the target element in this way:

The *dog* bit the boy.

Rather than call attention to the sentence at this time, the teacher writes other words on the board that have the same phonic element. The words should all be known words. Children are asked to look at the words and read them. It is suggested that the students, *rather than the teacher*, pronounce the words. Since language differences may exist between the teacher and the children, the sounds produced by the teacher may differ from those produced by the children; some confusion may arise.

Words that might be listed could include:

> Dick
> dot
> dig
> duck

Emphasis is placed upon the beginning sound as each is pronounced, but the phonic element is never separated from the word. Through questioning and discussion, the teacher would elicit the following from the students:

a. The words all start alike; and
b. The words all sound alike in the beginning.

2. Auditory discrimination

Now that students have seen and heard that the words start alike, the next step is to reinforce further the targeted phonic element through the student's listening vocabulary. A new group of words is read by one of the students, rather than by the teacher, again to avoid possible language confusion caused by differences in sound production between the teacher and the students. The students are now asked to decide whether or not these words begin like the group of words on the board. The new words are not written on the board. Words that might be used here could include:

dock	bank	deep
went	dark	rich

Finally, students are asked to generate words that begin the same way as the targeted phonic element:

dumb	do	Doug	dear

3. Word blending

If students are successful with the first two steps of the teaching procedure, they will be ready to learn to generalize from known words how the targeted phonic element sounds in new words. A sight word is written on the board, and below this word, another one with the targeted element:

> mad
> dad

Students are asked to focus on the similarities and differences between the word that they know and the new word with the phonic element which they are learning. They should observe that:

a. The words end alike;
b. They sound alike at the end; and
c. They differ in the beginning.

Once students have observed the above, the teacher draws their attention to the fact that the new word starts like the group of words on the board.

Students are now asked to interchange the beginning consonant elements; thus, the *m* is replaced with a *d*. Students must remember how words with *d* sound in order to pronounce the new word, *dad*. This process is continued with a few more pairs of words, to ensure that students can use their newly learned phonic element. Other pairs that might be used are:

bay	rip	fairy
day	dip	dairy

4. Contextual application

The last step in this teaching strategy requires that students apply their new learning in an actual reading situation, where phonic learning is more natural than in isolation. Students are now asked to read their newly acquired words in short sentences:

My dad is at work.
What day is today?
Dip your brush in the paint.
Milk comes from a dairy.

After reading these sentences successfully, the students are asked to go back to the original sentence that started the lesson and read it:

The *dog* bit the boy.

Students may respond to the original sentence in different ways. Some may rhyme "log" with "dog," substituting the initial consonant; others may have mastered the sound of *d* and use it in conjunction with context clues to decode *dog*. The important thing to remember is that nowhere in the lesson was the *d* separated from real words, thus avoiding any distortion that may result when the students sound letters in isolation.

Cautions and Comments

Substantial claims have been made by proponents of both synthetic and analytic phonics approaches as to which is the better method. Certainly, the more holistic approach taken by analytic phonics seems to be the more appropriate learning strategy. However, at this time there is no well-founded longitudinal research that would enable us to choose between the two approachs. Research that bears on the influence of the variations in these approaches upon oral reading performance has yielded predictable results. As Allington (1984) indicated:

> The errors of children in meaning-emphasis programs continue to reflect greater sensitivity to contextual constraints, while those of readers in code-emphasis programs reflect greater sensitivity to graphemic cues and less awareness of context. (P. 848)

Two comments are in order concerning the use of either analytic or synthetic phonics. First, some professionals argue that the exclusive use of one approach over the other limits students' chances to master phonic principles. Moving back and forth between the two approaches may be a productive procedure if it enhances the students' abilities to deal with the abstract principles of phonics. It also may prove to be nonproductive, causing confusion rather than developing understanding.

Secondly, no matter which approach is chosen, it must be remembered that the ultimate test of a student's ability to use phonics is whether or not the student is able to read successfully for meaning and to apply such skills in contextual situations. Regardless of the method used, it is possible that a student would acquire adequate phonic skills and still remain a poor reader. With respect to either the analytic or the synthetic phonic method, it would seem imperative that students' newly acquired phonic understandings be applied to actual reading situations. For a further discussion of this comment, the reader is directed to the Cautions and Comments section under Synthetic Word Families.

REFERENCES

Allington, R. L. 1984. Oral reading. In *Handbook of reading research*, edited by P. D. Pearson, R. Barr, M. L. Kamil, and P. Mosenthal. New York: Longman. Presents a review of research findings dealing with oral reading including the effects of different phonics approaches.

Durkin, D. 1972. *Phonics, linguistics, and reading*. New York: Teachers College. Provides a complete description of the content of phonics.

———. 1983. *Teaching them to read*. 4th ed. Boston: Allyn and Bacon, 177–205. Describes both the content of and the various teaching procedures used in phonics.

Johnson, D. D., and P. D. Pearson. 1978. *Teaching reading vocabulary*. New York: Holt, Rinehart & Winston. Examines word identification in both the analytic and the synthetic approaches.

———. 1984. *Teaching reading vocabulary*. New York: Holt, Rinehart & Winston. A revised edition of their earlier book.

Mazurkiewicz, A. T. 1976. *Teaching about Phonics*. New York: St. Martins, 1976. Provides a thorough description of teaching phonics.

SYNTHETIC WORD FAMILIES

Purpose

The purpose of synthetic word families is to (1) increase vocabulary through the use of consonant substitution and (2) aid students in word identification skills by employing the strategy of blending letter sounds with contrasting word elements.

Rationale

Word families are word elements that contain both vowel and consonant elements, to which can be synthetically blended an initial consonant element. For instance, the word family-*at* can be blended or "slid" with the sounds of *b,c,f,* and *h* to form *bat, cat, fat,* and *hat*. Word families have also been variously referred to as phonograms, graphemic bases, and spelling patterns; they form the basis for reading systems claiming a linguistic approach.

The use of word families is based upon the principle that English is an alphabetic writing system employing a methodical code that is easily broken. This code consists of many contrasting patterns (word families), which the student can take advantage of when learning to read. Therefore, reading instruction centered around the patterns of language and the contrasting elements that may be generated from those patterns might be highly conducive to success in identifying unknown words and in learning to read. Less importance is placed on learning words in context, since instruction with synthetic word families begins with parts and proceeds to form wholes.

When using word families in conjunction with consonant substitution, the instructor can capitalize on the principle of minimal contrast and the student's knowledge of letter sounds. After a model word (a known word) has been explored for its elements, the word family (vowel and consonant elements) can be used to generate new words through consonant substitution. Learning is accomplished by building upon what is already known, varying that known element only minimally. Thus, the identification of new words is centered around maximum similarity and minimum difference—the maximum similarity being the word family, and the minimum difference being the synthetically blended consonant.

Intended Audience

The use of synthetic word families is commonly associated with beginning reading instruction in the primary grades. Although synthetic word families are intended to be used as the total reading program, they may also be used as a supplement for other materials designed to teach word identification skills.

Description of the Procedure

Some background information is in order before dealing with the teaching procedure. The following would be representative of the use of synthetic word families in books known as linguistic readers:

> Nat is a cat.
> Is Nat fat?
> Nat is fat.
> Nat is a fat cat.[1]

The above is a prime example of the use of initial consonant substitution and minimal constrasts within the word family-*at*.

Aukerman (1971) has described the variety of ways word families are used in linguistic readers. Synthetic word families are built upon a base sound which may be a sound in any position—beginning, medial, or ending. For instance, using the short vowel sound of *a* (aah) with both initial and final consonant substitution, a number of combinations may be generated:

fa (fat)	pa (pal)	na (nab)
da (dad)	sa (sad)	va (van)
ma (mad)	ba (bat)	la (lap)
	or	
at	ax (axe)	ap (apt)
am	ad (add)	ak (ack)
an (ant)	ag	as

Nonsense combinations are encouraged in linguistic material, since they may be parts of meaningful words that the student may meet later.

A second method would be to use a medial position and word family, such as *an*, and build words or nonwords that are larger in length:

ban	bans	band
bant	banx	banp
bang	banz	bank

Using different initial consonant sounds, numerous other combinations may be built, both with and without meaning.

---

[1]C. C. Fries, A. C. Fries, R. Wilson, and M. K. Randolph. *Merrill Lingustic Readers: First Reader*. (Columbus, Ohio: Charles E. Merrill, 1965), 4.

Word pairs may also be used as follows:

lamp	belt	tilt	band
ramp	felt	pilt	cand

On the other hand, if more regularity is desired, an identical base with the five short vowel sounds could be used, to which initial consonant sounds might be added:

b-all	g-all	p-all
c-all	h-all	s-all
f-all	m-all	t-all
	or	
b-ell	j-ell	p-ell
d-ell	m-ell	s-ell
f-ell	n-ell	t-ell

Used in the previously mentioned ways, the synthetic word family concept can produce innumerable word combinations.

To present a more manageable application of synthetic word families, and to show how they may be fit into a teaching procedure to augment other types of instruction in word identification, we will focus our discussion of synthetic word families on (1) prior concepts, (2) teacher guidance, and (3) student independence.

1. Prior concepts

There are certain prior concepts or learnings that students may need to have before the teacher can initiate a synthetic word families approach. These include (1) a small bank of known words, (2) rhyming words, and (3) consonant sounds.

A first pedagogical principle is that learning proceeds from the known to the unknown. In accordance with this principle, the synthetic word families approach begins with a small bank of known words to serve as a referent from which to generate new words. It is recommended that whole words, rather than elements of words, be used to initiate this procedure. For example, *b-ell* might be easier to learn than *-ell*.

Students must be sensitive to rhyme. They must be able to recognize that those words which look alike at their end (possess the same word family) probably rhyme in most cases. Additionally, students must know which parts of rhyming words sound alike, and which parts do not. To this end, students should be given auditory discrimination activities to ensure that they can differentiate between the rhyming and nonrhyming words.

Finally, knowledge of individual consonant sounds is necessary, so that students may effectively synthesize these sounds with word families. Needless to say, it will be difficult to rhyme words without a knowledge of consonant sounds.

2. Teacher guidance

Again, as with most teaching procedures, it must not be assumed that even if students have mastered all necessary prerequisites, they will be thus able to use word families effectively to improve word identification abilities. The teacher must guide the students toward independence.

Initially, teachers should select a model word which is part of the student's known vocabulary. New words are generated by using (1) the same word family as the model word and (2) differing beginning consonant sounds, which may be placed next to the model. An example might be:

dog
bog
fog
hog
log

Through observation and teacher encouragement, students will see that the new words look like the model except for the initial consonant. Students who have mastered consonant sounds will be able to read the minimally contrasting words. By doing this, students will recognize that all words sound alike. The teacher may point out that detecting word family elements can aid in pronouncing unfamiliar words.

Exercises as described above should be continued by using other words the students know as a basis and blending known consonant sounds to them. Gradually, the teacher should allow the students to generate new words. Later on, the use of diagraphs and blends as possible initial substitutes should be explored and demonstrated.

By going through these exercises diligently, the teacher can be confident that the students are able to use the concept of synthetic word families in substitution exercises. However, there may not be any transfer to "real" reading and to student independence from these exercises alone.

3. Student independence

Exercises like these do not necessarily ensure that students will be able to match mentally the word families they know with the unfamiliar words they encounter in reading. To help students gain independence in using word families, Cunningham, Moore, Cunningham and Moore (1983) have recommended a teaching procedure to aid students in mentally processing word matches to identify unfamiliar words in their reading.

The first step in this strategy is to create five cards with known words for each student. For instance, the five word cards may be: *tell, can, dog, it,* and *bump*. The teacher writes a word on the board, such as *bell*, and students are expected to find a match among their cards. This is followed by the teacher, or more preferably, by a student volunteer, demonstrating how the words look alike (word family), how they differ (initial consonant), and pronouncing both words. Searching through their small bank of word cards to secure a match will aid students in eventually gaining the facility to match words on their own when reading print. Word cards are continually added, and this procedure is continued, until students have mastered fifteen word cards as well as possible matches.

The second step of this strategy is for students to match a word printed on the board without the aid of the word cards. This is the point where students start to use their total mental processes to provide a match. All fifteen words are used in this step.

The third step involves the extension of the fifteen words to include all the words the students know. A new model word is given, and students are asked to figure out the unknown word by attempting to match it with a known word in their heads. In this way, they gain further independence in using synthetic word families to decode unknown words.

The fourth and final step is for students to apply this concept to their reading. When a student encounters difficult words, the teacher should encourage the student to think of a word family which ends like the unknown word, to aid in identifying it. It is here that students face the true test of using synthetic word families, i.e., word families to aid in decoding unknown words.

Some further specific examples of strategies which support the use of synthetic methods of word identification are described in Unit 11, which deals with multisensory strategies for teaching reading.

Cautions and Comments

When using synthetic word families as an aid to improving word recognition, teachers need to be aware of some possible problems. For example, using word families in isolation without helping students use them in actual reading situations may be problematic. Students need to be shown the relevance of word families to reading text selections. Indeed, the use of word families may deteriorate into a "game of word calling" if students are merely asked to play with words, no matter how exciting this activity may become. Furthermore, students taught using synthetic methods may be prone to become overdependent upon graphic clues.

Some problems may arise in generating new words using word families. Nonsense words, though advocated by linguistic approaches to reading, should be avoided. By definition, these words are meaningless, despite the linguistic consistency they provide. They are likely to contribute to readers substituting nonsense words for unknown words in text where real words should apply.

The second area of concern is that of irregular words. For instance, does *bow* rhyme with *cow* or *row*? Furthermore, consonant sounds may become distorted when sounded separately, as with the sound of *b-buh*. Should *bat* be pronounced as *bah-at*?

An alternate use of synthetic word families has been developed by LaPray (1972) for use with poor readers. Those students who have mastered little else in reading except their name are asked to list spontaneously their names and other words which they may know. Utilizing the few words generated, new words can be built from their known parts. For example, if a student lists only *Bill, dog,* and *mom,* new words may be built and learned, first by sound and then by context, by putting them into a short phrase or sentence.

Finally, to leave the reader "some food for thought," Kenneth Goodman's (1976) comments on the efficacy of phonic instruction are worthy to note.

> You have to put skills in the context of meaning. That's where they have the most value. That's where they maintain their proper proportion. And there they won't lead to the development of problems which eventually interfere with learning to read. In fact, children learn best this way because skills taught in context don't result in incorrect generalizations which then have to be overcome.
>
> Take the common emphasis on phonic skills. When you isolate a letter or a sound, you make it more abstract, and you also change its relative value. If I give kids the sentence, "The girl is in the garden," I can talk about the initial letter of girl and the sound that it relates to. But if I give the lesson backwards, if I start with the sound of g, then I'm saying that each letter has a value—a meaning. That's not true. The value is dependent on the sequence that it's in. And the importance of noticing and using a particular graphic cue is exaggerated because in context it works together with everything else. (P.7)

REFERENCES

Aukerman, R. C. 1984. *Approaches to beginning reading.* 2d ed. New York: John Wiley and Sons. 177–220. Discusses the use of synthetic word families as one basic approach to phonics instruction. Also describes, in detail, linguistically-oriented materials used in beginning reading instruction.

Cunningham, P. M., S. A. Moore, J. W. Cunningham, and D. W. Moore. 1983. *Reading in elementary classrooms: Strategies and observations.* New York: Longman. Advocates the use of consonant substitution with word families to build signal vocabulary.

Durkin, D. 1983. *Teaching them to read.* 4th ed. Boston: Allyn and Bacon. Describes different phonic approaches, but especially synthetic.

Goodman, K. 1976. *Reading: A Conversation with Kenneth Goodman.* Glenview, Ill.: Scott, Foresman.

LaPray, M. 1972. *Teaching children to become independent readers.* New York: Center for Applied Research in Education. Advocates the use of synthetic word families as a means to establish success-oriented instruction with students experiencing reading difficulties.

SYLLABARIES

Purpose

The purpose of syllabaries is to

1. Teach word identification skills through the use of the syllable as the unit of instruction; and
2. Use a comparison-contrast strategy to decode words by preceding from known word parts to unknown word parts.

Rationale

The syllabary method of improving word recognition skills is based upon the use of the syllable as the unit of pronunciation. It is an alternative to traditional phonics which is based upon the use of phoneme/grapheme correspondence.

Phonemes, the basic sounds of language, become distorted when pronounced in isolation, i.e., the sound of the letter *b* pronounced in isolation is *buh*. Some students seem to have difficulty learning to pronounce these units and even more trouble blending them together, i.e., *buh-ah-tuh = bat*. Though the use of phonics to decode unknown words presents difficulty to some, most students do have the facility to segment words into syllables (Gibson and Levin 1975).

The syllabary, seemingly a more natural unit of pronunciation for some students, may provide a sound means to overcome those phonological problems by beginning with those units (syllables) that are more easily recognized and pronounced in isolation (Gleitman and Rozin 1973). To illustrate this point with the word *paper*, note the difference in ease of pronunciation between *puh-aper* (only first letter sound in isolation) versus *pa-per* (two syllables in isolation). This premise and the use of a comparison-contrast strategy to decode unknown words form the basis of the syllabary, which was developed as a means to teach word recognition skills.

There are some differences among the teacher strategies advocated by the various materials for teaching beginning readers decoding skills; however, it can be inferred that (1) certain rules must be applied by readers to identify unfamiliar words, and (2) they must be applied in some certain order. To identify an unknown word, readers are taught to apply an ordered set of syllabication rules and then to apply phonic rules with each of the individual syllables.

Cunningham provides this example with the word *recertify* to illustrate the word identification processes a reader might typically use:

1. Reader decides on the number of syllables by counting the vowels (remembering that the *y* at the end of a word is a vowel): four vowels = four syllables.

2. Reader divides the word inyllables by applying the following ordered rules:
    a. Divide between a root word and a prefix: *re certify*.
    b. Divide between two intervocalic consonants (except consonant, of course): *re cer tify*.
    c. Divide before a single intervocalic consonant: *re cer ti fy*.
3. Reader applies rules to the letters in each syllable.
    a. *re:* ends in a vowel—long *e* sound; think long *e* sound—blend with *r*—pronounce *rē*.
    b. *cer:* *c* before *e, i,* or *y* usually has the *s* sound; *e* is controlled by *r*. Blend *c* with *er*—pronounce *ser*.
    c. *ti:* just like first syllable, if it ends in a vowel; try the long sound—pronounce *tī*.
    d. *fy:* when it is a vowel rather than a consonant, *y* can be pronounced as in *cry* or as in *daddy*. Try *fī*.
4. Reader blends all four syllables together: *re ser ti fi*. Reader does not recognize word as one he or she has heard before or knows a meaning for, so reader tries different sound correspondences.
5. Reader tries a different sound for the syllables. Perhaps it is a *y* as in *Daddy: rē ser tī fē*. Still not a word reader knows; perhaps this is a word the reader has never heard of before?
6. Finally, reader remembers about unaccented syllables and tries a schwa in different places until he happens upon the correct pronunciation: *rē ser t'fī*. "Oh, like what happens if you forget to renew your license and have to be recertified to get another license."
7. Reader continues reading.

Source: Cunningham 1975−76, 129−30. Reprinted with permission of the International Reading Association.

Though it may seem difficult, if not impossible, for this process to take place in a reader's mind as he or she attempts to identify an unknown word, this is the current mode of word identification processes that is advocated and taught to elementary school students.

To provide an alternative to the theory that students apply an ordered set of rules in word identification, Cunningham (1975−76) proposes a synthesized theory of mediated word identification, based upon these premises:

1. Words and word parts are stored in the human memory.
2. Word identification does not involve the application of teacher-taught rules; rather, it involves a search through this memory-store, comparing the unknown with the known.
3. Unfamiliar words not recognized on sight are segmented into units.
4. These units are compared/contrasted with known words, with word parts, or with fragments, for identification.

5. Recombining the units results in a word for which the reader knows a meaning or a sound referent.
6. Readers form their own rules (they are not taught rules) for decoding unfamiliar words by comparing/contrasting the unknown with the known.

Applying the synthesized theory of word identification to previous example with *recertify*, it can be assumed that the reader has numerous words and word parts in his memory-store and has also developed the ability to compare the unknown to the known. Segmenting an unfamiliar word occurs not by successively applying adult-taught syllabication rules, but by recognizing known parts in the unknown whole.

The reader can identify the unfamiliar whole *recertify* through a variety of comparisons such as:

1. If *certify* is in the reader's-memory store, along with either the word part *re* or other words beginning with *re (reexamine; relay)*, the resulting combination of the two parts is tested against words for which the reader has sound and/or meaning referents.
2. If *certify* is not in the reader's store, it might be segmented into more manageable units. For instance, the reader might have *identify* or *sanctify* segmented *tify*. The reader could identify *re* as described. *Cer* might be secured from parts of *certainly* or *ceramics*. Again, the reader would combine parts for comparison against the reader's sound and/or meaning referents.
3. If a wrong match is chosen from the reader's word-store (*recreation* instead of *relay*, or *ceremony* instead of *certainly*), the reader will be unable to identify it as there will be not sound or meaning referent. The reader will reenter his or her memory store for a more appropriate match.

Intended Audience

Gleitman and Rozin (1973) suggested three possible ways to incorporate the use of the syllabary in reading instruction in the elementary grades. First, it may be used as an introductory system to make phonics utility more accessible to students. Secondly, the syllabary may be used as a substitute for teaching many phonics principles, thus minimizing the quantity of instruction in that area. Finally, Gleitman and Rozin recommend that the syllabary could be used as a remedial approach to word recognition in cases where students cannot master phonics principles. It is the latter use that Cunningham (1975–76) demonstrated successfully in a study investigating the use of the syllable as a means to improve word recognition skills. Therefore, the syllabary seems most appropriate for augmenting other forms of word recognition instruction for beginning readers or for readers experiencing difficulty with sound/symbol relationships.

Description of the Procedure

To employ the syllabary strategy to improve readers' word identification skills, the teacher would follow these steps:

1. Teacher-dominated training;
2. Student-oriented practice; and
3. Meaningful reading

1. Teacher-dominated training

The teacher must not assume that students will readily grasp the thrust of the syllabary. Teachers should start with familiar one-syllable words before moving on to less familiar polysyllabic words. Beginning the training with familiar monosyllabic words ensures students will be able to call upon their own word-store.

The teacher might begin with words like *pen, sill, for,* and *wind* to illustrate how words like *penny, pencil, silly, before, windy, window,* and *windowsill* may be identified. In this way, words or word parts that are known become established in the word-store, enabling the students to use these known words in comparing unknown polysyllabic words. For example, knowledge of the words *wind* and *silly* will enable a student to make the appropriate comparisons to identify the word *windowsill.* Teacher questioning should accompany this step of acquainting students with the use of the syllabary to insure the match between syllables and the known word parts. Gleitman and Rozin (1973) have recommended the use of pictures as an aid to identifying unknown words by their syllabic parts. Some examples are shown:

be   fore   penn   y

2. Student-oriented practice

At this point in the strategy, the students are ready to begin more independent work with the concept of the syllabary. Polysyllabic words are introduced for students to decode using the comparison/contrast strategy. Work may be done individually, but is probably best accomplished in pairs or in small groups, until students have a firm grasp of the concept. An illustration of this type of practice follows.

Words like *sleepless, blanket,* and *pillow* might be introduced. The teacher is cautioned that it may be necessary to guide the students through a few practice words before they can work independently. For instance, using the syllabary to decode *sleepless*, the teacher can show children *less*, which might be a word in their memory-store or a word part, as in *unless*.

Again, the teacher is illustrating how to compare unknown words to known words or word parts in the students word-stores. As students gain skill and confidence in using the comparison/contrast strategy, more complex words may be introduced. It is suggested that as students are exposed to new words, these words be written on word cards for review and reinforcement. The comparisons students have made from their word-stores may be written on the back of the card and may be referred to by the student if any difficulty arises during the review. Review with flash cards may be accomplished by pairing the students.

3. Meaningful reading

It is to be remembered that the implementation and usage of the syllabary has occurred only when unknown words were seen in isolation. The ultimate test of any form of word identification occurs when the student becomes able to decode unknown words from a meaningful context. Hence, the follow-up step in the use of the syllabary is to develop students' ability to deal with unknown words in story reading.

It is recommended that a short story consisting of a few paragraphs be constructed, using many of the words students have studied in isolation. Variations of those words or similar words should also be incorporated. For example, the polysyllabic words used in Section 2, student-oriented practice, should be used, but the teacher should attempt to use the variations (*sleeping; pill*) as well. In this way, the teacher can be assured that the comparison/ contrast word identification strategy is being successfully implemented and has been transferred to "real" reading. An illustration of a short story using these words is included.

> Nim looked very sleepy.
> He threw his pillow on the floor.
> He removed his blanket.
> He had not gotten to sleep.
> It had been a sleepless night.

Cautions and Comments

There are apparent merits to a word identification strategy employing the syllabary; however, there are also a number of cautions that teachers should be aware of. First, although the syllable may be more easily pronounced in isolation than a phoneme, there are thousands of separate syllables in the English language. The task of dealing with each of these units might be overwhelming. For this reason, it should be used in conjunction with sound/ symbol relationships.

Second, dialect differences in readers make for differences in syllable pronunciations. What may seem to be an obvious comparison with an individual's word-store may be obvious only to the teacher who also has a particular dialectical pattern. The students may not necessarily be contemplating the "obvious" comparison, because of differences in their speech.

Third, the syllable is very much influenced by the stress it receives, i.e., the sound shifts with the stress (Goodman 1973). For example, *site* becomes *situate* by adding more meaning units to the original word. This could very easily produce confusion for the young reader.

Despite these problems, the syllabary approach has been supported by research. Cunningham (1975–76, 1979) found differences between a group trained to use the syllabary concept and a control group, when both groups attempted to decode unknown words.

REFERENCES

Cunningham, P. M. 1975–76. Investigating a synthesized theory of mediated word identification. *Reading Research Quarterly* 11:127–43. Reports the results of an experiment designed to improve the word identification abilities of second graders using a syllabary approach.

———. 1978. A compare/contrast theory of mediated word identification. *Reading Teacher* 32:774–78. Reports a follow-up to the earlier study with fourth and fifth grade students.

Gibson, E. J., and H. Levin. 1975. *The psychology of reading*. Cambridge: MIT Press. Describes the use of the syllabic method as a means to learn to read in various languages.

Gleitman, L., and P. Rozin. 1973. Teaching reading by use of a syllabary. *Reading Research Quarterly* 8:447–83. Reports the successful use of the syllabary with pictures as an introductory method to teach reading to both inner-city and suburban children.

Goodman, K. S. 1973. The 13th easy way to make learning to read difficult. *Reading Research Quarterly* 8:484–93. Challenges the use of the syllabary as a means of teaching word identification skills.

Rozin, P., and L. R. Gleitman. 1977. The structure and acquisition of reading II: The reading process and the acquisition of the alphabetic principle. In *Toward a psychology of reading*, edited by A. Reber and O. Scarborough. Hillsdale, N.J.: Erlbaum, 55–142. Describes research, theory, and practice built around the syllabary approach.

GOODMAN'S READING
STRATEGY LESSONS

Purpose

The purpose of the reading strategy lessons (Y. Goodman and Burke 1972) is to increase students' awareness of the language and thought clues available during reading. The lessons are intended to (1) help readers focus on aspects of written language not being processed effectively, and (2) support and strengthen readers' use of clues already being used.

Rationale

Reading strategy lessons are based upon Kenneth Goodman's (1967, 1975) notions of reading that suggest there are certain universal reading processes. These processes are applied by all readers with varying levels of proficiency across different reading material. Toward the end of acquiring meaning, these processes include

1. The reader selecting the appropriate and necessary language cues to make predictions;
2. The reader verifying these predictions; and
3. The reader reprocessing language cues if predictions prove untenable.

A diagram developed by Goodman, Burke, and Sherman (1974) depicts these notions.

Proficient Silent Reading Model*

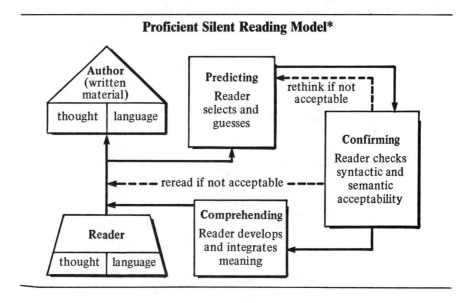

*The reader selects the appropriate language cues in order to *predict* as best he can, based upon his knowledge of language and his background experience. He *confirms* his predictions by testing these hypotheses or predictions. He does this by checking the syntactic and semantic acceptability of what he thinks he is reading against his knowledge of language and the world. Finally, he *comprehends* those items he believes to be significant. He integrates this new meaning or knowledge into established meaning system. He then interacts with the print again. The process is continuous, and as we read, we constantly add, alter, or reorganize the meanings. (Y. M. Goodman, Burke, and Sherman, 1972, 18. Used by permission of the author.)

The general goal of the reading strategy lessons is to involve students in a meaningful reading situation that does not distract them from reading with understanding. To this end, some general guidelines are suggested:

1. The language of the material used should be similar to the language of the reader and of worthy literary quality;
2. The language of the material should not be ambiguous;
3. The language of the material should use redundant information naturally;
4. The content of the material used should be both interesting and significant to readers;
5. Lessons should afford students the opportunity to apply learnings from strategy lessons to actual reading situations;
6. Lessons should be related to students' ongoing learning experiences; and
7. Lessons should be initiated when students' needs arise and terminate with students' boredom, disinterest, or accomplishment.

Intended Audience

It is suggested that almost all readers can benefit from reading strategy lessons. The lessons may expand proficient readers' actual reading experiences and help them to build confidence. They can improve and support the strategies used by readers who exhibit evidence of effective, but inconsistent, use of strategies, *or* for whom the development of effective strategies has been disrupted.

Description of the Procedure

Reading strategy lessons are planned situations in which the use and availability of selected reading strategies are highlighted and reinforced. The situations are not intended to be panaceas for reading difficulties. Instead, teacher insight and teacher adaptation of the various strategies are suggested as essential if the needs of students at specific times are to be met.

The following description presents selected and representative strategy lessons. These descriptions have been organized under these headings:

1. Meeting the needs of inefficient readers;
2. Meeting the needs of inconsistent readers; and
3. Meeting the needs of proficient readers.

1. Meeting the needs of inefficient readers

Y. Goodman (1975) describes inefficient readers this way:

They use effective reading strategies occasionally in short phrases or sections of written material, but in most reading situations, these readers tend to omit words they think they do not know; they do not predict acceptable grammatical or semantic structures as they read; they read word for word using sounding out techniques without concern for meaning. They do everything they were taught to do in an isolated and unrelated fashion. They look for little words in big words and find fat/her an acceptable solution for father. They separate words between two middle consonants and often read lit/tul for little and prit/tee for pretty. When they do make occasional effective use of reading strategies, they lack confidence in deciding which strategy is most effective. They regress and correct in situations when it is inefficient to do so. For example, if such a reader reads can't for cannot because of the use of an appropriate predicting strategy, this is corrected when the reader picks up additional graphic cues. Such readers often think that graphic input is the most significant aspect of reading. Reading is not to discover something new or for enjoyment, it is to satisfy another person.*

According to Goodman (1975), inefficient readers need first to realize that they are effective language users and that these abilities can help in reading. To this end, strategy lessons by which students become aware of the utility of their language cueing systems are suggested. For example, cloze procedures similar to the following are suggested to enable students to become more aware of their use of grammatical and meaning cues:

"Stop!" said John. "Stop! Stop!" He could see that the little red _____ was heading straight for the bridge that had been washed away in the last storm. The driver of the _____ must have heard John. He hit the brakes and the _____ stopped. Its motor stopped and the driver jumped out.

To deal with some of the specific inefficiencies of readers, other strategies are suggested.

a. For readers whose omissions or substitutions result in meaning loss, teachers are urged to encourage them to make meaningful substitutions for omissions. Students might produce words that have some related meaning or words with a close meaning. This might be done incidentally, by encouraging the reader to ask, "What word could go in this spot?" "Why do you think so?" The teacher might take a more systematic approach too, using exercises like these:

1. Present the students a passage with systematic deletions of words or phrases and encourage readers to use the context to suggest alternative possibilities.

*From: Yetta M. Goodman, "Reading Strategy Lessons: Expanding Reading Effectiveness." In *Help for the Reading Teacher: New Directions in Research*, edited by W. Page. NCTE and ERIC, 39. Copyright © 1975 by the National Council of Teachers of English. Reprinted with permission.

They _____ around the pool.
_____ enjoyed swimming.
The children ran for the bus. They had slept late. Just as they arrived at the bus stop, _____ .

2. Present the students with a passage containing nonsense words for significant verbs or nouns and have students replace these with real words.

The buemt hopped through the grass and disappeared into its burrow. The buemt had a little tail of white fur and long ears. The buemt loved to nibble on leaves.

3. Present the students either a passage containing intentional significant miscues, or have the students prepare a passage containing certain intentional miscues. The readers task would be to locate these miscues.

b. For the readers who have developed habitual associations between words or phrases that have close graphic or phonic similarities, such as *for-from, saw-was, though-thought*, lessons using carefully controlled linguistic material are suggested. For example, the students might be asked to read or write stories which use or elicit one of the confused words or use both words nonambiguously.

The following is an example of a suggested method for dealing with students' confusions between *was* and *saw*. First, present the student with sentences containing one of the habitually associated words. For example, "It was father." In this setting, it is not likely that students will produce "It saw father." When the students show evidence of being able to handle one of the habitually associated words, introduce the students to material in which both words are used nonambiguously.

2. Meeting the needs of the inconsistent reader

Y. Goodman (1975) describes inconsistent readers in the following statement:

These readers use effective reading strategies when the material is highly interesting to them or when it is easy because it has a low concept load. However, when these readers find themselves reading material which is complex, they use less efficient reading strategies. They stop searching for meaning and end up sounding out or word calling. When asked how they handle any particular reading problem, such readers often say they sound words out; they may be unaware that they use context to read or they may believe the teacher disapproves of it. Strategy lessons help these readers become aware of the various effective reading strategies they already use when reading easy material, permitting them to transfer effective reading strategies to more difficult reading materials.*

As described by Goodman and Burke in the manual *Reading Miscue Inventory* (1972), inconsistent readers include the reader who makes some effective use of reading strategies and the reader who makes moderately effective use of reading strategies. In natural reading situations, it is suggested that these readers be encouraged to make judgments while reading. They should be encouraged to ask self-monitoring questions, such as, "Does what I am reading make sense?" "If it doesn't, what should I do about it?" If the material is not making sense, it is suggested that the readers be encouraged either to continue to see if the selection will begin to make sense, or to judge whether to move to an alternative selection.

Strategy lessons for these readers are designed to develop their awareness of the transfer value of effective reading strategies from easy to difficult material. For example, in the context of easy material, readers might become aware of the strategies used to deal with unfamiliar words and to differentiate the significance of words.

Here is an example of a strategy lesson serving these purposes. It is taken from Goodman's article, "Reading Strategy Lessons: Expanding Reading Effectiveness" (1975). This story uses a concept or word which is probably not well known.

> The boy was looking for Petoskies. He was walking slowly to make sure he wouldn't miss them. He usually found a number of them each time he went looking for them. They were not easy to find because they were the same color as the sand. He enjoyed looking for Petoskies on the beach. He was helping his mother, too, since she used them in her work. She was an artist and made jewelry with them. Petoskies are usually bluish gray in their natural state with the fossils in them somewhat darker. When Petoskies are polished, the gray color becomes lighter and the fossils take on a brown character. Petoskies are found only on the shores of the Great Lakes.

To aid students gain meaning for the unknown word, the teacher would:

> Put this story on an overhead projector and use it with a small group of readers. Tell them not to worry about pronouncing every word as they read. Cover the entire story and move the cover down, exposing one more sentence with each move. As each sentence is exposed, ask the children to tell what the word (point to Petoskies) means. After each sentence, ask the children to revise their guesses

*From : Yetta M. Goodman, "Reading Strategy Lessons: Expanding Reading Effectiveness." In *Help for the Reading Teacher: New Directions in Research*, edited by W. Page. NCTE and ERIC, 138. Copyright © 1975 by the National Council of Teachers and English. Reprinted with permission.

about the word. Do not pronounce the word for the children, nor should you ask them to pronounce it. If any reader does say the word, the pronunciation should be accepted without comment. Only after the story is completely exposed and the meaning of Petoskies fully discussed should you ask for variations in pronunciation and finally tell the group how you think it may be pronounced. This is an interesting lesson because many teachers may not pronounce Petoskies the same way the people who polish and sell these stones do.*

Other strategy lessons for these readers might be to have students judge the significance or insignificance of words, phrases, or sentences contained in a selection. For example, students might be asked to read a selection and either delete or underline redundant words.

3. Meeting the needs of proficient readers

Proficient readers are considered to be using reading strategies effectively. Therefore, reading strategy lessons afford these readers an opportunity to develop confidence in the use of these strategies. Specifically, strategy lessons might broaden and deepen their reading experiences. To deepen the readers' experiences, they might be encouraged to anticipate plot, theme, and events, to perceive subtleties and inferential meaning, to realize the influence of background and experience upon interpretation, and to appreciate that other readers have different interpretations about the same reading experience. To broaden their reading experiences, such students might be given the opportunity to read a variety of different types of reading materials in varying literary styles. Obviously, attention should be centered upon improving their reading-to-learn abilities.

Cautions and Comments

Reading strategy lessons represent an attempt to extend Goodman's notions of the reading process to classroom practices. According to this view, learning to read "ought not to be very much more difficult than the process by which one learns the oral mode of language. That is, provided that the same principles of relevance, meaningfulness, and motivation for communication which characterized the learning of oral language have been adhered to" (Cambourne 1976–77, 610). The ramification of this notion for instruction, specifically phonic instruction, lies in the following assumptions: decoding to speech or sound is not a necessary step between grapheme and reading for meaning; a hierarchy of subskills is not a necessary aspect of learning reading; maximizing the internalized knowledge of a reader should be encouraged; beginning

*From: Yetta M. Goodman, "Reading Strategy Lessons: Expanding Reading Effectiveness." In *Help for the Reading Teacher: New Directions in Research*, edited by W. Page. NCTE and ERIC, 138. Copyright © 1975 by the National Council of Teachers of English. Reprinted with permission.

readers use the same process as fluent readers and should learn to read as naturally; and phonics analysis is neither useful nor necessary.

In terms of the latter assumption, Goodman has been critical of both the emphasis upon phonics and the methodologies proposed. He has claimed that phonic approaches to reading are preoccupied with the erroneous notion that reading requires precise letter identification. That is, he disagrees with the notion that reading involves exact, detailed, sequential perception and identification of letters, words, and spelling patterns. His main argument is that we do not and cannot read letter by letter. A good reader is so efficient in sampling and predicting that he uses the least available information necessary. A less proficient reader needs the confidence to engage in sampling and predicting; encouraging less proficient readers to use too many cues, to be cautious, may detract from the readers' addressing meaning.

Along this line of reasoning, the strategy lessons are not intended to be exhaustive, but to illustrate to teachers ways they might develop their own strategies, based upon a reasonable understanding of the reader and the strategy lessons' rationale. In this regard, the suggestions are sufficiently explicit for appropriate instructional adaptations at most levels. They do need further amplification, though, especially to meet the needs of primary-level and advanced high-school students. Finally, those teachers needing more background before they construct their own strategy lesson with Goodman's ideas are directed to the reference section that follows.

REFERENCES

Allen, P. D. and D. J. Watson, eds. 1976. *Findings of research in miscue analysis: Classroom implications*. National Council for Teachers of English and Educational Resources Information Center. Includes a collection of articles addressing an extended discussion of the research base of Goodman's ideas and its relevance to instruction.

Cambourne, B. 1976−77. Getting to Goodman: An analysis of the Goodman model of reading with some suggestions for evaluation. *Reading Research Quarterly* 12:605−36. Describes the major features of Goodman's model, its implications and how it might be reevaluated.

Goodman, K. S. 1965. A linguistic study of cues and miscues in reading. *Elementary English* 42:639−43. Presents aspects of Goodman's research and the bases for reading strategy lessons.

———. 1967. Reading: A psycholinguistic guessing game. *Journal of the Reading Specialist* 6:126−35. Presents Goodman's original definition of reading and describes its ramifications.

———. 1975. The reading process. In *Language and reading*, edited by S. S. Smiley and J. C. Towner. Bellingham: Western Washington State College. Presents an updated model of Goodman's reading process that revises and expands upon the earlier model.

Goodman, K. S., and C. L. Burke. 1970. When a child reads: A psycholinguistic analysis. *Elementary English* 47:121–29. Describes the reading process using data collected on students' miscues during reading.

Goodman, K. S., and Y. M. Goodman. 1979. Learning to read is natural. In *Theory and practice of early reading*, edited by L. B. Resnick and P. A. Weaver. Hillsdale, NJ: Erlbaum. Presents a discussion of the rationale behind a wholistic view of reading and teaching reading.

———. 1982. A whole-language comprehension-centered view of reading development. In *Basic skills issues and choices: Approach to basic skills instruction* (Vol. 2), edited by L. Reed and S. Ward. St. Louis: CEMREL. Describes a whole-language comprehension-centered reading program and suggests ways to implement such a program in the classroom, including modifying a basal reader program.

Goodman, Y. M. 1975. Reading strategy lessons: Expanding reading effectiveness. In *Help for the reading teacher: New directions in research*, edited by W. Page. National Council of Teachers of English and Educational Resources Information Center, 34–41. Presents the rationale for and several examples of reading strategy lessons.

Goodman, Y. M., and C. L. Burke. 1972. *Reading miscue inventory*. New York: Macmillan. A manual with suggestions for using strategy lessons, based upon students' identified needs.

———. 1980. *Reading strategies: Focus on comprehension*. New York: Holt, Rinehart, & Winston. Presents a resource book of reading strategies for teachers.

Goodman, Y. M., C. L. Burke, and B. Sherman. 1974. *Strategies in reading*. New York: Macmillan. A handbook of reading strategies that provides the theory and practice of Strategy Lessons.

Smith, F., ed. 1973. *Psycholinguistics and reading*. New York: Holt, Rinehart & Winston. Presents a series of articles addressing the relevance of psycholinguistics to reading.

11

Multisensory Strategies for Teaching Reading

UNIT OVERVIEW

The Unit and Its Theme

Starting from the premise that stimulation of several channels of sensory input reinforces learning, a number of specific variations of multisensory techniques have developed over the years. Indeed, multisensory strategies for teaching reading date back to ancient Greek and Roman education, where methods of tracing were used and recommended by notables such as Plato. In these various strategies, visual, auditory, kinesthetic, and tactile modalities are stimulated; therefore, they are often referred to as VAKT methods. Although the acceptability of using these processes without any emphasis upon comprehension may be questioned, the VAKT approaches described herein have had some reported success. While techniques suggested in the VAKT strategies could be incorporated into a classroom reading curriculum, they are designed and suggested for use when there are students with severe reading disabilities. Most of these approaches include techniques to improve spelling and writing skills, as well as reading skills. In the present unit, however, only the reading aspects of some of the more noted multisensory strategies will be presented.

The reader should be cautioned to examine carefully both the theoretical bases and the intent of a multisensory strategy prior to implementation. The effectiveness of a procedure should not be judged in terms of the efficiency with which it programs or sequences experiences. Instead, the effectiveness of an approach should be judged from whether it meets the needs of students who will be expected to read for meaning.

The Strategies

In this unit, six representative techniques have been labeled multisensory strategies and selected for inclusion. Three of the six techniques described here involve what might be considered traditional VAKT strategies. The remaining strategies place a heavy emphasis upon phonics instruction in association with traditional VAKT learning techniques.

Fernald Technique

With respect to multisensory approaches, the Fernald technique has been perhaps the most widely used VAKT approach. It represents a comprehensive approach to developing reading abilities from low to normal ability.

Cooper Method

The Cooper method represents one of several modifications of the Fernald technique, which purports to give students a foothold in reading. This method proposes a variation upon Fernald's tracing technique which proposes tracing in sand and the use of a controlled vocabulary as the initial source for learning words.

Modality Blocking Procedure

The modality blocking procedure was developed by Harriet and Harold Blau; it is based upon the Fernald technique and represents an attempt to avoid overstimulation of modalities. The technique systematically blocks the visual modality so that overstimulation of the various modalities will not happen concurrently. This procedure is purported to be successful with "disabled" readers of all ages.

Gillingham-Stillman Method

The Gillingham-Stillman method represents one of several multisensory approaches which emphasizes students' auditory channels in learning to read. Based upon the theories of Samuel Orton, the Gillingham-Stillman procedure provides an alphabetic method by which words are built through associations involving students' visual, auditory, and kinesthetic processes. It purports to provide teachers of "disabled" readers a systematic approach to teach reading in a progression from letters to words, from words to sentences, and from sentences to stories.

Hegge-Kirk-Kirk Method

The Hegge-Kirk-Kirk method represents another multisensory approach that emphasizes learning to read through auditory channels in association with visual and kinesthetic stimulation. As with the Gillingham-Stillman method, it purports to provide teachers of "disabled" readers with systematic drills to teach reading through sound blending, word families, and, eventually, sentence and story reading.

Monroe Methods

The Monroe methods represent still another multisensory approach in which sound blending is merged with kinesthetic responses to ensure learning. For teachers of "disabled" readers, it purports to provide various methods of approach for the difficulties these readers incur in beginning reading.

FERNALD TECHNIQUE

Purpose

The Fernald technique (Fernald 1943) has two basic purposes:

1. To teach the student to write and read words correctly; and
2. To extend the student's reading to various materials other than personal compositions.

Rationale

Fernald claims that many cases of reading disability, both "partial" and 'extreme," are due to teachers' failure to use methods that allow students to learn in the manner most appropriate to their individual abilities. Fernald claims the use of limited methods blocks the learning process. As an alternative, Fernald's own procedure, which incorporates a multisensory strategy, purportedly caters to the varied needs of individuals.

Intended Audience

The Fernald technique is intended for use with cases of "extreme" and "partial reading disability." "Extreme disability" refers to the totally disabled student with zero reading ability. "Partial disability" refers to the student with some reading skills, who is unable to acquire adequate reading skills within the instructional framework of the class. It is intended that the teacher use the procedure on a one-to-one basis with each student; however, the technique can be adapted for use with groups.

Description of the Procedure

Fernald divides her technique into four stages in accord with varying levels of individual reading ability and development. In the first stage, the student traces the word with a finger, saying each part of the word aloud as it is traced, until it can be written without looking at the copy. By the final stage, the student is eager to read. The student can begin to generalize about words and to identify new ones.

Stage One

The first stage is highly structured and for this reason will be described in some detail. In this stage, the student selects any word or words that he or she wants to learn, regardless of length. Each word is written with crayon on a strip of paper in large, chalkboard size cursive writing, or manuscript print. The student then traces the word with finger contact, pronouncing each part of the word as it is traced. This tracing procedure is repeated as many times as necessary until the student can write the word on a separate piece of paper without looking at the copy. As new words are learned in this manner, they are placed in an alphabetized word file by the student.

After several words are taught in this way, the student begins to realize that he or she can read and write words. At this time, "story writing" activities are introduced. Subsequent learning of words occurs whenever the student cannot write a word for the story. Sometimes the student may have to learn every word by this tracing technique before the story can be written. After the words are learned and the story is written, the story is typed by the teacher within twenty-four hours. The story is then read by the student, who proceeds to file the words under the proper letter in the word file.

The following points are stressed by Fernald for using this initial stage:

1. For maximum efficiency, unknown words should always be traced with the finger in contact with the paper;
2. In order to avoid breaking the word into meaningless units, the student should write the word from memory rather than from copy;
3. Similarly, if any error or interruption occurs during the student's writing of the word, the word should be rewritten entirely; and
4. To ensure the student understands the meaning of the word, words should always be used in context.

A FERNALD DIALOGUE FOR STAGE ONE

The following dialogue between a student and teacher is presented to illustrate the use of the first stage of the Fernald technique with a "totally disabled" reader.

TEACHER: Good morning, my name is Mr. Stewart and I'm your teacher. Please sit here at my side.

STUDENT: Oh, all right.

TEACHER: I have a new way of learning to read which I'd like you to try. Many bright people have had the same difficulty you have had in learning to read and have learned easily by this new method. Now, give me any word that you want to learn to read.

STUDENT: Dinosaur.

TEACHER: Dinosaur?

STUDENT: Dinosaur.

TEACHER: Now, watch what I do and listen to what I say. Are you ready?

STUDENT: Yeah.

[The teacher should use a crayon and a piece of paper which is approximately four inches by twelve inches.

1. The teacher says the word before writing it.
2. As the word is written, each syllable is said.
3. If the word is written in cursive style (as the word is said again), the *i*'s are crossed and the *i*'s are dotted, etc.
4. As the word is said again, each syllable is underlined.
5. The word is said again.]

TEACHER: Now again, watch what I do and listen to what I say. Are you ready?

STUDENT: Yeah.

TEACHER: [The teacher follows exactly the steps as above, only the teacher uses a finger instead of a crayon.] I want you to do exactly as I did until you think you can write the word without looking at it. Now watch again what I do and listen to what I say. Ready? [Teacher repeats tracing procedure.]

STUDENT: Let me try.

TEACHER: Do what I did and say what I said until you can write the word without looking at it.

STUDENT: [The student traces the word following the procedure demonstrated.]

TEACHER: [Teacher checks student's tracing technique. Whenever the student hesitates or makes an error, the teacher stops the student and, if necessary, demonstrates the technique again. The number of times the student traces the word is recorded.]

STUDENT: (After several tracings): I think I know the word now.

TEACHER: [Teacher removes copy of word and places a blank sheet of paper and a crayon in front of the student.] Write the word on this piece of paper using the same procedure. [If the student makes a mistake, the student is stopped immediately. Do not erase the word. Instead, fold or turn paper over and allow the student to try again.]

STUDENT: [Student writes the word using the same procedure followed when tracing the word.] Finished.

TEACHER: Are you correct?

> STUDENT: I sure am.
> TEACHER: Check and see if you are correct.
> STUDENT: [Student turns over the copy and compares attempt.]
> TEACHER: Were you correct?
> STUDENT: Yeah.
> TEACHER: Do you think you can write it correctly twice? Try writing the word again. [The teacher turns copies of the word down and gives student another blank sheet of paper.]
> [Student proceeds to write the word correctly a second time.]
> TEACHER: Check to see if you are correct again.
> [Student checks word.]
> TEACHER: Congratulations! That's great! Now place the word in your word file under the proper letter.
> [Student proceeds to place word under the letter *d* in the word file.]
> TEACHER: Now tell me another word you wish to learn.

Two, three, or maybe four words might be learned using this same procedure during a single sessions over each of the first few days. As soon as the student realizes that words can be learned by this procedure, "story writing" is started. Words are learned as they are needed for the story the student is writing.

Stage Two

The length of the tracing period (stage one) will vary from student to student and is phased out when the student is able to learn without it. This becomes evident when there is a decrease in the number of tracings required to learn a word, and when some words are learned with single or no tracings. At the point when the need for any tracing disappears, the student is ready to embark upon stage two. On the average, the tracing period lasts about two months, with a range from one to eight months.

During stage two, the student learns words simply by looking at the word while saying it over and over. As with stage one, words to be learned are derived from unknown words in stories the student has written. These words are presented to the student in print or in cursive form for study. The word is learned by saying the word several times, over and over again, until it can be written from memory.

Stage Three

Stage three is basically the same as stage two, except that the student has now reached the stage where learning occurs merely by looking at a word and saying it. The student is permitted to read anything and as much as he or she desires. Whenever an unknown word is met, the student is told the word. At this stage, the student learns directly from the printed page. It has become unnecessary to write or print each new word on a card. The student looks at the word in print, pronounces it a number of times, and then is able to write it from memory. As with the previous stage, after reading new words are reviewed, filed, and, at a later stage, reviewed again.

Stage Four

In stage four, the student is able to recognize new words from their resemblance to words or parts of words already learned. As with stage three, the student is expected to read a variety of materials. However, unlike stage three, the student is able to work out many words. For example, such words might be learned from the context, or from generalizations about words or word parts. The student is told only those words for which it is not possible to determine the meaning. For purposes of retention, such words are usually written down by the student.

Fernald emphasizes the need for student involvement in the content of what is being read. For this reason, she suggests that the student be encouraged to survey a paragraph to clear up the meaning of unknown words prior to reading. She argues that this will prevent distraction and enable the student to concentrate on the content of the reading material. Toward the goal of reading for meaning, she discourages the sounding out of words during reading, either by the teacher or by a student, and suggests that any word that the student does not know be provided.

Cautions and Comments

Empirical evidence of the success of the Fernald technique comes from various studies. Kress and Johnson (1970), Berres and Eyer (1970), Enstrom (1970), and Coterell (1972) have all reported positive results with this approach. Fernald herself provides a great deal of documented support for the strategy's success in *Remedial Techniques in Basic School Subjects* (1943).

While there seems to be a consensus that the Fernald technique yields positive results and has several desirable features, there also seems to be agreement that it suffers from some major drawbacks.

On the positive side, the desirable features of the Fernald method include:

1. It reinforces the acquisition of word form cues, and the ability to use context;
2. Methods seem consistent with aims and take into account variations in the child's rate of learning and specific needs and interests; and
3. Motivation and reading of interesting materials are emphasized.

On the negative side, objections to the use of the technique include:

1. The procedure tends to be very time consuming and demanding of the teacher's time, especially in the early stages. Often more

expedient methods for teaching "disabled" readers could be developed;

2. Reading books is deemed important, but delayed;
3. Syllabic division within words may distort the pronunciation of certain words, e.g. fat/her; and
4. Readers may develop who are too busy sounding out words to either concentrate on meaning or understand the purposes of reading. In this respect, it can be argued that Fernald suggests the need, but not the methods by which students will read for meaning.

REFERENCES

Berres, F., and J. T. Eyer. 1970. John. In *Casebook on reading disability*, edited by A. J. Harris. New York: David McKay, 25–47. Describes a case history example of the use of the procedure.

Bond, G. L., and M. A. Tinker. 1973. *Reading difficulties: Their diagnosis and correction*. 3d ed. Englewood Cliffs, N.J.: Prentice-Hall, 498–501. Presents a brief discussion of the procedure and its uses.

Chall, J. 1967. *Learning to read: The great debate*. New York: McGraw-Hill, 170–72. Presents a brief discussion of aspects of Fernald's work with disabled readers.

Coterell, G. 1972. A case of severe learning disability. *Remedial Education* 7:5–9. Describes an example of the procedure's successful use.

Enstrom, E. A. 1970. A key to learning. *Academic Therapy* 5:295–97. Describes a successful example using the procedure.

Fernald, G. 1943. *Remedial techniques in basic school subjects*. New York: McGraw-Hill. Presents a detailed description of the procedure and results of its use.

Gearhart, B. R. 1973. *Learning disabilities: Educational strategies*. St. Louis: C. V. Mosby, 76–90. Presents a detailed discussion of the procedure and provides examples of its use through case histories.

Harris, A. J., and E. R. Sipay. 1975. *How to increase reading ability*. 6th ed. New York: David McKay, 393–96. Presents a brief discussion of the procedure and its use with students experiencing reading difficulty.

Kaluger, G., and C. J. Kolson. 1969. *Reading and learning disabilities*. Columbus, Ohio: Charles E. Merrill, 263–67. Presents a theoretical discussion of the procedure and its use.

Kress, R. A., and M. S. Johnson. 1970. Martin. In *Casebook on reading disability*, edited by A. J. Harris. New York: David McKay, 1–24. Describes an example of the use of the procedure through a case history.

Meyer, C. A. 1978. Reviewing the literature on Fernald's technique of remedial reading. *The Reading Teacher* 31: 614–19. Reviews studies examining the effectiveness of Fernald's technique.

COOPER METHOD

Purpose

Using a modification of the Fernald technique, the Cooper method (1947) is a multisensory approach for beginning reading instruction with "disabled" readers.

Rationale

Cooper's method is in accord with Fernald's claim for VAKT procedures in the view that many cases of reading disability can be overcome by the use of methods that allow students to learn in the manner most appropriate to their individual abilities. But, as an alternative to the Fernald technique, Cooper proposes a different method of tracing and the use of a controlled vocabulary. With respect to the latter, words the student wishes to learn are selected by the student from a controlled vocabulary list.

Intended Audience

The Cooper method is intended for use with students with reading problems. As with the Fernald technique, it is intended for use on a one-to-one basis, but can be adapted for use with groups.

Description of the Procedure

The Cooper method, like the Fernald technique, involves extensive stimulation of the student's visual, auditory, kinesthetic, and tactile modalities. Unlike the Fernald technique, it consists of having the student select words from a controlled vocabulary list, derived from preprimers, and tracing words in a shallow sand tray. The Cooper method consists of the following steps:

1. Teacher prepares a shallow tray of sand or salt which corresponds in size to a shoebox lid. The bottom of the box or tray may be painted to make the tracings stand out;
2. The student is positioned in front of the sand tray at a desk;
3. The student is presented with a list of words from which to select;
4. With the student watching, the teacher prints the selected word on a small card and pronounces it;
5. As the word is pronounced, the student examines the card;
6. Using the index and second fingers, the student writes the word in the sand, with teacher guidance of the hand, if necessary;
7. The student compares the word written in the sand with the word written on the card;
8. The sand is shaken to erase the word and the word is written again in the sand;

9. If an error occurs, the process is repeated from Step 6 until the word can be reproduced without the copy; and

10. The student uses the word in a sentence, either orally or in writing.

When the student has acquired the vocabulary of three preprimers, book reading is introduced.

Cautions and Comments

Cooper's method differs from the Fernald technique in two major respects: the use of sand and controlled vocabulary. The use of a sand or salt tray for writing words appears to be more efficient, economical, and perhaps more motivating. The benefits of using a controlled vocabulary, however, have yet to be substantiated. Spache and Spache (1977) offer a discussion of the efficacy of controlled vocabulary, and the interested reader might refer to the disadvantages they cite.

As with all of the multisensory approaches described in Unit 11, the Cooper method proposes procedures for teaching a student to read that appear to contradict what is known about how and why a student reads. In particular, purposeful reading seems delayed until the student has acquired certain word identification skills. Unfortunately, the emphasis upon word and letter level accuracy may detract from the students' use of context in word identification and prompt word by word reading with little understanding.

REFERENCES

Cooper, J. L. 1947. A procedure for teaching non-readers. *Education* 67: 494–99. Presents a detailed discussion of his technique and its origin.

Kaluger, G., and C. J. Kolson. 1969. *Reading and learning disabilities*. Columbus, Ohio: Charles E. Merrill, 266–67. Discusses the Cooper method and makes suggestions for its use.

Spache, G. D., and E. B. Spache. 1977. *Reading in the elementary school*. Boston: Allyn and Bacon, 44–45. Discusses the problems arising from vocabulary controls.

MODALITY BLOCKING PROCEDURE

Purpose

The purpose of the modality blocking procedure (Blau and Blau 1968), is to teach "the severely handicapped reader" to read by avoiding interference caused by the visual modality during word identification.

Rationale

Basic to the modality blocking procedure is the theory that, in some cases, learning to read may be blocked by the visual modality. It is argued that, in contrast to reading, students learn to speak because there is no interference from the visual modality. Furthermore, it is argued that whenever two or more types of information, such as visual and auditory, are delivered to the brain simultaneously a breakdown in processing may occur. For these reasons, Blau and Blau (1968) suggest that the visual input must be cut off rather than reinforced, as it tends to be in other multisensory approaches.

Intended Audience

The modality blocking technique is intended for use on an individual basis with students who have difficulty reading. In general, it has been suggested for use with either readers who have minimal reading ability or with more advanced readers who are having word identification difficulties. The technique must be administered on a one-to-one basis, but a trained aide can implement it also.

Description of the Procedure

The modality blocking approach represents a modification of the Fernald technique. It entails a nonvisual AKT method for developing word identification. The following steps are involved in the approach:

1. A word is selected from either the student's spelling list, compositions, dictated stories, reading stories, or textbook, or in accordance with structured phonic material. As Blau and Blau suggest, students often learn to spell words several years above their reading level, so there should be few restrictions on their source for words.
2. The student is placed in front of a chalkboard, a flannel graph board, or a magnetic board. The procedure and its purpose are explained to the student.
3. The student is blindfolded, or eyes are closed.
4. The teacher or the aide traces the word to be learned on the student's back. As it is traced, the teacher or the aide spells the word aloud, letter by letter. This continues until the student can identify the letters and spell the word.
5. Usually, if overloading of the sensory modes does not result, or the student masters the procedure with ease, three-dimensional plastic or wooden letters are placed in front of the blindfolded student. As the teacher traces the spoken letters on the student's back, the student traces the three-dimensional letters.
6. The three-dimensional letters are scrambled, and the student, still blindfolded, arranges the letters in proper sequence.
7. The blindfold is removed, and the student sees the word.

8. The student writes the word on paper or at the board, and then on a file card for future review.

Blau and Blau have indicated that once a word has been mastered using this technique, it is readily recognized visually. Also, they claim that as a result of the procedure, learning appears to mature and, subsequently, word recognition, spelling, and comprehension appear to improve at a faster rate than might be expected.

Cautions and Comments

Blau and Blau (1968) reported success with students of varying ages using their modality blocking procedure or nonvisual AKT. Without questioning the legitimacy of these claims, both the rationale for this approach and its overall effectiveness need further substantiation.

The strategy is directed toward the improvement of word recognition skills and does not provide for either the improvement or the development of other reading skills. As with other multisensory strategies, the procedure places a heavy emphasis upon the acquisition of word identification skills from the part to the whole. In so doing, students are forced to learn skills which seem purposeless and rote. As has been suggested in our previous discussions of multisensory strategies, often students either fail to transfer these skills to actual reading situations, or overemphasize their importance.

REFERENCES

Blau, H., and H. Blau. 1968. A theory of learning to read. *The Reading Teacher* 22:126−29, 144. Describes the procedure and its rationale, and discusses examples of its use with selected students.

Gearhart, B. R. 1973. *Learning disabilities: Educational strategies*. St. Louis: C. V. Mosby, 89−90. Presents a detailed discussion of steps involved in using the procedure.

Harris, A. J., and E. R. Sipay. 1975. *How to increase reading ability*. 6th ed. New York: David McKay, 396. Discusses the procedure in conjunction with a discussion of various other multisensory approaches.

GILLINGHAM-STILLMAN METHOD

Purpose

The purpose of the Gillingham-Stillman method (Gillingham and Stillman 1973) is to provide the reader, "disabled" or "potentially disabled," who has a specific language difficulty, with a method for learning to read that is consistent with the evolution of language functions.

Rationale

Gillingham and Stillman (1973) argue that students with specific language disabilities will learn to read successfully only with methods that are consistent with the evolution of language functions. The system they have suggested is based upon the theoretical position and work of Samuel Orton. As suggested in the foreword to Gillingham and Stillman's 1965 text, *Remedial Training for Children with Specific Disabilities in Reading, Spelling, and Penmanship*, their goal was to organize remedial techniques to make them consistent with Orton's (1937) working hypothesis.

According to Gillingham and Stillman, Orton hypothesized that specific language disabilities he observed may have been due to hemispherical dominance in specific areas of the brain. He related certain instances of reading disability to the difficulty students might potentially have when dealing with inconsistencies that result from mixed dominance. Mirror writing and reversals seemed to be evidence of these difficulties.

The method, as it was developed by Gillingham and Stillman, purports to be new, different, and exclusive. It purports to be new and different in that it provides a "phonetic method" consistent with the evolution of language functions. It purports to be exclusive in that students using it engage in this and only this method. Gillingham and Stillman have claimed that the best teachers for this method are those familiar with traditional reading and spelling instruction. These teachers, it is argued, are cognizant of the need for and utility of Gillingham and Stillman's method.

Intended Audience

The Gillingham-Stillman method is intended for use with students who, due to specific language disabilities, have had or may have difficulty learning to read or spell. These "disabled readers" or "potentially disabled readers" should not include students who show either low mental abilities or sensory deficiencies. The method is intended for use with third graders through sixth graders, but has been adapted for use with older and younger students.

Description of the Procedure

To introduce students to the system, Gillingham and Stillman suggest a narrative entitled "The Growth of Written Language." The narrative is intended to provide a positive mind-set; it traces, with examples, the evolution of communications from spoken language to picture writing to alphabetic writing. The narrative ends with a description of the Gillingham-Stillman method and an explanation to the students that the difficulty they have incurred with reading it is not unique. As Gillingham and Stillman (1973) suggest, the latter message might be handled as follows:

> Now I am going to begin with you in an entirely different way. We are going to use the Alphabetic Method. You are going to learn the

sounds of the letters, then build them into words. You will find it real fun and it will be nice for you to be attempting something which you can do.

There are a great many children, more than you have any idea of, who have had the same kind of trouble that you have. Some of them have grown to be famous men and women. Boys and girls now doing well in college and business were taught to read and write as I am going to teach you. (P. 37)

Thereafter, a sequence of exercises beginning with the learning of letters and letter sounds, then blending sound to words, and finally to sentence and story reading is suggested. Within this framework, the technique will be described in this sequence: (1) letters, (2) words, (3) sentences and stories, and (4) others.

1. Letters

The first principle of the technique is to teach the sounds represented by letters and then build these into words. To this end, each word family is taught by associations involving visual, auditory, and kinesthetic processes.

There are three associative processes involved. The first associative process involves two parts:

a. The teacher shows the student a letter and says it. It is then repeated by the student.
b. The same procedure is followed for the sound represented by the letter. The teacher says it. The student repeats it.

The second associative process involves responding with the name of a letter to the sound represented by the letter. That is, the teacher makes the sound represented by the letter and the student names the letter represented.

The third associative process involves learning the letter form. Learning of letter forms takes place in the following manner:

a. The teacher writes and explains the letter form.
b. The student traces the teacher's lines, copies them, writes the word from memory, and then writes the word without looking at what is being written.

There are several guidelines for the teacher to follow across these associative processes:

a. Letters are always introduced by a key word, such as *b*, would be presented in the context of *boy*; when the *b* card is shown, the pupil would be expected to respond with *boy*.
b. Drill cards are used to introduce each letter, provide repetition, and improve the accuracy of sound production.

c. Students learn to differentiate vowels and consonants by the manner of their production and through the use of different colored cards, e.g., white for consonants, salmon for vowels.

d. The first letters presented to the student should represent clear sounds and nonreversible letter forms.

e. An "echo" speech procedure in which the teacher drills the student in reproducing sounds is suggested for students incurring pronunciation difficulties.

f. For reinforcement purposes, students who know the name and sound represented by a letter are asked to respond to the names of letters with the sounds they represent.

g. In instances where writing takes place, cursive writing is preferred and suggested over manuscript writing.

2. Words

After ten letters are well known, blending them into words begins. Drill cards forming a word are placed in front of the student, and the student is required to blend the sounds represented by these letters, such as *h-i-m*, *t-a-p*, *a-t*, *i-f*, *h-i-p*. It is the teacher's responsibility to devise ways of drilling words effectively. These words, printed on colored cards, are placed in what has been termed the student's "Jewel Case." Time drills are imposed; in some instances, students' growth in accuracy is graphed.

After a few days of sound blending, the student is required to reverse the procedure and analyze words into the component sounds. For example, the teacher might say the word *m-a-p* slowly and have students name and find the cards for each sound. As further reinforcement, the student might write the word. As the student writes the word, each letter is named and then the word is spoken.

Typically not more than one or two additional sounds are introduced each day. When a letter might represent more than one sound, only one of the sounds would be introduced. As word families are introduced, the drill card and "Jewel Case" card files are expanded. On a single day, the various activities might be organized as follows:

EXAMPLE OF DAILY LESSONS

(45 minutes to 60 minutes)
Practice in Association I   Selected Word Families
Practice in Association II   Same Selected Word Families
Practice in Association III Same Selected Word Families
(sometimes traced; written to dictation, simultaneous oral spelling)
Drill Words for Reading
Drill Words for Spelling and Writing

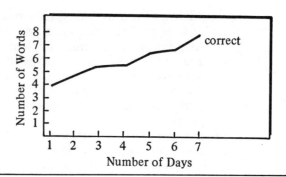

3. Sentences and stories

After students can read and write any three-letter "perfectly phonetic" word, sentence and story reading is begun. It begins with simple, highly structured stories, referred to as "Little Stories," which are presented to the student to read and write.

Several of these "Little Stories" are available from Gillingham and Stillman. The following is an example:

Pat sat on the mat.
She had a hat.
The hat was on Pat.
A rat sat on the mat.
Pat ran.
The rat ran.

For both sentence and story reading, students are required to prepare silently. Their task is to read the story or sentence silently until they can read it perfectly. Any words with which the students may have difficulty are either sounded out, or, in cases where words may be unfamiliar, such as "phonetically irregular words," pronunciation is provided. The students are encouraged to be accurate and to avoid guessing. For sentence and story writing, "Little Stories" are dictated by the teacher. As the teacher dictates the story avoiding unnecessary repetitions, the students write the words.

4. Other

As the students' reading skills develop, the teacher may want to use further guidance provided by Gillingham and Stillman:

a. Students learn that polysyllabic words are formed by syllables in the same way monosyllabic words are formed by letters. To this end, students are presented with and asked to combine detached syllables, and are taught to identify the appropriate accent by trying the accent on each syllable.

b. Dictionary use is taught for the purpose of identifying the pronunciation of words.
c. To deal with a few selected words which are "phonetically irregular," whole-word drill is suggested.
d. Finally, until the student completes a major portion of the phonics program, he or she is discouraged from reading independently.

Gillingham and Stillman suggested that the technique would yield substantial benefits, assuming sufficient time is provided. At a minimum, they suggest the technique requires a commitment of five lessons per week for no less than two years. Eventually, they suggest, the student will be able to return to a regular class; but unless returning students can read their texts and assignments fluently, they should be assisted in reading them.

Cautions and Comments

There appear to be several important similarities and differences between the Gillingham-Stillman technique and the previous multisensory approaches. Both the Gillingham-Stillman and Fernald techniques emphasize constant reinforcement and repetition through the use of visual, auditory, and kinesthetic modalities, both prefer cursive writing to manuscript, and both attempt to develop a positive mindset in the reader prior to the commencement of remediation. In terms of differences, Gillingham and Stillman insist upon a letter-by-letter, structured, synthetic phonics approach, in contrast to Fernald's concern that students not proceed letter by letter but select their own words to learn, and initially learn through all modalities.

While the Gillingham-Stillman technique purports to yield positive results, there are reasons to caution potential users. First, very few contemporary authorities still accept the theoretical position of Orton as tenable. Second, students who learn by these methods may have a tendency to emphasize pronunciation over meaning. This synthetic letter-by-letter approach, with its emphasis upon word-perfect reading places an undue emphasis upon the mechanics rather than reading for meaning. For a further discussion of these points, the reader should refer to the cautions and comments sections of the various strategies presented in Unit 10: Identification Strategies.

REFERENCES

Chall, J. 1967. *Learning to read: The great debate.* New York: McGraw-Hill, 169–70. Presents an evaluation and discussion of Orton's notions of reading disability and Orton's suggestions for remedial reading methods.

Gearhart, B. R. 1973. *Learning disabilities: Educational strategies.* St. Louis: C. V. Mosby, 103–7. Presents a detailed discussion of the major aspects of the technique.

Gillingham, A., and B. W. Stillman. 1973. *Remedial training for children with specific disability in reading, spelling and penmanship*. 7th ed. Cambridge, Mass.: Educators Publishing Service. Provides the rationale and history, and serves as the manual for the Gillingham-Stillman technique.

Harris, A. J., and E. R. Sipay. 1975. *How to increase reading ability*. 6th ed. New York: David McKay, 369–97. Discusses briefly the theory and procedure of the technique.

Kaluger, G., and C. J. Kolson. 1969. *Reading and learning disabilities*. Columbus, Ohio: Charles E. Merrill, 267–68. Presents a brief summary and discussion of this and other techniques.

Orton, J. 1966. The Orton-Gillingham approach. In *The disabled reader*, edited by J. Money. Baltimore: Johns Hopkins University Press, 119–46. Summarizes Orton's theory and discusses the technique.

Orton, S. 1937. *Reading, writing, and speech problems in children*. New York: W. W. Norton. Discusses Orton's theory for specific disabilities in reading.

HEGGE-KIRK-KIRK METHOD

Purpose

The purpose of the Hegge-Kirk-Kirk method (1955) is to provide a systematic synthetic phonic system for "disabled readers" that emphasizes sound blending and kinesthetic experiences in a programmed learning presentation.

Rationale

The Hegge-Kirk-Kirk method was developed by the authors during their work with "mentally retarded students classified as disabled readers." The method is a programmed synthetic phonic system; it emphasizes sound blending and kinesthetic experience. It reflects the influence of Fernald's technique and the work of Marion Monroe (1932). Its presentation follows some of the features of programmed learning: (1) the principle of minimal change; (2) overlearning through repetition and review; (3) prompting and confirmation; (4) teaching one response for each symbol; and (5) providing the student immediate knowledge of success by social reinforcement.

Intended Audience

The Hegge-Kirk-Kirk approach is designed to be used with students who have the following characteristics:

1. The reading status of the student is below the fourth grade,
2. The student has a severe specific reading disability,

3. The student is educable in sound blending,
4. The student has no extreme visual and auditory deficiencies, and
5. The student is motivated and cooperative.

Description of the Procedure

The Hegge-Kirk-Kirk method begins by providing the student auditory training in sound blending, and practice in writing and vocalizing letter sounds. Printed lessons then provide the student with two-or-three-letter words, in which the student sounds each element separately and then blends the sounds into a word. A "graphovocal method" supplements these lessons by having the student write words as their components are pronounced and blended.

The discussion of the teaching of the Hegge-Kirk-Kirk approach will focus upon (1) preparation for the method, (2) implementing the method, and (3) sentence and story reading.

1. Preparation for the method

Preparation for the method involves soliciting the student's cooperation and using an initial training period. The student's cooperation is solicited through a careful explanation of the intent and nature of the procedure to be used. The initial training period exposes the student to the methods used and presents tasks that can and should be readily mastered prior to implementing the procedure. The student is taught some letters and the sounds they represent. The student is shown that words are formed by blending these sounds. An example of the interaction that might occur between student and teacher in this initial period is included here:

> **TEACHER:** Writes *a* on the board. Tells student that it sounds like a baby's cry, *a-a-a*. The teacher erases letter.
>
> **STUDENT:** Writes letter from memory and says sound represented by the letter. (This may be done several times.)
>
> **TEACHER:** Other letters are introduced in similar fashion, and then a word composed of these letters is presented to the student. Teacher asks the student to name the sounds represented by the letters in the word.
>
> **STUDENT:** Names these sounds one at a time.
>
> **TEACHER:** Places other words on the board and asks student to blend the sounds to form a word. The teacher explains that knowing the sounds represented by letters allows the student to form many words and that this can help improve reading.

2. Implementing the Method

During the initial training period, the student is expected to have mastered most of the consonants and short vowel sounds and to be capable of blending three sounds into a word. It is at this time the Hegge-Kirk-Kirk method ıs implemented. It consists of repeated practice in blending specific sounds. Overlearning via repetition is the rule, with an emphasis upon accuracy rather than rate. The student begins with the short *a* sound and proceeds to blend orally long lists of words or word families containing no other vowel sounds, such as *sat, mat, rat,* and *fat.* To this end, Hegge, Kirk, and Kirk provide a total of fifty-five drill exercises and some thirty-seven supplementary exercises. The drill exercises purportedly deal with all the common vowel sounds, consonant sounds, combination sounds, and advanced sounds. The supplementary exercises deal with exceptions to the drills.

Here are some portions of the Hegge-Kirk-Kirk drill and supplementary exercises:

		Drill 2				Supplementary Exercise			
		o					*alk*		
hot	pot	not	rot	got		talk	chalk	walk	balk	stalk
sob	rob	mob	fob	bob		stalked			
hop	mop	top	pop	lop			*oe*		
cog	fog	hog	jog	bog		toe	doe	foe	joe	hoe
sod	rod	nod	hod	pod		tiptoe		goes	

3. Sentences and story reading

While Hegge, Kirk, and Kirk admitted that the drills in themselves would not teach reading to the student, they argued that the drills were essential in developing correct responses to written symbols, attacking new words, and starting a student in reading. Sentence and story reading, they suggest, must be introduced to supplement the drill material.

It is suggested that sentence reading can be implemented in conjunction with the drills. At the discretion of the teacher, students might be presented sentences composed of the same words being drilled. If these sentences include unknown, "phonetically irregular" words, these words would be taught as whole words.

Story reading poses a different type of problem. Hegge, Kirk, and Kirk suggested that primers and first reading books often are too elementary in content for the age of the intended student. They advised, therefore, the elimination of story reading until the student can read more advanced material. Ideally, the material should be interesting in content and "phonetically consistent." Insofar as transferring the knowledge acquired from sound blending to stories, Hegge, Kirk, and Kirk suggested that teachers should not assume that students can transfer their knowledge of derived sound blending to reading from a story. Instead, teachers should aid the student either by naming "phonetically irregular" words or by blending unknown "phonetically regular" words.

When story reading begins, the drills continue to provide support with the introduction of new sounds and practice in blending larger units. As students move beyond sound blending, the drills and exercises are displaced by word study and reading.

Cautions and Comments

The method proposed by Hegge-Kirk-Kirk has been used for over forty years, and throughout this period it has been purportedly successful with "disabled" readers of normal and subnormal abilities. As a synthetic phonic approach, the method is well organized and articulated. It has several of the same characteristics as programmed learning lessons, including small steps, repetition, review, and feedback. In many ways, the approach resembles the Gillingham-Stillman technique, but does not seem to be as flexible to manage.

There are several reasons why the potential user of this approach should be cautioned. In view of contemporary psycholinguistic research and thinking, the approach places undue and inappropriate emphasis upon learning, indeed overlearning, the sounds represented by the letters and sound blending (Zarske 1982). In this regard, the approach apparently assumes that the "disabled" reader should not and maybe cannot read for meaning until certain word identification skills are acquired. Many authorities (Smith 1973) would suggest that acquisition and overlearning of these skills may have the reverse effect and hinder reading. For example, students learning these skills may never develop an understanding of what is entailed in purposeful reading. These students may become "word callers" who have a great deal of difficulty understanding what they have read. As Smith (1973) has suggested, reading for meaning is easier and should not be displaced by "reading words." It has the potential, as Smith aptly states, to be an easy way to make learning to read difficult.

REFERENCES

Bond, G. L., and M. A. Tinker. 1973. *Reading difficulties: Their diagnosis and correction.* 3d ed. Englewood Cliffs, N.J.: Prentice-Hall, 518. Presents a brief discussion of the procedure and similar techniques.

Hegge, T., S. Kirk, and W. Kirk. 1955. *Remedial reading drills*, Ann Arbor: George Wehr. Presents a detailed description of the procedure, its rationale, utility, and drill exercises.

Kaluger, G., and C. J. Kolson. 1963. *Reading and learning difficulties.* Columbus, Ohio: Charles E. Merrill, 269. Presents a brief discussion of the procedure and similar techniques.

Kirk, S. A. 1983. *Educating exceptional children.* 4th ed. Boston: Houghton Mifflin. Discusses the theory, method, and development of the procedure.

Monroe, M. 1932. *Children who cannot read.* Chicago: University of Chicago Press. Describes the Monroe methods, their rationale, and their utility with disabled readers.

Smith, F., ed. 1973. *Psycholinguistics and reading*. New York: Holt, Rinehart & Winston. Presents a point of view to reading directly in opposition to this approach.

Zarske, J. A. 1982. Neuropsychological intervention approaches for handicapped children. *Journal of Research and Development in Education* 15: 66–75. Reviews the literature and research on various approaches including Hegge, Kirk, and Kirk.

MONROE METHODS

Purpose

The purpose of the Monroe methods (1932) is to overcome a student's impediments to reading by providing drills and devices that involve motor responses to synthetic word recognition instruction.

Rationale

Monroe proposed drills and devices to reduce the student's errors in reading, to build up discriminations not being made, and to utilize to the fullest discriminations that are being made. She claimed that just as two individuals may think of the same object differently, so different individuals learn to read differently. From this standpoint, she suggested the use of "the possible secondary or vicarious steps in word recognition that are not usually presented in ordinary instruction" (Monroe 1932, 111). In accordance with an individual's abilities and needs, methods would be selected requiring motor responses whenever possible. As reasons for stressing motor responses, she suggested that:

1. Motor responses are more easily observed by the teacher and student;
2. Motor responses are probably a part of the normal reading process, and movement serves to intensify this process;
3. Motor responses reinforce and develop precise discriminations of the auditory and visual features of words; and
4. Motor responses assist in directing attention to learning.

Furthermore, as Monroe (1932) noted:

> To the usual child, the emphasis on motor response as outlined here, and the placement of the secondary links in the learning process, may be an unnecessary procedure, detracting from the enjoyment through the mechanical devices for recognition of words. The child who has not learned to read, however, and who for the first time finds that he can succeed in reading simple words and

sentences, even if by somewhat laborious methods, finds a new interest and enthusiasm for reading, and a new respect for his own capacities. (P. 113)

Intended Audience

The Monroe methods are intended for those students who deviate to the extent that they have failed or are failing to read by ordinary procedures. Ideally, the methods are intended for use on a one-to-one basis, but can and have been used with small groups.

Description of the Procedure

Monroe's methods have as their ultimate goal the development of the ability to read fluently, "comprehendingly, accurately, pleasurably, and with as little effort as possible" (Monroe 1932, 136). The methods described herein are seen as a means to this end for disabled readers. These methods are intended to be modified to meet the errors or difficulties they attempt to overcome. They address:

1. Faulty vowels and consonants;
2. Reversals;
3. Additions of sounds;
4. Omission of sounds;
5. Substitution of words; and
6. Repetition of words.

1. Faulty vowels and consonants

Monroe suggested that there are many sources for the type of difficulty when students need help in discriminating speech sounds, in establishing association with letters, and in sequencing these sounds into words. Monroe suggested three steps to this end.

  a. The first step is to develop the student's ability to discriminate speech sounds. In this step, students are presented with cards containing pictures of several objects beginning with the same consonant or containing the same vowel. These pictures may be obtained from magazines. Examples of the objects used are:

b, as in *boy; book*
e, as in *pen; hen*

To develop discrimination, the student is presented with cards containing unlike sounds, for example, *m* compared with *s*. The student is instructed to articulate clearly the sound represented by either the letter *s* or *m*, then name the pictured object. If the name of the object begins with the sound the student is asked to articulate, then the student retains the card. As the student proceeds, more difficult discriminations are presented. For example, *s* compared with *sh*. Where the student appears confused, an attempt is made to develop discrimination by articulated movements. To provide variety in the activity, the student is asked to generate words for beginning sounds.

b. The second step involves establishing associations between letters and their most frequent sounds. The suggested procedure involves a sounding-tracing technique. The student traces over a letter written by the teacher, while simultaneously articulating the sound. The procedure is repeated until the student can look at the letter and articulate the sound it represents on sight. Monroe suggested that usually five or six consonant sounds can be learned at one sitting. After the student has retained the associations for five or six consonant sounds, a short vowel sound is presented. The student then is taught to blend the consonants and vowels to form words. From this point, the words learned are listed systematically, traced manually, and reviewed frequently. The student begins to proceed through word family drills. The method was illustrated by Monroe (1932) with the following example:

> The teacher wrote the word to be learned in large handwriting on a piece of paper. She said to the child, "See this word? This word is man. Say man. Now let me see how slowly you can say man, like this, m-a-n. Now I want you to do two things at the same time. Take your pencil and trace over this word while you say m-a-n slowly. Be sure to speak quickly enough and write slowly enough that you will come out just even." (P. 120)

Monroe gave a series of word lists to be learned in this manner. These lists begin with words composed of three sounds, including one short vowel, and end with words containing several syllables. Recall is checked by presenting the students with the words printed on cards. The student is instructed to articulate the separate sounds and to blend them.

As a variation of the tracing method, Monroe proposed substitution or a "sound-dictation" method. The "sound-dictation" method entails the student's writing the words as the teacher dictates the sounds, then re-reading the list.

c. As soon as the student has acquired a vocabulary of a number of words, the next step can be introduced. This step can be implemented concurrently with step (b). The step entails having the students read stories with a controlled phonetic language. "Phonetically irregular" words would be avoided, but if added to the stories, these words would be taught by tracing and by whole-word methods.

2. Reversals

To overcome difficulties incurred as a result of reversals, Monroe made various suggestions for providing cues to direction. The tracing-sounding method described for vowels and consonants was suggested for dealing with many of the more discrete reversals of letters and words. To develop a consistent direction for reading words, it was suggested that the student be instructed to follow, using the sliding motion of a pencil or a finger, the letters within words, then to follow the words within lines and to follow lines on a page. If the student's motor control proves too inaccurate for this approach, then retyping of the selection leaving more space between the lines was suggested. In some cases, Monroe suggested having the students underline, or write the words under each line. In extreme cases, she suggested presenting the students with words on cards, printed in large and raised type. With eyes closed, the student traces the word until it can be differentiated.

3. Addition of sounds

Monroe claimed that sounds are added to words, such as *tack* and *track*, either due to student confusion of one word with another or as a result of a previous error. To cope with the former case, she suggested auditory and visual drilling to eradicate the confusion. To cope with the latter, no special drill was suggested. Monroe claimed the correction of the previous error was sufficient to eliminate these errors.

4. Omission of sounds

Monroe suggested that the omission of sounds occurred as a result either of speech defects and discrimination difficulties, or of an overstress on speed of reading. To correct these difficulties, she suggested either speech-training, sound-tracing, training in dividing words into syllables, or encouraging a slower reading rate.

5. Substitution of words

Monroe expressed differentiated concern for the substitution of words. She suggested that instances of meaningful substitution of words, such as *father* for *dad*, should be overlooked, but meaningless substitutions, such as *day* for *dad*, should be corrected. To cope with the latter, she suggested either moving the student to easier material or increasing the student's reading vocabulary.

6. Repetition of words

Monroe suggested several methods for dealing with occurrences of repetition of words. In cases where other errors cause the repetition, no specific drill was suggested. She claimed these types of repetition decrease with the treatment of other errors. In cases of habitual repetition, she suggested that the habit be made obvious to the student, by both the teacher and the student reading in unison. In cases where reversals accompany repetitions, manual guidance in the direction of reading was suggested. In cases of repetition that occur as a result of students stalling for time, she suggested no specific method but claimed that this kind of repetition would be eliminated with the acquisition of word analysis skills.

7. Omission of words

Monroe associated word omission with excessive reading speed. To cope with this type of error, she suggested slowing the reader's rate, either through the use of unison reading or by retyping the stories, leaving increased spacing between the lines of print.

Cautions and Comments

Monroe (1932) claimed that for twenty-seven disabled readers whose reading ability placed them halfway through the first grade, the average gain was 1.3 grades after approximately twenty-six hours of instruction (over an eight-month period) with her methods. In comparison, a control group gained only 0.14 grades. Monroe suggested that her methods were means to an end and not ends in themselves. As she stated:

> Although our methods stressed the mechanics of word-recognition, we utilized the recognition of words, not as an end in itself, but as a means to accomplish the final goal of reading, i.e., the comprehension of meaning. (P. 136)

The question arises: Do the students reach these ends by these means? Monroe claimed they do. As she suggested:

> Re-examinations of children taught by these methods show that after the initial start in reading is made, the children become more and more like normal readers. The secondary links, while utilized extensively by the children at first, become less in evidence and seem to disappear. Speed of reading develops gradually without specific pressure. Words are grouped into phrases and larger thought units. After remedial training, reading takes on the characteristics of normal performance until the child meets a strange, unfamiliar, or forgotten word. The mechanical links thereupon immediately become evident as the child attacks the word. Incipient

tracing or articulary movements appear until the word is recognized and the child proceeds with the reading. Thus, it appears that the child ultimately builds up an organization of responses which is very similar to the usual reading performance of unselected children, although the underlying steps in building the organization are somewhat different. (P. 114)

Inasmuch as Monroe's methods are similar to those suggested by the Gillingham-Stillman and Hegge-Kirk-Kirk procedures, many of the criticisms suggested previously are again relevant. While the procedures suggested by Monroe are less insensitive to individual differences and do not divorce word recognition from comprehension, these procedures do seem to place undue emphasis upon a synthetic-letter and word-by-word type of reading.

REFERENCES

Bond, G. L., and M. A. Tinker. 1973. *Reading difficulties: Their diagnosis and correction.* 3d ed. Englewood Cliffs, N.J.: Prentice-Hall, 501−4. Presents a discussion and evaluation of Monroe's methods.

Chall, J. 1967. *Learning to read: The great debate.* New York: McGraw-Hill, 166−68. Presents a discussion of Monroe's methods and research on the disabled reader.

Monroe, M. 1932. *Children who cannot read.* Chicago: University of Chicago Press. Describes the methods, their rationale, their utility, and potential use with disabled readers.

Index